Advanced Topics in C

Core Concepts in Data Structures

Noel Kalicharan

Apress

Advanced Topics in C: Core Concepts in Data Structures

Copyright © 2013 by Noel Kalicharan

This work is subject to copyright. All rights are reserved by the Publisher, whether the whole or part of the material is concerned, specifically the rights of translation, reprinting, reuse of illustrations, recitation, broadcasting, reproduction on microfilms or in any other physical way, and transmission or information storage and retrieval, electronic adaptation, computer software, or by similar or dissimilar methodology now known or hereafter developed. Exempted from this legal reservation are brief excerpts in connection with reviews or scholarly analysis or material supplied specifically for the purpose of being entered and executed on a computer system, for exclusive use by the purchaser of the work. Duplication of this publication or parts thereof is permitted only under the provisions of the Copyright Law of the Publisher's location, in its current version, and permission for use must always be obtained from Springer. Permissions for use may be obtained through RightsLink at the Copyright Clearance Center. Violations are liable to prosecution under the respective Copyright Law.

ISBN-13 (pbk): 978-1-4302-6400-2

ISBN-13 (electronic): 978-1-4302-6401-9

Trademarked names, logos, and images may appear in this book. Rather than use a trademark symbol with every occurrence of a trademarked name, logo, or image we use the names, logos, and images only in an editorial fashion and to the benefit of the trademark owner, with no intention of infringement of the trademark.

The use in this publication of trade names, trademarks, service marks, and similar terms, even if they are not identified as such, is not to be taken as an expression of opinion as to whether or not they are subject to proprietary rights.

While the advice and information in this book are believed to be true and accurate at the date of publication, neither the authors nor the editors nor the publisher can accept any legal responsibility for any errors or omissions that may be made. The publisher makes no warranty, express or implied, with respect to the material contained herein.

President and Publisher: Paul Manning
Lead Editor: Steve Anglin
Technical Reviewers: Stefan Turalski and Massimo Nardone
Editorial Board: Steve Anglin, Ewan Buckingham, Gary Cornell, Louise Corrigan, Morgan Ertel, Jonathan Gennick, Jonathan Hassell, Robert Hutchinson, Michelle Lowman, James Markham, Matthew Moodie, Jeff Olson, Jeffrey Pepper, Douglas Pundick, Ben Renow-Clarke, Dominic Shakeshaft, Gwenan Spearing, Matt Wade, Tom Welsh
Coordinating Editor: Kevin Shea
Copy Editor: Kim Wimpsett
Compositor: SPi Global
Indexer: SPi Global
Artist: SPi Global
Cover Designer: Anna Ishchenko

Distributed to the book trade worldwide by Springer Science+Business Media New York, 233 Spring Street, 6th Floor, New York, NY 10013. Phone 1-800-SPRINGER, fax (201) 348-4505, e-mail `orders-ny@springer-sbm.com`, or visit `www.springeronline.com`.

For information on translations, please e-mail `rights@apress.com`, or visit `www.apress.com`.

Apress and friends of ED books may be purchased in bulk for academic, corporate, or promotional use. eBook versions and licenses are also available for most titles. For more information, reference our Special Bulk Sales–eBook Licensing web page at `www.apress.com/bulk-sales`.

Any source code or other supplementary materials referenced by the author in this text is available to readers at `www.apress.com`. For detailed information about how to locate your book's source code, go to `www.apress.com/source-code`.

To Harry Ramnarine, a remarkably gifted man who, I believe, has come closest to unlocking the secrets of the universe and without whose timely intervention in my life this book may never have been written.

Contents at a Glance

Contents

About the Author

Dr. Noel Kalicharan is a senior lecturer in computer science at the University of the West Indies (UWI) in St. Augustine, Trinidad. For more than 36 years, he has taught programming courses to people at all levels, from children to senior citizens. He has been teaching algorithms and programming, among other things, at UWI since 1976.

In 1988, he developed and hosted a 26-program television series entitled *Computers: Bit by Bit*. This series taught computer literacy and programming to the general public. He is always looking for innovative ways to teach logical thinking skills, which go hand in hand with programming skills. His efforts resulted in two games —BrainStorm! and Not Just Luck—which won him the Prime Minister's Award for Invention and Innovation in 2000 and 2002, respectively.

He has written 16 computing books and is a computer science author for Cambridge University Press, which published his international successes, *Introduction to Computer Studies* and *C by Example*. The C book has received glowing reviews from readers from diverse countries such as Australia, Brazil, Canada, France, India, and Scotland. Many rate it as having "the best treatment of pointers," one of the more difficult C topics to master. *Advanced Topics in C* is written in a more leisurely style.

In 2010, Kalicharan was designated as a Trinidad & Tobago Icon in Computer Science by the National Institute for Higher Education, Research, Science, and Technology (NIHERST). In 2011, he was bestowed with a national award, the Public Service Medal of Merit (Gold), for his contribution to education. In 2012, he was given a lifetime award for "Excellence in Education" by the Ministry of Education of Trinidad and Tobago.

In 2012, he created a system called DigitalMath (`www.digitalmath.tt`), which is an ingenious way to do arithmetic with your hands. With it, you can do addition, subtraction, multiplication, and division quickly, accurately, and with confidence, using just your fingers.

Born in Lengua Village in Princes Town, Trinidad, he received his primary education at the Lengua Presbyterian School and his secondary education at Naparima College. He is a graduate of the University of the West Indies, Jamaica; the University of British Columbia, Canada; and the University of the West Indies, Trinidad.

About the Author

About the Technical Reviewer

Massimo Nardone earned a master's of science degree in computing science from the University of Salerno, Italy. He worked as a PCI QSA and senior lead IT security/cloud architect for many years, and currently he leads the Security Consulting Team in Hewlett Packard Finland. With more than 19 years of work experience in SCADA, cloud computing, IT infrastructure, mobile, security, and WWW technology areas for both national and international projects, Massimo has worked as a project manager, software engineer, research engineer, chief security architect, and software specialist. In addition, he worked as a visiting lecturer and supervisor for exercises at the Networking Laboratory of the Helsinki University of Technology (Helsinki University of Technology TKK became part of Aalto University) for the course Security of Communication Protocols. He holds four international patents (PKI, SIP, SAML, and Proxy areas). This book is dedicated to the memory of Harri Uolevi Bremer (1945–2013).

Preface

This book assumes you have a working knowledge of basic programming concepts such as variables, constants, assignment, selection (`if...else`), and looping (`while`, `for`). It also assumes you are comfortable with writing functions and working with arrays. If you are not, it is recommended that you study *C Programming: A Beginner's Course* (`www.amazon.com/C-Programming-A-Beginners-Course/dp/1438287844/`) or any other introductory C programming book before tackling the material in this book.

The emphasis is not on teaching advanced concepts of the C language per se but, rather, on using C to teach advanced programming concepts that any aspiring programmer should know. The major topics covered include elementary sorting methods (selection, insertion), searching (sequential, binary), merging, structures, pointers, linked lists, stacks, queues, recursion, random numbers, files (text, binary, random access, indexed), binary tress, advanced sorting methods (heapsort, quicksort, mergesort, Shell sort), and hashing (a very fast way to search).

Chapter 1 deals with sorting a list using selection and insertion sort, searching a list using sequential and binary search, and merging two ordered lists.

Chapter 2 introduces an important concept: structures. Structures allow you to group a set of related data and manipulate them as one. This chapter shows you how to search and sort an array of structures and how to create useful user-defined types using `typedef` and `struct`.

Chapter 3 covers the sometimes elusive but powerful concept of pointers. Many programmers will tell you that this is probably the most difficult concept to grasp and the one that gives them the most headaches. I hope that, after reading this chapter, you will agree that it does not have to be so.

Chapter 4 deals with linked lists—an important data structure in its own right but also the foundation for more advanced structures such as trees and graphs. We will explain how to create a linked list, how to add to and delete from a linked list, how to build a sorted linked list, and how to merge two sorted linked lists.

Chapter 5 is devoted specifically to stacks and queues, perhaps the most useful kinds of linear lists. They have important applications in computer science. We will show you how to implement stacks and queues using arrays and linked lists and how to evaluate an arithmetic expression by converting it to postfix form.

Chapter 6 introduces a powerful programming methodology: recursion. There is no doubt that recursion takes a bit of getting used to. But, once you've mastered the topic, you will be able to solve a whole new world of problems that would be difficult to solve using traditional, nonrecursive techniques. Among other interesting problems, we will show you how to solve the Towers of Hanoi problem and how to escape from a maze.

We all like to play games. But what lurks inside these game-playing programs? Random numbers. Chapter 7 shows you how to use random numbers to play some simple games and simulate real-life situations. We will explain how to write an arithmetic drill program, how to play the perfect game of Nim, and how to simulate a queue at a supermarket checkout counter or bank, among others. We will also discuss a novel use of random numbers—estimating numerical values like π (pi).

Almost anything you need to store on a computer must be stored in a file. We use text files for storing the kinds of documents we create with a text editor or word processor. We use binary files for storing photographic image files, sound files, video files, and files of records. Chapter 8 shows how to create and manipulate text and binary files. It also explains how to work with two of the most useful kinds of files: random access and indexed.

Chapter 9 introduces that most versatile data structure—the binary tree. A binary tree combines the advantages of an array and a linked list without the disadvantages. For example, a binary search tree allows you to search in "binary search time" (as with a sorted array) and insert/delete with the facility of linked lists.

The sorting methods (selection, insertion) discussed in Chapter 1 are simplistic in that they get the job done but will be slow if given a large number of items (a million, say) to sort. For example, they will take about six days (!) to sort a million items on a computer that can process a million comparisons per second. Chapter 10 discusses some faster sorting methods, namely, heapsort, quicksort, and Shell sort. Heapsort and quicksort will sort the million items on the same computer in less than a minute, while Shell sort will take slightly more than one minute.

Chapter 11 is devoted to hashing, one of the fastest ways to search. It covers hashing fundamentals and discusses several ways to resolve collisions, the key to the performance of any hashing algorithm.

Our goal is to provide a good grasp of advanced programming techniques as well as a basic understanding of important data structures (linked lists, stacks, queues, binary trees) and how they can be implemented in C. We hope this will whet your appetite for a deeper study of this exciting, essential area of computer science.

Many of the exercises require you to write a program. Not providing answers for these was deliberate. Our experience is that, in our fast-food culture, students do not spend the necessary time to figure out the solutions when answers are available. In any case, the goal of the programming exercises is for you to write the programs.

Programming is an iterative process. When you compile and run your solutions, you will know whether you are correct. If you are not, you must try to figure out why the program does not work, make improvements, and try again. The only way to learn programming well is to write programs to solve new problems. Providing answers will short-circuit this process without any benefits.

The programs in *Advanced Topics in C* conform to the C99 standard. They can be compiled with any compiler that conforms to C99. However, for this book, we used Code::Blocks (`http://sourceforge.net/projects/codeblocks/`). Code::Blocks is a free, open source, cross-platform C/C++ IDE built to meet the needs of the most demanding users. It is also easy to use. You can download a version of Code::Blocks that includes the minGW C compiler but it can be used with any other C compiler.

The code for the examples shown in this book is available on the Apress web site, `www.apress.com`. You can find a link to it on the book's information page; go to the Source Code/Downloads tab, which is in the Related Titles section of the page.

Thank you for taking the time to read and study this book. We hope your experience will be a successful, enjoyable, and rewarding one.

—Noel Kalicharan

CHAPTER 1

Sorting, Searching, and Merging

In this chapter, we will explain the following:

- How to sort a list of items using selection and insertion sort
- How to add a new item to a sorted list so that the list remains sorted
- How to sort an array of strings
- How to sort related (parallel) arrays
- How to search a sorted list using *binary search*
- How to search an array of strings
- How to write a program to do a frequency count of words in a passage
- How to merge two sorted lists to create one sorted list

1.1 Sorting an Array: Selection Sort

Sorting is the process by which a set of values are arranged in ascending or descending order. There are many reasons to sort. Sometimes we sort in order to produce more readable output (for example, to produce an alphabetical listing). A teacher may need to sort her students in order by name or by average score. If we have a large set of values and we want to identify duplicates, we can do so by sorting; the repeated values will come together in the sorted list.

Another advantage of sorting is that some operations can be performed faster and more efficiently with sorted data. For example, if data is sorted, it is possible to search it using binary search—this is much faster than using a sequential search. Also, merging two separate lists of items can be done much faster than if the lists were unsorted.

There are many ways to sort. In this chapter, we will discuss two of the "simple" methods: *selection* and *insertion* sort. In Chapter 10, we will look at more sophisticated ways to sort. We start with selection sort.

Consider the following list of numbers stored in a C array, `num`:

num

57	48	79	65	15	33	52
0	1	2	3	4	5	6

Sorting num in ascending order using *selection sort* proceeds as follows:

1st pass

- Find the smallest number in the entire list, from positions 0 to 6; the smallest is 15, found in position 4.
- Interchange the numbers in positions 0 and 4. This gives us the following:

num

15	48	79	65	57	33	52
0	1	2	3	4	5	6

2nd pass

- Find the smallest number in positions 1 to 6; the smallest is 33, found in position 5.
- Interchange the numbers in positions 1 and 5. This gives us the following:

num

15	33	79	65	57	48	52
0	1	2	3	4	5	6

3rd pass

- Find the smallest number in positions 2 to 6; the smallest is 48, found in position 5.
- Interchange the numbers in positions 2 and 5. This gives us the following:

num

15	33	48	65	57	79	52
0	1	2	3	4	5	6

4th pass

- Find the smallest number in positions 3 to 6; the smallest is 52, found in position 6.
- Interchange the numbers in positions 3 and 6. This gives us the following:

num

15	33	48	52	57	79	65
0	1	2	3	4	5	6

5th pass

- Find the smallest number in positions 4 to 6; the smallest is 57, found in position 4.
- Interchange the numbers in positions 4 and 4. This gives us the following:

num

15	33	48	52	57	79	65
0	1	2	3	4	5	6

6th pass

- Find the smallest number in positions 5 to 6; the smallest is 65, found in position 6.
- Interchange the numbers in positions 5 and 6. This gives us the following:

num

15	33	48	52	57	65	79
0	1	2	3	4	5	6

The array is now completely sorted. Note that once the 6th largest (65) has been placed in its final position (5), the largest (79) would automatically be in the last position (6).

In this example, we made six passes. We will count these passes by letting the variable h go from 0 to 5. On each pass, we find the smallest number from positions h to 6. If the smallest number is in position s, we interchange the numbers in positions h and s.

In general, for an array of size n, we make n-1 passes. In our example, we sorted seven numbers in six passes. The following is a pseudocode outline of the algorithm for sorting num[0..n-1]:

```
for h = 0 to n - 2
   s = position of smallest number from num[h] to num[n-1]
   swap num[h] and num[s]
endfor
```

We can implement this algorithm as follows, using the generic parameter, list:

```
void selectionSort(int list[], int lo, int hi) {
//sort list[lo] to list[hi] in ascending order
   int getSmallest(int[], int, int);
   void swap(int[], int, int);
   for (int h = lo; h < hi; h++) {
      int s = getSmallest(list, h, hi);
      swap(list, h, s);
   }
}
```

The two statements in the for loop *could* be replaced by this:

```
swap(list, h, getSmallest(list, h, hi));
```

We can write getSmallest and swap as follows:

```
int getSmallest(int list[], int lo, int hi) {
//return location of smallest from list[lo..hi]
   int small = lo;
   for (int h = lo + 1; h <= hi; h++)
      if (list[h] < list[small]) small = h;
   return small;
}
```

```
void swap(int list[], int i, int j) {
//swap elements list[i] and list[j]
   int hold = list[i];
   list[i] = list[j];
   list[j] = hold;
}
```

To test whether selectionSort works properly, we write Program P1.1. Only main is shown. To complete the program, just add selectionSort, getSmallest, and swap.

Program P1.1

```
#include <stdio.h>
#define MaxNumbers 10
int main() {
   void selectionSort(int [], int, int);
   int num[MaxNumbers];
   printf("Type up to %d numbers followed by 0\n", MaxNumbers);
   int n = 0, v;
   scanf("%d", &v);
   while (v != 0 && n < MaxNumbers) {
      num[n++] = v;
      scanf("%d", &v);
   }
   if (v != 0) {
      printf("More than %d numbers entered\n", MaxNumbers);
      printf("First %d used\n", MaxNumbers);
   }
   //n numbers are stored from num[0] to num[n-1]
   selectionSort(num, 0, n-1);
   printf("\nThe sorted numbers are\n");
   for (int h = 0; h < n; h++) printf("%d ", num[h]);
   printf("\n");
}
```

The program requests up to ten numbers (as defined by MaxNumbers), stores them in the array num, calls selectionSort, and then prints the sorted list.

The following is a sample run of the program:

```
Type up to 10 numbers followed by 0
57 48 79 65 15 33 52 0
The sorted numbers are
15 33 48 52 57 65 79
```

Note that if the user enters more than ten numbers, the program will recognize this and sort only the first ten.

1.1.1 Analysis of Selection Sort

To find the smallest of *k* items, we make *k*-1 comparisons. On the first pass, we make *n*-1 comparisons to find the smallest of *n* items. On the second pass, we make *n*-2 comparisons to find the smallest of *n*-1 items. And so on, until the last pass where we make one comparison to find the smaller of two items. In general, on the *j*th pass, we make *n-j* comparisons to find the smallest of *n-j*+1 items. Hence:

```
total number of comparisons = 1 + 2 + ...+ n-1 = ½ n(n-1) » ½ n2
```

We say selection sort is of order $O(n^2)$ ("big O *n* squared"). The constant ½ is not important in "big O" notation since, as *n* gets very big, the constant becomes insignificant.

On each pass, we swap two items using three assignments. Since we make *n*-1 passes, we make 3(*n*-1) assignments in all. Using "big O" notation, we say that the number of assignments is $O(n)$. The constants 3 and 1 are not important as *n* gets large.

Does selection sort perform any better if there is order in the data? No. One way to find out is to give it a sorted list and see what it does. If you work through the algorithm, you will see that the method is oblivious to order in the data. It will make the same number of comparisons every time, regardless of the data.

As we will see, some sorting methods, such as mergesort and quicksort (see Chapters 6 and 10) require extra array storage to implement them. Note that selection sort is performed "in place" in the given array and does not require additional storage.

As an exercise, modify the programming code so that it counts the number of comparisons and assignments made in sorting a list using selection sort.

1.2 Sorting an Array: Insertion Sort

Consider the same array as before:

num

57	48	79	65	15	33	52
0	1	2	3	4	5	6

Now, think of the numbers as cards on a table that are picked up one at a time, in the order they appear in the array. Thus, we first pick up 57, then 48, then 79, and so on, until we pick up 52. However, as we pick up each new number, we add it to our hand in such a way that the numbers in our hand are all sorted.

When we pick up 57, we have just one number in our hand. We consider one number to be sorted.

When we pick up 48, we add it in front of 57 so our hand contains the following:

```
48 57
```

When we pick up 79, we place it after 57 so our hand contains the following:

```
48 57 79
```

When we pick up 65, we place it after 57 so our hand contains the following:

```
48 57 65 79
```

At this stage, four numbers have been picked up, and our hand contains them in sorted order.

When we pick up 15, we place it before 48 so our hand contains the following:

```
15 48 57 65 79
```

When we pick up 33, we place it after 15 so our hand contains the following:

```
15 33 48 57 65 79
```

Finally, when we pick up 52, we place it after 48 so our hand contains the following:

```
15 33 48 52 57 65 79
```

The numbers have been sorted in ascending order.

The method described illustrates the idea behind *insertion sort*. The numbers in the array will be processed one at a time, from left to right. This is equivalent to picking up the numbers from the table, one at a time. Since the first number, by itself, is sorted, we will process the numbers in the array starting from the second.

When we come to process `num[h]`, we can assume that `num[0]` to `num[h-1]` are sorted. We insert `num[h]` among `num[0]` to `num[h-1]` so that `num[0]` to `num[h]` are sorted. We then go on to process `num[h+1]`. When we do so, our assumption that `num[0]` to `num[h]` are sorted will be true.

Sorting `num` in ascending order using insertion sort proceeds as follows:

1st pass

- Process `num[1]`, that is, 48. This involves placing 48 so that the first two numbers are sorted; `num[0]` and `num[1]` now contain the following:

num

48	57
0	1

The rest of the array remains unchanged.

2nd pass

- Process `num[2]`, that is, 79. This involves placing 79 so that the first three numbers are sorted; `num[0]` to `num[2]` now contain the following:

num

48	57	79
0	1	2

The rest of the array remains unchanged.

3rd pass

- Process `num[3]`, that is, 65. This involves placing 65 so that the first four numbers are sorted; `num[0]` to `num[3]` now contain the following:

num

48	57	65	79
0	1	2	3

The rest of the array remains unchanged.

4th pass

- Process `num[4]`, that is, `15`. This involves placing `15` so that the first five numbers are sorted. To simplify the explanation, think of 15 as being taken out and stored in a simple variable (key, say) leaving a "hole" in `num[4]`. We can picture this as follows:

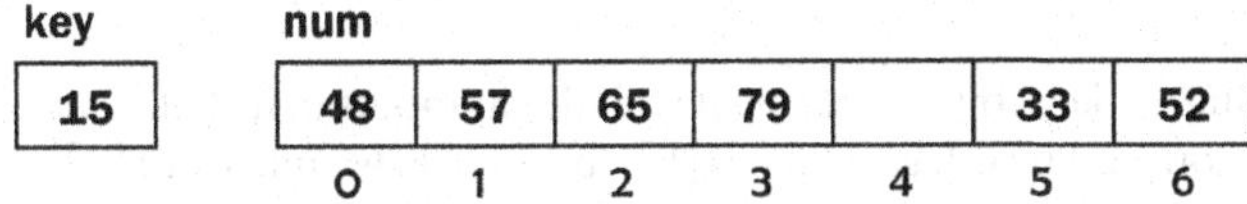

The insertion of `15` in its correct position proceeds as follows:

- Compare `15` with `79`; it is smaller, so move `79` to location `4`, leaving location `3` free. This gives the following:

key: 15

num						
48	57	65		79	33	52
0	1	2	3	4	5	6

- Compare `15` with `65`; it is smaller, so move `65` to location `3`, leaving location `2` free. This gives the following:

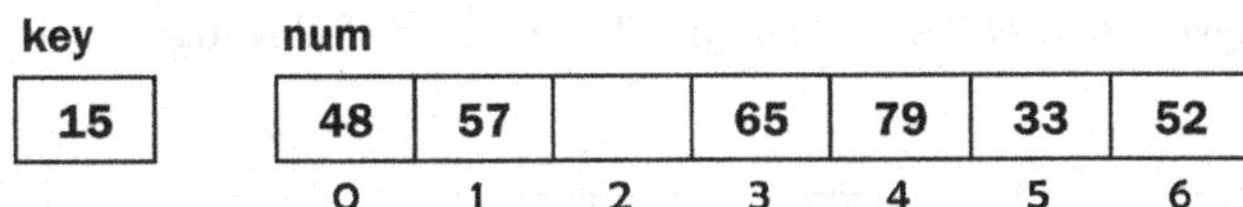

- Compare `15` with `57`; it is smaller, so move `57` to location `2`, leaving location `1` free. This gives the following:

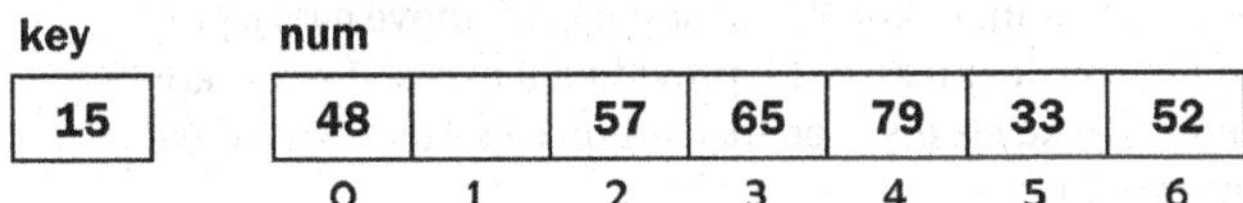

- Compare `15` with `48`; it is smaller, so move `48` to location `1`, leaving location `0` free. This gives the following:

key: 15

num						
	48	57	65	79	33	52
0	1	2	3	4	5	6

- There are no more numbers to compare with 15, so it is inserted in location 0, giving the following:

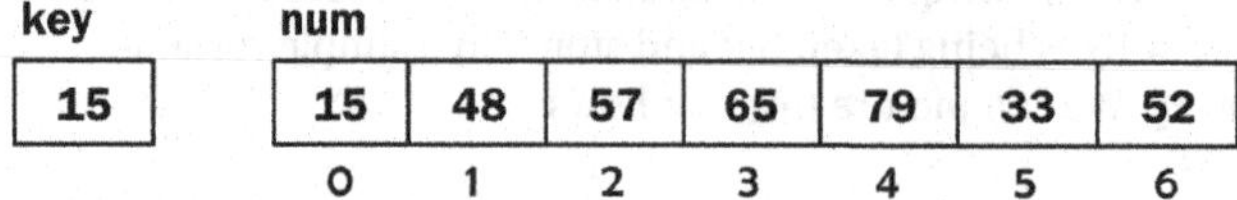

- We can express the logic of placing 15 (key) by comparing it with the numbers to its left, starting with the nearest one. As long as key is less than num[k], for some k, we move num[k] to position num[k + 1] and move on to consider num[k-1], providing it exists. It won't exist when k is actually 0. In this case, the process stops, and key is inserted in position 0.

5th pass

- Process num[5], that is, 33. This involves placing 33 so that the first six numbers are sorted. This is done as follows:
    - Store 33 in key, leaving location 5 free;
    - Compare 33 with 79; it is smaller, so move 79 to location 5, leaving location 4 free.
    - Compare 33 with 65; it is smaller, so move 65 to location 4, leaving location 3 free.
    - Compare 33 with 57; it is smaller, so move 57 to location 3, leaving location 2 free.
    - Compare 33 with 48; it is smaller, so move 48 to location 2, leaving location 1 free.
    - Compare 33 with 15; it is bigger, so insert 33 in location 1. This gives the following:

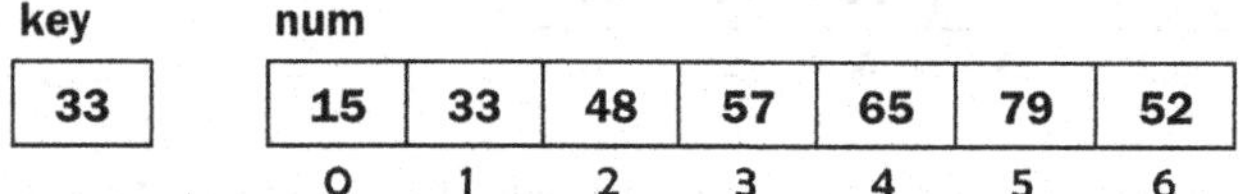

- We can express the logic of placing 33 by comparing it with the numbers to its left, starting with the nearest one. As long as key is less than num[k], for some k, we move num[k] to position num[k + 1] and move on to consider num[k-1], providing it exists. If key is greater than or equal to num[k] for some k, then key is inserted in position k+1. Here, 33 is greater than num[0] and so is inserted into num[1].

6th pass

- Process num[6], that is, 52. This involves placing 52 so that the first seven (all) numbers are sorted. This is done as follows:
    - Store 52 in key, leaving location 6 free.
    - Compare 52 with 79; it is smaller, so move 79 to location 6, leaving location 5 free.
    - Compare 52 with 65; it is smaller, so move 65 to location 5, leaving location 4 free.

- Compare 52 with 57; it is smaller, so move 57 to location 4, leaving location 3 free.
- Compare 52 with 48; it is bigger, so insert 52 in location 3. This gives the following:

key

52

num

15	33	48	52	57	65	79
0	1	2	3	4	5	6

The array is now completely sorted.

The following is an outline of how to sort the first n elements of an array, num, using insertion sort:

```
for h = 1 to n - 1 do
   insert num[h] among num[0] to num[h-1] so that num[0] to num[h] are sorted
endfor
```

Using this outline, we write the function insertionSort using the parameter list.

```
void insertionSort(int list[], int n) {
//sort list[0] to list[n-1] in ascending order
   for (int h = 1; h < n; h++) {
      int key = list[h];
      int k = h - 1; //start comparing with previous item
      while (k >= 0 && key < list[k]) {
         list[k + 1] = list[k];
         --k;
      }
      list[k + 1] = key;
   } //end for
} //end insertionSort
```

The while statement is at the heart of the sort. It states that as long as we are within the array (k >= 0) and the current number (key) is less than the one in the array (key < list[k]), we move list[k] to the right (list[k + 1] = list[k]) and move on to the next number on the left (--k).

We exit the while loop if k is equal to -1 or if key is greater than or equal to list[k], for some k. In either case, key is inserted into list[k + 1].

If k is -1, it means that the current number is smaller than all the previous numbers in the list and must be inserted in list[0]. But list[k + 1] *is* list[0] when k is -1, so key is inserted correctly in this case.

The function sorts in ascending order. To sort in descending order, all we have to do is change < to > in the while condition, like this:

```
while (k >= 0 && key > list[k])
```

Now, a key moves to the left if it is *bigger*.

We write Program P1.2 to test whether insertionSort works correctly. Only main is shown. Adding the function insertionSort completes the program.

Program P1.2

```
#include <stdio.h>
#define MaxNumbers 10
int main() {
   void insertionSort(int [], int);
   int num[MaxNumbers];
   printf("Type up to %d numbers followed by 0\n", MaxNumbers);
   int n = 0, v;
   scanf("%d", &v);
   while (v != 0 && n < MaxNumbers) {
      num[n++] = v;
      scanf("%d", &v);
   }
   if (v != 0) {
      printf("More than %d numbers entered\n", MaxNumbers);
      printf("First %d used\n", MaxNumbers);
   }
   //n numbers are stored from num[0] to num[n-1]
   insertionSort(num, n);
   printf("\nThe sorted numbers are\n");
   for (int h = 0; h < n; h++) printf("%d ", num[h]);
   printf("\n");
}
```

The program requests up to ten numbers (as defined by `MaxNumbers`), stores them in the array `num`, calls `insertionSort`, and then prints the sorted list.

The following is a sample run of the program:

```
Type up to 10 numbers followed by 0
57 48 79 65 15 33 52 0
The sorted numbers are
15 33 48 52 57 65 79
```

Note that if the user enters more than ten numbers, the program will recognize this and sort only the first ten.

We could easily generalize `insertionSort` to sort a *portion* of a list. To illustrate, we rewrite `insertionSort` (calling it `insertionSort1`) to sort `list[lo]` to `list[hi]` where `lo` and `hi` are passed as arguments to the function.

Since element `lo` is the first one, we start processing elements from `lo+1` until element `hi`. This is reflected in the `for` statement. Also now, the lowest subscript is `lo`, rather than `0`. This is reflected in the `while` condition `k >= lo`. Everything else remains the same as before.

```
void insertionSort1(int list[], int lo, int hi) {
//sort list[lo] to list[hi] in ascending order
   for (int h = lo + 1; h <= hi; h++) {
      int key = list[h];
      int k = h - 1; //start comparing with previous item
      while (k >= lo && key < list[k]) {
         list[k + 1] = list[k];
         --k;
      }
```

```
        list[k + 1] = key;
    } //end for
} //end insertionSort1
```

1.2.1 Analysis of Insertion Sort

In processing item *j*, we can make as few as one comparison (if `num[j]` is bigger than `num[j-1]`) or as many as *j*-1 comparisons (if `num[j]` is smaller than all the previous items). For random data, we would expect to make ½(*j*-1) comparisons, on average. Hence, the average total number of comparisons to sort *n* items is as follows:

$$\sum_{j=2}^{n} \frac{1}{2}(j-1) = \frac{1}{2}\{1+2+\ldots+n-1\} = \frac{1}{4}n(n-1) \approx \frac{1}{4}n^2$$

We say insertion sort is of order $O(n^2)$ ("big O n squared"). The constant ¼ is not important as n gets large.

Each time we make a comparison, we also make an assignment. Hence, the total number of assignments is also $\frac{1}{4}n(n-1) \approx \frac{1}{4}n^2$.

We emphasize that this is an average for random data. Unlike selection sort, the actual performance of insertion sort depends on the data supplied. If the given array is already sorted, insertion sort will quickly determine this by making n-1 comparisons. In this case, it runs in O(n) time. One would expect that insertion sort will perform better the more order there is in the data.

If the given data is in descending order, insertion sort performs at its worst since each new number has to travel all the way to the beginning of the list. In this case, the number of comparisons is $\frac{1}{2}n(n-1) \approx \frac{1}{2}n^2$. The number of assignments is also $\frac{1}{2}n(n-1) \approx \frac{1}{2}n^2$.

Thus, the number of comparisons made by insertion sort ranges from n-1 (best) to $\frac{1}{4}n^2$ (average) to $\frac{1}{2}n^2$ (worst). The number of assignments is always the same as the number of comparisons.

As with selection sort, insertion sort does not require extra array storage for its implementation.

As an exercise, modify the programming code so that it counts the number of comparisons and assignments made in sorting a list using insertion sort.

1.3 Inserting an Element in Place

Insertion sort uses the idea of adding a new element to an already sorted list so that the list remains sorted. We can treat this as a problem in its own right (nothing to do with insertion sort). Specifically, given a sorted list of items from `list[m]` to `list[n]`, we want to add a new item (`newItem`, say) to the list so that `list[m]` to `list[n + 1]` are sorted.

Adding a new item increases the size of the list by 1. We assume that the array has room to hold the new item. We write the function `insertInPlace` to solve this problem.

```
void insertInPlace(int newItem, int list[], int m, int n) {
//list[m] to list[n] are sorted
//insert newItem so that list[m] to list[n+1] are sorted
   int k = n;
   while (k >= m && newItem < list[k]) {
      list[k + 1] = list[k];
      --k;
   }
   list[k + 1] = newItem;
} //end insertInPlace
```

Using `insertInPlace`, we can rewrite `insertionSort` (calling it `insertionSort2`) as follows:

```
void insertionSort2(int list[], int lo, int hi) {
//sort list[lo] to list[hi] in ascending order
   void insertInPlace(int, int [], int, int);
   for (int h = lo + 1; h <= hi; h++)
      insertInPlace(list[h], list, lo, h - 1);
} //end insertionSort2
```

1.4 Sorting an Array of Strings

Consider the problem of sorting a list of names in alphabetical order. In C, each name is stored in a character array. To store several names, we need a two-dimensional character array. For example, we can store eight names as shown in Figure 1-1.

	0	1	2	3	4	5	6	7	8	9	10	11	12	13	14
0	T	a	y	l	o	r	,		V	i	c	t	o	r	\0
1	D	u	n	c	a	n	,		D	e	n	i	s	e	\0
2	R	a	m	d	h	a	n	,		K	a	m	a	l	\0
3	S	i	n	g	h	,		K	r	i	s	h	n	a	\0
4	A	l	i	,		M	i	c	h	a	e	l	\0		
5	S	a	w	h	,		A	n	i	s	a	\0			
6	K	h	a	n	,		C	a	r	o	l	\0			
7	O	w	e	n	,		D	a	v	i	d	\0			

Figure 1-1. *Two-dimensional character array*

Doing so will require a declaration such as the following:

```
char list[8][15];
```

To cater for longer names, we can increase `15`, and to cater for more names, we can increase `8`.

The *process* of sorting `list` is essentially the same as sorting an array of integers. The major difference is that whereas we use < to compare two numbers, we must use `strcmp` to compare two names. In the function `insertionSort` shown at the end of Section 1.3, the `while` condition changes from this:

```
while (k >= lo && key < list[k])
```

to the following, where key is now declared as `char key[15]`:

```
while (k >= lo && strcmp(key, list[k]) < 0)
```

Also, we must now use `strcpy` (since we can't use = for strings) to assign a name to another location. Here is the complete function:

```
void insertionSort3(int lo, int hi, int max, char list[][max]) {
//Sort the strings in list[lo] to list[hi] in alphabetical order.
//The maximum string size is max - 1 (one char taken up by \0).
```

```
   char key[max];
   for (int h = lo + 1; h <= hi; h++) {
      strcpy(key, list[h]);
      int k = h - 1; //start comparing with previous item
      while (k >= lo && strcmp(key, list[k]) < 0) {
         strcpy(list[k + 1], list[k]);
         --k;
      }
      strcpy(list[k + 1], key);
   } //end for
} //end insertionSort3
```

Note the declaration of list (char list[][max]) in the parameter list. The size of the first dimension is left unspecified, as for one-dimensional arrays. The size of the second dimension is specified using the parameter max; the value of max will be specified when the function is called. This gives us a bit more flexibility since we can specify the size of the second dimension at run time.

We write a simple main routine to test insertionSort3 as shown in Program P1.3.

Program P1.3

```
#include <stdio.h>
#include <string.h>
#define MaxNameSize 14
#define MaxNameBuffer MaxNameSize+1
#define MaxNames 8
int main() {
   void insertionSort3(int, int, int max, char [][max]);
   char name[MaxNames][MaxNameBuffer] = {"Taylor, Victor", "Duncan, Denise",
      "Ramdhan, Kamal", "Singh, Krishna", "Ali, Michael",
      "Sawh, Anisa", "Khan, Carol", "Owen, David" };

   insertionSort3(0, MaxNames-1, MaxNameBuffer, name);
   printf("\nThe sorted names are\n\n");
   for (int h = 0; h < MaxNames; h++) printf("%s\n", name[h]);
} //end main
```

The declaration of name initializes it with the eight names shown in Figure 1-1. When run, the program produces the following output:

```
The sorted names are
Ali, Michael
Duncan, Denise
Khan, Carol
Owen, David
Ramdhan, Kamal
Sawh, Anisa
Singh, Krishna
Taylor, Victor
```

1.5 Sorting Parallel Arrays

It is quite common to have related information in different arrays. For example, suppose, in addition to name, we have an integer array id such that id[h] is an identification number associated with name[h], as shown in Figure 1-2.

	name	id
0	Taylor, Victor	3050
1	Duncan, Denise	2795
2	Ramdhan, Kamal	4455
3	Singh, Krishna	7824
4	Ali, Michael	6669
5	Sawh, Anisa	5000
6	Khan, Carol	5464
7	Owen, David	6050

Figure 1-2. *Two arrays with related information*

Consider the problem of sorting the names in alphabetical order. At the end, we would want each name to have its correct ID number. So, for example, after the sorting is done, name[0] should contain "Ali, Michael" and id[0] should contain 6669.

To achieve this, each time a name is moved during the sorting process, the corresponding ID number must also be moved. Since the name and ID number must be moved "in parallel," we say we are doing a *parallel sort* or we are sorting *parallel arrays*.

We rewrite insertionSort3 to illustrate how to sort parallel arrays. We simply add the code to move an ID whenever a name is moved. We call it parallelSort.

```
void parallelSort(int lo, int hi, int max, char list[][max], int id[]) {
//Sort the names in list[lo] to list[hi] in alphabetical order, ensuring that
//each name remains with its original id number.
//The maximum string size is max - 1 (one char taken up by \0).
   char key[max];
   for (int h = lo + 1; h <= hi; h++) {
      strcpy(key, list[h]);
      int m = id[h];          // extract the id number
      int k = h - 1;          //start comparing with previous item
      while (k >= lo && strcmp(key, list[k]) < 0) {
         strcpy(list[k + 1], list[k]);
         id[k + 1] = id[k];  // move up id number when we move a name
         --k;
      }
      strcpy(list[k + 1], key);
      id[k + 1] = m;          // store the id number in the same position as the name
   } //end for
} //end parallelSort
```

We test parallelSort by writing the following main routine:

```
#include <stdio.h>
#include <string.h>
#define MaxNameSize 14
#define MaxNameBuffer MaxNameSize+1
#define MaxNames 8
int main() {
   void parallelSort(int, int, int max, char [][max], int[]);
   char name[MaxNames][MaxNameBuffer] = {"Taylor, Victor", "Duncan, Denise",
      "Ramdhan, Kamal", "Singh, Krishna", "Ali, Michael",
      "Sawh, Anisa", "Khan, Carol", "Owen, David" };
   int id[MaxNames] = {3050,2795,4455,7824,6669,5000,5464,6050};

   parallelSort(0, MaxNames-1, MaxNameBuffer, name, id);
   printf("\nThe sorted names and IDs are\n\n");
   for (int h = 0; h < MaxNames; h++) printf("%-18s %d\n", name[h], id[h]);
} //end main
```

When run, it produces the following output:

```
The sorted names and IDs are
Ali, Michael      6669
Duncan, Denise    2795
Khan, Carol       5464
Owen, David       6050
Ramdhan, Kamal    4455
Sawh, Anisa       5000
Singh, Krishna    7824
Taylor, Victor    3050
```

1.6 Binary Search

Binary search is a fast method for searching a list of items for a given one, *providing the list is sorted* (either ascending or descending). To illustrate the method, consider a list of 13 numbers, sorted in ascending order and stored in an array num[0..12].

num

17	24	31	39	44	49	56	66	72	78	83	89	96
0	1	2	3	4	5	6	7	8	9	10	11	12

Suppose we want to search for 66. The search proceeds as follows:

1. First, we find the middle item in the list. This is 56 in position 6. We compare 66 with 56. Since 66 is bigger, we know that if 66 is in the list at all, it *must* be *after* position 6, since the numbers are in ascending order. In our next step, we confine our search to locations 7 to 12.

2. Next, we find the middle item from locations 7 to 12. In this case, we can choose either item 9 or item 10. The algorithm we will write will choose item 9, that is, 78.

3. We compare 66 with 78. Since 66 is smaller, we know that if 66 is in the list at all, it *must* be *before* position 9, since the numbers are in ascending order. In our next step, we confine our search to locations 7 to 8.

4. Next, we find the middle item from locations 7 to 8. In this case, we can choose either item 7 or item 8. The algorithm we will write will choose item 7, that is, 66.

5. We compare 66 with 66. Since they are the same, our search ends successfully, finding the required item in position 7.

Suppose we were searching for 70. The search will proceed as described above until we compare 70 with 66 (in location 7).

1. Since 70 is bigger, we know that if 70 is in the list at all, it *must* be *after* position 7, since the numbers are in ascending order. In our next step, we confine our search to locations 8 to 8. This is just one location.

2. We compare 70 with item 8, that is, 72. Since 70 is smaller, we know that if 70 is in the list at all, it *must* be *before* position 8. Since it can't be after position 7 *and* before position 8, we conclude that it is not in the list.

At each stage of the search, we confine our search to some portion of the list. Let us use the variables `lo` and `hi` as the subscripts that define this portion. In other words, our search will be confined to `num[lo]` to `num[hi]`.

Initially, we want to search the entire list so that we will set `lo` to 0 and `hi` to 12, in this example.

How do we find the subscript of the middle item? We will use the following calculation:

```
mid = (lo + hi) / 2;
```

Since integer division will be performed, the fraction, if any, is discarded. For example, when `lo` is 0 and `hi` is 12, `mid` becomes 6; when `lo` is 7 and `hi` is 12, `mid` becomes 9; and when `lo` is 7 and `hi` is 8, `mid` becomes 7.

As long as `lo` is less than or equal to `hi`, they define a nonempty portion of the list to be searched. When `lo` is equal to `hi`, they define a single item to be searched. If `lo` ever gets bigger than `hi`, it means we have searched the entire list and the item was not found.

Based on these ideas, we can now write a function `binarySearch`. To be more general, we will write it so that the calling routine can specify which portion of the array it wants the search to look for the item.

Thus, the function must be given the item to be searched for (`key`), the array (`list`), the start position of the search (`lo`), and the end position of the search (`hi`). For example, to search for the number 66 in the array `num`, shown earlier, we can issue the call `binarySearch(66, num, 0, 12)`.

The function must tell us the result of the search. If the item is found, the function will return its location. If not found, it will return -1.

```
int binarySearch(int key, int list[], int lo, int hi) {
//search for key from list[lo] to list[hi]
//if found, return its location; otherwise, return -1
   while (lo <= hi) {
      int mid = (lo + hi) / 2;
      if (key == list[mid]) return mid; // found
      if (key < list[mid]) hi = mid - 1;
      else lo = mid + 1;
   }
   return -1; //lo and hi have crossed; key not found
} //end binarySearch
```

If item contains a number to be searched for, we can write code as follows:

```
int ans = binarySearch(item, num, 0, 12);
if (ans == -1) printf("%d not found\n", item);
else printf("%d found in location %d\n", item, ans);
```

If we want to search for `item` from locations `i` to `j`, we can write the following:

```
int ans = binarySearch(item, num, i, j);
```

1.7 Searching an Array of Strings

We can search a sorted array of strings (names in alphabetical order, say) using the same technique we used for searching an integer array. The major differences are in the declaration of the array and the use of `strcmp`, rather than == or <, to compare two strings. The following is the string version of `binarySearch`:

```
int binarySearch(int lo, int hi, char key[], int max, char list[][max]) {
//search for key from list[lo] to list[hi]
//if found, return its location; otherwise, return -1
   while (lo <= hi) {
      int mid = (lo + hi) / 2;
      int cmp = strcmp(key, list[mid]);
      if (cmp == 0) return mid; // found
      if (cmp < 0) hi = mid - 1;
      else lo = mid + 1;
   }
   return -1; //lo and hi have crossed; key not found
} //end binarySearch
```

The function can be tested with `main` shown in Program P1.4.

Program P1.4

```
#include <stdio.h>
#include <string.h>
#define MaxNameSize 14
#define MaxNameBuffer MaxNameSize+1
#define MaxNames 8
int main () {
   int binarySearch(int, int, char [], int max, char [][max]);
   int n;
   char name[MaxNames][MaxNameBuffer] = {"Ali, Michael","Duncan, Denise",
      "Khan, Carol","Owen, David", "Ramdhan, Kamal",
      "Sawh, Anisa", "Singh, Krishna", "Taylor, Victor"};
   n = binarySearch(0, 7, "Ali, Michael", MaxNameBuffer, name);
   printf("%d\n", n);  //will print 0, location of Ali, Michael
   n = binarySearch(0, 7, "Taylor, Victor", MaxNameBuffer, name);
   printf("%d\n", n); //will print 7, location of Taylor, Victor
   n = binarySearch(0, 7, "Owen, David", MaxNameBuffer, name);
   printf("%d\n", n); //will print 3, location of Owen, David
```

```
    n = binarySearch(4, 7, "Owen, David", MaxNameBuffer, name);
    printf("%d\n", n); //will print -1, since Owen, David is not in locations 4 to 7
    n = binarySearch(0, 7, "Sandy, Cindy", MaxNameBuffer, name);
    printf("%d\n", n); //will print -1 since Sandy, Cindy is not in the list
} //end main
```

This sets up the array name with the names in alphabetical order. It then calls binarySearch with various names and prints the result of each search.

One may wonder what might happen with a call like this:

```
n = binarySearch(5, 10, MaxNameBuffer, "Sawh, Anisa", name);
```

Here, we are telling binarySearch to look for "Sawh, Anisa" in locations 5 to 10 of the given array. However, locations 8 to 10 do not exist in the array. The result of the search will be unpredictable. The program may crash or return an incorrect result. The onus is on the calling program to ensure that binarySearch (or any other function) is called with valid arguments.

1.8 Example: Word Frequency Count

Let's write a program to read an English passage and count the number of times each word appears. The output consists of an alphabetical listing of the words and their frequencies.

We can use the following outline to develop our program:

```
while there is input
   get a word
   search for word
   if word is in the table
      add 1 to its count
   else
      add word to the table
      set its count to 1
   endif
endwhile
print table
```

This is a typical "search and insert" situation. We search for the next word among the words stored so far. If the search succeeds, we need only increment its count. If the search fails, the word is put in the table, and its count set to 1.

A major design decision here is how to search the table, which, in turn, will depend on where and how a new word is inserted in the table. The following are two possibilities:

1. A new word is inserted in the next free position in the table. This implies that a sequential search must be used to look for an incoming word since the words would not be in any particular order. This method has the advantages of simplicity and easy insertion, but searching takes longer because more words are put in the table.

2. A new word is inserted in the table in such a way that the words are always in alphabetical order. This may entail moving words that have already been stored so that the new word may be slotted in the right place. However, since the table is in order, a binary search can be used to search for an incoming word.

For (2), searching is faster, but insertion is slower than in (1). Since, in general, searching is done more frequently than inserting, (2) might be preferable.

Another advantage of (2) is that, at the end, the words will already be in alphabetical order and no sorting will be required. If (1) is used, the words will need to be sorted to obtain the alphabetical order.

We will write our program using the approach in (2). The complete program is shown as Program P1.5.

Program P1.5

```
#include <stdio.h>
#include <string.h>
#include <ctype.h>
#include <stdlib.h>
#define MaxWords 50
#define MaxLength 10
#define MaxWordBuffer MaxLength+1
int main() {
   int getWord(FILE *, char[]);
   int binarySearch(int, int, char [], int max, char [][max]);
   void addToList(char[], int max, char [][max], int[], int, int);
   void printResults(FILE *, int max, char [][max], int[], int);
   char wordList[MaxWords][MaxWordBuffer], word[MaxWordBuffer];
   int frequency[MaxWords], numWords = 0;

   FILE * in = fopen("passage.txt", "r");
   if (in == NULL){
      printf("Cannot find file\n");
      exit(1);
   }

   FILE * out = fopen("output.txt", "w");
   if (out == NULL){
      printf("Cannot create output file\n");
      exit(2);
   }

   for (int h = 0; h < MaxWords; h++) frequency[h] = 0;

   while (getWord(in, word) != 0) {
      int loc = binarySearch (0, numWords-1, word, MaxWordBuffer, wordList);
      if (strcmp(word, wordList[loc]) == 0) ++frequency[loc]; //word found
      else //this is a new word
         if (numWords < MaxWords) { //if table is not full
            addToList(word, MaxWordBuffer, wordList, frequency, loc, numWords-1);
            ++numWords;
         }
         else fprintf(out, "'%s' not added to table\n", word);
   }
   printResults(out, MaxWordBuffer, wordList, frequency, numWords);
} // end main
```

```
int getWord(FILE * in, char str[]) {
// stores the next word, if any, in str; word is converted to lowercase
// returns 1 if a word is found; 0, otherwise
   char ch;
   int n = 0;
   // read over white space
   while (!isalpha(ch = getc(in)) && ch != EOF) ; //empty while body
   if (ch == EOF) return 0;
   str[n++] = tolower(ch);
   while (isalpha(ch = getc(in)) && ch != EOF)
      if (n < MaxLength) str[n++] = tolower(ch);
   str[n] = '\0';
   return 1;
} // end getWord

int binarySearch(int lo, int hi, char key[], int max, char list[][max]) {
//search for key from list[lo] to list[hi]
//if found, return its location;
//if not found, return the location in which it should be inserted
//the calling program will check the location to determine if found
   while (lo <= hi) {
      int mid = (lo + hi) / 2;
      int cmp = strcmp(key, list[mid]);
      if (cmp == 0) return mid; // found
      if (cmp < 0) hi = mid - 1;
      else lo = mid + 1;
   }
   return lo; //not found; should be inserted in location lo
} //end binarySearch

void addToList(char item[], int max, char list[][max], int freq[], int p, int n) {
//adds item in position list[p]; sets freq[p] to 1
//shifts list[n] down to list[p] to the right
   for (int h = n; h >= p; h--) {
      strcpy(list[h+1], list[h]);
      freq[h+1] = freq[h];
   }
   strcpy(list[p], item);
   freq[p] = 1;
} //end addToList

void printResults(FILE *out, int max, char list[][max], int freq[], int n) {
   fprintf(out, "\nWords          Frequency\n\n");
   for (int h = 0; h < n; h++)
      fprintf(out, "%-15s %2d\n", list[h], freq[h]);
} //end printResults
```

When Program P1.5 was run with this data, it produced the output that follows:

```
The quick brown fox jumps over the lazy dog. Congratulations!
If the quick brown fox jumped over the lazy dog then
Why did the quick brown fox jump over the lazy dog?
To recuperate!
```

Here is the output:

```
Words        Frequency
brown             3
congratula        1
did               1
dog               3
fox               3
if                1
jump              1
jumped            1
jumps             1
lazy              3
over              3
quick             3
recuperate        1
the               6
then              1
to                1
why               1
```

The following are comments on Program P1.5:

- For our purposes, we assume that a word begins with a letter and consists of letters only. If you want to include other characters (such as a hyphen or apostrophe), you need change only the `getWord` function.
- `MaxWords` denotes the maximum number of distinct words catered for. For testing the program, we have used `50` for this value. If the number of distinct words in the passage exceeds `MaxWords` (50, say), any words after the 50th will be read but not stored, and a message to that effect will be printed. However, the count for a word already stored will be incremented if it is encountered again.
- `MaxLength` (we use `10` for testing) denotes the maximum length of a word. Strings are declared using `MaxLength+1` (defined as `MaxWordBuffer`) to cater for `\0`, which must be added at the end of each string.
- `main` checks that the input file exists and that the output file can be created. Next, it initializes the frequency counts to `0`. It then processes the words in the passage based on the outline shown at the start of Section 1.8.
- `getWord` reads the input file and stores the next word found in its string argument. It returns `1` if a word is found and `0`, otherwise. If a word is longer than `MaxLength`, only the first `MaxLength` letters are stored; the rest are read and discarded. For example, `congratulations` is truncated to `congratula` using a word size of `10`.

- All words are converted to lowercase so that, for instance, The and the are counted as the same word.
- binarySearch is written so that if the word is found, its location is returned. If the word is not found, then the location in which it *should* be inserted is returned. addToList is given the location in which to insert a new word. Words to the right of, and including, this location are shifted one position to make room for the new word.
- In declaring a *function prototype*, some compilers allow a two-dimensional array parameter to be declared as in char [][], with no size specified for either dimension. Others require that the size of the second dimension *must* be specified. Specifying the size of the second dimension should work on all compilers. In our program, we specify the second dimension using the parameter max, whose value will be supplied when the function is called.

1.9 Merging Ordered Lists

Merging is the process by which two or more ordered lists are combined into one ordered list. For example, given two lists of numbers, A and B, as follows:

```
A: 21 28 35 40 61 75
B: 16 25 47 54
```

they can be combined into one ordered list, C, as follows:

```
C: 16 21 25 28 35 40 47 54 61 75
```

The list C contains all the numbers from lists A and B. How can the merge be performed?

One way to think about it is to imagine that the numbers in the given lists are stored on cards, one per card, and the cards are placed face up on a table, with the smallest at the top. We can imagine the lists A and B as follows:

```
21    16
28    25
35    47
40    54
61
75
```

We look at the top two cards, 21 and 16. The smaller, 16, is removed and placed in C. This exposes the number 25.

The top two cards are now 21 and 25. The smaller, 21, is removed and added to C, which now contains 16 21. This exposes the number 28.

The top two cards are now 28 and 25. The smaller, 25, is removed and added to C, which now contains 16 21 25. This exposes the number 47.

The top two cards are now 28 and 47. The smaller, 28, is removed and added to C, which now contains 16 21 25 28. This exposes the number 35.

The top two cards are now 35 and 47. The smaller, 35, is removed and added to C, which now contains 16 21 25 28 35. This exposes the number 40.

The top two cards are now 40 and 47. The smaller, 40, is removed and added to C, which now contains 16 21 25 28 35 40. This exposes the number 61.

The top two cards are now 61 and 47. The smaller, 47, is removed and added to C, which now contains 16 21 25 28 35 40 47. This exposes the number 54.

The top two cards are now 61 and 54. The smaller, 54, is removed and added to C, which now contains 16 21 25 28 35 40 47 54. The list B has no more numbers.

We copy the remaining elements (61 75) of A to C, which now contains the following:

```
16 21 25 28 35 40 47 54 61 75
```

The merge is now completed.

At each step of the merge, we compare the smallest remaining number of A with the smallest remaining number of B. The smaller of these is added to C. If the smaller comes from A, we move on to the next number in A; if the smaller comes from B, we move on to the next number in B.

This is repeated until all the numbers in either A or B have been used. If all the numbers in A have been used, we add the remaining numbers from B to C. If all the numbers in B have been used, we add the remaining numbers from A to C.

We can express the logic of the merge as follows:

```
while (at least one number remains in both A and B) {
   if (smallest in A < smallest in B)
      add smallest in A to C
      move on to next number in A
   else
      add smallest in B to C
      move on to next number in B
   endif
}
if (A has ended) add remaining numbers in B to C
else add remaining numbers in A to C
```

1.9.1 Implementing the Merge

Assume that an array A contains *m* numbers stored in A[0] to A[m-1] and an array B contains *n* numbers stored in B[0] to B[n-1]. Assume that the numbers are stored in ascending order. We want to merge the numbers in A and B into another array C such that C[0] to C[m+n-1] contains all the numbers in A and B sorted in ascending order.

We will use integer variables i, j, and k to subscript the arrays A, B, and C, respectively. "Moving on to the next position" in an array can be done by adding 1 to the subscript variable. We can implement the merge with the following code:

```
i = 0;      //i points to the first (smallest) number in A
j = 0;      //j points to the first (smallest) number in B
k = -1;     //k will be incremented before storing a number in C[k]
while (i < m && j < n) {
   if (A[i] < B[j]) C[++k] = A[i++];
   else C[++k] = B[j++];
}
if (i == m) //copy B[j] to B[n-1] to C
   for ( ; j < n; j++) C[++k] = B[j];
else        // j == n, copy A[i] to A[m-1] to C
   for ( ; i < m; i++) C[++k] = A[i];
```

Program P1.6 shows a simple main function that tests the previous logic. We write the merge as a function that, given the arguments A, m, B, n, and C, performs the merge and returns the number of elements, m + n, in C. When run, the program prints the contents of C, like this:

```
16 21 25 28 35 40 47 54 61 75
```

Program P1.6

```
#include <stdio.h>
int main () {
   int merge(int[], int, int[], int, int[]);
   int A[] = {21, 28, 35, 40, 61, 75};
   int B[] = {16, 25, 47, 54};
   int C[20];
   int n = merge(A, 6 , B, 4, C);
   for (int h = 0; h < n; h++) printf("%d ", C[h]);
   printf("\n\n");
} //end main

int merge(int A[], int m, int B[], int n, int C[]) {
   int i = 0;  //i points to the first (smallest) number in A
   int j = 0;  //j points to the first (smallest) number in B
   int k = -1; //k will be incremented before storing a number in C[k]
   while (i < m && j < n) {
      if (A[i] < B[j]) C[++k] = A[i++];
      else C[++k] = B[j++];
   }
   if (i == m) ///copy B[j] to B[n-1] to C
      for ( ; j < n; j++) C[++k] = B[j];
   else // j == n, copy A[i] to A[m-1] to C
      for ( ; i < m; i++) C[++k] = A[i];
   return m + n;
} //end merge
```

As a matter of interest, we can also implement merge as follows:

```
int merge(int A[], int m, int B[], int n, int C[]) {
   int i = 0;  //i points to the first (smallest) number in A
   int j = 0;  //j points to the first (smallest) number in B
   int k = -1; //k will be incremented before storing a number in C[k]
   while (i < m || j < n) {
      if (i == m) C[++k] = B[j++];
      else if (j == n) C[++k] = A[i++];
      else if (A[i] < B[j]) C[++k] = A[i++];
      else C[++k] = B[j++];
   }
   return m + n;
} //end merge
```

The `while` loop expresses the following logic: as long as there is at least one element to process in either `A` *or* `B`, we enter the loop. If we are finished with `A` (`i == m`), copy an element from `B` to `C`. If we are finished with `B` (`j == n`), copy an element from `A` to `C`. Otherwise, copy the smaller of `A[i]` and `B[j]` to `C`. Each time we copy an element from an array, we add 1 to the subscript for that array.

While the previous version implements the merge in a straightforward way, it seems reasonable to say that this version is a bit neater.

EXERCISES 1

1. A survey of ten pop artists is made. Each person votes for an artist by specifying the number of the artist (a value from `1` to `10`). Each voter is allowed one vote for the artist of their choice. The vote is recorded as a number from `1` to `10`. The number of voters is unknown beforehand, but the votes are terminated by a vote of `0`. Any vote that is not a number from `1` to `10` is a spoiled vote. A file, `votes.txt`, contains the names of the candidates. The first name is considered as candidate 1, the second as candidate 2, and so on. The names are followed by the votes. Write a program to read the data and evaluate the results of the survey.

   Print the results in alphabetical order by artist name and in order by votes received (most votes first). Print all output to the file `results.txt`.

2. Write a program to read names and phone numbers into two arrays. Request a name and print the person's phone number. Use binary search to look up the name.

3. Write a program to read English words and their equivalent Spanish words into two arrays. Request the user to type several English words. For each, print the equivalent Spanish word. Choose a suitable end-of-data marker. Search for the typed words using binary search. Modify the program so that the user types Spanish words instead.

4. The *median* of a set of *n* numbers (not necessarily distinct) is obtained by arranging the numbers in order and taking the number in the middle. If *n* is odd, there is a unique middle number. If *n* is even, then the average of the two middle values is the median. Write a program to read a set of *n* positive integers (assume $n < 100$) and print their median; *n* is not given but `0` indicates the end of the data.

5. The *mode* of a set of *n* numbers is the number that appears most frequently. For example, the mode of `7 3 8 5 7 3 1 3 4 8 9` is `3`. Write a program to read a set of *n* positive integers (assume $n < 100$) and print their mode; *n* is not given, but `0` indicates the end of the data.

6. An array `chosen` contains `n` distinct integers arranged in no particular order. Another array `winners` contains `m` distinct integers arranged in *ascending* order. Write code to determine how many of the numbers in `chosen` appear in `winners`.

7. A multiple-choice examination consists of 20 questions. Each question has 5 choices, labeled *A, B, C, D, and E*. The first line of data contains the correct answers to the 20 questions in the first 20 *consecutive* character positions, for example:

   ```
   BECDCBAADEBACBAEDDBE
   ```

Each subsequent line contains the answers for a candidate. Data on a line consists of a candidate number (an integer), followed by one or more spaces, followed by the 20 answers given by the candidate in the next 20 *consecutive* character positions. An X is used if a candidate did not answer a particular question. You may assume all data is valid and stored in a file called `exam.dat`. Here is a sample line:

```
4325   BECDCBAXDEBACCAEDXBE
```

There are at most 100 candidates. A line containing a "candidate number" 0 indicates only the end of the data.

Points for a question are awarded as follows—correct answer: 4 points; wrong answer: -1 point; no answer: 0 points.

Write a program to process the data and print a report consisting of candidate number and the total points obtained by the candidate, *in ascending order by candidate number*. At the end, print the average number of points gained by the candidates.

8. A is an array sorted in descending order. B is an array sorted in descending order. Merge A and B into C so that C is in *descending* order.

9. A is an array sorted in descending order. B is an array sorted in descending order. Merge A and B into C so that C is in *ascending* order.

10. A is an array sorted in ascending order. B is an array sorted in descending order. Merge A and B into C so that C is in *ascending* order.

11. An array A contains integers that first increase in value and then decrease in value, for example:

17	24	31	39	44	49	36	29	20	18	13
0	1	2	3	4	5	6	7	8	9	75

It is unknown at which point the numbers start to decrease. Write efficient code to copy the numbers in A to another array B so that B is sorted in ascending order. Your code must take advantage of the way the numbers are arranged in A.

12. Two words are anagrams if one word can be formed by rearranging all the letters of the other word, for example: section, notices. Write a program to read two words and determine whether they are anagrams.

Write another program to read a list of words and find all sets of words such that words within a set are anagrams of each other.

CHAPTER 2

Structures

In this chapter, we will explain the following:

- What a structure is
- How to declare a structure
- How to use `typedef` to work with structures more conveniently
- How to work with an array of structures
- How to search an array of structures
- How to sort an array of structures
- How to declare *nested* structures
- How to use structures to manipulate fractions
- How to use structures to solve a "voting" problem
- How structures can be passed to a function

2.1 Defining Structures

In C, a structure is a collection of one or more variables, possibly of different types, grouped together under a single name for convenient handling.

There are many situations in which we want to process data about a certain entity or object but the data consists of items of various types. For example, the data for a student (the *student record*) may consist of several *fields* such as a name, address and telephone number (all of type string), number of courses taken (integer), fees payable (floating-point), names of courses (string), grades obtained (character), and so on.

The data for a car may consist of manufacturer, model and registration number (string), seating capacity and fuel capacity (integer), and mileage and price (floating-point). For a book, we may want to store author and title (string), price (floating-point), number of pages (integer), type of binding—hardcover, paperback, spiral (string)—and number of copies in stock (integer).

Suppose we want to store data for 100 students in a program. One approach is to have a separate array for each field and use subscripts to link the fields together. Thus, `name[i]`, `address[i]`, `fees[i]`, and so on, refer to the data for the *i*th student.

The problem with this approach is that if there are many fields, the handling of several parallel arrays becomes clumsy and unwieldy. For example, suppose we want to pass a student's data to a function via the parameter list. This will involve the passing of several arrays. Also, if we are sorting the students by name, say, each time two names are interchanged, we have to write statements to interchange the data in the other arrays as well. In such situations, C structures are convenient to use.

2.2 How to Declare a Structure

Consider the problem of storing a date in a program. A date consists of three parts: the day, the month, and the year. Each of these parts can be represented by an integer. For example, the date "September 14, 2006" can be represented by the day, 14; the month, 9; and the year 2006. We say that a date consists of three *fields*, each of which is an integer.

If we want, we can also represent a date by using the *name* of the month, rather than its number. In this case, a date consists of three fields, one of which is a string and the other two are integers.

In C, we can declare a *date type* as a *structure* using the keyword `struct`. Consider this declaration:

```
struct date {int day, month, year;};
```

It consists of the word `struct` followed by some name we choose to give to the structure (`date`, in the example); this is followed by the declarations of the fields enclosed in left and right braces. Note the semicolon at the end of the declaration just before the right brace—this is the usual case of a semicolon ending a declaration. The right brace is followed by a semicolon, ending the `struct` declaration.

We could also have written the declaration as follows, where each field is declared individually:

```
struct date {
   int day;
   int month;
   int year;
} ;
```

This could be written as follows, but the former style is preferred for its readability:

```
struct date {int day; int month; int year;};
```

Given the `struct` declaration, we can declare variables of type `struct date`, as follows:

```
struct date dob; //to hold a "date of birth"
```

This declares `dob` as a "structure variable" of type `date`. It has three fields called `day`, `month`, and `year`. This can be pictured as follows:

	day	month	year
dob	14	11	2013

We refer to the day field as `dob.day`, the month field as `dob.month`, and the year field as `dob.year`. In C, the period (`.`), as used here, is referred to as the *structure member operator.*

In general, *a field is specified by the structure variable name, followed by a period, followed by the field name.*

We could declare more than one variable at a time, as follows:

```
struct date borrowed, returned; //for a book in a library, say
```

Each of these variables has three fields: `day`, `month`, and `year`. The fields of `borrowed` are referred to by `borrowed.day`, `borrowed.month`, and `borrowed.year`. The fields of `returned` are referred to by `returned.day`, `returned.month`, and `returned.year`.

In this example, each field is an int and can be used in any context in which an int variable can be used. For example, to assign the date "November 14, 2013" to dob, we can use this:

```
dob.day = 14;
dob.month = 11;
dob.year = 2013;
```

This can be pictured as follows:

	day	month	year
dob	14	11	2013

We can also read values for day, month, and year with the following:

```
scanf("%d %d %d", &dob.day, &dob.month, &dob.year);
```

If today was a struct date variable holding a date, we could assign all the fields of today to dob, say, with the following:

```
dob = today;
```

This one statement is equivalent to the following:

```
dob.day = today.day;
dob.month = today.month;
dob.year = today.year;
```

We can print the "value" of dob with this:

```
printf("The party is on %d/%d/%d\n", dob.day, dob.month, dob.year);
```

For this example, this will print the following:

```
The party is on 14/11/2013
```

Note that each field has to be printed individually. We could also write a function printDate, say, which prints a date given as an argument. For example, given this...

```
void printDate(struct date d) {
   printf("%d/%d/%d \n", d.day, d.month, d.year);
}
```

The following call...

```
printDate(dob);
```

will print this:

```
14/11/2013
```

We note, in passing, that C provides a date and time structure, `tm`, in the standard library. In addition to the date, it provides, among other things, the time to the nearest second. To use it, your program must be preceded by the following:

```
#include <time.h>
```

The construct `struct date` is a bit cumbersome to use, compared to single word types such `int` or `double`. Fortunately, C provides us with `typedef` to make working with structures a little more convenient.

2.2.1 typedef

We can use `typedef` to give a name to some existing type, and this name can then be used to declare variables of that type. We can also use `typedef` to construct shorter or more meaningful names for predefined C types or for user-declared types, such as structures. For example, the following statement declares a new type-name `Whole`, which is synonymous with the predefined type `int`:

```
typedef int Whole;
```

Note that `Whole` appears in the same position as a variable would, not right after the word `typedef`. We can then declare variables of type `Whole`, as follows:

```
Whole amount, numCopies;
```

This is exactly equivalent to the following:

```
int amount, numCopies;
```

For those accustomed to the term `real` of languages like Pascal or FORTRAN, the following statement allows them to declare variables of type `Real`:

```
typedef float Real;
```

In this book, we use at least one uppercase letter to distinguish type names declared using `typedef`.

We could give a short, meaningful name, `Date`, to the date structure shown earlier with the following declaration:

```
typedef struct date {
   int day;
   int month;
   int year;
} Date;
```

Recall that C distinguishes between uppercase and lowercase letters so that `date` is different from `Date`. We could, if we wanted, have used any other identifier, such as `DateType`, instead of `Date`.

We could now declare "structure variables" of type `Date`, such as the following:

```
Date dob, borrowed, returned;
```

Notice how much shorter and neater this is compared to the following:

```
struct date dob, borrowed, returned;
```

Since there is hardly any reason to use this second form, we could omit date from the earlier declaration and write this:

```
typedef struct {
   int day;
   int month;
   int year;
} Date;
```

Thereafter, we can use Date whenever the struct is required. For example, we can rewrite printDate as follows:

```
void printDate(Date d) {
   printf("%d/%d/%d \n", d.day, d.month, d.year);
}
```

To pursue the date example, suppose we want to store the "short" name—the first three letters, for example Aug—of the month. We will need to use a declaration such as this:

```
typedef struct {
   int day;
   char month[4]; //one position for \0 to end string
   int year;
} Date;
```

We can represent the date "November 14, 2013" in a Date variable dob with the following:

```
dob.day = 14;
strcpy(dob.month, "Nov");
dob.year = 2013;
```

And we can write printDate as follows:

```
void printDate(Date d) {
   printf("%s %d, %d \n", d.month, d.day, d.year);
}
```

The following call...

```
printDate(dob);
```

will print this:

```
Nov 14, 2013
```

Suppose we want to store information about students. For each student, we want to store their name, age, and gender (male or female). Assuming that a name is no longer than 30 characters, we could use the following declaration:

```
typedef struct {
   char name[31];
   int age;
   char gender;
} Student;
```

We can now declare variables of type Student, as follows:

```
Student stud1, stud2;
```

Each of stud1 and stud2 will have its own fields—name, age, and gender. We can refer to these fields with this:

```
stud1.name    stud1.age    stud1.gender
stud2.name    stud2.age    stud2.gender
```

As usual, we can assign values to these fields or read values into them. And, if we want, we can assign all the fields of stud1 to stud2 with the following statement:

```
stud2 = stud1;
```

2.3 Working with an Array of Structures

Suppose we want to store data on 100 students. We will need an array of size 100, and each element of the array will hold the data for one student. Thus, each element will have to be a structure—we need an "array of structures."

We can declare the array with the following, similar to how we say "int pupil[100]" to declare an integer array of size 100:

```
Student pupil[100];
```

This allocates storage for pupil[0], pupil[1], pupil[2], ..., up to pupil[99]. Each element pupil[j] consists of three fields that can be referred to as follows:

```
pupil[j].name    pupil[j].age    pupil[j].gender
```

First we will need to store some data in the array. Assume we have data in the following format (name, age, gender):

```
"Jones, John" 24 M
"Mohammed, Lisa" 33 F
"Singh, Sandy" 29 F
"Layne, Dennis" 49 M
"END"
```

Suppose the data are stored in a file input.txt and in is declared as follows:

```
FILE * in = fopen("input.txt", "r");
```

If str is a character array, assume we can call the function getString(in, str) to store the next data string in quotes in str without the quotes. Also assume that readChar(in) will read the data and return the next nonwhitespace character.

Exercise: Write the functions getString and readChar.

We can read the data into the array pupil with the following code:

```
int n = 0;
char temp[31];
getString(in, temp);
```

```
while (strcmp(temp, "END") != 0) {
   strcpy(pupil[n].name, temp);
   fscanf(in, "%d", &pupil[n].age);
   pupil[n].gender = readChar(in);
   n++;
   getString(in, temp);
}
```

At the end, n contains the number of students stored, and pupil[0] to pupil[n-1] contain the data for those students.

To ensure that we do not attempt to store more data than we have room for in the array, we should check that n is within the bounds of the array. Assuming that MaxItems has the value 100, this can be done by changing the while condition to the following:

```
while (n < MaxItems && strcmp(temp, "END") != 0)
```

or by inserting the following just after the statement n++; inside the loop:

```
if (n == MaxItems) break;
```

2.4 Searching an Array of Structures

With the data stored in the array, we can manipulate it in various ways. For instance, we can write a function to search for a given name. Assuming the data is stored in no particular order, we can use a sequential search as follows:

```
int search(char key[], Student list[], int n) {
//search for key in list[0] to list[n-1]
//if found, return the location; if not found, return -1
   for (int h = 0; h < n; h++)
      if (strcmp(key, list[h].name) == 0) return h;
   return -1;
} //end search
```

Given the previous data, the following call:

```
search("Singh, Sandy", pupil, 4)
```

will return 2, and the following call will return -1:

```
search("Layne, Sandy", pupil, 4)
```

2.5 Sorting an Array of Structures

Suppose we want the list of students in alphabetical order by name. It will be required to sort the array pupil. The following function uses an insertion sort to do the job. The *process* is identical to sorting an int array, say, except that the name field is used to govern the sorting.

```
void sort(Student list[], int n) {
//sort list[0] to list[n-1] by name using an insertion sort
   for (int h = 1; h < n; h++) {
      Student temp = list[h];
      int k = h - 1;
      while (k >= 0 && strcmp(temp.name, list[k].name) < 0) {
         list[k + 1] = list[k];
         k = k - 1;
      }
      list[k + 1] = temp;
   } //end for
} //end sort
```

Observe this statement:

```
list[k + 1] = list[k];
```

This assigns *all* the fields of `list[k]` to `list[k + 1]`.

If we want to sort the students in order by age, all we need to change is the `while` condition. To sort in *ascending* order, we write this:

```
while (k >= 0 && temp.age < list[k].age) //move smaller numbers to the left
```

To sort in *descending* order, we write this:

```
while (k >= 0 && temp.age > list[k].age) //move bigger numbers to the left
```

We could even separate the list into male and female students by sorting on the `gender` field. Since *F* comes before *M* in alphabetical order, we can put the females first by writing this:

```
while (k >= 0 && temp.gender < list[k].gender) //move Fs to the left
```

And we can put the males first by writing this:

```
while (k >= 0 && temp.gender > list[k].gender ) //move Ms to the left
```

2.6 How to Read, Search, and Sort a Structure

We illustrate the ideas discussed earlier in Program P2.1. The program performs the following:

- Reads data for students from a file, `input.txt`, and stores them in an array of structures
- Prints the data in the order stored in the array
- Tests `search` by reading several names and looking for them in the array
- Sorts the data in alphabetical order by name
- Prints the sorted data

The program also illustrates how the functions `getString` and `readChar` may be written. `getString` lets us read a string enclosed within *any* "delimiter" characters. For example, we could specify a string as `$John Smith$` or `"John Smith"`. This is a very flexible way of specifying a string. *Each* string can be specified with its own delimiters, which could be different for the next string. It is particularly useful for specifying strings that may include special characters such as the double quotes without having to use an escape sequence like `\"`.

Program P2.1

```
#include <stdio.h>
#include <stdlib.h>
#include <string.h>
#include <ctype.h>
#define MaxStudents 100
#define MaxNameLength 30
#define MaxNameBuffer MaxNameLength+1
typedef struct {
   char name[MaxNameBuffer];
   int age;
   char gender;
} Student;

int main() {
   Student pupil[MaxStudents];
   char aName[MaxNameBuffer];
   void getString(FILE *, char[]);
   int getData(FILE *, Student[]);
   int search(char[], Student[], int);
   void sort(Student[], int);
   void printStudent(Student);
   void getString(FILE *, char[]);

   FILE * in = fopen("input.txt", "r");
   if (in == NULL) {
      printf("Error opening file: %s.\n", strerror(errno));
      exit(1);
   }

   int numStudents = getData(in, pupil);
   if (numStudents == 0) {
      printf("No data supplied for students");
      exit(1);
   }

   printf("\n");
   for (int h = 0; h < numStudents; h++) printStudent(pupil[h]);
   printf("\n");

   getString(in, aName);
   while (strcmp(aName, "END") != 0) {
      int ans = search(aName, pupil, numStudents);
      if (ans == -1) printf("%s not found\n", aName);
      else printf("%s found at location %d\n", aName, ans);
      getString(in, aName);
   }

   sort(pupil, numStudents);
   printf("\n");
   for (int h = 0; h < numStudents; h++) printStudent(pupil[h]);
} //end main
```

```
void printStudent(Student t) {
   printf("Name: %s Age: %d Gender: %c\n", t.name, t.age, t.gender);
} //end printStudent

int getData(FILE *in, Student list[]) {
   char temp[MaxNameBuffer];
   void getString(FILE *, char[]);
   char readChar(FILE *);

   int n = 0;
   getString(in, temp);
   while (n < MaxStudents && strcmp(temp, "END") != 0) {
      strcpy(list[n].name, temp);
      fscanf(in, "%d", &list[n].age);
      list[n].gender = readChar(in);
      n++;
      getString(in, temp);
   }
   return n;
} //end getData

int search(char key[], Student list[], int n) {
//search for key in list[0] to list[n-1]
//if found, return the location; if not found, return -1
   for (int h = 0; h < n; h++)
      if (strcmp(key, list[h].name) == 0) return h;
   return -1;
} //end search

void sort(Student list[], int n) {
//sort list[0] to list[n-1] by name using an insertion sort
   for (int h = 1; h < n; h++) {
      Student temp = list[h];
      int k = h - 1;
      while (k >= 0 && strcmp(temp.name, list[k].name) < 0) {
         list[k + 1] = list[k];
         k = k - 1;
      }
      list[k + 1] = temp;
   } //end for
} //end sort

void getString(FILE * in, char str[]) {
//stores, in str, the next string within delimiters
// the first non-whitespace character is the delimiter
// the string is read from the file 'in'

   char ch, delim;
   int n = 0;
   str[0] = '\0';
   // read over white space
   while (isspace(ch = getc(in))) ; //empty while body
   if (ch == EOF) return;
```

```
    delim = ch;
    while (((ch = getc(in)) != delim) && (ch != EOF))
       str[n++] = ch;
    str[n] = '\0';
 } // end getString

 char readChar(FILE * in) {
    char ch;
    while (isspace(ch = getc(in))) ; //empty while body
    return ch;
 } //end readChar
```

If the file input.txt contains the following data:

```
"Jones, John" 24 M
"Mohammed, Lisa" 33 F
"Singh, Sandy" 29 F
"Layne, Dennis" 49 M
"Singh, Cindy" 16 F
"Ali, Imran" 39 M
"Kelly, Trudy" 30 F
"Cox, Kerry" 25 M
"END"
"Kelly, Trudy"
"Layne, Dennis"
"Layne, Cindy"
"END"
```

the program prints this:

```
Name: Jones, John Age: 24 Gender: M
Name: Mohammed, Lisa Age: 33 Gender: F
Name: Singh, Sandy Age: 29 Gender: F
Name: Layne, Dennis Age: 49 Gender: M
Name: Singh, Cindy Age: 16 Gender: F
Name: Ali, Imran Age: 39 Gender: M
Name: Kelly, Trudy Age: 30 Gender: F
Name: Cox, Kerry Age: 25 Gender: M

Kelly, Trudy found at location 6
Layne, Dennis found at location 3
Layne, Cindy not found

Name: Ali, Imran Age: 39 Gender: M
Name: Cox, Kerry Age: 25 Gender: M
Name: Jones, John Age: 24 Gender: M
Name: Kelly, Trudy Age: 30 Gender: F
Name: Layne, Dennis Age: 49 Gender: M
Name: Mohammed, Lisa Age: 33 Gender: F
Name: Singh, Cindy Age: 16 Gender: F
Name: Singh, Sandy Age: 29 Gender: F
```

2.7 Nested Structures

C allows us to use a structure as part of the definition of another structure—a structure within a structure, called a *nested* structure. Consider the student structure. Suppose that, instead of age, we want to store the student's date of birth. This might be a better choice since a student's date of birth is fixed, whereas his age changes, and the field would have to be updated every year.

We could use the following declaration:

```
typedef struct {
   char name[31];
   Date dob;
   char gender;
} Student;
```

If `mary` is a variable of type `Student`, then `mary.dob` refers to her date of birth. But `mary.dob` is *itself* a `Date` structure. If necessary, we can refer to *its* fields with `mary.dob.day`, `mary.dob.month`, and `mary.dob.year`.

If we want to store a name in a more flexible way, for example, first name, middle initial, and last name, we could use a structure like this:

```
typedef struct {
   char first[21];
   char middle;
   char last[21];
} Name;
```

The `Student` structure now becomes the following, which contains two structures, `Name` and `Date`:

```
typedef struct {
   Name name;
   Date dob;
   char gender;
} Student;
```

If `st` is a variable of type `Student`,

`st.name` refers to a structure of the type `Name`,
`st.name.first` refers to the student's first name, and
`st.name.last[0]` refers to the first letter of her last name.

Now, if we want to sort the array `pupil` by last name, the `while` condition becomes the following:

```
while (k >= 0 && strcmp(temp.name.last, pupil[k].name.last) < 0)
```

A structure may be nested as deeply as you want. The dot (`.`) operator associates from left to right. If `a`, `b` and `c` are structures, like this:

```
a.b.c.d
```

is interpreted as follows:

```
((a.b).c).d
```

2.8 Working with Fractions

Consider the problem of working with fractions, where a fraction is represented by two integer values: one for the numerator and the other for the denominator. For example, is represented by the two numbers 5 and 9.

We will use the following structure to represent a fraction:

```
typedef struct {
   int num;
   int den;
} Fraction;
```

If a is variable of type `Fraction`, we can store in a with this:

```
a.num = 5;
a.den = 9;
```

This can be pictured as follows:

	num	den
a	5	9

We can also read two values representing a fraction and store them in a with a statement such as this:

```
scanf("%d %d", &a.num, &a.den);
```

We can write a function to print a fraction. For example, the following will print `5/9` when called with `printFraction(a)`:

```
void printFraction(Fraction f) {
   printf("%d/%d", f.num, f.den);
}
```

2.8.1 Manipulating Fractions

We can write functions to perform various operations on fractions. For instance, since the following is true:

$$\frac{a}{b}+\frac{c}{d}=\frac{ad+bc}{bd}$$

we can write a function to add two fractions as follows:

```
Fraction addFraction(Fraction a, Fraction b) {
   Fraction c;
   c.num = a.num * b.den + a.den * b.num;
   c.den = a.den * b.den;
   return c;
}
```

Similarly, we can write functions to subtract, multiply, and divide fractions.

```
Fraction subFraction(Fraction a, Fraction b) {
   Fraction c;
   c.num = a.num * b.den - a.den * b.num;
   c.den = a.den * b.den;
   return c;
}

Fraction mulFraction(Fraction a, Fraction b) {
   Fraction c;
   c.num = a.num * b.num;
   c.den = a.den * b.den;
   return c;
}

Fraction divFraction(Fraction a, Fraction b) {
   Fraction c;
   c.num = a.num * b.den;
   c.den = a.den * b.num;
   return c;
}
```

To illustrate their use, suppose we want to find the following:

$$\frac{2}{5} \text{ of } \left\{\frac{3}{7} + \frac{5}{8}\right\}$$

We can do this with the following statements:

```
Fraction a, b, c, sum, ans;
a.num = 2; a.den = 5;
b.num = 3; b.den = 7;
c.num = 5; c.den = 8;
sum = addFraction(b, c);
ans = mulFraction(a, sum);
printFraction(ans);
```

Strictly speaking, the variables `sum` and `ans` are not necessary, but we've used them to simplify the explanation. Since an argument to a function can be an expression, we could get the same result with this:

```
printFraction(mulFraction(a, addFraction(b, c)));
```

When run, this code will print the following, which is the correct answer:

```
118/280
```

However, if you want, you can write a function to reduce a fraction to its lowest terms. This can be done by finding the highest common factor (HCF) of the numerator and denominator. You then divide the numerator and denominator by their HCF. For example, the HCF of `118` and `280` is `2` so `118/280` reduces to `59/140`. Writing this function is left as an exercise.

2.9 A Voting Problem

This example will be used to illustrate several points concerning the passing of arguments to functions. It further highlights the differences between array arguments and simple-variable arguments. We will show how a function can return more than one value to a calling function by using a structure.

- *Problem*: In an election, there are seven candidates. Each voter is allowed one vote for the candidate of their choice. The vote is recorded as a number from 1 to 7. The number of voters is unknown beforehand, but the votes are terminated by a vote of 0. Any vote that is not a number from 1 to 7 is an invalid (spoiled) vote.
- *Exercise*: A file, `votes.txt`, contains the names of the candidates. The first name is considered as candidate 1, the second as candidate 2, and so on. The names are followed by the votes. Write a program to read the data and evaluate the results of the election. Print all output to the file, `results.txt`.

Your output should specify the total number of votes, the number of valid votes, and the number of spoiled votes. This is followed by the votes obtained by each candidate and the winner(s) of the election.

Here's the raw data:

```
Victor Taylor
Denise Duncan
Kamal Ramdhan
Michael Ali
Anisa Sawh
Carol Khan
Gary Owen

3 1 2 5 4 3 5 3 5 3 2 8 1 6 7 7 3 5
6 9 3 4 7 1 2 4 5 5 1 4 0
```

Your program should send the following output to `results.txt`:

```
Invalid vote: 8
Invalid vote: 9

Number of voters: 30
Number of valid votes: 28
Number of spoilt votes: 2

Candidate       Score

Victor Taylor     4
Denise Duncan     3
Kamal Ramdhan     6
Michael Ali       4
Anisa Sawh        6
Carol Khan        2
Gary Owen         3

The winner(s):
Kamal Ramdhan
Anisa Sawh
```

We now explain how we can solve this problem using C structures. Consider these declarations:

```
typedef struct  {
   char name[31];
   int numVotes;
} PersonData;
PersonData candidate[8];
```

Here, candidate is an array of structures. We will use candidate[1] to candidate[7] for the seven candidates; we will not use candidate[0]. This will allow us to work more naturally with the votes. For a vote (v, say), candidate[v] will be updated. If we used candidate[0], we would have the awkward situation where for a vote v, candidate[v-1] would have to be updated.

An element candidate[h] is not just a single data item but a structure consisting of two fields. These fields can be referred to as follows:

```
candidate[h].name and candidate[h].numVotes
```

To make the program flexible, we will define symbolic constants with this:

```
#define MaxCandidates 7
#define MaxNameLength 30
#define MaxNameBuffer MaxNameLength+1
```

and change the earlier declarations to the following:

```
typedef struct  {
   char name[MaxNameBuffer];
   int numVotes;
} PersonData;
PersonData candidate[MaxCandidates+1];
```

The solution is based on the following outline:

```
initialize
process the votes
print the results
```

The function initialize will read the names from the file in and set the vote counts to 0. The file is passed as an argument to the function. We will read a candidate's name in two parts (first name and last name) and then join them together to create a single name that we will store in person[h].name. Data will be read for max persons. Here is the function:

```
void initialize(PersonData person[], int max, FILE *in) {
   char lastName[MaxNameBuffer];
   for (int h = 1; h <= max; h++) {
      fscanf(in, "%s %s", person[h].name, lastName);
      strcat(person[h].name, " ");
      strcat(person[h].name, lastName);
      person[h].numVotes = 0;
   }
} //end initialize
```

Processing the votes will be based on the following outline:

```
get a vote
while the vote is not 0
   if the vote is valid
      add 1 to validVotes
      add 1 to the score of the appropriate candidate
   else
      print invalid vote
      add 1 to spoiltVotes
   endif
   get a vote
endwhile
```

After all the votes are processed, this function will need to return the number of valid and spoiled votes. But how can a function return more than one value? It can if the values are stored in a structure and the structure returned as the "value" of the function.

We will use the following declaration:

```
typedef struct {
   int valid, spoilt;
} VoteCount;
```

And we will write processVotes as follows:

```
VoteCount processVotes(PersonData person[], int max, FILE *in, FILE *out) {
   VoteCount temp;
   temp.valid = temp.spoilt = 0;

   int v;
   fscanf(in, "%d", &v);
   while (v != 0) {
      if (v < 1 || v > max) {
         fprintf(out, "Invalid vote: %d\n", v);
         ++temp.spoilt;
      }
      else {
         ++person[v].numVotes;
         ++temp.valid;
      }
      fscanf(in, "%d", &v);
   } //end while
   return temp;
} //end processVotes
```

Next, we write main, preceded by the compiler directives and the structure declarations.

```
#include <stdio.h>
#include <string.h>
#define MaxCandidates 7
#define MaxNameLength 30
#define MaxNameBuffer MaxNameLength+1
```

```
typedef struct  {
   char name[MaxNameBuffer];
   int numVotes;
} PersonData;
PersonData candidate[MaxCandidates];

typedef struct {
   int valid, spoilt;
} VoteCount;

int main() {
   void initialize(PersonData[], int, FILE *);
   VoteCount processVotes(PersonData[], int, FILE *, FILE *);
   void printResults(PersonData[], int, VoteCount, FILE *);

   PersonData candidate[MaxCandidates+1];
   VoteCount count;
   FILE *in = fopen("votes.txt", "r");
   FILE *out = fopen("results.txt", "w");

   initialize(candidate, MaxCandidates, in);
   count = processVotes(candidate, MaxCandidates, in, out);
   printResults(candidate, MaxCandidates, count, out);

   fclose(in);
   fclose(out);
} //end main
```

The declarations of `PersonData` and `VoteCount` come before `main`. This is done so that other functions can refer to them, without having to repeat the entire declarations. If they were declared in `main`, then the names `PersonData` and `VoteCount` would be known only in `main`, and other functions would have no access to them.

Now that we know how to read and process the votes, it remains only to determine the winner(s) and print the results. We will delegate this task to the function `printResults`.

Using the sample data, the array `candidate` will contain the values shown in Figure 2-1 after all the votes have been tallied (remember, we are not using `candidate[0]`).

	name	numVotes
1	Victor Taylor	4
2	Denise Duncan	3
3	Kamal Ramdhan	6
4	Michael Ali	4
5	Anisa Sawh	6
6	Carol Khan	2
7	Gary Owen	3

Figure 2-1. *The array* `candidate` *after votes are processed*

To find the winner, we must first find the largest value in the array. To do this, we will call a function `getLargest` with the following, which will set `win` to the *subscript* of the largest value in the `numVotes` field from `candidate[1]` to `candidate[7]` (since `MaxCandidates` is 7):

```
int win = getLargest(candidate, 1, MaxCandidates);
```

In our example, `win` will be set to 3 since the largest value, 6, is in position 3. (6 is also in position 5, but we just need the largest value, which we can get from either position.)

Here is `getLargest`:

```
int getLargest(PersonData person[], int lo, int hi) {
//returns the index of the highest vote from person[lo] to person[hi]
   int big = lo;
   for (int h = lo + 1; h <= hi; h++)
      if (person[h].numVotes > person[big].numVotes) big = h;
   return big;
} //end getLargest
```

Now that we know the largest value is in `candidate[win].numVotes`, we can "step through" the array, looking for those candidates with that value. This way, we will find all the candidates, if there is more than one, with the highest vote and declare them as winners.

An outline of `printResults` is as follows:

```
printResults
   print the number of voters, valid votes and spoilt votes
   print the score of each candidate
   determine and print the winner(s)
```

The details are given in the function `printResults`:

```
void printResults(PersonData person[], int max, VoteCount c, FILE *out) {
   int getLargest(PersonData[], int, int);
   fprintf(out, "\nNumber of voters: %d\n", c.valid + c.spoilt);
   fprintf(out, "Number of valid votes: %d\n", c.valid);
   fprintf(out, "Number of spoilt votes: %d\n", c.spoilt);
   fprintf(out, "\nCandidate       Score\n\n");

   for (int h = 1; h <= max; h++)
      fprintf(out, "%-15s %3d\n", person[h].name, person[h].numVotes);

   fprintf(out, "\nThe winner(s)\n");
   int win = getLargest(person, 1, max);
   int winningVote = person[win].numVotes;
   for (int h = 1; h <= max; h++)
      if (person[h].numVotes == winningVote)
         fprintf(out, "%s\n", person[h].name);
} //end printResults
```

Suppose it were required to print the names of the candidates in *descending* order by numVotes. To do this, the structure array candidate must be sorted in descending order using the numVotes field to control the sorting. This could be done by the following function call:

```
sortByVote(candidate, 1, MaxCandidates);
```

sortByVote uses an insertion sort and is written using the formal parameter person (any name will do), as shown here:

```
void sortByVote(PersonData person[], int lo, int hi) {
//sort person[lo..hi] in descending order by numVotes
   PersonData insertItem;
   for (int h = lo + 1; h <= hi; h++) { // process person[lo+1] to person[hi]
      // insert person h in its proper position
      insertItem = person[h];
      int k = h -1;
      while (k >= lo && insertItem.numVotes > person[k].numVotes) {
         person[k + 1] = person[k];
         --k;
      }
      person[k + 1] = insertItem;
   }
} //end sortByVote
```

Observe that the structure of the function is pretty much the same as if we were sorting a simple integer array. The major difference is in the while condition where we must specify which field is used to determine the sorting order. (In this example, we also use >, rather than <, since we are sorting in descending order rather than ascending order.) When we are about to process person[h], we copy it to the temporary structure, insertItem. This frees person[h] so that person[h-1] may be shifted into position h, if necessary. To shift an array element to the right, we use the following simple assignment:

```
person[k + 1] = person[k];
```

This moves the entire structure (two fields, in this example).

If we need to sort the candidates in alphabetical order, we could use the function sortByName:

```
void sortByName(PersonData person[], int lo, int hi) {
//sort person[lo..hi] in alphabetical order by name
   PersonData insertItem;
   for (int h = lo + 1; h <= hi; h++) { // process person[lo+1] to person[hi]
      // insert person j in its proper position
      insertItem = person[h];
      int k = h -1;
      while (k > 0 && strcmp(insertItem.name, person[k].name) < 0) {
         person[k + 1] = person[k];
         --k;
      }
      person[k + 1] = insertItem;
   }
} //end sortByName
```

The function sortByName is identical with sortByVote except for the while condition, which specifies which field is used in comparisons and the use of < for sorting in ascending order. Note the use of the standard string function, strcmp, for comparing two names. If strcmp(s1, s2) is negative, it means that the string s1 comes before the string s2 in alphabetical order.

As an exercise, rewrite the program for solving the voting problem so that it prints the results in descending order by votes and in alphabetical order.

2.10 Passing Structures to Functions

In the voting problem, we saw examples where candidate, an array of structures, was passed to various functions. We now discuss some other issues that arise in passing a structure to a function.

Consider a structure for a "book type" with the following fields:

```
typedef struct {
   char author[31];
   char title[51];
   char binding;            //paperback, hardcover, spiral, etc.
   double price;
   int quantity;            //quantity in stock
} Book;
Book text;
```

This declares a new type called Book, and text is declared as a variable of type Book.

We could pass individual fields to functions in the usual way; for a simple variable, its value is passed, but, for an array variable, its address is passed. Thus:

```
fun1(text.quantity);    // value of text.quantity is passed
fun2(text.binding);     // value of text.binding is passed
fun3(text.price);       // value of text.price is passed
```

but,

```
fun4(text.title);       // address of array text.title is passed
```

We could even pass the first letter of the title, as follows:

```
fun5(text.title[0]);    // value of first letter of title is passed
```

To pass the entire structure, we use this:

```
fun6(text);
```

Of course, the header for each of these functions must be written with the appropriate parameter type.

In the last example, the fields of text are copied to a temporary place (called the *run-time heap*), and the copy is passed to fun6; that is, the structure is passed "by value." If a structure is complicated or contains arrays, the copying operation could be time-consuming. In addition, when the function returns, the values of the structure elements must be removed from the heap; this adds to the overhead—the extra processing required to perform a function call.

To avoid this overhead, the *address* of the structure could be passed. We will show how to do this when we discuss pointers in the next chapter.

EXERCISES 2

1. Do Chapter 1, Exercise 1 using structures.
2. Write a program to read names and phone numbers into a structure array. Request a name and print the person's phone number. Use binary search to look up the name.
3. Do Chapter 1, Exercise 3 using a structure array to hold the words.
4. Do Chapter 1, Exercise 6 using a structure to hold a candidate's data.
5. Write a function that, given two date structures, `d1` and `d2`, returns `-1` if `d1` comes before `d2`, `0` if `d1` is the same as `d2`, and `1` if `d1` comes after `d2`.
6. Write a function that, given two date structures, `d1` and `d2`, returns the number of days that `d2` is ahead of `d1`. If `d2` comes before `d1`, return a negative value.
7. A time in 24-hour clock format is represented by two numbers; for example, `16 45` means the time `16:45`, that is, 4:45 p.m. Using a structure to represent a time, write a function that, given two time structures, `t1` and `t2`, returns the number of minutes from `t1` to `t2`. For example, if the two given times are `16 45` and `23 25`, your function should return `400`.
8. Modify the function so that it works as follows: if `t2` is less than `t1`, take it to mean a time for the *next* day. For example, given the times `20:30` and `6:15`, take this to mean 8.30 p.m. to 6.15 a.m. of the next day. Your function should return `585`.
9. A length, specified in meters and centimeters, is represented by two integers. For example, the length 3m 75cm is represented by `3 75`. Using a structure to represent a length, write functions to compare, add, and subtract two lengths.
10. A file contains the names and distances jumped by athletes in a long-jump competition. Using a structure to hold a name and distance (which is itself a structure as in 8), write a program to read the data and print a list of names and distance jumped in order of merit (best jumper first).
11. At a school's bazaar, activities were divided into stalls. At the close of the bazaar, the manager of each stall submitted information to the principal consisting of the name of the stall, the income earned, and its expenses. Here's some sample data:

    ```
    Games 2300.00 1000.00
    Sweets 900.00 1000.00
    ```

    Using a structure to hold a stall's data, write a program to read the data and print a report consisting of the stall name and net income (income - expenses), *in order of decreasing net income* (that is, with the most profitable stall first and the least profitable stall last). In addition, print the number of stalls, the total profit or loss of the bazaar, and the stall(s) that made the most profit. Assume that a line containing `xxxxxx` only ends the data.

12. A data file contains registration information for six courses—CS20A, CS21A, CS29A, CS30A, CS35A, and CS36A. Each line of data consists of a seven-digit student registration number followed by six (ordered) values, each of which is `0` or `1`. A value of `1` indicates that the student is registered for the corresponding course; `0` means the student is not. Thus, `1 0 1 0 1 1` means that the student is registered for CS20A, CS29A, CS35A, and CS36A, but not for CS21A and CS30A. You may assume that there are no more than 100 students and a registration number `0` ends the data. Write a program to read the data and produce a class list for each course. Each list consists of the registration numbers of those students taking the course.

CHAPTER 3

Pointers

In this chapter, we will explain the following:

- What a pointer is
- How to declare pointer variables
- How to dereference a pointer
- How a function can change the value of a variable in a "calling" function
- Some issues involved in passing an array as an argument to a function
- How to work with character pointers
- The meaning of pointer arithmetic
- How to use pointers to structures
- How to use pointers to functions to write general-purpose routines
- What are `void` pointers and how to use them

3.1 Defining Pointers

In C, arguments to functions are passed "by value." Suppose the function `test` is called with the variable `num` as an argument.

```
test(num);
```

The value of `num` is copied to a temporary location, and this location is passed to `test`. In this scenario, `test` has no access whatsoever to the original argument `num` and, hence, cannot change it in any way.

Does this mean that a function can never change the value of a variable in another function? It can, but in order to do so, it must have access to the address of the variable—the location in memory where the variable is stored.

If a computer has 1 million bytes of memory, its memory locations range from 0 to 999,999. Among other things, memory locations are used for storing the values of variables. Suppose a variable `num` has the value `36` and this value is stored at memory location `5000`. We say the storage address (or, simply, the address) of `num` is `5000`.

The operator `&`, when applied to a variable, returns the address of the variable. For example, suppose `num` is stored at address `5000`. Then the value of `&num` is `5000`.

The term *pointer* is used to refer to an address in memory. A pointer variable is one that can hold the address of a memory location.

If ptr is a pointer variable, we can assign a value to it.

```
ptr = &num;
```

This statement stores the *address* of num (whatever it may be) in ptr. We say that ptr "points to" num.

But how do we declare ptr to be a pointer variable? First, we observe that, in C, a given pointer variable can "point to" values of one type only (see "3.8 Void Pointers"). The declaration of the pointer variable specifies the type. For example, the following declaration is read as int pointer ptr and declares ptr to be a *pointer* variable, which can "point to" (hold the address of) int values only:

```
int *ptr;
```

Of course, since ptr can assume only one value at a time, it can point to only one integer at any given time. The declaration could also have been written as follows:

```
int* ptr;
```

or

```
int * ptr;
```

■ **Caution** If you want to declare three pointers to int, it might be tempting to use this:

```
int* a, b, c;
```

However, this would be wrong. As written, only a is a pointer variable; b and c are just int. This might be more obvious had it been written as follows:

```
int *a, b, c;
```

The correct way to declare a, b, and c as pointers is as follows:

```
int *a, *b, *c;
```

Suppose the address of num is 5000 and the value of num is 17. This statement assigns the value 5000 to ptr:

```
ptr = &num;
```

Assuming ptr is stored at location 800, this can be pictured as follows:

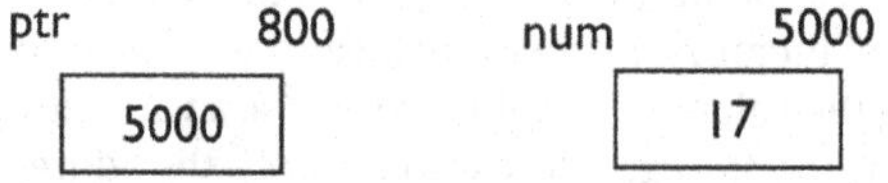

```
ptr        800        num        5000
 ┌──────────┐          ┌──────────┐
 │   5000   │          │    17    │
 └──────────┘          └──────────┘
```

We use *ptr to refer to "the value pointed at by ptr"[1] (in effect, the value of num), and it can be used in any context that an integer can. For example, if m is int, then the following assigns the value 24 (17 + 7) to m:

```
m = *ptr + 7;
```

It is sometimes helpful to think of * and & as cancelling out each other. For instance, if ptr = &num, then we can use the following:

```
*ptr ≡ *(&num) ≡ num;
```

An interesting assignment is as follows:

```
num = *ptr + 1;
```

This is exactly equivalent to the following:

```
num = num + 1;
```

It could even be written like this:

```
(*ptr)++;
```

This says to increment whatever ptr is pointing at. The brackets around *ptr are necessary. Without the brackets, *ptr++ would mean "take the value pointed to by ptr and then increment the value of ptr" (see "3.5 Pointer Arithmetic" for what it means to increment a pointer). To increment num by a value other than 1 (5, say), you could write this:

```
(*ptr) += 5;
```

In many respects, ptr is just like any other variable, and we can change its value if necessary. For example, the following assigns the address of m to ptr:

```
ptr = &m;
```

The old value of ptr is lost. Now ptr points to the value of m rather than num.

3.2 Passing Pointers as Arguments

Consider the problem of getting a function to change the value of a variable in the "calling" function. Specifically, we will attempt to write a function to add 6 to its integer argument. A naive attempt might be Program P3.1. The comments are for reference only.

Program P3.1

```
#include <stdio.h>
int main() {
   void test(int);
   int n = 14;
```

[1]Getting the value pointed to is called *dereferencing* the pointer.

```
   printf("%d\n", n);          // before calling test
   test(n);
   printf("%d\n", n);          //after return from test
} //end main

void test(int a) {
   a = a + 6;
   printf("%d\n", a);          // within test
} //end test
```

When run, this program will print the following:

```
14              (before calling test)
20              (within test)
14              (after return from test)
```

At the end, the value of n is still 14. Clearly, test was unable to change the value of n.

As written, there is no way for test to change the value of n (declared in main) since it has no access to n. The only way test can change the value of n is if the address of n is passed to test. This can be achieved by calling test with this:

```
test(&n);
```

But now, since the actual argument is a pointer, we must change the definition of the formal parameter in test so that it is also a pointer. Program P3.2 incorporates the changes.

Program P3.2

```
#include <stdio.h>
int main() {
   void test(int *);
   int n = 14;
   printf("%d\n", n);          // before calling test
   test(&n);
   printf("%d\n", n);          // after return from test
} //end main

void test(int *a) {
   *a = *a + 6;
   printf("%d\n", *a);         // within test
} //end test
```

The following function prototype indicates that the argument to test is an integer pointer:

```
void test(int *);
```

The formal parameter a is declared accordingly. The integer value "pointed at" by a is denoted by *a. When test is called with the following, the address of n (5000, say) is passed to it:

```
test(&n);
```

test, therefore, has access to whatever value is stored at this address and may change it if desired. In this case, it adds 6 to the value at location 5000, effectively adding 6 to the value of n. When run, Program P3.2 will print the following:

```
14      (before calling test)
20      (within test)
20      (after return from test)
```

At the end, the value of n in main has been changed to 20 by the function test.

It should now be clear why it is necessary to put the ampersand (&) in front of variables when we use the standard input function scanf(...) to read data. The only way scanf(...) can put a value into an actual argument is if its address is passed to it. For example, in the following statement, the address of n is passed to scanf:

```
scanf("%d", &n);
```

This enables scanf to store the value read in the location occupied by n.

For the cognoscenti, even with pointers, it is still true that, in C, arguments are passed by value and a function *cannot* change the value of an original argument passed to it. Suppose ptr = &n and consider the following call:

```
test(ptr);
```

The value of the argument, ptr, is determined. Suppose it is 5000. This value is copied to a temporary location, and this location is passed to test where it is known as a. Thus, the value of a is 5000.

When interpreted as an address, this is the address of the variable n, in main. Thus, the function has access to n and can change it, if desired. But note that test cannot change the value of the *original* argument ptr since only a copy of ptr was passed. However, as we have seen, it can change the value *pointed to* by ptr.

3.3 More on Passing an Array as an Argument

We have learned that when an array name is used as an actual argument, the address of its first element is passed to the function. Consider Program P3.3.

Program P3.3

```
#include <stdio.h>
int main() {
   void test(int val[], int max);
   int j, list[5];

   for (j = 0; j < 5; j++) list[j] = j;
   test(list, 5);
   for (j = 0; j < 5; j++) printf("%d ", list[j]);
   printf("\n");
} //end main

void test(int val[], int max) {
// add 25 to each of val[0] to val[max - 1]
   int j;
   for (j = 0; j < max; j++) val[j] += 25;
} //end test
```

When run, this program prints the following:

```
25 26 27 28 29
```

In main, the elements list[0] to list[4] are set to 0, 1, 2, 3, and 4, respectively.

When the following call is made, the address of list[0] is passed to test where it becomes known as val[0]:

```
test(list, 5);
```

The function adds 25 to each of val[0] to val[4]. But since val[0] to val[4] occupy the same storage as list[0] to list[4], the function effectively adds 25 to list[0], list[1], list[2], list[3], and list[4].

The call

```
test(list, 5);
```

could be replaced by the following since, in both cases, the address of the first element of list is passed to the function:

```
test(&list[0], 5);
```

In other words, an array name *is* a pointer—the address of the first element of the array.

An interesting variation is the following call:

```
test(&list[2], 3);
```

Here, the address of element list[2] is passed to test. In the function, this address is matched with val[0]. The net effect is the following:

```
val[0]  matches with   list[2];
val[1]  matches with   list[3];
val[2]  matches with   list[4];
```

These elements are incremented by 25 so that the program prints this:

```
0  1  27  28  29
```

In case you are wondering, it would be invalid to attempt something like this:

```
test(&list[2], 5);
```

This implies that, starting at list[2], there are at least five elements in the array, and, in our case, there are only three. What would happen is that, in the function, val[3] and val[4] would be associated with the locations in memory immediately following list[4]. The contents of these locations would be altered with unpredictable consequences.

3.4 Character Pointers

Suppose word is declared as an array of characters.

```
char word[20];
```

We have emphasized that the array name word is a synonym for the address of its first element, word[0]. Thus:

```
word ≡ &word[0]
```

In effect, word "points to" the first character of the array and is, in fact, a pointer—a *character* pointer, to be more precise. However, word is not a pointer variable but, rather, a pointer *constant*. We can't change its value, which is the address of word[0].

Whenever a string constant appears in a program, the characters without the quotes are stored somewhere in memory; \0 is added at the end, and the address of the first character is used in place of the string. For example, in the following

```
printf("Enter a number:");
```

what is actually passed to printf is a character pointer whose value is the address of the first character of the following string, stored somewhere in memory and terminated by \0:

```
Enter a number:
```

Consider this declaration:

```
char *errorMessage;
```

It is permitted to write the following:

```
errorMessage = "Cannot divide by 0\n";
```

The effect is that the characters of the string (properly terminated by \0) are stored somewhere in memory (starting at address 800, say), and the address of the first character (800) is assigned to errorMessage. This can be used as follows:

```
printf("%s", errorMessage);
```

or, simply, as follows:

```
printf(errorMessage);
```

Note that errorMessage is a pointer variable whose value can be changed, if desired. For example, the following sets errorMessage to point to the new string:

```
errorMessage = "Negative argument to square root\n";
```

Of course, the string previously pointed at by errorMessage now becomes inaccessible. If we wanted to save the old value of errorMessage, we could have done something like the following, assuming that oldMessage is also a character pointer:

```
oldMessage = errorMessage;
```

It is important to observe that this assignment simply stores the (pointer) value of errorMessage in oldMessage. No characters are copied. For example, suppose the following was stored starting at address 500:

```
"Cannot divide by 0\n"
```

After the assignment above, the value of oldMessage is 500 and, hence, points to the string. There is nothing wrong or invalid in having several variables point to the same location. It is the same as, for instance, several integer variables having the same value.

3.5 Pointer Arithmetic

We saw earlier that a pointer variable could be assigned to another pointer variable. C also permits us to increment and decrement pointer variables, but these operations have special meanings when applied to pointers.

Consider the following:

```
char *verse = "The day is done";
```

The string "The day is done" is stored somewhere in memory, and verse is assigned the address of the first character, T. In addition:

```
verse + 1  is the address of 'h';
verse + 2  is the address of 'e';
verse + 3  is the address of ' ';
           etc.
```

If required, we could change the value of verse with constructions such as this:

```
verse++;
verse += j;
```

As an example, the following will print the characters of the string pointed at by verse, one per line:

```
while (*verse != '\0')
   printf("%c\n", *verse++);
```

*verse refers to the character currently pointed at by verse. After this character has been printed, verse is incremented to point to the next character.

The previous discussion relates to character pointers. But suppose ptr is a pointer to integers. What is the meaning of this:

```
ptr + 1 or ptr + k?
```

To illustrate the ideas involved, consider an integer array num declared as follows:

```
int num[5];
```

We know by now that the name num refers to the address of num[0]. What is new is the following:

```
num + 1  is the address of  num[1];
num + 2  is the address of  num[2];
num + 3  is the address of  num[3];
num + 4  is the address of  num[4];
```

This holds true regardless of how many storage locations are occupied by an integer. For example, suppose an integer occupies 4 bytes and the address of num[0] is 800.

The value of the array name num is 800, and the value of, say, num + 1 (pointer arithmetic) is the address of num[1], that is, 800 + 4 = 804. Similarly:

```
the value of num + 2  is 808;
the value of num + 3  is 812;
the value of num + 4  is 816;
```

In general, suppose a pointer, p, is declared to point at a type of value that occupies k locations of storage. Incrementing p by 1 has the effect of adding k to the current value of p so that p now points to the *next* item of the type that p is declared to point at.

Thus, using pointer arithmetic, "adding 1" means getting the address of the next item (no matter how many locations away), and "adding j" means getting the address of the jth item beyond the current one. Thus, p + j is the address of the jth element beyond the one pointed to by p.

Since, for example, num + 2 is the address of num[2], i.e., &num[2], it follows that *(num + 2) is equivalent to *(&num[2]), that is, num[2]. (Think of * and & as cancelling each other.)

The following prints the values in the array num, one per line:

```
for (int h = 0 ; h < 5; h++)
   printf("%d\n", *(num + h));
```

*(num + h) could be replaced by num[h], and the effect would be the same.

You might wonder, in this example, about the meaning of num + 5. Theoretically, this is the address of element num[5], but this element does not exist. However, it is not invalid to attempt to use num + 5. But if, for instance, we attempt to print *(num + 5), we will print whatever happens to be stored in memory at the address designated by num + 5 or, worse, get a memory access or address error. In either case, the moral is that you must not attempt to refer to array elements you have not declared and, hence, for which storage has not been allocated.

We will illustrate the intimate relationship between arrays and pointers by writing two versions of a function, length, which finds the length of a string.

Suppose word is declared as follows:

```
char word[MaxLength];  // MaxLength is a symbolic constant
```

Then in order to find the length of a string stored in word, you can call the following function:

```
length(word);
```

length assumes that word consists of characters terminated by \0. The value returned is the number of characters excluding \0. Since what is passed to the function is the address of the first character (in other words, &word[0]), the function can be written with the formal parameter declared either as an array or as a pointer. Which version is used has no effect on how the function is called. First we write the array version.

```
int length(char string[]) {
   int n = 0;
   while (string[n] != '\0') n++;
   return n;
}
```

Now we write the pointer version.

```
int length(char *strPtr) {  // string pointer
   int n = 0;
   while (*strPtr != '\0') {
      n++;
      strPtr++;
   }
   return n;
}
```

We could even increment `strPtr` as part of the `while` test, giving the following:

```
int length(char *strPtr) {
   int n = 0;
   while (*strPtr++ != '\0') n++;
   return n;
}
```

Which version is better? It depends on your point of view. Whereas the array version is more readable, the pointer version is more efficient. In the array version, it is clear that at each step we are looking at the `n`th element of the string. This is not so obvious in the pointer version. However, evaluating `string[n]` requires evaluation of the subscript `n`, which is then converted into the address of element `n`. The pointer version deals with the address directly.

We have mentioned that an array name is a constant and, hence, its value can't be changed. There may appear to be a conflict in that the function, when passed the array name, increments it (`strPtr++`) to move on to the next character.

But remember that the formal parameter in the function definition *is* a variable. When the function is called with `length(word)`, say, the value of `word` (the address of the first character) is copied to a temporary location, and this location is passed to the function, where it is known as `strPtr`. The effect is that `strPtr` is simply initialized to the value of `word`. Incrementing `strPtr` in the function has no effect on the value of `word` in the calling function.

3.6 Pointers to Structures

Just as it is possible to take the address of an `int` or `double` variable, so too can we take the address of a structure variable. In Chapter 2, we mentioned that when we make the call `fun6(text);`, where `text` is a structure variable of type `Book`, the fields of `text` are copied to the run-time heap and the copy is passed to `fun6`. That is, the structure is passed "by value." If a structure is complicated or contains arrays, the copying operation could be time-consuming. In addition, when the function returns, the values of the structure elements must be removed from the heap, and this adds to the overhead—the extra processing required to perform a function call.

To avoid this overhead, the address of the structure could be passed, as follows:

```
fun7(&text);
```

Of course, in fun7, the corresponding formal parameter must be declared appropriately, such as the following:

```
void fun7(Book *bp)
```

Now, only a single value (the address) has to be copied to (and later removed from) the heap. And given the address, the function has access to the original argument text and can change it, if desired.

It is also possible to pass the address of an individual field to a function. For array fields, this happens automatically, as follows:

```
fun4(text.title);       // address of text.title is passed
```

For simple variables, the structure name (*not* the field name) must be preceded by &, as follows:

```
fun3(&text.price);       // address of text.price is passed
```

For example, we could read values for price and quantity with this:

```
scanf("%lf %d", &text.price, &text.quantity); //"lf" since price is double
```

Using the declaration

```
typedef struct {
   char name[31];
   int age;
   char gender;
} Student;
```

consider the following:

```
Student child, *sp;
```

This declares child to be a structure variable of type Student. It also declares sp to be a pointer to a structure of the type Student. In other words, the values that sp can assume are addresses of variables of type Student. For example, the following statement is valid and assigns the *address* of the structure variable child to sp:

```
sp = &child;
```

If the fields of child are stored starting at memory location 6000, then the value 6000 is assigned to sp.

As with pointers to other types, *sp refers to the structure that sp is pointing at. In this example, *sp is a synonym for child. We can refer to the fields of the structure that sp is pointing at by using the dot operator (.), as follows:

```
(*sp).name, (*sp).age and (*sp).gender
```

The brackets around *sp are required since . has higher precedence than *. Without them, *sp.age, for instance, would be interpreted as *(sp.age). This implies that sp.age is a pointer; since it is not, it will produce an error.

Pointers to structures occur so frequently in C that a special alternative notation is provided. If sp is pointing to a structure of type Student, then we can use -> (a minus sign followed by a greater-than sign) to specify a field, as follows:

```
sp -> name       refers to the 'name' field,
sp -> age        refers to the 'age' field, and
sp -> gender     refers to the 'gender' field,
```

We will see many examples of the use of pointers to structures in the next chapter.
The following list summarizes valid operations on structures:

- A field can be accessed using the "structure member" (`.`) operator, as in `text.author`.
- A structure variable can be assigned the value of another structure variable of the same type.
- The address-of operator `&` can be applied to a structure name to give the address of the structure, for example, `&text`. `&` can also be applied to an element of a structure. However, `&` must precede the structure name, not the field name. For example, `&text.price` is valid, but `text.&price` and `&price` are not.
- If `p` is a pointer to a structure, then `*p` refers to the structure. For example, if `p` contains the address of the structure, `text` then

  ```
  (*p).title   //brackets required since . has higher precedence than *
  ```

  refers to the `title` field. However, the *structure pointer* (arrow) operator `->` (a minus sign immediately followed by `>`) is more commonly used to refer to a field, as in:

  ```
  p -> title
  ```

3.7 Pointers to Functions

In the same way that an array name is the address of its first element, so too a function name is the address of the function. To put it another way, a function name is a *pointer* to the function in much the same way that an array name is a pointer to the array. In C, a pointer to a function can be manipulated in much the same way as other pointers; in particular, it can be passed to functions. This is especially handy for writing general-purpose routines.

Consider the problem of producing two-column tables such as tables of squares, reciprocals, square roots, weight conversions, temperature conversions, and so on. In each table, the first column consists of an ascending sequence of integers, and the second has the associated values.

We could write separate functions for each type of table we wanted to produce. But we could also write *one* function (called `makeTable`, say) that produced the various tables. Which specific table is produced depends on which function is passed to `makeTable`.

How do we specify a function as a parameter? Consider the following function definition:

```
void makeTable(int first, int last, double (*fp) (int)) {
   for (int j = first; j <= last; j++)
      printf("%2d   %0.3f\n", j, (*fp)(j));
}
```

The heading says that `makeTable` takes three arguments; the first two are integers and the third, `fp`, is a pointer to a function that takes an `int` argument and returns a `double` value. The brackets around `*fp` in the following are necessary:

```
double (*fp) (int)
```

If they are omitted, the following would mean that `fp` is a function returning a pointer to a `double`, which is quite different from what is intended:

```
double *fp (int)
```

In the printf statement, the function call (*fp) (j) is interpreted as follows:

- fp is a pointer to a function; *fp *is* the function.
- j is the actual argument to the function call; the brackets around j are the usual brackets around a function's argument(s).
- The value returned by the call should be a double, which would match the %f specification.
- The brackets around *fp are necessary since () has higher precedence than *. Without them, *fp(j) would be equivalent to *(fp(j)), which is meaningless in this context.

But how do we use makeTable to produce a table of reciprocals, say? Suppose we want to produce the table from 1 to 10. We would like to use a statement such as the following to get the required table, where reciprocal is a function that takes an int value and returns a double value—the reciprocal of the integer:

```
makeTable(1, 10, reciprocal);
```

It could be written as follows:

```
double reciprocal(int x) {
   return 1.0 / x;
}
```

Note that in the following call the function name reciprocal is a pointer to a function, so it matches the third parameter of makeTable:

```
makeTable(1, 10, reciprocal);
```

Program P3.4 shows all the pieces put together in one complete program.

Program P3.4

```
#include <stdio.h>
int main() {
   void makeTable(int, int, double (*fp) (int));
   double reciprocal(int);
   makeTable(1, 10, reciprocal);
} //end main

void makeTable(int first, int last, double (*fp) (int)) {
   for (int h = first; h <= last; h++)
      printf("%2d   %0.3f\n", h, (*fp)(h));
} //end makeTable

double reciprocal(int x) {
   return 1.0 / x;
} //end reciprocal
```

When run, Program P3.4 produces the following output:

```
1        1.000
2        0.500
3        0.333
4        0.250
5        0.200
6        0.167
7        0.143
8        0.125
9        0.111
0        0.100
```

If we now want to create a table of squares, all we need are the following.
Here's the function prototype in `main`:

```
double square(int);
```

Here's the function call in `main`:

```
makeTable(1, 10, square);
```

Here's the function definition:

```
double square(int x) {
   return x * x;
}
```

As another example, consider the problem of evaluating the following definite integral using the Trapezoidal Rule with *n* strips:

$$\int_a^b f(x)dx$$

The rule states that an approximation to the previous integral is given by the following, where $h = (b - a)/n$:

$$h\{ (f(a) + f(b))/2 + f(a+h) + f(a+2h) + \ldots + f(a + (n-1)h) \}$$

We want to write a general function `integral`, which, given `a`, `b`, `n`, and a function, `f`, returns the value of the integral. To evaluate the integrals of different functions, we would need only to pass the appropriate function to `integral`. Consider the following version of `integral`:

```
double integral(double a, double b, int n, double (*fp) (double)) {
   double h, sum;
   h = (b - a) / n;
   sum = ((*fp)(a) + (*fp)(b)) / 2.0;
   for (int j = 1; j < n ; j++)
      sum += (*fp)(a + j * h);
   return h * sum;
} //end integral
```

The following declaration says that `fp` is a pointer to a function that takes a `double` argument and returns a `double` value:

```
double (*fp) (double)
```

`*fp` denotes the function, and `(*fp)(a)` is a call to the function with argument `a`.

To show how `integral` can be used, suppose we want to find an approximation to the following using 20 strips:

$$\int_0^2 (x^2 + 5x + 3)dx$$

We would need to write a function such as `quadratic`.

```
double quadratic(double x) {
   return x * x + 5.0 * x + 3.0;
}
```

The following call would return the value of the integral:

```
integral(0, 2, 20, quadratic)
```

3.8 Void Pointers

As we have emphasized, a pointer variable in C can point to only one type of value. However, C allows the declaration and use of `void` (also called *generic*) pointers—pointers that may point to any type of object. For example, the following declares `pv` as a `void` pointer:

```
void *pv;
```

And the following declares `getNode` as a function that returns a `void` pointer:

```
void *getNode(int size);
```

Any valid address can be assigned to a `void` pointer. In particular, a pointer to `int` (or `double` or `float`, and so on) can be assigned to a `void` pointer variable. Given `double d, *dp;`, you can write the following:

```
dp = &d; //assign the address of d to dp
pv = dp; //assign a double pointer to a void pointer variable
```

Even though `pv` and `dp` have the same pointer value after the previous assignment, it is invalid to think of `*pv` as a `double`. In other words, we should not attempt to dereference a `void` pointer. However, if we *know* that `pv` contains a double pointer, we can tell this to C using a cast and dereference it, like this:

```
* (double *) pv
```

`void` pointers are useful for writing general-purpose functions where you do not want to restrict a function to returning a specific type of pointer. Also, declaring a function parameter as a `void` pointer allows the actual argument to be any type of pointer.

For example, suppose we want to write a function to accept an address and print the value stored at that address. If we know that the address will be a double pointer, say, we can write the function like this:

```
void dprint(double *p) {
   printf("%0.3lf\n", *p); //print to 3 decimal places
}
```

But what if we want the function to work no matter what type of pointer is passed? We can try to specify the parameter as a void pointer, as follows, but this won't work:

```
void vprint(void *p) {   //this won't work
   printf("%0.3lf\n", *p);
}
```

Remember that an address is just a positive integer (8000, say). When this number is sent to the function, vprint will not know what type of value is stored at that address, so it will not know how to interpret *p in printf. (In dprint, shown earlier, it *knows* that *p is a double value.)

So, in addition to the pointer, we need to tell the function what type of value is stored so the pointer can be dereferenced correctly. We can do this via another argument (t, say). To illustrate, we write the following function assuming t = 1 means an int pointer is passed and t = 2 means a double pointer is passed:

```
void print(void *p, int t){
   if (t == 1) printf("%d\n", *(int *) p);
      else if (t == 2) printf("%0.3lf\n", *(double *) p);
      else printf("error: unknown type\n");
} //end print
```

Consider the following code:

```
int n = 375;
double d = 2.71865;
print(&n, 1); //int pointer passed
print(&d, 2); //double pointer passed
```

When executed, this will print the following:

```
375
2.719
```

The function print can be easily extended to handle other types.

C permits a void pointer to be assigned to any other type of pointer, as follows:

```
float *fp =  pv;
```

However, it is up to you to ensure that the assignment makes sense. For instance, if pv contains an int pointer, it makes no sense to assign it to a float pointer variable. On the other hand, if you *know* that pv contains a float pointer, then the assignment is meaningful.

Programming note: if you use a C++ compiler to compile your C programs, you will get an error if you try to assign a void pointer to another pointer type. You will need to cast the void pointer to the appropriate type before assigning, as follows:

```
fp = (float *) pv;
```

Even though assigning a void pointer without casting is permitted in C, good programming practice dictates you should use a cast anyway.

EXERCISES 3

1. What is meant by "an argument is passed by value"?
2. Which type of argument in C is not passed by value? How is it passed?
3. How is it possible for a function to change the value of an actual argument?
4. In main, there are two int variables, a and b. Write a function that, when called, interchanges the values of a and b so that the change is known in main.
5. In main, there are three int variables, a, b, and c. Write a function that, when called, stores the sum of a and b in c so that c is changed in main.
6. Explain the differences between a character pointer and a character array.
7. The character pointer msgPtr is pointing to a string of characters. What happens when msgPtr is assigned to another character pointer, oldPtr?
8. How is a pointer similar to an integer?
9. How does pointer arithmetic differ from ordinary integer arithmetic?
10. What is the difference between num[j] and *(num + j)?
11. If ps is a pointer to a structure that contains an int field score, what is the difference between (*ps).score and ps -> score?
12. If a function *f* is continuous in the interval [*a*, *b*] and *f*(*a*)*f*(*b*) < 0, then, since *f* changes sign, there must exist some *c* in [*a*, *b*] for which *f*(*c*) = 0. Assume there is one such *c*. It can be found as follows:

    - Bisect the interval [*a*, *b*].
    - Determine in which half *f* changes sign.

    This is repeated giving a sequence of intervals, each smaller than the last and each containing *c*. The procedure can be terminated when the interval is arbitrarily small or *f* is 0 at one of the endpoints.

    Write a function that, given *f*, *a*, and *b*, returns an approximation to *c*. Test your function using the function 5x2 + 3x - 14 with a solution in the interval [1, 2].

13. Write a function to calculate the value of the following definite integral using Simpson's rule (below) with *n* strips; *n* must be even:

$$\int_a^b f(x)dx$$

An approximation to the integral is given by the following, where $h = (b - a)/n$:

$$\frac{h}{3}\{(f(a)+4f(a+h)+2f(a+2h)+\ldots+2f(a+(n-2)h)+4f(a+(n-1)h)+f(b)\}$$

Test your function on some simple integrals.

What happens if the number of strips increases?

14. What is a `void` pointer? How are `void` pointers useful?

15. An `int` pointer is assigned to a void pointer variable, `vp`. How can we print the value pointed to by `vp`?

16. It is permitted to assign a `void` pointer to another type of pointer variable. What should you be mindful of in making such an assignment?

17. Apart from `void` pointers, where else can you use the word `void` in C?

CHAPTER 4

Linked Lists

In this chapter, we will explain the following:

- The notion of a linked list
- How to write declarations for working with a linked list
- How to count the nodes in a linked list
- How to search for an item in a linked list
- How to find the last node in a linked list
- The difference between static storage and dynamic storage allocation
- How to allocate and free storage in C using `malloc`, `calloc`, `sizeof`, and `free`
- How to build a linked list by adding a new item at the end of the list
- How to insert a node into a linked list
- How to build a linked list by adding a new item at the head of the list
- How to delete items from a linked list
- How to build a linked list by adding a new item in such a way that the list is always sorted
- How to use linked lists to determine whether a phrase is a palindrome
- How to save a linked list
- The differences between using linked lists and arrays for storing a list of items
- How to represent a linked list using arrays
- How to merge two sorted linked lists
- The concept of a circular list and a doubly linked list

4.1 Defining Linked Lists

When values are stored in a one-dimensional array ($x[0]$ to $x[n]$), say), they can be thought of as being organized as a "linear list." Consider each item in the array as a *node*. A linear list means that the nodes are arranged in a linear order such that the following is true:

```
x[0] is the first node
x[n] is the last node
```

```
if 0 < k <= n, then x[k] is preceded by x[k - 1]
if 0 <= k < n then x[k ] is followed by x[k + 1]
```

Thus, given a node, the "next" node is assumed to be in the next location, if any, in the array. The order of the nodes is the order in which they appear in the array, starting from the first. Consider the problem of inserting a new node between two existing nodes, $x[k]$ and $x[k + 1]$.

This can be done only if $x[k + 1]$ and the nodes after it are moved to make room for the new node. Similarly, the deletion of $x[k]$ involves the movement of the nodes $x[k+1]$, $x[k + 2]$, and so on. Accessing any given node is easy; all we have to do is provide the appropriate index (subscript).

In many situations, we use an array for representing a linear list. But we can also represent such a list by using an organization in which each node in the list points *explicitly* to the next node. This new organization is referred to as a *linked list*.

In a (singly) linked list, each node contains a pointer that points to the next node in the list. We can think of each node as a cell with two components, like this:

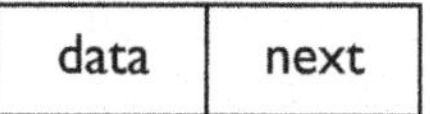

where `data` can actually be one or more fields (depending on what needs to be stored in a node), and `next` points to the next node of the list. (You can use any names you want instead of `data` and `next`.)

Since the `next` field of the last node does not point to anything, we must set it to a special value called the *null pointer*. In C, the null pointer value is denoted by the standard identifier `NULL`, defined in `<stdlib.h>` and `<stdio.h>`.

In addition to the cells of the list, we need a pointer variable (`top`, say) that points to the first item in the list. If the list is empty, the value of `top` is `NULL`.

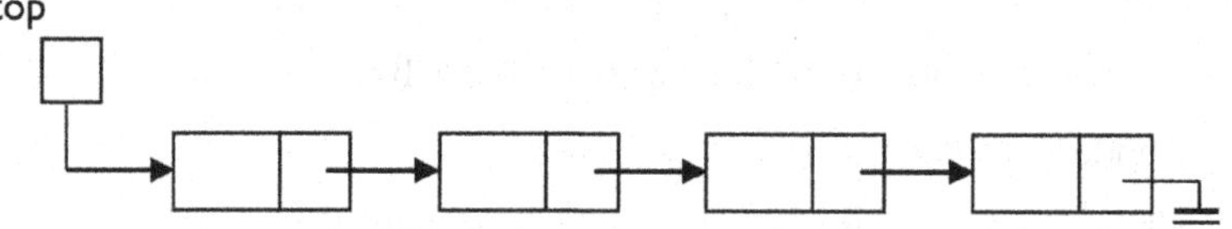

The electrical earth symbol is used to represent the null pointer:

Traversing a linked list is like going on a treasure hunt. You are told where the first item is. This is what `top` does. When you get to the first item, it directs you to where the second item is (this is the purpose of `next`). When you get to the second item, it tells you where the third item is (via `next`), and so on. When you get to the last item, its null pointer tells you that you are at the end of the hunt (the end of the list).

How can we represent a linked list in a C program? Since each node consists of at least two fields, we will need to use a `struct` to define the format of a node. The `data` component can consist of one or more fields (possibly including structures, perhaps nested). The type of these fields will depend on what kind of data needs to be stored.

But what is the type of the `next` field? We know it's a pointer, but a pointer to what? It's a pointer to a structure that is just like the one being defined![1] As an example, suppose the data at each node is a positive integer. We can define the node as follows (using `num` instead of `data`):

```
struct node {
   int num;
   struct node *next;
};
```

[1]This is usually called a *self-referencing structure*.

Or we define it using typedef, like this:

```
typedef struct node {
   int num;
   struct node *next;
} Node, *NodePtr; // we also declare a name for "struct node *"
```

The variable top can now be defined as a pointer to a node, like this:

```
Node *top;
```

or

```
NodePtr top;
```

As explained earlier, the struct declaration of node, as we have written it, does not allocate any storage for any variables. It simply specifies the form that such variables will take. However, the declaration of top does allocate storage, but only for a pointer to a node. The value of top can be the address of a node, but, so far, there are no nodes in the list. How can storage be allocated to nodes of the list? We will see how to do this in Section 4.2, but first we will look at some basic operations that may be performed on a linked list.

4.2 Basic Operations on a Linked List

For illustrative purposes, let's assume we have a linked list of integers. We ignore, for the moment, how the list might be built.

4.2.1 Counting the Nodes in a Linked List

Perhaps the simplest operation is to count the number of nodes in a list. To illustrate, we write a function that, given a pointer to a linked list, returns the number of nodes in the list.

Before we write the function, let's see how we can traverse the items in the list, starting from the first one. Suppose top points to the head of the list. Consider the following code:

```
NodePtr curr = top;
while (curr != NULL) curr = curr -> next;
```

Initially, curr points to the first item, if any, in the list. If it is not NULL, the following statement is executed:

```
curr = curr -> next;
```

This sets curr to point to "whatever the current node is pointing to," in effect, the next node. For example, consider the following list:

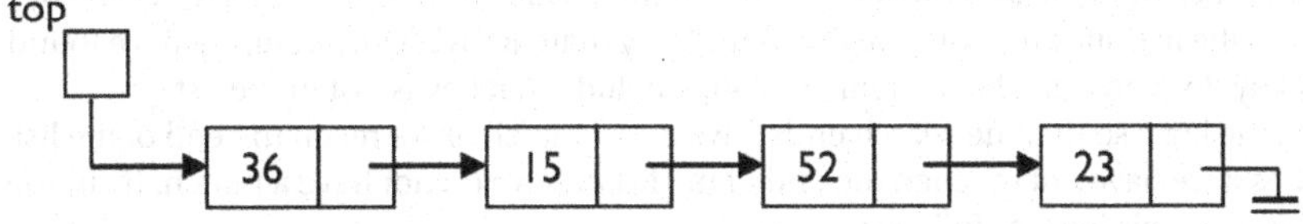

Initially, curr points to (the node containing) 36. Since curr is not NULL, it is set to point to whatever 36 is pointing to, that is, (the node containing) 15.

The while condition is tested again. Since curr is not NULL, curr = cur -> next is executed, setting curr to point to whatever 15 is pointing to, that is, 52.

The while condition is tested again. Since curr is not NULL, curr = cur -> next is executed, setting curr to point to whatever 52 is pointing to, that is, 23.

The while condition is tested again. Since curr is not NULL, curr = cur -> next is executed, setting curr to point to whatever 23 is pointing to, that is, NULL.

The while condition is tested again. Since curr *is* NULL, the while loop is no longer executed.

Note that each time curr is not NULL, we enter the while loop. But the number of times that curr is *not* NULL is the same as the number of items in the list. So, to count the number of items in the list, we just have to count how many times the while body is executed.

To do this, we use a counter initialized to 0 and increment it by 1 inside the while loop. We can now write the function as follows (we call it length):

```
int length(NodePtr top) {
   int n = 0;
   NodePtr curr = top;
   while (curr != NULL) {
      n++;
      curr = curr -> next;
   }
   return n;
} //end length
```

Note that if the list is empty, curr will be NULL the first time, and the while loop will not be executed. The function will return 0, the correct result.

Strictly speaking, the variable curr is not necessary. The function will work fine if we omit curr and replace curr by top in the function. At the end of the execution of the function, top will be NULL.

You may be worried that you have lost access to the list, but do not be. Remember that top in length is a *copy* of whatever variable (head, say) is pointing to the list in the calling function. Changing top has no effect whatsoever on head. When length returns, head is still pointing to the first item in the list.

4.2.2 Searching a Linked List

Another common operation is to search a linked list for a given item. For example, given the following list, we may want to search for the number 52:

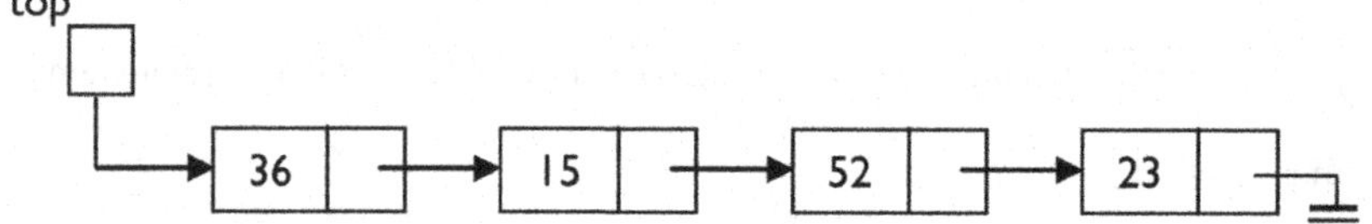

Our search should be able to tell us that 52 is in the list. On the other hand, if we searched for 25, our search should report that 25 is not in the list.

Suppose the number we are searching for is stored in the variable key. The search proceeds by comparing key with each number in the list, starting from the first one. If key matches with any item, we have found it. If we get to the end of the list and key does not match any item, we can conclude that key is not in the list.

We must write the logic so that the search ends if we find a match *or* we reach the end of the list. Put another way, the search continues if we have not reached the end of the list *and* we do not have a match. If curr points to some item in the list, we can express this logic as follows:

```
while (curr != NULL && key != curr -> num) curr = curr -> next;
```

C guarantees that the operands of && are evaluated from left to right and evaluation ceases as soon as the truth value of the expression is known, in this case, as soon as one operand evaluates to `false` or the entire expression has been evaluated. We take advantage of this by writing the condition `curr != NULL` first. If `curr` *is* `NULL`, the && is false, and the second condition `key != curr -> num` is not evaluated.

If we wrote the following and `curr` happens to be `NULL`, our program will crash when it tries to retrieve `curr -> num`:

```
while (key != curr -> num && curr != NULL) curr = curr -> next; //wrong
```

In effect, this asks for the number pointed to by `curr`, but if `curr` is `NULL`, it does not point to anything. We say we are trying to "dereference a `NULL` pointer," which is an error.

Let's write the search as a function that, given a pointer to the list and `key`, returns the node containing `key` if it is found. If it's not found, the function returns `NULL`.

We assume the node declaration from the previous section. Our function will return a value of type `NodePtr`. Here it is:

```
NodePtr search(NodePtr top, int key) {
   while (top != NULL && key != top -> num)
      top = top -> next;
   return top;
} //end search
```

If `key` is not in the list, `top` will become `NULL`, and `NULL` will be returned. If `key` is in the list, the `while` loop is exited when `key is equal to top -> num`; at this stage, `top` is pointing to the node containing `key`, and this value of `top` is returned.

4.2.3 Finding the Last Node in a Linked List

Sometimes we need to find the pointer to the last node in a list. Recall that the last node in the list is distinguished by its `next` pointer being `NULL`. Here is a function that returns a pointer to the last node in a given list. If the list is empty, the function returns `NULL`.

```
NodePtr getLast(NodePtr top) {
   if (top == NULL) return NULL;
   while (top -> next != NULL)
      top = top -> next;
   return top;
} //end getLast
```

We get to the `while` statement if `top` is not `NULL`. It therefore makes sense to ask about `top -> next`. If this is not `NULL`, the loop is entered, and `top` is set to this non-`NULL` value. This ensures that the `while` condition is defined the next time it is executed. When `top -> next` *is* `NULL`, `top` is pointing at the last node, and this value of `top` is returned.

4.3 Dynamic Storage Allocation: malloc, calloc, sizeof, free

Consider the problem of reading positive integers (terminated by `0`) and building a linked list that contains the numbers in the order in which they were read. For example, consider the following data:

```
36 15 52 23 0
```

Say we want to build the following linked list:

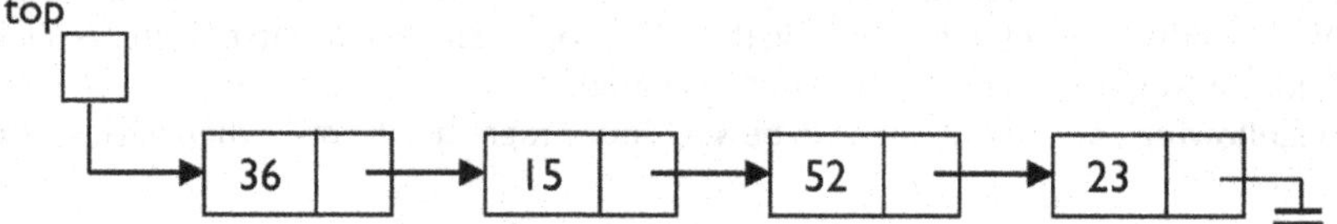

One question that arises is, how many nodes will there be in the list? This, of course, depends on how many numbers are supplied. One disadvantage of using an array for storing a linear list is that the size of the array must be specified beforehand. If, when the program is run, it finds that it needs to store more items than this size allows, it may have to be aborted.

With the linked list approach, whenever a new node must be added to the list, storage is allocated for the node, and the appropriate pointers are set. Thus, we allocate just the right amount of storage for the list—no more, no less.

We do use extra storage for the pointers, but this is more than compensated for by more efficient use of storage as well as easy insertions and deletions. Allocating storage "as needed" is usually referred to as *dynamic storage allocation*. (On the other hand, array storage is referred to as *static* storage.)

In C, storage can be allocated dynamically by using the standard functions `malloc` and `calloc`. In order to use these functions (and `free`, later), your program must be preceded by this header line:

```
#include <stdlib.h>
```

This line is also needed to use `NULL`, the null pointer definition in C.

4.3.1 malloc

The prototype for `malloc` is as follows, where `size_t` is an implementation-defined unsigned integer type defined in the standard header `<stddef.h>`:

```
void *malloc(size_t size);
```

Typically, `size_t` is the same as `unsigned int` or `unsigned long int`. For all intents and purposes, we can think of `size` as a positive integer.

`malloc` allocates `size` bytes of memory and returns a pointer to the first byte. The storage is *not* initialized. If `malloc` is unable to find the requested amount of storage, it returns `NULL`.

When your program calls `malloc`, it is important to verify that the requested storage has been successfully allocated. To use the storage allocated, the pointer returned must be assigned to a pointer variable of the appropriate type. For example, assuming that `cp` is a character pointer, the following statement allocates 20 bytes of storage and stores the address of the first byte in `cp`:

```
cp = malloc(20);
```

To be safe, your program should check that `cp` is not `NULL` before continuing.

In general, a pointer to one type may not be *directly* assigned to a pointer of another type; however, assignment is possible if an explicit cast is used. For example, given these declarations:

```
int *ip;
double *dp;
```

the following assignment is invalid:

```
ip = dp;        // wrong
```

However, it is valid to write the following:

```
ip = (int *) dp;          // right
```

but it is up to the programmer to ensure that this assignment is meaningful.

On the other hand, values of type `void *` may be assigned to pointers of other types without using a cast. In the previous example, no cast is required to assign the `void *` returned by `malloc` to the character pointer `cp`. However, even though assigning a `void` pointer without casting is permitted in C, good programming practice dictates that you should use a cast anyway. In the previous example, it is better to use this:

```
char *cp = (char *) malloc(20);
```

4.3.2 calloc

The prototype for `calloc` is as follows:

```
void *calloc(size_t num, size_t size);
```

`calloc` allocates `num * size` bytes of memory and returns a pointer to the first byte. (Another way of looking at it is that `calloc` allocates enough memory for an array of `num` objects each of size `size`.) All bytes returned are initialized to `0`. If `calloc` is unable to find the requested amount of storage, it returns `NULL`.

When your program calls `calloc`, it is important to verify that the requested storage has been successfully allocated. To use the storage allocated, the pointer returned must be assigned to a pointer variable of the appropriate type. As an example, assuming that `cp` is a character pointer, the following statement allocates 10 × 20 = 200 bytes of storage and stores the address of the first byte in `cp`:

```
char *cp = calloc(10, 20);
```

To be safe, the program should check that `cp` is not `NULL` before continuing. As mentioned, it is good programming practice to use this:

```
char *cp = (char *) calloc(10, 20);
```

`calloc` is useful for allocating storage for arrays. For example, if we know that a `double` variable occupies 8 bytes and we want to allocate space for 25 elements, we could use this:

```
double *dp = (double *) calloc(25, 8);
```

When executed, `dp` will point to the first element of the array, `dp + 1` will point to the second, and, in general, `dp + j - 1` will point to the `j`th element.

If we do not know the size of a type, and even if we do, we should use `sizeof` (see the next section).

4.3.3 sizeof

`sizeof` is a standard unary operator that returns the number of bytes needed for storing its argument. For example, the following returns the number of bytes needed for storing an `int` variable:

```
sizeof (int)
```

The argument to sizeof is either a type or a variable. If it is a type (like int or float or double), it must be enclosed in parentheses. If it is a variable or a type defined using typedef, the parentheses are optional. For example, if root is a variable of type double, then both sizeof root and sizeof (root) are valid and return the number of bytes needed for storing root. Similarly, sizeof Book and sizeof (Book) are both valid and return the number of bytes needed for storing a Book structure (see Section 2.10).

sizeof is used mainly for writing portable code, where the code depends on the number of bytes needed for storing various data types. For example, an integer may occupy 2 bytes on one machine but 4 bytes on another. Using sizeof (int) (instead of 2 or 4) in your program ensures that the program will work on either machine.

sizeof is used quite often with the functions malloc and calloc. For example, the following statement allocates enough storage for storing a double variable and assigns the address of the first byte to dp:

```
double *dp = malloc(sizeof (double));
```

Another example is as follows:

```
float *fp = calloc(10, sizeof (float));
```

Here, storage is allocated for 10 floats, and the address of the first is stored in fp.

You can also use type names defined with typedef as the argument to sizeof. Using the previous declarations, the following allocates enough storage for one Node structure and assigns the address of the first byte to np:

```
Node *np = malloc(sizeof (Node));
```

4.3.4 free

The function free is related to malloc and calloc. It is used to free storage acquired by calls to malloc and calloc. Its prototype is as follows:

```
void free(void *ptr);
```

It releases the storage pointed to by ptr. For example, to free the storage pointed to by np, shown earlier, you could use this:

```
free(np);
```

Observe that even though free expects a void pointer, it is not necessary to explicitly cast np (a Node pointer) into a void pointer. Of course, it is perfectly acceptable, but a bit cumbersome, to use this:

```
free((void *) np);
```

It is a **fatal error** to attempt to free storage not obtained by a call to malloc or calloc, using pointers to memory that has been freed and freeing pointers twice.

■ **Note** Alert readers may wonder how C knows how much memory to free. Easy. For each block allocated (using malloc, say), C keeps track of its size, usually by storing the size adjacent to the block.

4.4 Building a Linked List: Adding New Item at the Tail

Consider again the problem of building a linked list of positive integers in the order in which they are given. Say the incoming numbers are (0 terminates the data) as follows:

```
36 15 52 23 0
```

And say we want to build the following linked list:

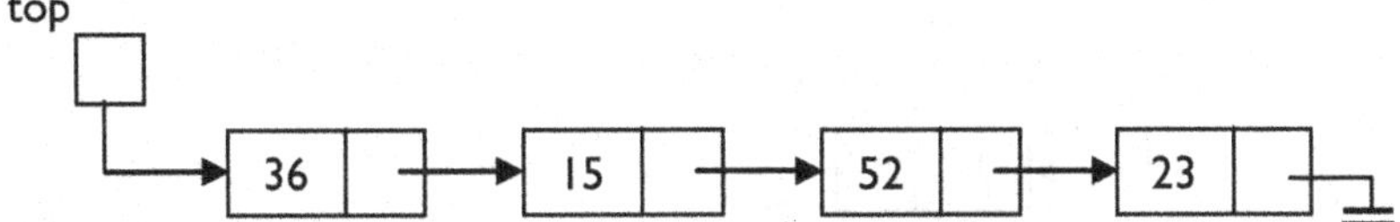

In our solution, we start with an empty list. Our program will reflect this with the following statement:

```
top = NULL;
```

The symbolic constant NULL, denoting the null pointer value, is defined in <stdio.h> and <stdlib.h>. When we read a new number, we must do the following:

1. Allocate storage for a node.
2. Put the number in the new node.
3. Make the new node the last one in the list.

We assume the following declaration for defining a node:

```
typedef struct node {
   int num;
   struct node *next;
} Node, *NodePtr;
```

Let's write a function called makeNode that, given an integer argument, allocates storage for the node, stores the integer in it, and returns a pointer to the new node. It will also set the next field to NULL. Here is makeNode:

```
NodePtr makeNode(int n) {
   NodePtr np = (NodePtr) malloc(sizeof (Node));
   np -> num = n;
   np -> next = NULL;
   return np;
}
```

Consider the following call:

```
makeNode(36);
```

First, storage for a new node is allocated. Assuming an int occupies 4 bytes and a pointer occupies 4 bytes, the size of Node is 8 bytes. So, 8 bytes are allocated starting at address 4000, say. This is illustrated by the following:

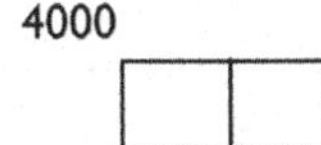

makeNode then stores 36 in the num field and NULL in the next field, giving us this:

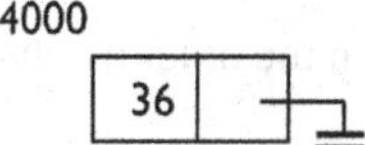

The value 4000 is then returned by makeNode.

When we read the first number, we must create a node for it and set top to point to the new node. In our example, when we read 36, we must create the following:

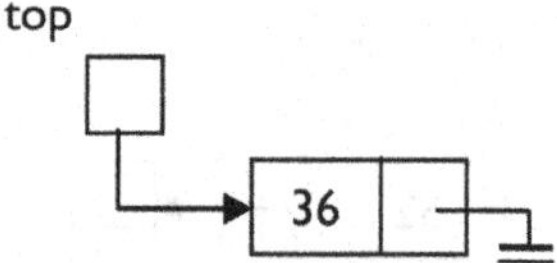

If n contains the new number, this can be accomplished with a statement such as this:

```
if (top == NULL) top = makeNode(n);
```

From the previous example, makeNode returns 4000, which is stored in top. Effectively, top now "points to" the node containing 36. There are no arrows inside the computer, but the effect is achieved with the following:

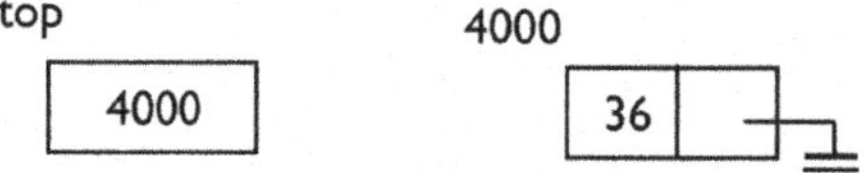

For each subsequent number, we must set the next field of the current last node to point to the new node. The new node becomes the last node. Suppose the new number is 15. We must create this:

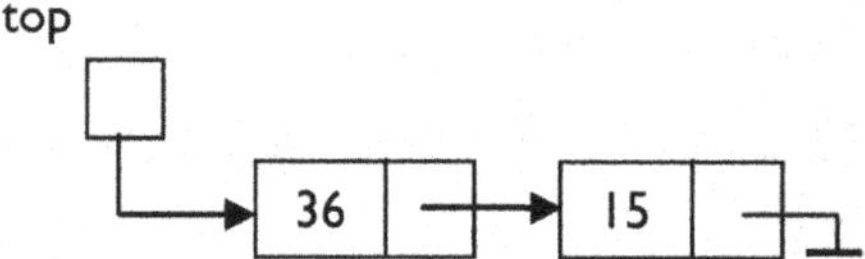

But how do we find the last node of the existing list? One method is to start at the top of the list and follow the next pointers until we encounter NULL. This is time-consuming if we have to do it for each new number. A better approach is to keep a pointer (last, say) to the last node of the list. This pointer is updated as new nodes are added. The code for this could be written like this:

```
np = makeNode(n);                  //create a new node
if (top == NULL) top = np;         //set top if first node
else last -> next = np;            //set last -> next for other nodes
last = np;                         //update last to  new node
```

Suppose there is just one node in the list; this is also the last node. In our example, the value of last will be 4000. Suppose the node containing 15 is stored at location 2000. We have the following situation:

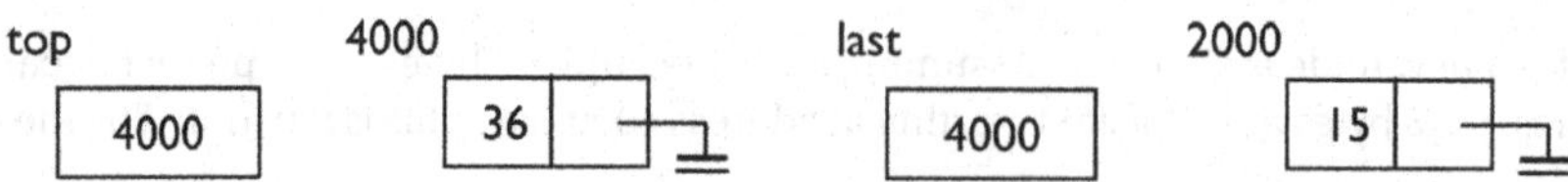

The previous code will set the next field at location 4000 to 2000 and set last to 2000. The following is the result:

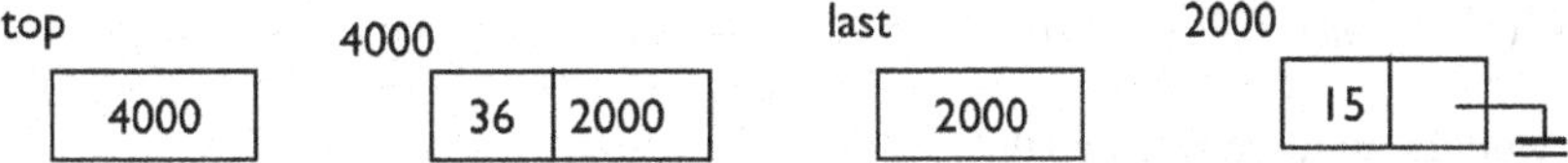

Now top (4000) points to the node containing 36; this node's next field is 2000 and, hence, points to the node containing 15. This node's next field is NULL, indicating the end of the list. The value of last is 2000, which is the address of the last node in the list.

Program P4.1 reads the numbers and creates the linked list as discussed. To verify that the list has been built correctly, we should print its contents. The function printList traverses the list from the first node to the last, printing the number at each node.

Program P4.1

```
#include <stdio.h>
#include <stdlib.h>
typedef struct node {
   int num;
   struct node *next;
} Node, *NodePtr;

int main() {
   void printList(NodePtr);
   NodePtr makeNode(int);
   int n;
   NodePtr top, np, last;

   top = NULL;
   if (scanf("%d", &n) != 1) n = 0;
   while (n != 0) {
      np = makeNode(n);    //create a new node containing n
      if (top == NULL) top = np;    //set top if first node
      else last -> next = np;    //set last -> next for other nodes
      last = np;    //update last to  new node
      if (scanf("%d", &n) != 1) n = 0;
   }
   printList(top);
} //end main

NodePtr makeNode(int n) {
   NodePtr np = (NodePtr) malloc(sizeof (Node));
   np -> num = n;
   np -> next = NULL;
   return np;
} //end makeNode

void printList(NodePtr np) {
   while (np != NULL) {  // as long as there's a node
      printf("%d\n", np -> num);
      np = np -> next;  // go on to the next node
   }
} //end printList
```

The following statement deserves some mention:

```
if (scanf("%d", &n) != 1) n = 0;
```

Normally, we would simply have written this:

```
scanf("%d", &n);
```

But, here, we take advantage of the value returned by scanf to do some error checking.

When scanf is called, it stores data in the requested variable(s) and returns the number of values successfully stored. So, if we ask it to read one value, it should return 1 unless some error occurred (like end-of-file being reached or non-numeric data found when a number was expected). If we ask it to read two values and only one is assigned, it will return 1.

In this program, if a value was not successfully read into n, scanf will return 0. In this case, n is set to 0, forcing an exit from the while loop.

4.5 Insertion into a Linked List

A list with one pointer in each node is called a *one-way*, or *singly linked*, list. One important characteristic of such a list is that access to the nodes is via the "top of list" pointer and the pointer field in each node. (However, other explicit pointers may point to specific nodes in the list, for example, the pointer last, shown earlier, which pointed to the last node in the list.) This means that access is restricted to being sequential. The only way to get to node 4, say, is via nodes 1, 2, and 3. Since we can't access the *k*th node directly, we will not be able, for instance, to perform a binary search on a linked list. The great advantage of a linked list is that it allows for easy insertions and deletions anywhere in the list.

Suppose we want to insert a new node between the second and third nodes. We can view this simply as insertion after the second node. For example, suppose prev points to the second node and np points to the new node.

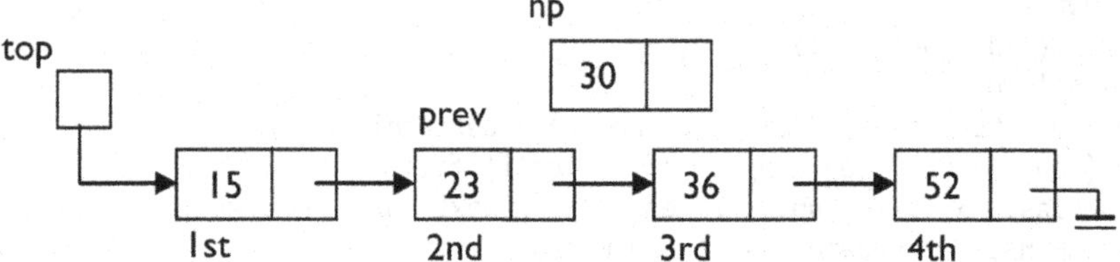

We can insert the new node by setting its next field to point to the third node and the next field of the second node to point to the new node. Note that the second node is all we need to do the insertion; *its* next field will give us the third node. The insertion can be done with this:

```
np -> next = prev -> next;
prev -> next = np;
```

The first statement says, "Let the new node point to whatever the second node is pointing at, in other words, the third node." The second statement says, "Let the second node point to the new node." The net effect is that the new node is inserted between the second and the third. The new node becomes the third node, and the original third node becomes the fourth node. This changes the previous list into this:

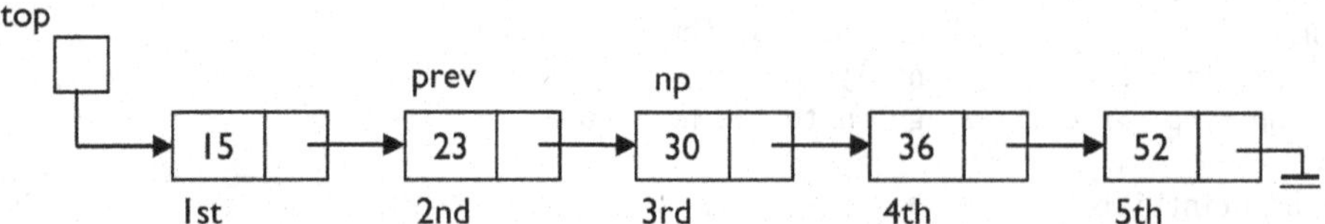

Does this code work if prev were pointing at the last node so that we are, in fact, inserting after the last node? Yes. If prev is the last node, then prev -> next is NULL. Therefore, the following statement sets np -> next to NULL so that the new node becomes the last node:

```
np -> next = prev -> next;
```

As before, prev -> next is set to point to the new node. This is illustrated by changing this:

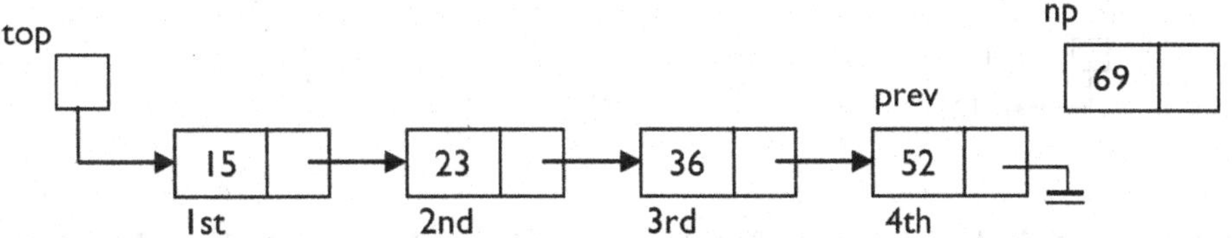

to this:

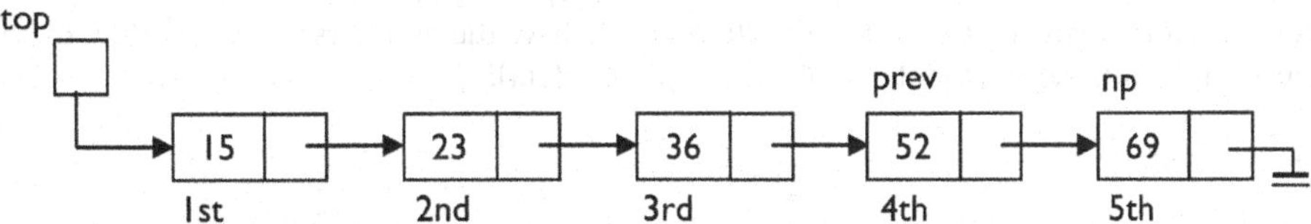

In many situations, it is required to insert a new node at the head of the list. That is, we want to make the new node the first node. Assuming that np points to the new node, we want to convert this:

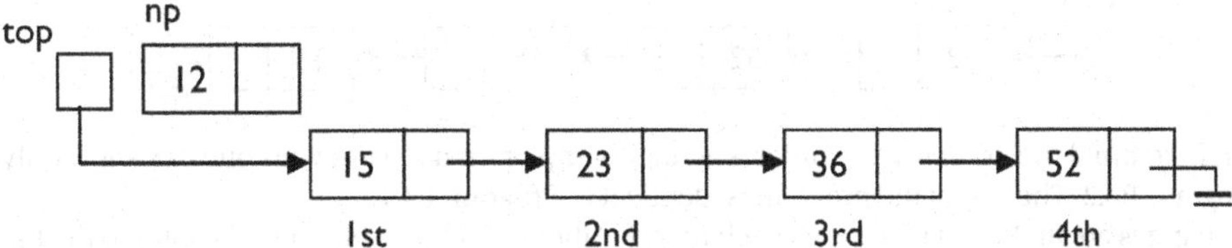

to this:

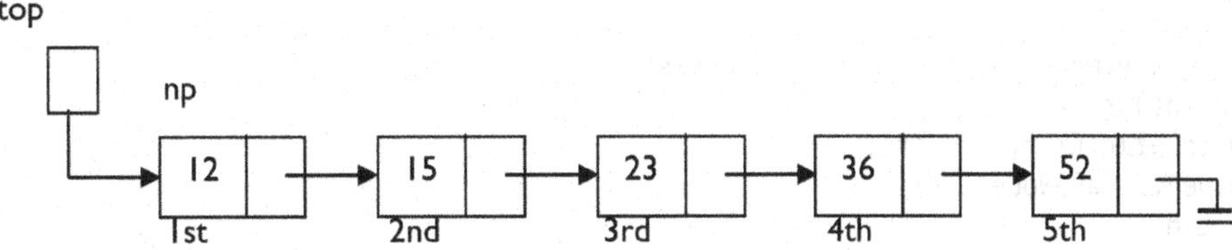

This can be done with the code:

```
np -> next = top;
top = np;
```

The first statement sets the new node to point to whatever top is pointing at (that is, the first node), and the second statement updates top to point to the new node.

You should observe that the code works even if the list is initially empty (that is, if `top` is `NULL`). In this case, it converts this:

into this:

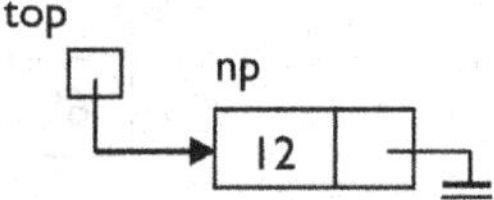

4.6 Building a Linked List: Adding a New Item at the Head

Consider again the problem of building a linked list of positive integers but, this time, we insert each new number at the head of the list rather than at the end. The resulting list will have the numbers in reverse order to how they are given. Say the incoming numbers are as follows (`0` terminates the data):

```
36 15 52 23 0
```

And say we want to build the following linked list:

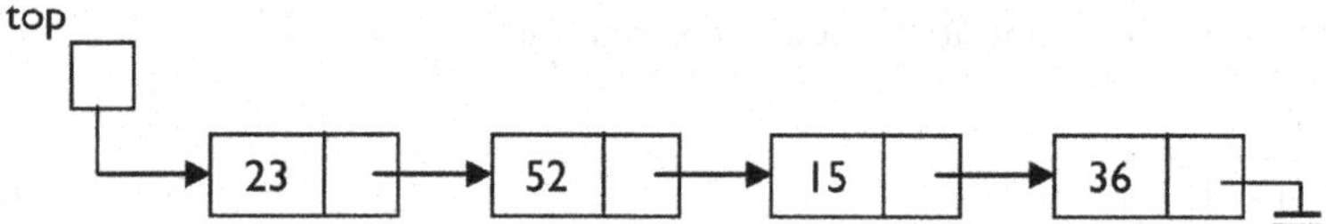

The program to build the list in reverse order is actually simpler than the previous one. We show only the `main` function of Program P4.2. The rest of the program is identical to Program P4.1.

The only changes are in the `while` loop. As each new number is read, we set its link to point to the first node, and we set `top` to point to the new node, making it the (new) first node.

Program P4.2

```
//add new numbers at the head of the list
int main() {
   void printList(NodePtr);
   NodePtr makeNode(int);
   int n;
   NodePtr top, np;
   top = NULL;
   if (scanf("%d", &n) != 1) n = 0;
   while (n != 0) {
      np = makeNode(n);    //create a new node containing n
      np -> next = top;    //set link of new node to first node
      top = np;   //set top to point to new node
      if (scanf("%d", &n) != 1) n = 0;
   }
   printList(top);
} //end main
```

Program P4.1 inserts incoming numbers at the tail of the list. This is an example of adding an item to a queue. A *queue* is a linear list in which insertions occur at one end and deletions (see the next section) occur at the other end.

Program P4.2 inserts incoming numbers at the head of the list. This is an example of adding an item to a stack. A *stack* is a linear list in which insertions and deletions occur at the same end. In stack terminology, when we add an item, we say the item is *pushed* onto the stack. Deleting an item from a stack is referred to as *popping* the stack.

We will treat with stacks and queues more fully in Chapter 5.

4.7 Deletion from a Linked List

Deleting a node from the top of a linked list is accomplished by doing this:

```
top = top -> next;
```

This says let `top` point to whatever the first node was pointing at (that is, the second node, if any). Since `top` is now pointing at the second node, effectively the first node has been deleted from the list. This statement changes the following:

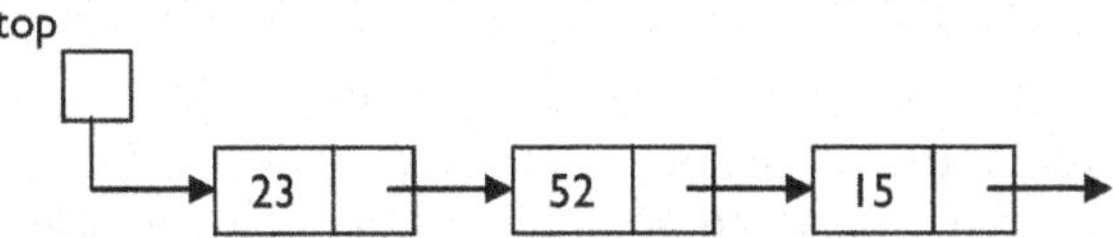

to this:

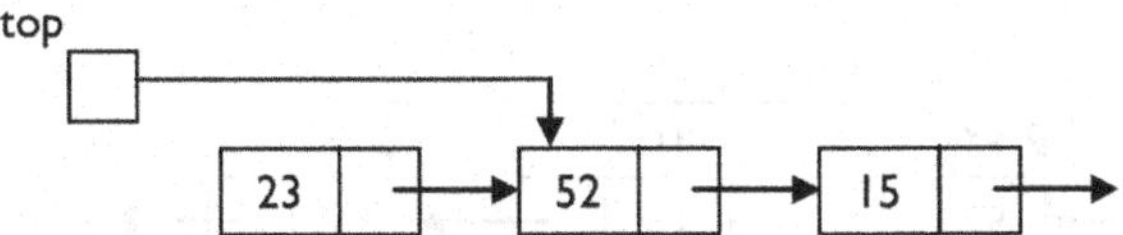

Of course, before we delete, we should check that there is something to delete, in other words, that `top` is not `NULL`. If there is only one node in the list, deleting it will result in the empty list; `top` will become `NULL`.

Deleting an arbitrary node from a linked list requires more information. Suppose `curr` (for "current") points to the node to be deleted. Deleting this node requires that we change the `next` field of the *previous* node. This means we must know the pointer to the previous node; suppose it is `prev` (for "previous"). Then deletion of node `curr` can be accomplished by doing this:

```
prev -> next = curr -> next;
```

This changes the following:

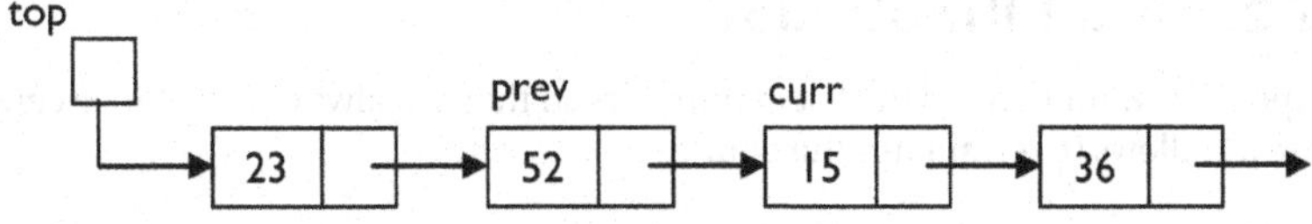

to this:

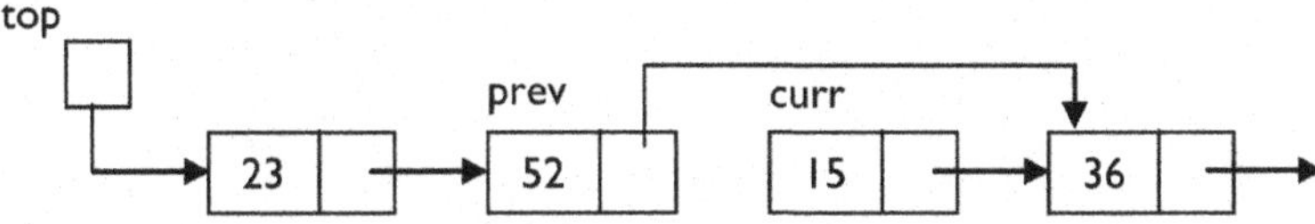

Effectively, the node pointed to by curr is no longer in the list—it has been deleted.

You may wonder what happens to nodes that have been deleted. In our earlier discussion, *deletion* meant "logical deletion." That is, as far as processing the list is concerned, the deleted nodes are not present. But the nodes are still in memory, occupying storage, even though we may have lost the pointers to them.

If we have a large list in which many deletions have occurred, then there will be a lot of "deleted" nodes scattered all over memory. These nodes occupy storage even though they will never, and cannot, be processed. We may need to delete them physically from memory.

As discussed in Section 4.3, C provides us with a function, free, to free the storage space occupied by nodes that we need to delete. The space to be freed should have been obtained by a call to malloc or calloc. The function call free(p) frees the space pointed to by p.

To illustrate its use, deleting the first node of the list can be accomplished by doing the following, where old is the same kind of pointer as top:

```
old = top;            // save the pointer to the node to be deleted
top = top -> next;  // set top to point to the 2nd node, if any
free(old);            // free the space occupied by the first node
```

To delete a node from elsewhere in the list where curr points to the node to be deleted and prev points to the previous node, we can use this:

```
prev -> next = curr -> next; // logical deletion
free(curr);                  // free the space occupied by the deleted node
```

The free statement will change the following:

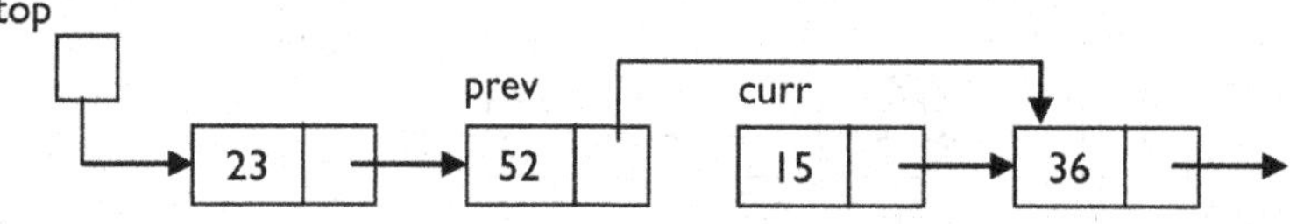

to this:

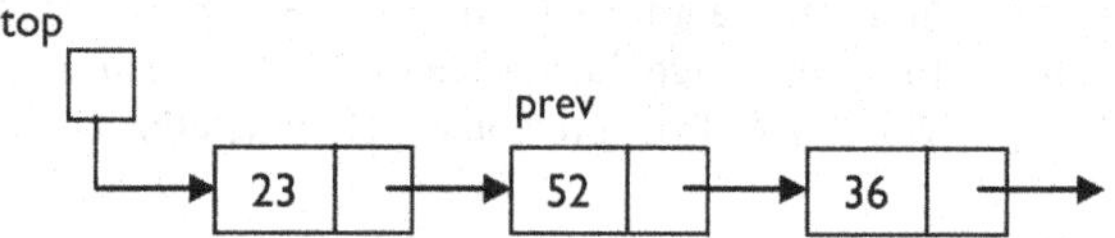

The storage occupied by curr no longer exists as far as our program is concerned.

4.8 Building a Sorted Linked List

As a third possibility, suppose we want to build the list of numbers so that it is always sorted in ascending order. Say the incoming numbers are as follows (0 terminates the data):

```
36 15 52 23 0
```

And say we want to build the following list:

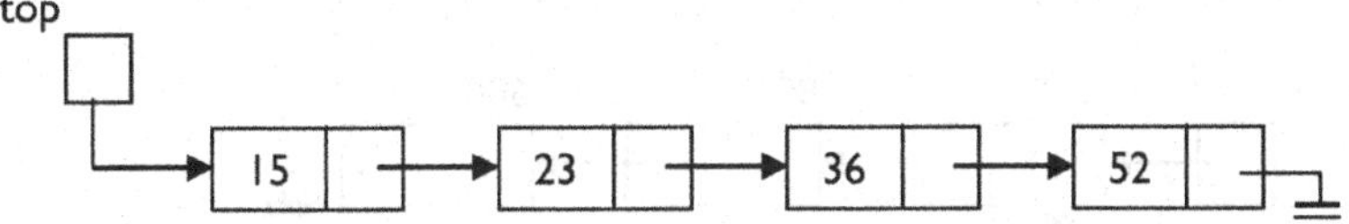

When a new number is read, it is inserted in the existing list (which is initially empty) in its proper place. The first number is simply added to the empty list.

Each subsequent number is compared with the numbers in the existing list. As long as the new number is greater than a number in the list, we move down the list until the new number is smaller than, or equal to, an existing number or we come to the end of the list.

To facilitate the insertion of the new number, before we leave a node and move on to the next one, we must save the pointer to it in case the new number must be inserted after this node. However, we can know this only when we compare the new number with the number in the next node.

To illustrate these ideas, consider the following sorted list and suppose we want to add a new number (`30`, say) to the list so that it remains sorted:

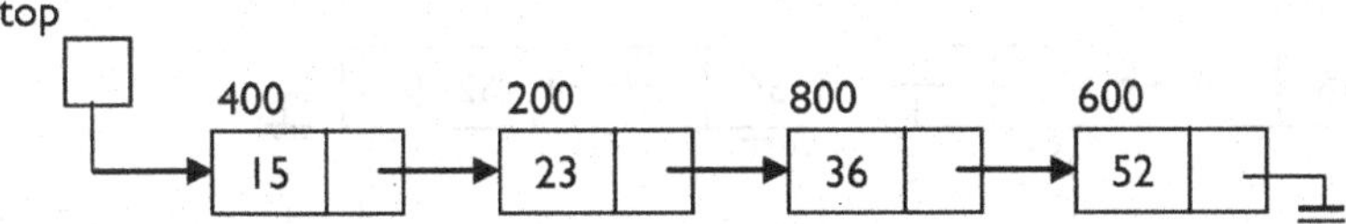

Assume the number before a node is the address of the node. Thus, the value of `top` is `400`.

First, we compare `30` with `15`. It is bigger, so we move on to the next number, `23`, remembering the address (`400`) of `15`.

Next, we compare `30` with `23`. It is bigger, so we move on to the next number, `36`, remembering the address (`200`) of `23`. We no longer need to remember the address (`400`) of `15`.

Next, we compare `30` with `36`. It is smaller, so we have found the number *before* which we must insert `30`. This is the same as inserting `30` *after* `23`. Since we have remembered the address of `23`, we can now perform the insertion.

We will use the following code to process the new number, `n`:

```
prev = NULL;
curr = top;
while (curr != NULL && n > curr -> num) {
   prev = curr;
   curr = curr -> next;
}
```

Initially, `prev` is `NULL` and `curr` is `400`. The insertion of 30 proceeds as follows:

- `30` is compared with `curr -> num`, `15`. It is bigger, so we set `prev` to `curr` (`400`) and set `curr` to `curr -> next`, `200`; `curr` is not `NULL`.
- `30` is compared with `curr -> num`, `23`. It is bigger, so we set `prev` to `curr` (`200`) and set `curr` to `curr -> next`, `800`; `curr` is not `NULL`.
- `30` is compared with `curr -> num`, `36`. It is smaller, so we exit the `while` loop with `prev` being `200` and `curr` being `800`.

We have the following situation:

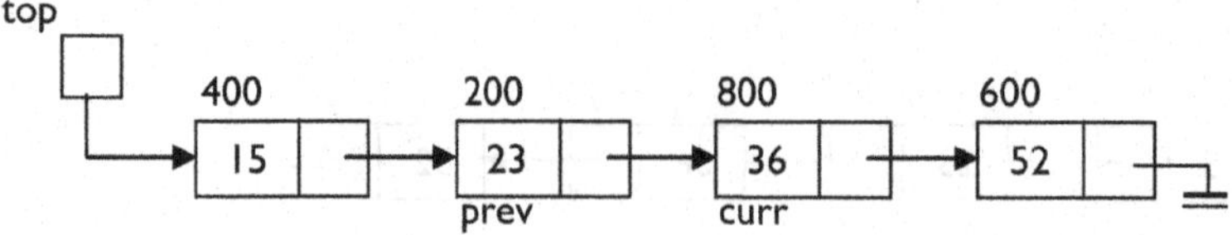

If the new number is stored in a node pointed to by np, we can now add it to the list (except at the head, see next) graphic, with the following code:

```
np -> next = curr;  //we could also use prev -> next for curr
prev -> next = np;
```

This will change the following:

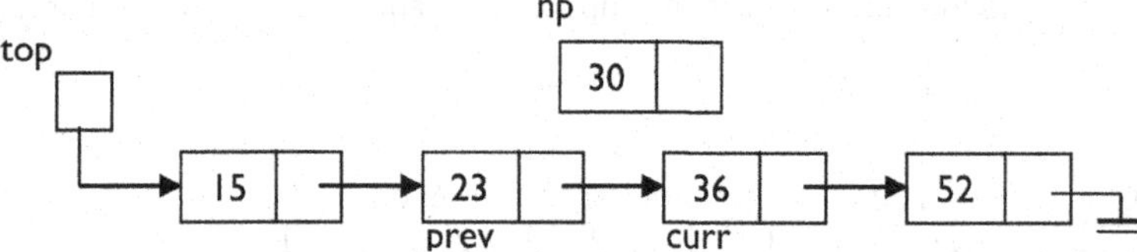

to the following:

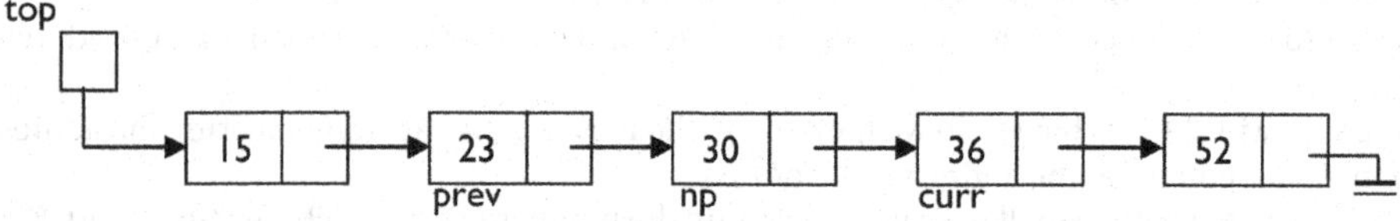

As an exercise, verify that this code will work if the number to be added is bigger than all the numbers in the list. Hint: when will the while loop exit?

If the number to be added is *smaller* than all the numbers in the list, it must be added at the head of the list and becomes the new first node in the list. This means the value of top has to be changed to the new node.

The while loop shown previously will work in this case as well. The while condition will be false on the very first test (since n will be smaller than curr -> num). On exit, we simply test whether prev is still NULL; if it is, the new node must be inserted at the top of the list.

If the list were initially empty, the while loop will exit immediately (since curr will be NULL). In this case also, the new node must be inserted at the top of the list, becoming the only node in the list.

Program P4.3 contains all the details. The insertion of a new node in its proper position in the list is delegated to the function addInPlace. This function returns a pointer to the top of the modified list.

Program P4.3

```
#include <stdio.h>
#include <stdlib.h>

typedef struct node {
   int num;
   struct node *next;
} Node, *NodePtr;
```

```
int main() {
   void printList(NodePtr);
   NodePtr addInPlace(NodePtr, int);
   int n;
   NodePtr top = NULL;
   if (scanf("%d", &n) != 1) n = 0;
   while (n != 0) {
      top = addInPlace(top, n);
      if (scanf("%d", &n) != 1) n = 0;
   }
   printList(top);
} //end main

NodePtr addInPlace(NodePtr top, int n) {
// This functions inserts n in its ordered position in a (possibly empty)
// list pointed to by top, and returns a pointer to the new list
   NodePtr np, curr, prev, makeNode(int);

   np = makeNode(n);
   prev = NULL;
   curr = top;
   while (curr != NULL && n > curr -> num) {
      prev = curr;
      curr = curr -> next;
   }
   if (prev == NULL) { //new number must be added at the top
      np -> next = top;
      return np; //the top of the list has changed to the new node
   }
   np -> next = curr;
   prev -> next = np;
   return top; //the top of the list has not changed
} //end addInPlace

NodePtr makeNode(int n) {
   NodePtr np = (NodePtr) malloc(sizeof (Node));
   np -> num = n;
   np -> next = NULL;
   return np;
} // end makeNode

void printList(NodePtr np) {
   while (np != NULL) {  // as long as there's a node
      printf("%d\n", np -> num);
      np = np -> next;  // go on to the next node
   }
} //end printList
```

4.9 Example: Palindrome

Consider the problem of determining whether a given string is a *palindrome* (the same when spelled forward or backward). The following are examples of palindromes (ignoring case, punctuation, and spaces):

```
civic
Racecar
Madam, I'm Adam.
A man, a plan, a canal, Panama.
```

If all the letters were of the same case (upper or lower) and the string (`word`, say) contained no spaces or punctuation marks, we *could* solve the problem as follows:

```
compare the first and last letters
if they are different, the string is not a palindrome
if they are the same, compare the second and second to last letters
if they are different, the string is not a palindrome
if they are the same, compare the third and third to last letters
```

We continue until we find a nonmatching pair (and it's not a palindrome) or there are no more pairs to compare (and it is a palindrome).

This method is efficient, but it requires us to be able to access any letter in the word directly. This is possible if the word is stored in an array and we use a subscript to access any letter. However, if the letters of the word are stored in a linked list, we cannot use this method since we can access the letters only sequentially.

To illustrate how linked lists may be manipulated, we will use linked lists to solve the problem using the following idea:

1. Store the original phrase in a linked list, one character per node.
2. Create another list containing the letters only of the phrase, all converted to lowercase and stored in reverse order; call this list1.
3. Reverse list1 to get list2.
4. Compare list1 with list2, letter by letter, until we get a mismatch (the phrase is not a palindrome) or we come to the end of the lists (the phrase is a palindrome).

Consider the phrase `Damn Mad!`; this will be stored as follows:

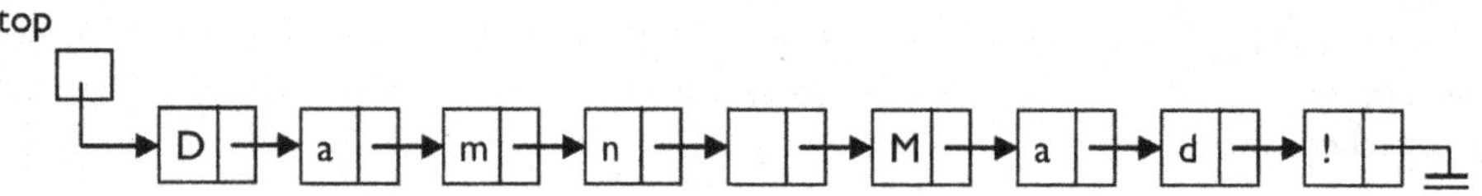

Step 2 will convert it to this:

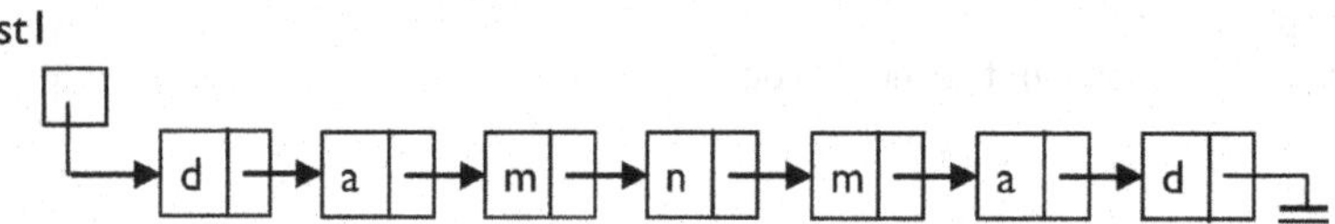

Step 3 will reverse this list to get the following:

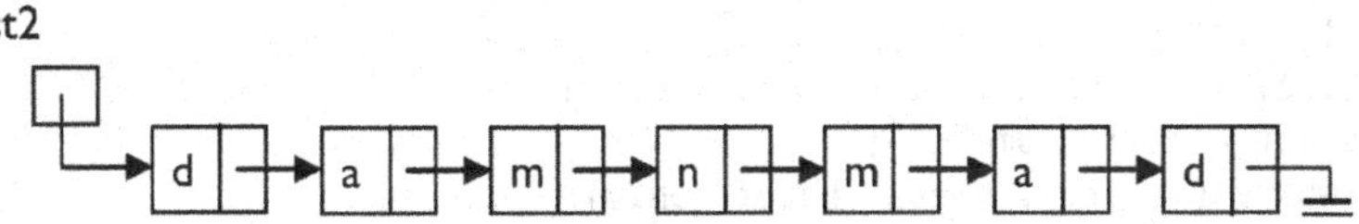

Comparing `list1` and `list2` will reveal that `Damn Mad!` is a palindrome.

We will write a program that prompts the user to type a phrase and tells her if it is a palindrome. It then prompts for another phrase. To stop, the user must press Enter.

We will write a function, `getPhrase`, that will read the data and store the characters of the phrase in a linked list, one character per node. The function will return a pointer to the list. This function must build the linked list in the order in which the characters are read—each new character is added at the end of the list.

We will write another function, `reverseLetters`, which, given a pointer to a list of characters, creates another list containing the letters only, all converted to lowercase and stored in reverse order. As each letter is encountered, it is converted to lowercase and added to the *front* of the new list.

To complete the job, we will write a function called `compare` that implements step 4 in the previous list.

These functions are shown in Program P4.4, which solves the palindrome problem. The following is a sample run of the program:

```
Type a phrase. (To stop, press "Enter" only): Damn Mad!
is a palindrome
Type a phrase. (To stop, press "Enter" only): So Many Dynamos!
is a palindrome
Type a phrase. (To stop, press "Enter" only): Rise to vote, sir.
is a palindrome
Type a phrase. (To stop, press "Enter" only): Thermostat
is not a palindrome
Type a phrase. (To stop, press "Enter" only): A Toyota's a Toyota.
is a palindrome
Type a phrase. (To stop, press "Enter" only):
```

Program P4.4

```
#include <stdio.h>
#include <stdlib.h>
#include <ctype.h>

typedef struct node {
   char ch;
   struct node * next;
} Node, *NodePtr;

int main() {
   NodePtr getPhrase();
   NodePtr reverseLetters(NodePtr);
   int compare(NodePtr, NodePtr);
   NodePtr phrase, s1, s2;

   printf("Type a phrase. (To stop, press 'Enter' only): ");
   phrase = getPhrase();
```

```
   while (phrase != NULL) {
      s1 = reverseLetters(phrase);
      s2 = reverseLetters(s1);
      if (compare(s1, s2) == 0) printf("is a palindrome\n");
      else printf("is not a palindrome\n");
      printf("Type a word. (To stop, press 'Enter' only): ");
      phrase = getPhrase();
   }
} //end main

NodePtr getPhrase() {
   NodePtr top = NULL, last, np;
   char c = getchar();
   while (c != '\n') {
      np = (NodePtr) malloc(sizeof(Node));
      np -> ch = c;
      np -> next = NULL;
      if (top == NULL) top = np;
      else last -> next = np;
      last = np;
      c = getchar();
   }
   return top;
} //end getPhrase

NodePtr reverseLetters(NodePtr top) {
   NodePtr rev = NULL, np;
   char c;
   while (top != NULL) {
      c = top -> ch;
      if (isalpha(c)) { // add to new list
         np = (NodePtr) malloc(sizeof(Node));
         np -> ch = tolower(c);
         np -> next = rev;
         rev = np;
      }
      top = top -> next; //go to next character of phrase
   }
   return rev;
} //end reverseLetter

int compare(NodePtr s1, NodePtr s2) {
//return -1 if s1 < s2, +1 if s1 > s2 and 0 if s1 = s2
   while (s1 != NULL) {
      if (s1 -> ch < s2 -> ch) return -1;
      else if (s1 -> ch > s2 -> ch) return 1;
      s1 = s1 -> next;
      s2 = s2 -> next;
   }
   return 0;
}
```

■ **Note** The solution presented was used mainly to show how linked lists can be manipulated. The palindrome problem can be solved more efficiently using arrays, where we would have direct access to any character of the given phrase. For instance, we would be able to compare the first and last letters directly. Even in the solution presented here, we could clean up the phrase as it is being input by retaining letters only and converting them to lowercase. As an exercise, write a program to solve the problem using arrays.

4.10 Saving a Linked List

When we create a linked list, the actual "pointer" value in a node is determined at runtime depending on where in memory storage for the node is allocated. Each time the program is run, the pointer values will change. So, what do we do if, having created a linked list, we need to save it for later use?

Since it would be useless to save the pointer values, we must save the contents of the nodes in such a way that we would be able to re-create the list when needed. The simplest way to do this is to write the items to a file (see Chapter 8) in the order that they appear in the linked list. Later, we can read the file and re-create the list as each item is read.

Sometimes we may want to compact a linked list into an array. One reason might be that the linked list is sorted and we want to search it quickly. Since we are restricted to a sequential search on a linked list, we can transfer the items to an array where we can use a binary search.

For example, suppose we have a linked list of at most 50 integers pointed to by `top`. If `num` and `next` are the fields of a node, we can store the integers in an array called `saveLL` with the following code:

```
int saveLL[50], n = 0;
while (top != NULL & n < 50) {
   saveLL[n++] = top -> num;
   top = top -> next;
}
```

On completion, the value of `n` will indicate how many numbers were saved. They will be stored in `saveLL[0..n-1]`.

4.11 Arrays vs. Linked Lists

Arrays and linked lists are the two common ways to store a linear list, and each has its advantages and disadvantages.

The big difference between the two is that we have direct access to any element of an array by using a subscript, whereas to get to any element of a linked list, we have to traverse the list starting from the top.

If the list of items is unsorted, we must search the list using a sequential search whether the items are stored in an array or a linked list. If the list is sorted, it is possible to search the array using a binary search. Since binary search requires direct access to an element, we cannot perform a binary search on a linked list. The only way to search a linked list is sequential.

Inserting an item at the tail of a list stored in an array is easy (assuming there is room), but inserting an item at the head requires that all the other items be moved to make room for the new one. Inserting an item in the middle would require about half of the items to be moved to make room for the new one. Inserting an item anywhere in a linked list is easy since it requires setting/changing just a couple links.

Similarly, deleting an item from a linked list is easy regardless of where the item is located (head, tail, middle). Deleting an item from an array is easy only if it is the last one; deleting any other item would require other items to be moved to "close the space" previously occupied by the deleted item.

Maintaining an array in sorted order (when new items are added) is cumbersome since each new item has to be inserted "in place," and, as we've seen, this would normally require that other items be moved. However, finding the *location* in which to insert the item can be done quickly using a binary search.

Finding the *position* at which to insert a new item in a sorted linked list must be done using a sequential search. However, once the position is found, the item can be quickly inserted by setting/changing a couple links.

Table 4-1 summarizes the strengths and weaknesses of storing a list of items in an array versus storing them in a linked list.

Table 4-1. *Storing List of Items in an Array vs. in Linked List*

Array	Linked List
Direct access to any element	Must traverse list to get to element
If unsorted, sequential search	If unsorted, sequential search
If sorted, binary search	If sorted, sequential search
Easy-to-insert item at the tail of the list	Easy to insert item anywhere in the list
Must move items to insert anywhere but the tail	Easy to insert item anywhere in the list
Deletion (except the last one) requires items to be moved	Deletion of any item is easy
Need to move items when adding a new item to a sorted list	Adding a new item to a sorted linked list is easy
Can use binary search on a sorted list to find the position at which to insert new item	Must use sequential search to find the position at which to insert new item in a sorted linked list

4.12 Storing a Linked List Using Arrays

We have seen how to create a linked list using dynamic storage allocation. When we need to add another node to a linked list, we request the storage for that node. If we need to delete a node from a linked list, we first delete it logically by changing pointers and then physically by freeing the storage occupied by the node.

It is also possible to represent a linked list using arrays. Consider, once again, the following linked list:

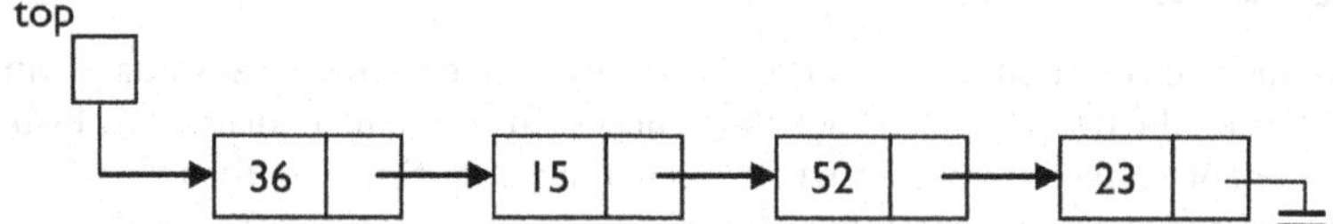

We can store this as follows:

top: 5

	data	next
0		
1	15	7
2		
3	23	-1
4		
5	36	1
6		
7	52	3
8		
9		

Here, the links (pointers) are merely array subscripts. Since an array subscript is just an integer, `top` is an `int` variable, and `next` is an `int` array. In this example, the data happens to be integers (so `data` is an `int` array), but it could be of any other type, even a structure. (Typically, you would use a `struct` array, with `next` being one of the fields and the other fields holding the data.)

The value of `top` is 5, so this says that the first item in the list is found at array index 5; `data[5]` holds the data (36, in this case), and `next[5]` (1, in this case) tells us where to find the next (second) item in the list.

So, the second item is found at array index 1; `data[1]` holds the data (15), and `next[1]` (7) tells us where to find the next (third) item in the list.

The third item is found at array index 7; `data[7]` holds the data (52), and `next[7]` (3) tells us where to find the next (fourth) item in the list.

The fourth item is found at array index 3; `data[3]` holds the data (23), and `next[3]` (-1) tells us where to find the next item in the list. Here, we use -1 as the null pointer, so we've come to the end of the list. Any value that cannot be confused with a valid array subscript can be used to denote the null pointer, but it is common to use -1.

All the operations described in this chapter for working with linked lists (for example, adding, deleting, and traversing) can be performed in a similar manner on linked lists stored using arrays. The main difference is that, previously, if `curr` points to the current node, `curr -> next` points to the next node. Now, if `curr` points to the current node, `next[curr]` points to the next node.

One disadvantage of using arrays to store a linked list is that you must have some idea of how big the list is expected to be in order to declare the arrays. Another is that storage for deleted items cannot be freed. However, the storage can be reused to store new items.

4.13 Merging Two Sorted Linked Lists

In Section 1.8, we considered the problem of merging two ordered lists. There, we showed how to solve the problem when the lists were stored in arrays. We now will show how to solve the same problem when the lists are stored as linked lists.

Suppose the given lists are as follows:

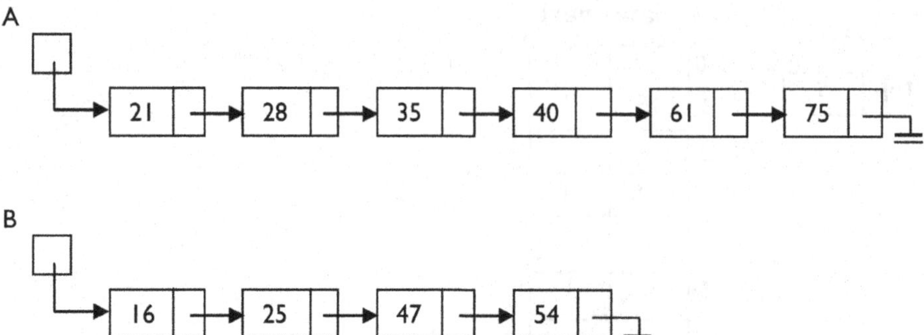

We want to create one linked list with all the numbers in ascending order, like this:

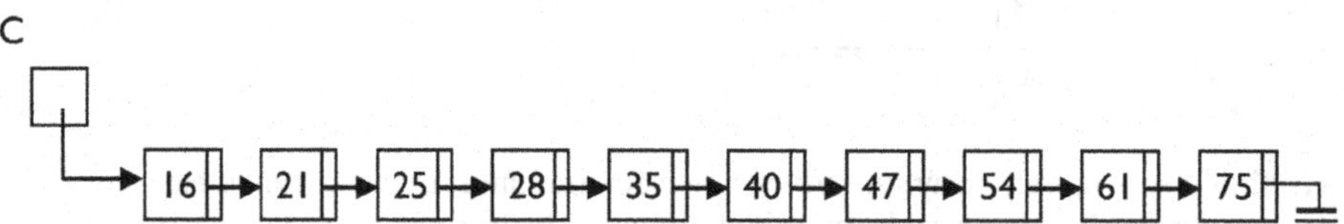

We could create the merged list by creating a new node for each number that we add to the list C. In other words, we leave the lists A and B untouched. However, we will perform the merge by *not* creating any new nodes. All numbers will remain in their original nodes. We will simply adjust pointers to create the merged list. At the end, the lists A and B will no longer exist.

We will use the same algorithm that we used in Section 1.9. Here it is for easy reference:

```
while (at least one number remains in A and B) {
   if (smallest in A < smallest in B)
      add smallest in A to C
      move on to next number in A
   else
      add smallest in B to C
      move on to next number in B
   endif
}
if (A has ended) add remaining numbers in B to C
else add remaining numbers in A to C
```

We assume that the nodes of the lists are defined like this:

```
typedef struct node {
   int num;
   struct node *next;
} Node, *NodePtr;
```

and A, B, and C are declared like this:

```
NodePtr A, B, C = NULL;
```

A and B point to the given lists, and C will point to the merged list. Initially, C is NULL. Each new number must be added at the tail of C. To make this easy to do, we will keep a pointer to the current last node in C (we call it `last`).

The previous algorithm translates into the code shown here. To keep the presentation simple for now, this code assumes that both A and B are nonempty. We will deal with an empty A or B later.

```
NodePtr C = NULL, last == NULL;
while (A != NULL && B != NULL) {
   if (A -> num < B -> num) {
      //add node pointed to by A to the tail of C;
      A = A -> next ;
   }
   else {
      //add node pointed to by B to the tail of C;
      B = B -> next ;
   }
}
if (A == NULL) last -> next = B;
else last -> next = A;
```

Note the last `if` statement and how easy it is to "add the remaining elements" of a list to C. All we have to do is set the current last node of C to point to the list (A or B).

To complete the translation, we must show how to add a node (pointed to by N, say) to the tail of C. If C is empty, N becomes the only node in the list. If C is not empty, the current last node of C is set to point to N. In either case, N becomes the current last node of C. Thus, the following:

```
//add node pointed to by A to the tail of C;
```

is translated into this:

```
if (C == NULL) C = A; else last -> next = A;
last = A;
```

The case for adding the node pointed to by B is handled by replacing A with B.

In Program P4.5, we write a function called `merge` that, given the sorted lists A and B, performs the merge and returns a pointer to the merged list. This function also deals with the case when either A or B is empty. We test `merge` by using the code from Program P4.1 to create two sorted lists, merge them, and print the merged list.

Recall that Program P4.1 builds a list in the order in which the numbers are supplied. Thus, you must enter the numbers for a list in ascending order. As an exercise, you can use code from Program P4.3 to build the lists in ascending order regardless of the order in which the numbers are supplied.

A sample run of Program P4.5 is shown here:

```
Enter numbers for the first list (0 to end)
2 4 6 8 10 12 0
Enter numbers for the second list (0 to end)
1 3 5 7 0

The merged list is
1 2 3 4 5 6 7 8 10 12
```

Program P4.5

```
#include <stdio.h>
#include <stdlib.h>
typedef struct node {
   int num;
   struct node *next;
} Node, *NodePtr;

int main() {
   void printList(NodePtr);
   NodePtr makeList(void);
   NodePtr merge(NodePtr, NodePtr);
   NodePtr A, B;

   printf("Enter numbers for the first list (0 to end)\n");
   A = makeList();
   printf("Enter numbers for the second list (0 to end)\n");
   B = makeList();
   printf("\nThe merged list is\n");
   printList(merge(A, B));
} //end main

NodePtr makeList() {
   NodePtr makeNode(int), np, top, last;
   int n;
   top = NULL;
   if (scanf("%d", &n) != 1) n = 0;
   while (n != 0) {
      np = makeNode(n);   //create a new node containing n
      if (top == NULL) top = np;   //set top if first node
      else last -> next = np;   //set last -> next for other nodes
      last = np;   //update last to  new node
      if (scanf("%d", &n) != 1) n = 0;
   }
   return top;
} //end makeList

NodePtr makeNode(int n) {
   NodePtr np = (NodePtr) malloc(sizeof (Node));
   np -> num = n;
   np -> next = NULL;
   return np;
} //end makeNode

void printList(NodePtr np) {
   while (np != NULL) {  // as long as there's a node
      printf("%d ", np -> num);
      np = np -> next;  // go on to the next node
   }
   printf("\n\n");
} //end printList
```

```
NodePtr merge(NodePtr A, NodePtr B) {
   NodePtr C = NULL, last = NULL;
   // check if either A or B is empty
   if (A == NULL) return B;
   if (B == NULL) return A;
   //both lists are non-empty
   while (A != NULL && B != NULL) {
      if (A -> num < B -> num) {
         if (C == NULL) C = A; else last -> next = A;
         last = A;
         A = A -> next ;
      }
      else {
         if (C == NULL) C = B; else last -> next = B;
         last = B;
         B = B -> next ;
      }
   } //end while
   if (A == NULL) last -> next = B;
   else last -> next = A;
   return C;
} //end merge
```

4.14 Circular and Two-Way Linked Lists

So far, our discussion has been primarily about one-way (singly linked) lists. Each node contains one pointer that tells us the location of the next item. The last node has a null pointer, indicating the end of the list. While this is the most commonly used type of list, two common variations are the *circular* list and the *two-way* (or doubly linked) list.

4.14.1 Circular Lists

In a circular list, we let the last item point back to the first, as follows:

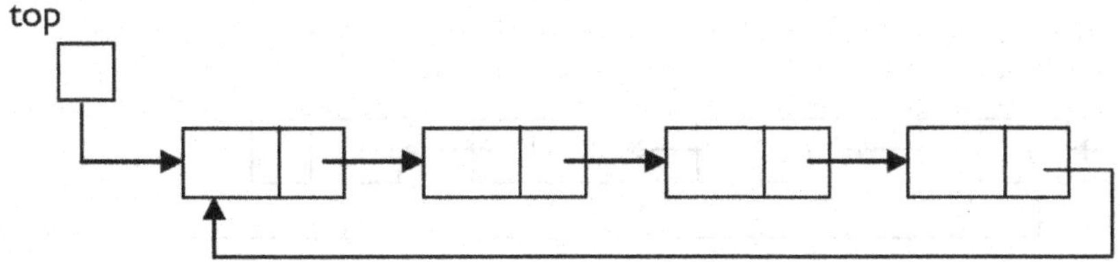

Now, there is no null pointer to tell us when we have reached the end of the list, so we must be careful in traversing that we do not end up in an infinite loop. In other words, say we were to write something like this:

```
NodePtr curr = top;
while (curr != NULL) {
   //do something with node pointed to by curr
   curr = curr -> next;
}
```

This loop will *never* terminate since curr never becomes NULL. To avoid this problem, we can save the pointer of our starting node and recognize when we have returned to this node. Here's an example:

```
NodePtr curr = top;
do {
   //do something with node pointed to by curr
   curr = curr -> next;
} while (curr != top) {
```

Alert readers will observe that since the body of a do...while loop is executed at least once, we should ensure that the list is not empty before going into the loop and trying to dereference a null pointer.

Circular lists are useful for representing situations that are, well, circular. For example, in a card or board game in which players take turns, we can represent the order of play using a circular list. If there are four players, they will play in the order 1, 2, 3, 4, 1, 2, 3, 4, 1, 2, and so on. After the last person plays, it's the turn of the first.

In the children's game *count-out*, the children are arranged in a circle and some variation of "eenie, meenie, mynie, mo; sorry, child, you've got to go" is used to eliminate one child at a time. The last remaining child wins the game.

We will write a program that uses a circular list to find the winner of the game described as follows:

The count-out game*: n children (numbered 1 to n) are arranged in a circle. A sentence consisting of m words is used to eliminate one child at a time until one child is left. Starting at child 1, the children are counted from 1 to m and the mth child is eliminated. Starting with the child after the one just eliminated, the children are again counted from 1 to m and the mth child eliminated. This is repeated until one child is left. Counting is done circularly, and eliminated children are not counted. Write a program to read values for n and m (> 0), play the game as described, and print the number of the last remaining child.*

It is possible to use an array (child, say) to solve this problem. To declare the array, we would need to know the maximum number (max, say) of children to cater for. We could set child[1] to child[n] to 1 to indicate that all *n* children are initially in the game. When a child (h, say) is eliminated, we would set child[h] to 0 and start counting out from the next child still in the game.

As the game progresses, several entries in child will be set to 0, and when we count, we must ensure that 0s are not counted. In other words, even when a child has been eliminated, we must still inspect the array item and skip it if 0. As more children are eliminated, we will need to inspect and skip more zero entries. This is the main disadvantage of using an array to solve this problem.

We can write a more efficient solution using a circular linked list. First, we create the list with *n* nodes. The value at each node is the child's number. For $n = 4$, the list will look like the following, assuming curr points to the first child:

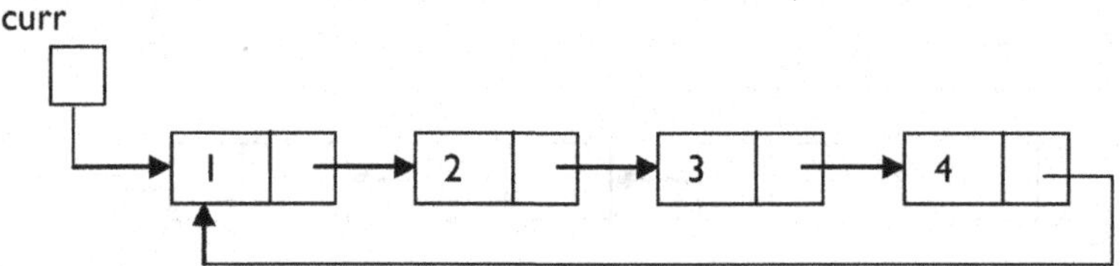

Suppose $m = 5$. We start counting from 1; when we reach 4, the count of 5 takes us back to child 1, which is eliminated. The list will look like this:

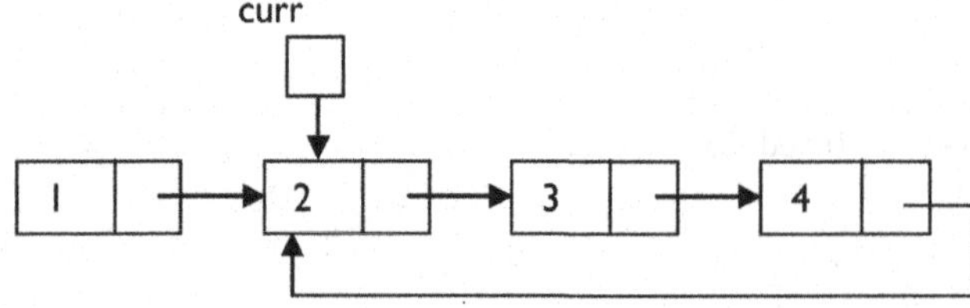

As shown, child 1 is no longer in the list; the storage for this node would be freed. We count to 5 again, starting from child 2. The count ends at child 3, which is eliminated by setting child 2's pointer to point to child 4. The list will look like this:

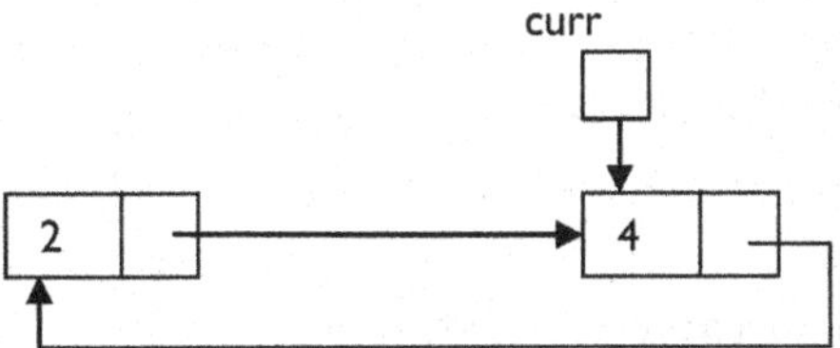

Finally, we count to 5 starting at child 4. The count ends at child 4, which is eliminated. Child 2 is the winner.

Note that this solution (as opposed to the array version) really does eliminate a child from the game by deleting its node. Eliminated children are neither inspected nor counted since they are gone! This is more in keeping with the way the game is played.

Program P4.6 plays the game and finds the winner as described earlier.

Program P4.6

```
#include <stdio.h>
#include <stdlib.h>

typedef struct node {
   int num;
   struct node *next;
} Node, *NodePtr;

int main() {
   NodePtr curr, linkCircular(int), playGame(NodePtr, int, int);
   int n, m;

   do {
      printf("Enter number of children and length of count-out: ");
      scanf("%d %d", &n, &m);
   } while (n < 1 || m < 1);

   curr = linkCircular(n); //link children in a circular list
   curr = playGame(curr, n-1, m); //eliminate n-1 children
   printf("The winning child: %d\n", curr -> num);
} //end main

NodePtr makeNode(int n) {
   NodePtr np = (NodePtr) malloc(sizeof (Node));
   np -> num = n;
   np -> next = NULL;
   return np;
} //end makeNode
```

```
NodePtr linkCircular(int n) {
   //link n children in a circular list; return pointer to first child
   NodePtr first, np, makeNode(int);

   first = np = makeNode(1);      //first child
   for (int h = 2; h <= n; h++) { //link the others
      np -> next = makeNode(h);
      np = np -> next;
   }
   np -> next = first; //set last child to point to first
   return first;
} //end linkCircular

NodePtr playGame(NodePtr first, int x, int m) {
   NodePtr prev, curr = first;
   //eliminate x children
   for (int h = 1; h <= x; h++) {
      //curr is pointing at the first child to be counted;
      //count m-1 more to get to the mth child
      for (int c = 1; c < m; c++) {
         prev = curr;
         curr = curr -> next;
      }
      //delete the mth child
      prev -> next = curr -> next;
      free(curr);
      curr = prev -> next; //set curr to the child after the one eliminated
   }
   return curr;
} //end playGame
```

4.14.2 Two-Way (Doubly Linked) Lists

As the name implies, each node will contain two pointers—one points to the next node, and the other points to the previous node. While this requires more work to implement and maintain, there are some advantages.

The obvious one is that it is now possible to traverse the list in both directions, starting from either end. If required, reversing the list is now a simple operation.

If we land at a node (the current node) in a singly linked list, there is no way to get to (or know) the previous node unless that information was kept as the list was traversed. With a doubly linked list, we have a direct pointer to the previous node so we can move in either direction.

One possible disadvantage is that more storage is required for the extra link. Another is that adding and deleting nodes is more complicated since more pointers have to be set.

EXERCISES 4

1. Write a function that, given a pointer to a linked list of integers, returns `1` if the list is sorted in ascending order and returns `0` otherwise.
2. Write code to reverse the nodes of a linked list by manipulating pointer fields only. No new nodes must be created.
3. Write a function to sort a linked list of integers as follows:
   (a) Find the largest value in the list.
   (b) Delete it from its position and insert it at the head of the list.
   (c) Starting from what is now the second element, repeat (a) and (b).
   (d) Starting from what is now the third element, repeat (a) and (b).

   Continue until the list is sorted.
4. Write a function to free all the nodes of a given linked list.
5. Write a function that takes three arguments—a pointer to a linked list of integers and two integers, `n` and `j`—and inserts `n` after the `j`th element of the list. If `j` is `0`, `n` is inserted at the head of the list. If `j` is greater than the number of elements in the list, `n` is inserted after the last one.
6. The characters of a string are held on a linked list, one character per node.
   (a) Write a function that, given a pointer to a string and two characters, `c1` and `c2`, replaces all occurrences of `c1` with `c2`.
   (b) Write a function that, given a pointer to a string and a character, `c`, deletes all occurrences of `c` from the string. Return a pointer to the modified string.
   (c) Write a function that, given a pointer to a string, converts all lowercase letters to uppercase, leaving all the other characters unchanged.
   (d) Write a function that creates a new list consisting of the letters only in the given list, all converted to lowercase and stored in alphabetical order. Return a pointer to the new list.
   (e) Write a function that, given pointers to two strings, determines whether the first is a substring of the other.
7. Write a function that, given an integer `n`, converts `n` to binary and stores each bit in one node of a linked list with the *least* significant bit at the head of the list and the *most* significant bit at the tail. For example, given `13`, the bits are stored in the order `1 0 1 1`, from head to tail. Return a pointer to the head of the list.
8. Write a function that, given a pointer to a linked list of bits stored as in 7, *traverses the list once* and returns the decimal equivalent of the binary number.

9. You are given two pointers, `b1` and `b2`, each pointing to a binary number stored as in 7. You must return a pointer to a newly created linked list representing the binary sum of the given numbers with the *least* significant bit at the head of the list and the *most* significant bit at the tail of the list. Write functions to do this in two ways:

   (i) Using the functions from 7 and 8

   (ii) Performing a "bit-by-bit" addition

10. Repeat exercises 7, 8, and 9, but this time, store the bits with the *most* significant bit at the head of the list and the *least* significant bit at the tail.

11. Two words are anagrams if one word can be formed by rearranging all the letters of the other word, for example *treason, senator*. A word is represented as a linked list with one letter per node of the list.

    Write a function that, given `w1` and `w2` each pointing to a word of lowercase letters, returns `1` if the words are anagrams and `0` if they are not. Base your algorithm on the following: for each letter in `w1`, search `w2` for it; if found, delete it and continue. Otherwise, return `0`.

12. The children's game of "count-out" is played as follows: *n* children (numbered 1 to *n*) are arranged in a circle. A sentence consisting of *m* words is used to eliminate one child at a time until one child is left.

    Starting at child 1, the children are counted from 1 to *m*, and the *m*th child is eliminated. Starting with the child after the one just eliminated, the children are again counted from 1 to *m*, and the *m*th child eliminated. This is repeated until one child is left. Counting is done circularly, and eliminated children are not counted.

    Write a program to read values for *n* and *m* and print the number of the last remaining child. Use a linked list to hold the children.

    Hint: Let the last node point to the first, creating a *circular* list.

13. The digits of an integer are held on a linked list in reverse order, one digit per node. Write a function that, given pointers to two integers, performs a digit-by-digit addition and returns a pointer to the digits of the sum stored in reverse order. Note: This idea can be used to add arbitrarily large integers.

CHAPTER 5

Stacks and Queues

In this chapter, we will explain the following:

- The notion of an abstract data type
- What a stack is
- How to implement a stack using an array
- How to implement a stack using a linked list
- How to create a header file for use by other programs
- How to implement a stack for a general data type
- How to convert an expression from infix to postfix
- How to evaluate an arithmetic expression
- What a queue is
- How to implement a queue using an array
- How to implement a queue using a linked list

5.1 Abstract Data Types

We are familiar with the notion of declaring variables of a given type (`double`, say) and then performing operations on those variables (for example, add, multiply, and assign) without needing to know **how** those variables are stored in the computer. In this scenario, the compiler designer can change the way a `double` variable is stored, and the programmer would not have to change any programs that use `double` variables. This is an example of an abstract data type.

An *abstract data type* is one that allows a user to manipulate the data type without any knowledge of how the data type is represented in the computer. In other words, as far as the user is concerned, all he needs to know are the operations that can be performed on the data type. The person who is implementing the data type is free to change its implementation without affecting the users.

In this chapter, we will show how to implement stacks and queues as abstract data types.

5.2 Stacks

A *stack* as a linear list in which items are added at one end and deleted from the same end. The idea is illustrated by a "stack of plates" placed on a table, one on top the other. When a plate is needed, it is taken from the top of the stack. When a plate is washed, it is added at the top of the stack. Note that if a plate is now needed, this "newest" plate is the one that is taken. A stack exhibits the "last in, first out" property.

To illustrate the stack idea, we will use a stack of integers. Our goal is to define a data type called `Stack` so that a user can declare variables of this type and manipulate it in various ways. What are some of these ways?

As indicated earlier, we will need to add an item to the stack; the term commonly used is *push*. We will also need to take an item off the stack; the term commonly used is *pop*.

Before we attempt to take something off the stack, it is a good idea to ensure that the stack has something on it, in other words, that it is not *empty*. We will need an operation that tests whether a stack is empty.

Given these three operations—*push*, *pop*, and *empty*—let's illustrate how they can be used to read some numbers and print them in reverse order. For example, say we have these numbers:

```
36 15 52 23
```

And say we want to print the following:

```
23 52 15 36
```

We can solve this problem by adding each new number to the top of a stack, `S`. After all the numbers have been placed on the stack, we can picture the stack as follows:

```
23        (top of stack)
52
15
36        (bottom of stack)
```

Next, we remove the numbers, one at a time, printing each as it is removed.

We will need a way of telling when all the numbers have been read. We will use `0` to end the data. The logic for solving this problem can be expressed as follows:

```
create an empty stack, S
read(num)
while (num != 0) {
   push num onto S
   read(num)
}
while (S is not empty) {
   pop S into num //store the number at the top of S in num
   print num
}
```

We now show how we can implement a stack of integers and its operations.

5.2.1 Implementing a Stack Using an Array

In the array implementation of a stack (of integers), we use an integer array (`ST`, say) for storing the numbers and an integer variable (`top`, say) that contains the index (subscript) of the item at the top of the stack.

Since we are using an array, we will need to know its size in order to declare it. We will need to have some information about the problem to determine a reasonable size for the array. We will use the symbolic constant `MaxStack`. If an attempt is made to push more than `MaxStack` elements onto the stack, we will report a *stack overflow* error.

We can use the following to define the data type Stack:

```
typedef struct {
   int top;
   int ST[MaxStack];
} StackType, *Stack;
```

Valid values for top will range from 0 to MaxStack-1. When we initialize a stack, we will set top to the invalid subscript, -1.

We can now declare a stack variable, S, with this:

```
Stack S;
```

Observe that Stack is declared as a pointer to the structure we call StackType. So, for instance, S is a pointer to a structure consisting of the variable top and the array ST. This is necessary since top and ST would need to be changed by the *push* and *pop* routines and the changes known to the calling function (main, say). This can be achieved by passing a pointer to them, in effect, the Stack variable.

To work with a stack, the first task is to create an empty stack. This is done by allocating storage for a StackType, assigning its address to a Stack variable, and setting top to -1. We can use the following:

```
Stack initStack() {
   Stack sp = (Stack) malloc(sizeof(StackType));
   sp -> top = -1;
   return sp;
}
```

In main, say, we can declare and initialize a stack, S, with this:

```
Stack S = initStack();
```

When this statement is executed, the situation in memory can be represented by that shown in Figure 5-1.

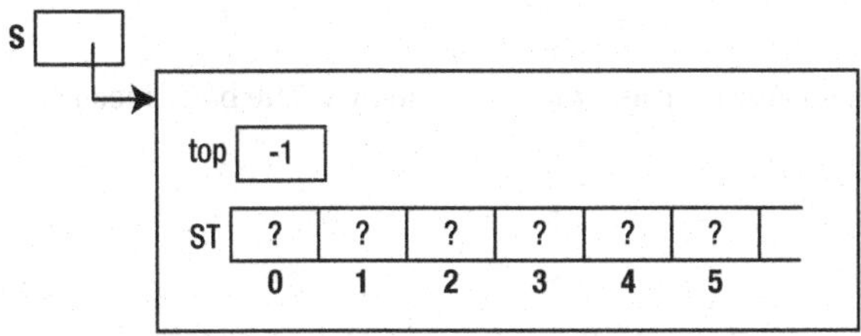

Figure 5-1. *Array representation of stack in memory*

This represents the empty stack. In working with stacks, we will need a function that tells us whether a stack is empty. We can use the following:

```
int empty(Stack S) {
   return (S -> top == -1);
}
```

This simply checks whether top has the value -1.

The major operations on a stack are *push* and *pop*. To push an item, n, onto a stack, we must store it in ST and update top to point to it. The basic idea is as follows:

```
add 1 to top
set ST[top] to n
```

However, we must guard against trying to add something to the stack when it is already full. The stack is full when top has the value MaxStack-1, the subscript of the last element. In this case, we will report that the stack is full and halt the program. Here is push:

```
void push(Stack S, int n) {
   if (S -> top == MaxStack - 1) {
      printf("\nStack Overflow\n");
      exit(1);
   }
   ++(S -> top);
   S -> ST[S -> top] = n;
}
```

To illustrate, after the numbers 36, 15, 52, and 23 have been pushed onto S, our picture in memory looks like Figure 5-2.

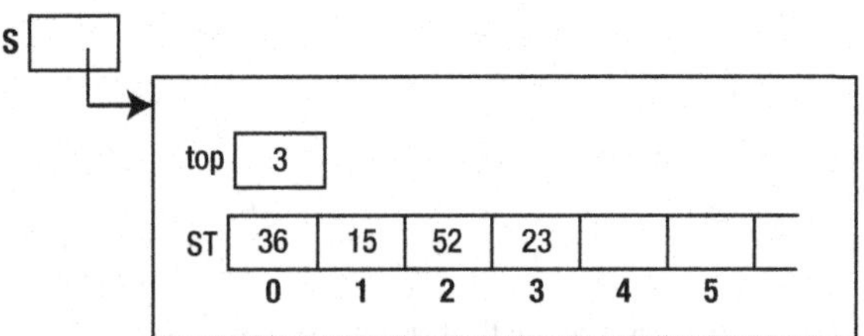

Figure 5-2. *Stack view after pushing 36, 15, 52, and 23*

Finally, to pop an item off the stack, we return the value in location top and decrease top by 1. The basic idea is as follows:

```
set hold to ST[top]
subtract 1 from top
return hold
```

Again, we must guard against trying to take something off an empty stack. What should we do if the stack is empty and pop is called? We could simply report an error and halt the program. However, it might be better to return some "rogue" value, indicating that the stack is empty. We take the latter approach in our function, pop.:

```
int pop(Stack S) {
   if (empty(S)) return RogueValue; //a symbolic constant
   int hold = S -> ST[S -> top];
   --(S -> top);
   return hold;
}
```

Note that even though we have written pop to do something reasonable if it is called and the stack is empty, it is better if the programmer establishes that the stack is *not* empty (using the empty function) before calling pop.

We now write Program P5.1, which reads some numbers, terminated by 0, and prints them in reverse order. The following shows a sample run of the program:

```
Enter some integers, ending with 0
1 2 3 4 5 6 7 8 9 0

Numbers in reverse order
9 8 7 6 5 4 3 2 1
```

Program P5.1

```
#include <stdio.h>
#include <stdlib.h>
#define RogueValue -9999
#define MaxStack 10

typedef struct {
   int top;
   int ST[MaxStack];
} StackType, *Stack;

int main() {
   Stack initStack();
   int empty(Stack);
   void push(Stack, int);
   int pop(Stack);
   int n;
   Stack S = initStack();
   printf("Enter some integers, ending with 0\n");
   scanf("%d", &n);
   while (n != 0) {
      push(S, n);
      scanf("%d", &n);
   }
   printf("Numbers in reverse order\n");
   while (!empty(S))
      printf("%d ", pop(S));
   printf("\n");
} //end main

Stack initStack() {
   Stack sp = (Stack) malloc(sizeof(StackType));
   sp -> top = -1;
   return sp;
} //end initStack

int empty(Stack S) {
   return (S -> top == -1);
} //end empty
```

```
void push(Stack S, int n) {
   if (S -> top == MaxStack - 1) {
      printf("\nStack Overflow\n");
      exit(1);
   }
   ++(S -> top);
   S -> ST[S -> top]= n;
} //end push

int pop(Stack S) {
   if (empty(S)) return RogueValue;
   int hold = S -> ST[S -> top];
   --(S -> top);
   return hold;
}  //end pop
```

It is important to observe that the code in `main` that uses the stack does so via the functions `initStack`, `push`, `pop`, and `empty` and makes no assumption about how the stack elements are stored. This is the hallmark of an abstract data type—it can be used without the user needing to know how it is implemented.

Next, we will implement the stack using a linked list, but `main` will remain the same for solving the problem of printing the numbers in reverse order.

5.2.2 Implementing a Stack Using a Linked List

The array implementation of a stack has the advantages of simplicity and efficiency. However, one major disadvantage is the need to know what size to declare the array. Some reasonable guess has to be made, but this may turn out to be too small (and the program has to halt) or too big (and storage is wasted).

To overcome this disadvantage, a linked list can be used. Now, we will allocate storage for an element only when it is needed.

The stack is implemented as a linked list with new items added at the head of the list. When we need to pop the stack, the item at the head is removed.

We will define a `Stack` data type as a pointer to the linked list, defined by its "top" variable. So, a `Stack` variable points to the variable that points to the first item in the linked list. As in the case of the array implementation, this is necessary so that changes made in the `push` and `pop` routines will be known in the calling function. We will use the following declarations:

```
typedef struct node {
   int num;
   struct node *next;
} Node, *NodePtr;

typedef struct {
   NodePtr top;
} StackType, *Stack;
```

After 36, 15, 52, and 23 (in that order) have been pushed onto a stack, `S`, we can picture it as shown in Figure 5-3. `S` is a pointer to `top`, which is a pointer to the linked list of stack elements.

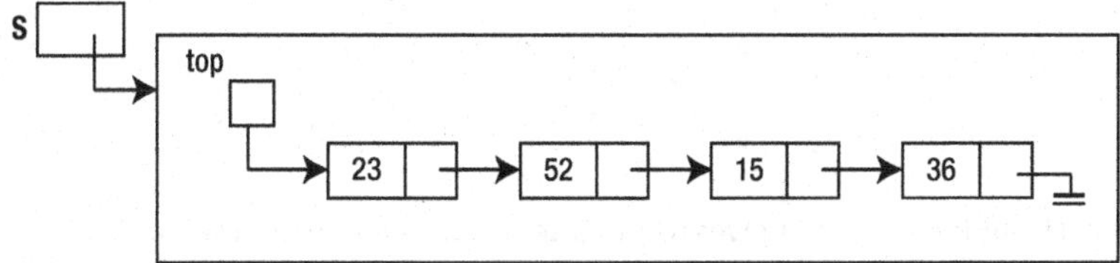

Figure 5-3. Stack view after pushing 36, 15, 52, and 23

The empty stack is represented as shown in Figure 5-4.

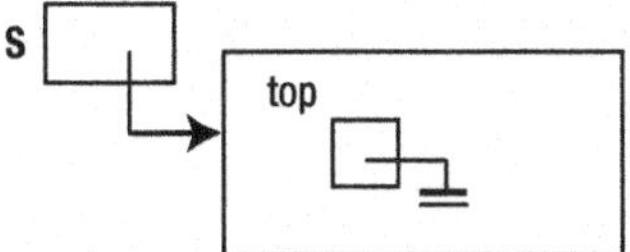

Figure 5-4. Empty stack

Creating an empty stack involves allocating storage for a `StackType` structure that consists of the single pointer variable, `top`, and setting `top` to `NULL`. Here is the function, `initStack`:

```
Stack initStack() {
   Stack sp = (Stack) malloc(sizeof(StackType));
   sp -> top = NULL;
   return sp;
}
```

We can test for an empty stack with this:

```
int empty(Stack S) {
   return (S -> top == NULL);
}
```

This simply checks whether `top` is `NULL`.

To push an item onto a stack, we need to allocate storage for a node and add it to the head of the list. Here is `push`:

```
void push(Stack S, int n) {
   NodePtr np = (NodePtr) malloc(sizeof(Node));
   np -> num = n;
   np -> next = S -> top;
   S -> top = np;
}
```

To pop an item from the stack, we first check whether the stack is empty. If it is, a rogue value is returned. If not, the item at the head of the list is returned and the node containing the item is deleted. Here is pop:

```
int pop(Stack S) {
   if (empty(S)) return RogueValue;
   int hold = S -> top -> num;
   NodePtr temp = S -> top;
```

```
    S -> top = S -> top -> next;
    free(temp);
    return hold;
}
```

Putting these functions together with `main` from Program P5.1 gives us Program P5.2, which reads a set of numbers, terminated by `0`, and prints them in reverse order.

Program P5.2

```
#include <stdio.h>
#include <stdlib.h>
#define RogueValue -9999

typedef struct node {
   int num;
   struct node *next;
} Node, *NodePtr;

typedef struct stackType {
   NodePtr top;
} StackType, *Stack;

int main() {
   Stack initStack();
   int empty(Stack);
   void push(Stack, int);
   int pop(Stack);
   int n;

   Stack S = initStack();
   printf("Enter some integers, ending with 0\n");
   scanf("%d", &n);
   while (n != 0) {
      push(S, n);
      scanf("%d", &n);
   }
   printf("Numbers in reverse order\n");
   while (!empty(S))
      printf("%d ", pop(S));
   printf("\n");
} //end main

Stack initStack() {
   Stack sp = (Stack) malloc(sizeof(StackType));
   sp -> top = NULL;
   return sp;
}

int empty(Stack S) {
   return (S -> top == NULL);
}
```

```
void push(Stack S, int n) {
   NodePtr np = (NodePtr) malloc(sizeof(Node));
   np -> num = n;
   np -> next = S -> top;
   S -> top = np;
}

int pop(Stack S) {
   if (empty(S)) return RogueValue;
   int hold = S -> top -> num;
   NodePtr temp = S -> top;
   S -> top = S -> top -> next;
   free(temp);
   return hold;
}
```

5.3 Creating a Stack Header File

Now that we have created a set of declarations/functions for manipulating an integer stack, we can put them together in one file so that *any* user can have access to them without having to repeat the code in their program. To illustrate, we create a file called `stack.h`, say, and put the following in it:

```
#include <stdlib.h>
#define RogueValue -9999

typedef struct node {
   int num;
   struct node *next;
} Node, *NodePtr;

typedef struct stackType {
   NodePtr top;
} StackType, *Stack;

Stack initStack() {
   Stack sp = (Stack) malloc(sizeof(StackType));
   sp -> top = NULL;
   return sp;
}

int empty(Stack S) {
   return (S -> top == NULL);
} //end empty

void push(Stack S, int n) {
   NodePtr np = (NodePtr) malloc(sizeof(Node));
   np -> num = n;
   np -> next = S -> top;
   S -> top = np;
} //end push
```

```
int pop(Stack S) {
   if (empty(S)) return RogueValue;
   int hold = S -> top -> num;
   NodePtr temp = S -> top;
   S -> top = S -> top -> next;
   free(temp);
   return hold;
} //end pop
```

Next, we put `stack.h` in the "include library" of C functions. Typically, most C compilers will have a folder called `include`. This is the same folder that contains files such as `stdio.h`, `string.h`, and so on. Simply put `stack.h` in this folder.[1] Now, any program that wants to use the stack functions must contain this declaration:

```
#include <stack.h>
```

For example, Program P5.2 can now be written as Program P5.3.

Program P5.3

```
#include <stdio.h>
#include <stack.h>

int main() {
   int n;
   Stack S = initStack();
   printf("Enter some integers, ending with 0\n");
   scanf("%d", &n);
   while (n != 0) {
      push(S, n);
      scanf("%d", &n);
   }
   printf("\nNumbers in reverse order\n");
   while (!empty(S))
      printf("%d ", pop(S));
   printf("\n");
}
```

Note how much shorter this program is, now that the stack declarations/functions are hidden away in `stack.h`.

5.4 A General Stack Type

To simplify our presentation, we have worked with a stack of integers. We remind you of those places in the program that are tied to the decision to use integers.

- In the declaration of `Node`, we declare an `int` called `num`.
- In `push`, we pass an `int` argument.
- In `pop`, we return an `int` result.

[1]Some compilers may already have a file called `stack.h`. In this case, you can add your declarations to this file or just use another name for your file.

No changes are needed in initStack and empty.

This means that if we need a stack of characters, for example, we will have to change int to char in all of the previously mentioned places. Similar changes will have to be made for stacks of other types.

It would be nice if we could minimize the changes needed when a different type of stack is required. We now will show how this could be done.

Our first generalization lets us have a stack of *any* type, including structures. So, for instance, if we have a structure representing a fraction (see Section 2.4 in Chapter 2), we can have a stack of fractions. We can also have stacks of primitive types such as int, char, and double. To this end, we declare a structure called StackData; this structure will contain the field or fields that will comprise a stack element.

Consider the following:

```
typedef struct {
   //declare all the data fields here
   char ch; //for example
} StackData;
```

Whichever kind of stack we want, we declare the data fields within the structure. In the earlier example, if we want a stack of characters, we declare one field of type char.

Now, a linked list node will consist of two fields: a data field of type StackData and a field that points to the next node. Here is its declaration:

```
typedef struct node {
   StackData data;
   struct node *next;
} Node, *NodePtr;
```

The only change from before is that we use StackData instead of int.

The major change in push is in the function heading. We change this:

```
void push(Stack S, int n)
```

to this:

```
void push(Stack S, StackData d)
```

In the function body, we change this:

```
np -> num = n;
```

to this:

```
np -> data = d;
```

The major change in pop is also in the function heading. We change this:

```
int pop(Stack S)
```

to this:

```
StackData pop(Stack S)
```

In the function body, we change this:

```
int hold = S -> top -> num;
```

to this:

```
StackData hold = S -> top -> data;
```

For variation, we will write pop such that if it is called and the stack is empty, a message is printed and the program halts.

With these changes, it is now easy to change the kind of stack we want to work with. We will need to change only the declaration of StackData, including the field or fields we want for our stack elements.

To illustrate, suppose we want to read a line of data and print it reversed. We need a stack of characters. We declare StackData as follows:

```
typedef struct {
  char ch;
} StackData;
```

Suppose the following statements are stored in an include file, stack.h:

```
#include <stdlib.h>

typedef struct node {
   StackData data;
   struct node *next;
} Node, *NodePtr;

typedef struct stackType {
   NodePtr top;
} StackType, *Stack;

Stack initStack() {
   Stack sp = (Stack) malloc(sizeof(StackType));
   sp -> top = NULL;
   return sp;
}

int empty(Stack S) {
   return (S -> top == NULL);
}

void push(Stack S, StackData d) {
   NodePtr np = (NodePtr) malloc(sizeof(Node));
   np -> data = d;
   np -> next = S -> top;
   S -> top = np;
}
```

```
StackData pop(Stack S) {
   if (empty(S)) {
      printf("\nAttempt to pop an empty stack\n");
      exit(1);
   }
   StackData hold = S -> top -> data;
   NodePtr temp = S -> top;
   S -> top = S -> top -> next;
   free(temp);
   return hold;
}
```

The StackData declaration is *not* included here. This is desirable since each user may need a different type of stack and must be given the opportunity to declare whatever she wants StackData to be. She can do this in her own program as illustrated in Program P5.4, which reads a line of input and prints it reversed.

Program P5.4

```
#include <stdio.h>

typedef struct {
   char ch;
} StackData;

#include <stack.h>

int main() {
   StackData temp;
   char c;
   Stack S = initStack();
   printf("Type some data and press Enter\n");
   while ((c = getchar()) != '\n') {
      temp.ch = c;
      push(S, temp);
   }
   printf("\nData in reverse order\n");
   while (!empty(S))
      putchar(pop(S).ch);
   putchar('\n');
} //end main
```

Note the placement of #include stack.h—it comes *after* the declaration of StackData. This is necessary since there are functions/declarations in stack.h that make reference to StackData.

Note also that the stack functions work with the data type StackData. Even though we want a "stack of characters," a character must be stored in a StackData variable (temp is used) before it can be pushed onto the stack. Similarly, pop returns a StackData value; we must retrieve the ch field of the value returned to get at the character.

The following is a sample run of Program P5.4:

```
Type some data and press Enter
Was it a rat I saw?

Data in reverse order
?was I tar a ti saW
```

As another example, if a programmer needs to work with a stack of fractions, she can use this:

```
typedef struct {
   int num;
   int den;
} StackData;
```

5.4.1 Example: Convert from Decimal to Binary

Consider the problem of converting a positive integer from decimal to binary. We can use an integer stack, S, to do this using repeated division by 2 and saving the remainders. Here is the algorithm:

```
initialize S to empty
read the number, n
while (n > 0) {
  push n % 2 onto S
   n = n / 2
}
while (S is not empty) print pop(S)
```

This algorithm is implemented as Program P5.5.

Program P5.5

```
#include <stdio.h>

typedef struct {
   int bit;
} StackData;

#include <stack.h>

int main() {
   StackData temp;
   int n;
   Stack S = initStack();
   printf("Enter a positive integer: ");
   scanf("%d", &n);
   while (n > 0) {
      temp.bit = n % 2;
      push(S, temp);
      n = n / 2;
   }
   printf("\nIts binary equivalent is ");
   while (!empty(S))
      printf("%d", pop(S).bit);
   printf("\n");
} //end main
```

Note, again, that each bit must be stored in a `StackData` variable (`temp` is used). A sample run of Program P5.5 is shown here:

```
Enter a positive integer: 99

Its binary equivalent is 1100011
```

5.5 Converting Infix to Postfix

Consider the expression 7 + 3 * 4. What is its value? Without any knowledge about which operation should be performed first, we would probably work out the value from left to right as (7 + 3 = 10) * 4 = 40. However, normal rules of arithmetic state that multiplication *has higher precedence* than addition. This means that, in an expression like 7 + 3 * 4, multiplication (*) is performed before addition (+). Knowing this, the value is 7 + 12 = 19.

We can, of course, force the addition to be performed first by using brackets, as in (7 + 3) * 4. Here, the brackets mean that + is done first.

These are examples of *infix* expressions; the operator (+, *) is placed *between* its operands. One disadvantage of infix expressions is the need to use brackets to override the normal *precedence rules*.

Another way of representing expressions is to use *postfix* notation. Here, the operator comes *after* its operands and there is no need to use brackets to specify which operations to perform first. For example, the postfix form of

```
7 + 3 * 4 is 7 3 4 * +
```

and the postfix form of

```
(7 + 3) * 4 is 7 3 + 4 *
```

One useful observation is that the operands appear in the same order in both the infix and postfix forms but operators differ in order and placement.

Why is postfix notation useful? As mentioned, we do not need brackets to specify the precedence of operators. More importantly, though, it is a convenient form for evaluating the expression.

Given the postfix form of an expression, it can be evaluated as follows:

```
initialize a stack, S, to empty
while we have not reached the end of the expression
   get the next item, x, from the expression
   if x is an operand, push it onto S
   if x is an operator, pop its operands from S, apply the operator and
            push the result onto S
endwhile
pop S; // this is the value of the expression
```

Consider the expression (7 + 3) * 4 whose postfix form is 7 3 + 4 *. It is evaluated by traversing from left to right.

1. The next item is 7; push 7 onto S; S contains `7`.
2. The next item is 3; push 3 onto S; S contains `7 3` (the top is on the right).
3. The next item is +; pop 3 and 7 from S; apply + to 7 and 3, giving 10; push 10 onto S; S contains `10`.
4. The next item is 4; push 4 onto S; S contains `10 4`.
5. The next item is *; pop 4 and 10 from S; apply * to 10 and 4, giving 40; push 40 onto S; S contains `40`.
6. We have reached the end of the expression; we pop S, getting 40—the result of the expression.

Note that when operands are popped from the stack, the first one popped is the second operand, and the second one popped is the first operand. This does not matter for addition and multiplication but would be important for subtraction and division. As an exercise, convert the following to postfix form and step through its evaluation using the earlier algorithm: (7 – 3) * (9 – 8 / 4).

The big question, of course, is how do we convert an infix expression to postfix? Before presenting the algorithm, we observe that it will use an *operator stack*. We will also need a *precedence table* that gives the relative precedence of the operators. Given any two operators, the table will tell us whether they have the same precedence (like + and -) and, if not, which has greater precedence.

As the algorithm proceeds, it will output the postfix form of the given expression.

Here is the algorithm:

1. Initialize a stack of operators, S, to empty.
2. Get the next item, x, from the infix expression; if none, go to step 8 (x is either an operand, a left bracket, a right bracket, or an operator).
3. If x is an operand, output x.
4. If x is a left bracket, push it onto S.
5. If x is a right bracket, pop items off S and output popped items until a left bracket appears on top of S; pop the left bracket and discard.
6. If x is an operator, then do the following:

```
while (S is not empty) and (a left bracket is not on top of S) and
   (an operator of equal or higher precedence than x is on top of S)
   pop S and output popped item
push x onto S
```

7. Repeat from step 2.
8. Pop S and output the popped item until S is empty.

You are advised to step through the algorithm for the following expressions:

```
3 + 5
7 - 3 + 8
7 + 3 * 4
(7 + 3) * 4
(7 + 3) / (8 - 2 * 3)
(7 - 8 / 2 / 2) * ((7 - 2) * 3 - 6)
```

Let's write a program to read a simplified infix expression and output its postfix form. We assume that an operand is a single-digit integer. An operator can be one of +, –, *, or /. Brackets are allowed. The usual precedence of operators apply: + and – have the same precedence, which is lower than that of * and /, which have the same precedence. The left bracket is treated as an operator with very low precedence, less than that of + and –.

We will implement this as a function `precedence` that, given an operator, returns an integer representing its precedence. The actual value returned is not important as long as the relative precedence of the operators is maintained. We will use the following:

```
int precedence(char c) {
   if (c == '(') return 0;
   if (c == '+' || c == '-') return 3;
   if (c == '*' || c == '/') return 5;
} //end precedence
```

We could also write precedence using a switch statement as follows:

```
int precedence(char c) {
   switch (c) {
      case '(': return 0;
      case '+':
      case '-': return 3;
      case '*':
      case '/': return 5;
   }//end switch
} //end precedence
```

The actual values 0, 3, and 5 are not important. Any values can be used as long as they represent the relative precedence of the operators.

We will need a function to read the input and return the next nonblank character. The end-of-line character will indicate the end of the expression. Here is the function (we call it getToken):

```
char getToken() {
   char ch;
   while ((ch = getchar()) == ' ') ; //empty body
   return ch;
} //end getToken
```

The operator stack is simply a stack of characters that we will implement using this:

```
typedef struct {
   char ch;
} StackData;
```

Step 6 of the algorithm requires us to compare the precedence of the operator on top of the stack with the current operator. This would be easy if we can "peek" at the element on top of the stack without taking it off. To do this, we write the function peek and add it to stack.h, the file containing our stack declarations/ functions.

```
StackData peek(Stack S) {
   if (!empty(S)) return S -> top -> data;
   printf("\nAttempt to peek at an empty stack\n");
   exit(1);
}
```

Putting all these together, we now write Program P5.6, which implements the algorithm for converting an infix expression to postfix.

The job of reading the expression and converting to postfix is delegated to readConvert. This outputs the postfix form to a character array, post. So as not to clutter the code with error checking, we assume that post is big enough to hold the converted expression. The function returns the number of elements in the postfix expression.

The function printPostfix simply prints the postfix expression.

The following is a sample run of Program P5.6:

```
Type an infix expression and press Enter
(7 - 8 / 2 / 2) * ((7 - 2) * 3 - 6)

The postfix form is
7 8 2 / 2 / - 7 2 - 3 * 6 - *
```

Program P5.6

```
#include <stdio.h>
#include <ctype.h>
typedef struct {
   char ch;
} StackData;

#include <stack.h>

int main() {
   int readConvert(char[]);
   void printPostfix(char[], int);
   char post[50];

   int n = readConvert(post);
   printPostfix(post, n);
} //end main

int readConvert(char post[]) {
   char getToken(void), token, c;
   int precedence(char);
   StackData temp;
   int h = 0;
   Stack S = initStack();
   printf("Type an infix expression and press Enter\n");
   token = getToken();
   while (token != '\n') {
      if (isdigit(token)) post[h++] = token;
      else if (token == '(') {
         temp.ch = token;
         push(S, temp);
      }
      else if (token == ')')
         while ((c = pop(S).ch) != '(') post[h++] = c;
      else {
         while (!empty(S) && precedence(peek(S).ch) >= precedence(token))
            post[h++] = pop(S).ch;
         temp.ch = token;
         push(S, temp);
      }
      token = getToken();
   } //end while
   while (!empty(S)) post[h++] = pop(S).ch;
   return h; //the size of the expression
} //end readConvert

void printPostfix(char post[], int n) {
   printf("\nThe postfix form is \n");
   for (int h = 0; h < n; h++) printf("%c ", post[h]);
   printf("\n");
} //end printPostfix
```

```
char getToken() {
   char ch;
   while ((ch = getchar()) == ' ') ; //empty body
   return ch;
} //end getToken

int precedence(char c) {
   if (c == '(') return 0;
   if (c == '+' || c == '-') return 3;
   if (c == '*' || c == '/') return 5;
} //end precedence
```

Program P5.6 assumes that the given expression is a valid one. However, it can be easily modified to recognize some kinds of invalid expressions. For instance, if a right bracket is missing, when we reach the end of the expression, there would be a left bracket on the stack. (If the brackets match, there would be none.) Similarly, if a left bracket is missing, when a right one is encountered and we are scanning the stack for the (missing) left one, we would not find it.

You are urged to modify Program P5.6 to catch expressions with mismatched brackets. You should also modify it to handle any integer operands, not just single-digit ones. Yet another modification is to handle other operations such as %, sqrt (square root), sin (sine), cos (cosine), tan (tangent), log (logarithm), exp (exponential), and so on.

5.5.1 Evaluating a Postfix Expression

Program P5.6 stores the postfix form of the expression in a character array, post. We now write a function that, given post, evaluates the expression and returns its value. The function uses the algorithm at the beginning of Section 5.5.

We will need an *integer* stack to hold the operands and intermediate results. Recall that we needed a *character* stack to hold the operators. We can neatly work with both kinds of stacks if we declare StackData as follows:

```
typedef struct {
   char ch;
   int num;
} StackData;
```

We use the char field for the operator stack and the int field for the operand stack. Here is eval:

```
int eval(char post[], int n) {
   int a, b, c;
   StackData temp;

   Stack S = initStack();
   for (int h = 0; h < n; h++) {
      if (isdigit(post[h])) {
         temp.num = post[h] - '0'; //convert to integer
         push(S, temp);
      }
      else {
         b = pop(S).num;
         a = pop(S).num;
         if (post[h] == '+') c = a + b;
         else if (post[h] == '-') c = a - b;
```

```
            else if (post[h] == '*') c = a * b;
            else c = a / b;
            temp.num = c;
            push(S, temp);
         } //end outer else
      } //end for
      return pop(S).num;
   } //end eval
```

We can test eval by adding it to Program P5.6 and putting its prototype, as follows, in `main`:

```
int eval(char[], int);
```

We also change the declaration of `StackData` to the one shown above and add the following as the last statement in `main`:

```
printf("\nIts value is %d\n", eval(post, n));
```

The following is a sample run of the modified program:

```
Type an infix expression and press Enter
(7 - 8 / 2 / 2) * ((7 - 2) * 3 - 6)

The postfix form is
7 8 2 / 2 / - 7 2 - 3 * 6 - *

Its value is 45
```

5.6 Queues

A *queue* is a linear list in which items are added at one end and deleted from the other end. Familiar examples are queues at a bank, a supermarket, a concert, or a sporting event. People are supposed to join the queue at the rear and exit from the front. We would expect that a queue data structure would be useful for simulating these real-life queues.

Queues are also found inside the computer. There may be several jobs waiting to be executed, and they are held in a queue. For example, several people may each request something to be printed on a network printer. Since the printer can handle only one job at a time, the others have to be queued.

These are the basic operations we want to perform on a queue:

- Add an item to the queue; we say *enqueue*.
- Take an item off the queue; we say *dequeue*.
- Check whether the queue is empty.
- Inspect the item at the head of the queue.

Like with stacks, we can easily implement the queue data structure using arrays or linked lists. We will use a queue of integers for illustration purposes.

5.6.1 Implementing a Queue Using an Array

In the array implementation of a queue (of integers), we use an integer array (QA, say) for storing the numbers and two integer variables (head and tail) that indicate the item at the head of the queue and the item at the tail of the queue, respectively.

Since we are using an array, we will need to know its size in order to declare it. We will need to have some information about the problem to determine a reasonable size for the array. We will use the symbolic constant MaxQ. In our implementation, the queue will be declared full if there are MaxQ-1 elements in it and we attempt to add another.

We use the following to define the data type Queue:

```
typedef struct {
   int head, tail;
   int QA[MaxQ];
} QType, *Queue;
```

Valid values for head and tail will range from 0 to MaxQ-1. When we initialize a queue, we will set head and tail to 0.

We can now declare a *queue variable*, Q, with this:

```
Queue Q;
```

Observe that Queue is declared as a pointer to the structure we call QType. So, for instance, Q is a pointer to a structure consisting of the variables head and tail and the array QA. This is necessary since head, tail, and QA would need to be changed by the enqueue and dequeue routines and the changes known to the calling function (main, say). This can be achieved by passing a pointer to them, in effect, the Queue variable.

To work with a queue, the first task is to create an empty queue. This is done by allocating storage for a QType, assigning its address to a Queue variable, and setting head and tail to 0. Later, we will see why 0 is a good value to use. We can use the following:

```
Queue initQueue() {
   Queue qp = (Queue) malloc(sizeof(QType));
   qp -> head = qp -> tail = 0;
   return qp;
}
```

In main, say, we can declare and initialize a queue, Q, with this:

```
Queue Q = initQueue();
```

When this statement is executed, the situation in memory can be represented as shown in Figure 5-5.

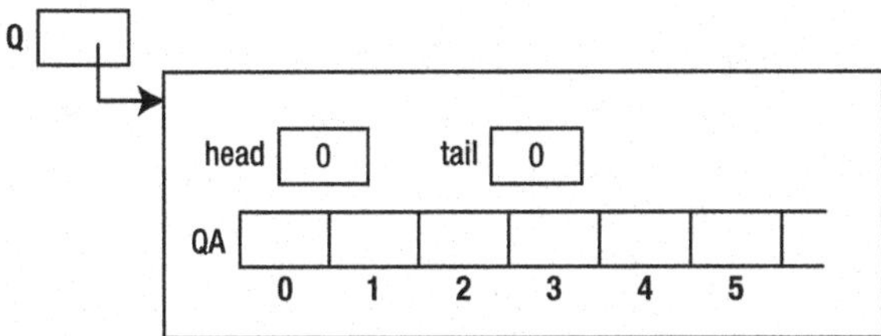

Figure 5-5. *Array representation of a queue*

This represents the empty queue. In working with queues, we will need a function that tells us whether a queue is empty. We can use the following:

```
int empty(Queue Q) {
   return (Q -> head == Q -> tail);
}
```

Shortly, we will see that given the way we will implement the enqueue and dequeue operations, the queue will be empty whenever head and tail have the same value. This value will not necessarily be 0. In fact, it may be any of the values from 0 to MaxQ-1, the valid subscripts of QA.

Consider how we might add an item to the queue. In a real queue, a person joins at the tail. We will do the same here by incrementing tail and storing the item at the location indicated by tail.

For example, to add 36, say, to the queue, we increment tail to 1 and store 36 in QA[1]; head remains at 0.

If we then add 15 to the queue, it will be stored in QA[2], and tail will be 2.

If we now add 52 to the queue, it will be stored in QA[3], and tail will be 3.

Our picture in memory will look like Figure 5-6.

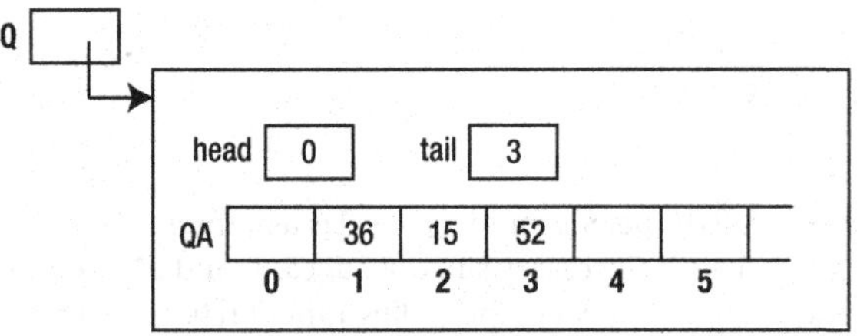

***Figure 5-6.** State of the queue after adding 36, 15, and 52*

Note that head points "just in front of" the item that is actually at the head of the queue, and tail points at the last item in the queue.

Now consider taking something off the queue. The item to be taken off is the one at the head. To remove it, we must first increment head and then return the value pointed to by head.

For example, if we remove 36, head will become 1, and it points "just in front of" 15, the item now at the head. Note that 36 still remains in the array, but, for all intents and purposes, it is not in the queue.

Suppose we now add 23 to the queue. It will be placed in location 4, with tail being 4 and head being 1. The picture now looks like Figure 5-7.

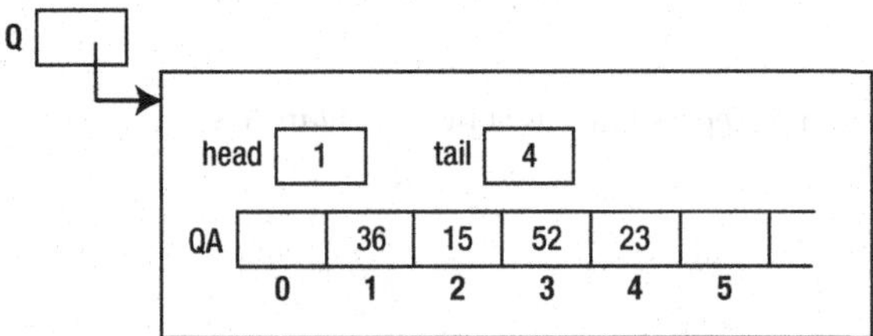

***Figure 5-7.** State of the queue after removing 36 and adding 23*

There are three items in the queue; 15 is at the head, and 23 is at the tail.

Consider what happens if we continuously add items to the queue without taking off any. The value of tail will keep increasing until it reaches MaxQ-1, the last valid subscript of QA. What do we do if another item needs to be added?

We *could* say that the queue is full and stop the program. However, there are two free locations, 0 and 1. It would be better to try to use one of these. This leads us to the idea of a *circular queue*. Here, we think of the locations in the array as arranged in a circle: location MaxQ-1 is followed by location 0.

So, if tail has the value MaxQ-1, incrementing it will set it to 0.

Suppose we had not taken off any item from the queue. The value of head would still be 0. Now, what if, in attempting to add an item, tail is incremented from MaxQ-1 to 0? It now has the same value as head. In this situation, we declare that the queue is full.

We do this even though nothing is stored in location 0, which is, therefore, available to hold another item. The reason for taking this approach is that it simplifies our code for detecting when the queue is empty and when it is full.

To emphasize, when the queue is declared full, it contains MaxQ-1 items.

We can now write enqueue, a function to add an item to the queue.

```
void enqueue(Queue Q, int n) {
   if (Q -> tail == MaxQ - 1) Q -> tail = 0;
   else ++(Q -> tail);
   if (Q -> tail == Q -> head) {
      printf("\nQueue is full\n");
      exit(1);
   }
   Q -> QA[Q -> tail] = n;
} //end enqueue
```

We first increment tail. If, by doing so, it has the same value as head, we declare that the queue is full. If not, we store the new item in position tail.

Consider the previous diagram. If we delete 15 and 52, it changes to that shown in Figure 5-8.

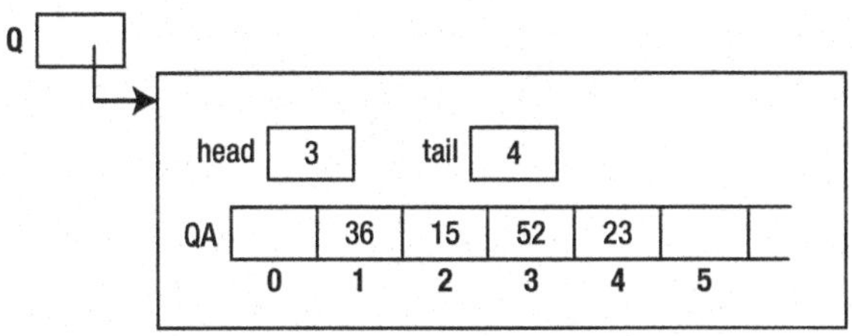

Figure 5-8. *Queue after removing 15, 52*

Now, head has the value 3, tail has the value 4, and there is one item in the queue, 23, in location 4. If we delete this last item, head and tail would both have the value 4, and the queue would be empty. This suggests that we have an empty queue when head has the same value as tail, as indicated earlier.

We can now write the function dequeue for removing an item from the queue.

```
int dequeue(Queue Q) {
   if (empty(Q)) {
      printf("\nAttempt to remove from an empty queue\n");
      exit(1);
   }
```

```
      if (Q -> head == MaxQ - 1) Q -> head = 0;
      else ++(Q -> head);
      return Q -> QA[Q -> head];
   } //end dequeue
```

If the queue is empty, an error is reported, and the program is halted. If not, we increment head and return the value in location head. Note, again, that if head has the value MaxQ-1, incrementing it sets it to 0.

As in the case of a stack, we can create a file called queue.h and store our declarations and functions in it so they can be used by other programs. So far, queue.h would contain the items shown here:

```
#include <stdlib.h>

typedef struct {
   int head, tail;
   int QA[MaxQ];
} QType, *Queue;

Queue initQueue() {
   Queue qp = (Queue) malloc(sizeof(QType));
   qp -> head = qp -> tail = 0;
   return qp;
}

int empty(Queue Q) {
   return (Q -> head == Q -> tail);
}

void enqueue(Queue Q, int n) {
   if (Q -> tail == MaxQ - 1) Q -> tail = 0;
   else ++(Q -> tail);
   if (Q -> tail == Q -> head) {
      printf("\nQueue is full\n");
      exit(1);
   }
   Q -> QA[Q -> tail] = n;
}

int dequeue(Queue Q) {
   if (empty(Q)) {
      printf("\nAttempt to remove from an empty queue\n");
      exit(1);
   }
   if (Q -> head == MaxQ - 1) Q -> head = 0;
   else ++(Q -> head);
   return Q -> QA[Q -> head];
}
```

To test our queue operations, we write Program P5.7, which reads an integer and prints its digits in reverse order. For example, if 12345 is read, the program prints 54321. The digits are extracted, from the right, and stored in a queue. The items in the queue are taken off, one at a time, and printed.

Program P5.7

```
#include <stdio.h>
#define MaxQ 10
#include <queue.h>

int main() {
   int n;
   Queue Q = initQueue();
   printf("Enter a positive integer: ");
   scanf("%d", &n);
   while (n > 0) {
      enqueue(Q, n % 10);
      n = n / 10;
   }
   printf("\nDigits in reverse order: ");
   while (!empty(Q))
      printf("%d", dequeue(Q));
   printf("\n");
}
```

Note the order of the header statements. The user is free to define the value of MaxQ; this value will be used by the declarations in queue.h.

5.6.2 Implementing a Queue Using a Linked List

As with stacks, we can implement a queue using linked lists. This has the advantage of us not having to decide beforehand how many items to cater for. We will use two pointers, head and tail, to point to the first and last items in the queue, respectively. Figure 5-9 shows the data structure when four items (36, 15, 52, and 23) are added to the queue.

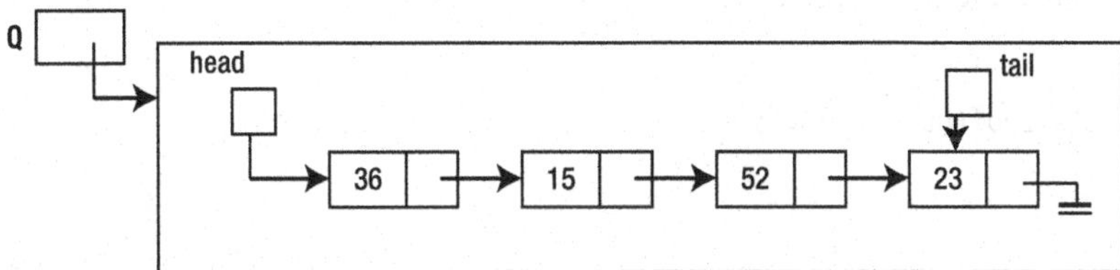

Figure 5-9. *Linked list representation of a queue*

We will implement the queue so that it works with a general data type that we will store in a structure called QueueData. We will use the following framework:

```
typedef struct {
   //declare all the data fields here
   int num; //for example
} QueueData;
```

Whichever kind of queue we want, we declare the data fields within the structure. In the earlier example, if we want a queue of integers, we declare one field of type `int`.

A linked list node will consist of two fields: a data field of type `QueueData` and a field that points to the next node. Here is its declaration:

```
typedef struct node {
   QueueData data;
   struct node *next;
} Node, *NodePtr;
```

We will define the `Queue` data type as a pointer to a structure containing two `NodePtrs`, `head` and `tail`, as follows:

```
typedef struct {
   NodePtr head, tail;
} QueueType, *Queue;
```

We can declare a queue with the following statement:

```
Queue Q;
```

The empty queue, `Q`, is represented by Figure 5-10.

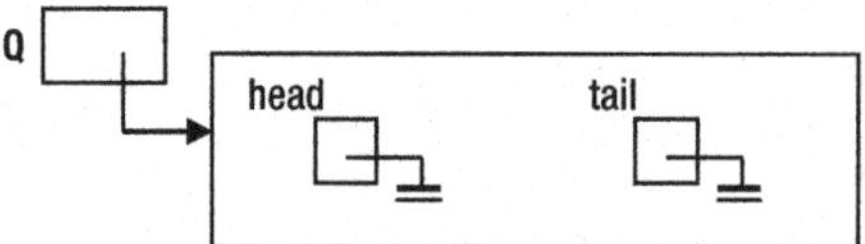

Figure 5-10. *An empty queue (linked list representation)*

Creating an empty queue involves allocating storage for a `QueueType` structure that consists of two variables, `head` and `tail`, and setting them to `NULL`. Here is the function, `initQueue`:

```
Queue initQueue() {
   Queue qp = (Queue) malloc(sizeof(QueueType));
   qp -> head = NULL;
   qp -> tail = NULL;
   return qp;
}
```

We can test for an empty queue with this:

```
int empty(Queue Q) {
   return (Q -> head == NULL);
}
```

This simply checks whether `head` is `NULL`.

To add an item to the queue, we need to allocate storage for a node and add it to the tail of the list. Here is enqueue:

```
void enqueue(Queue Q, QueueData d) {
   NodePtr np = (NodePtr) malloc(sizeof(Node));
   np -> data = d;
   np -> next = NULL;
   if (empty(Q)) {
      Q -> head = np;
      Q -> tail = np;
   }
   else {
      Q -> tail -> next = np;
      Q -> tail = np;
   }
}
```

If the queue is empty, the new item becomes the only one in the queue; head and tail are set to point to it. If the queue is not empty, the item at the tail is set to point to the new one, and tail is updated to point to the new one.

To take an item off the queue, we first check whether the queue is empty. If it is, we print a message and end the program. If not, the item at the head of the queue is returned, and the node containing the item is deleted.

If, by removing an item, head becomes NULL, it means that the queue is empty. In this case, tail is also set to NULL. Here is dequeue:

```
QueueData dequeue(Queue Q) {
   if (empty(Q)) {
      printf("\nAttempt to remove from an empty queue\n");
      exit(1);
   }
   QueueData hold = Q -> head -> data;
   NodePtr temp = Q -> head;
   Q -> head = Q -> head -> next;
   if (Q -> head == NULL) Q -> tail = NULL;
   free(temp);
   return hold;
} //end dequeue
```

As before, we can store all these declarations and functions, except QueueData, in a file called queue.h so that other programs can use them. The contents of queue.h are shown here:

```
#include <stdlib.h>

typedef struct node {
   QueueData data;
   struct node *next;
} Node, *NodePtr;

typedef struct queueType {
   NodePtr head, tail;
} QueueType, *Queue;
```

```
Queue initQueue() {
   Queue qp = (Queue) malloc(sizeof(QueueType));
   qp -> head = NULL;
   qp -> tail = NULL;
   return qp;
} //end initQueue

int empty(Queue Q) {
   return (Q -> head == NULL);
} //end empty

void enqueue(Queue Q, QueueData d) {
   NodePtr np = (NodePtr) malloc(sizeof(Node));
   np -> data = d;
   np -> next = NULL;
   if (empty(Q)) {
      Q -> head = np;
      Q -> tail = np;
   }
   else {
      Q -> tail -> next = np;
      Q -> tail = np;
   }
} //end enqueue

QueueData dequeue(Queue Q) {
   if (empty(Q)) {
      printf("\nAttempt to remove from an empty queue\n");
      exit(1);
   }
   QueueData hold = Q -> head -> data;
   NodePtr temp = Q -> head;
   Q -> head = Q -> head -> next;
   if (Q -> head == NULL) Q -> tail = NULL;
   free(temp);
   return hold;
} //end dequeue
```

To use these functions, a user only needs to declare what he wants QueueData to be. To illustrate, we rewrite Program P5.7, which reads an integer and prints its digits in reverse order. It is shown as Program P5.8.

Program P5.8

```
#include <stdio.h>
typedef struct {
   int num;
} QueueData;
#include <queue.h>
```

```
int main() {
   int n;
   QueueData temp;
   Queue Q = initQueue();
   printf("Enter a positive integer: ");
   scanf("%d", &n);
   while (n > 0) {
      temp.num = n % 10;
      enqueue(Q, temp);
      n = n / 10;
   }
   printf("\nDigits in reverse order: ");
   while (!empty(Q))
      printf("%d", dequeue(Q).num);
   printf("\n");
} //end main
```

Note that the declaration of QueueData must come before #include <queue.h>. Also, since enqueue expects a QueueData argument, the digits of the integer must be stored in the int field of a QueueData variable (temp is used) before being passed to enqueue.

Stacks and queues are important to systems programmers and compiler writers. We have seen how stacks are used in the evaluation of arithmetic expressions. They are also used to implement the "calling" and "return" mechanism for functions. Consider the situation where function A calls function C, which calls function B, which calls function D. When a function returns, how does the computer figure out where to return to? We show how a stack can be used to do this.

Assume we have the following situation, where a number, like 100, represents the *return address*, which is the address of the next instruction to be executed when the function returns:

```
function A      function B      function C      function D
    .               .               .               .
    C;              D;              B;              .
100:            200:            300:
    .               .               .               .
```

When A calls C, the address 100 is pushed onto a stack, S. When C calls B, 300 is pushed onto S. When B calls D, 200 is pushed onto S. At this stage, the stack looks like the following, and control is in D:

```
(bottom of stack) 100  300  200 (top of stack)
```

When D finishes and is ready to return, the address at the top of the stack (200) is popped and execution continues at this address. Note that this is the address immediately following the call to D.

Next, when B finishes and is ready to return, the address at the top of the stack (300) is popped, and execution continues at this address. Note that this is the address immediately following the call to B.

Finally, when C finishes and is ready to return, the address at the top of the stack (100) is popped, and execution continues at this address. Note that this is the address immediately following the call to C.

Naturally, queue data structures are used in simulating real-life queues. They are also used to implement queues in the computer. In a multiprogramming environment, several jobs may have to be queued while waiting on a particular resource such as processor time or a printer.

Stacks and queues are also used extensively in working with more advanced data structures such as trees and graphs. We will discuss trees in Chapter 9.

EXERCISES 5

1. What is an abstract data type?
2. What is a stack? What are the basic operations that can be performed on a stack?
3. What is a queue? What are the basic operations that can be performed on a queue?
4. Modify Program P5.6 to recognize infix expressions with mismatched brackets.
5. Program P5.6 works with single-digit operands. Modify it to handle any integer operands.
6. Modify Program P5.6 to handle expressions with operations such as %, square root, sine, cosine, tangent, logarithm, and exponential.
7. An integer array `post` is used to hold the postfix form of an arithmetic expression such that the following is true:

   A positive number represents an operand.

   -1 represents +.

   -2 represents -.

   -3 represents *.

   -4 represents /.

   0 indicates the end of the expression.
8. Show the contents of `post` for the expression `(2 + 3) * (8 / 4) - 6`.
9. Write a function `eval` that, given `post`, returns the value of the expression.
10. Write declarations/functions to implement a stack of `double` values.
11. Write declarations/functions to implement a queue of `double` values.
12. A priority queue is one in which items are added to the queue based on a priority number. Jobs with higher-priority numbers are closer to the head of the queue than those with lower-priority numbers. A job is added to the queue in front of all jobs of lower priority but after all jobs of greater or equal priority.
13. Write declarations and functions to implement a priority queue. Each item in the queue has a job number (integer) and a priority number. Implement, at least, the following functions: (i) initialize an empty queue, (ii) add a job in its appropriate place in the queue, (iii) delete and dispose of the job at the head of the queue, and (iv) given a job number, remove that job from the queue.
14. Ensure your functions work regardless of the state of the queue.
15. An input line contains a word consisting of lowercase letters only. Explain how a stack can be used to determine whether the word is a palindrome.
16. Show how to implement a queue using two stacks.
17. Show how to implement a stack using two queues.
18. A stack, `S1`, contains some numbers in arbitrary order. Using another stack, `S2`, for temporary storage, show how to sort the numbers in `S1` such that the smallest is at the top of `S1` and the largest is at the bottom.

CHAPTER 6

Recursion

In this chapter, we will explain the following:

- What a recursive definition is
- How to write recursive functions in C
- How to convert from decimal to binary
- How to print a linked list in reverse order
- How to solve Towers of Hanoi
- How to write an efficient power function
- How to sort using merge sort
- What are `static` variables
- How to use recursion to keep track of pending subproblems
- How to implement backtracking using recursion by finding a path through a maze

6.1 Recursive Definition

A *recursive definition* is one that is defined in terms of itself. Perhaps the most common example is the *factorial* function. The factorial of a non-negative integer, *n* (written as *n*!), is defined as follows:

```
0! = 1
n! = n(n - 1)!, n > 0
```

Here, *n*! is defined in terms of (*n* - 1)!, but what is (*n* - 1)! exactly? To find out, we must apply the definition of factorial! In this case, we have this:

```
(n - 1)! = 1, if (n - 1) = 0
(n - 1)! = (n - 1)(n - 2)! if (n - 1) > 0
```

So what is 3! now?

- Since 3 > 0, it is 3×2!
- Since 2 > 0, 2! is 2×1! and 3! is 3×2×1!
- Since 1 > 0, 1! is 1×0! and 3! is 3×2×1×0!
- Since 0! is 1, we have 3! is 3×2×1×1 = 6.

Loosely, we say that *n*! is the product of all integers from 1 to *n*.

Let's rewrite the definition using programming notation; we call it `fact`.

```
fact(0) = 1
fact(n) = n * fact(n - 1), n > 0
```

The recursive definition of a function consists of two parts.

- The *base* case, which gives the value of the function for a specific argument. This is also called the *anchor*, *end* case, or *terminating* case, and it allows the recursion to terminate eventually.
- The recursive (or general) case where the function is defined in terms of itself.

Shortly, we will write `fact` as a C function. Before we do, we give a nonmathematical example of a recursive definition. Consider how you might define *ancestor*. Loosely, we can say that an ancestor is one's parent, grandparent, or great-grandparent, and so on. But we can state this more precisely as follows:

```
a is an ancestor of b if
     (1) a is a parent of b, or
     (2) a is an ancestor of c and c is a parent of b
```

`(1)` is the base case and `(2)` is the general, recursive case where *ancestor* is defined in terms of itself.

A less serious example is the meaning of the acronym LAME. It stands for LAME, Another MP3 Encoder. Expanding LAME, we get LAME, Another MP3 Encoder, Another MP3 Encoder, and so on. We can say that LAME is a recursive acronym. It's not a true recursive definition, though, since it has no base case.

6.2 Writing Recursive Functions in C

We have seen many examples of functions that call other functions. What we have not seen is a function that calls itself—a *recursive function*. We start off with `fact`.

```
int fact(int n) {
   if (n < 0) return 0;
   if (n == 0) return 1;
   return n * fact(n - 1);
}
```

In the previous statement, we have a call to the function `fact`, the function we are writing. The function calls itself.

Consider the following statement:

```
int n = fact(3);
```

It is executed as follows:

1. `3` is copied to a temporary location, and this location is passed to `fact` where it becomes the value of `n`;.
2. Execution reaches the last statement, and `fact` attempts to return `3 * fact(2)`. However, `fact(2)` must be calculated before the return value is known. Think of this as just a call to a function `fact` with argument `2`.

3. As usual, 2 is copied to a temporary location, and this location is passed to fact where it becomes the value of n. If fact were a different function, there would be no problem. But since it's the *same* function, what happens to the first value of n? It has to be saved somewhere and reinstated when *this* call to fact finishes.

4. The value is saved on something called the *runtime stack*. Each time a function calls itself, its arguments (and local variables, if any) are stored on the stack before the new arguments take effect. Also, for each call, new local variables are created. Thus, each call has its own copy of arguments and local variables.

5. When n is 2, execution reaches the last statement, and fact attempts to return.

6. 2 * fact(1). However, fact(1) must be calculated before the return value is known. Think of this as just a call to a function fact with argument 1.

7. This call reaches the last statement, and fact attempts to return 1 * fact(0). However, fact(0) must be calculated before the return value is known. Think of this as just a call to a function fact with argument 0.

8. At this time, the runtime stack contains the arguments 3, 2, and 1. The call fact(0) reaches the second statement and returns a value of 1.

9. The calculation 1 * fact(0) can now be completed, returning 1 as the value of fact(1).

10. The calculation 2 * fact(1) can now be completed, returning 2 as the value of fact(2).

11. The calculation 3 * fact(2) can now be completed, returning 6 as the value of fact(3).

We should emphasize that this recursive version of fact is merely for illustrative purposes. It is not an efficient way to calculate a factorial—think of all the function calls, the stacking and unstacking of arguments, just to multiply the numbers from 1 to n. A more efficient function is as follows:

```
int fact(int n) {
   int f = 1;
   while (n > 0) {
      f = f * n;
      --n;
   }
   return f;
}
```

Another example of a function that can be defined recursively is the highest common factor (HCF) of two positive integers, m and n.

```
hcf(m, n) is
   (1) m, if n is 0
   (2) hcf(n, m % n), if n > 0
```

If m = 70 and n = 42, we have:

```
hcf(70, 42) = hcf(42, 70 % 42) = hcf(42, 28) = hcf(28, 42 % 28)
            = hcf(28, 14) = hcf(14, 28 % 14) = hcf(14, 0) = 14
```

We can write hcf as a recursive C function.

```
int hcf(int m, int n) {
   if (n == 0) return m;
   return hcf(n, m % n);
}
```

As a matter of interest, we can also write hcf as an iterative (as opposed to recursive) function, using Euclid's algorithm.

```
int hcf(int m, int n) {
   int r;
   while (n > 0) {
      r = m % n;
      m = n;
      n = r;
   }
   return m;
}
```

Effectively, this function does explicitly what the recursive function does implicitly.

Yet another example of a recursively defined function is that of the Fibonacci numbers. We define the first two Fibonacci numbers as 1 and 1. Each new number is obtained by adding the previous two. So, the Fibonacci sequence is 1, 1, 2, 3, 5, 8, 13, 21, and so on.

Recursively, we define the *n*th Fibonacci number, F(n), as follows:

```
F(0) = F(1) = 1
F(n) = F(n - 1) + F(n - 2), n > 1
```

This is a C function to return the *n*th Fibonacci number:

```
int fib(int n) {
   if (n == 0 || n == 1) return 1;
   return fib(n - 1) + fib(n - 2);
}
```

Again, we emphasize that while this function is neat, concise, and easy to understand, it is not efficient. For example, consider the calculation of F(5).

```
F(5) = F(4) + F(3) = F(3) + F(2) + F(3) = F(2) + F(1) + F(2) + F(3)
= F(1) + F(0) + F(1) + F(2) + F(3) = 1 + 1 + 1 + F(1) + F(0) + F(3)
= 1 + 1 + 1 + 1 + 1 + F(2) + F(1) =  1 + 1 + 1 + 1 + 1 + F(1) + F(0) + F(1)
= 1 + 1 + 1 + 1 + 1 + 1 + 1 + 1
= 8
```

Notice the number of function calls and additions that have to be made, whereas we can calculate F(5) straightforwardly using only four additions. You are urged to write an efficient, iterative function to return the *n*th Fibonacci number.

6.3 Converting a Decimal Number to Binary Using Recursion

In Section 5.4.1, we used a stack to convert an integer from decimal to binary. We will now show how to write a recursive function to perform the same task.

To see what needs to be done, suppose n is 13, which is 1101 in binary. Recall that n % 2 gives us the *last* bit of the binary equivalent of n. If, somehow, we have a way to print all but the last bit, we can then follow this with n % 2. But "printing all but the last bit" is the same as printing the binary equivalent of n/2.

For example, 1101 is 110 followed by 1; 110 is the binary equivalent of 6, which is 13/2, and 1 is 13 % 2. So, we can print the binary equivalent of n as follows:

```
print binary of n / 2
print n % 2
```

We use the same method to print the binary equivalent of 6. This is the binary equivalent of 6/2 = 3, which is 11, followed by 6 % 2, which is 0; this gives 110.

We use the same method to print the binary equivalent of 3. This is the binary equivalent of 3/2 = 1, which is 1, followed by 3 % 2, which is 1; this gives 11.

We use the same method to print the binary equivalent of 1. This is the binary equivalent of 1/2 = 0 followed by 1 % 2, which is 1; if we "do nothing" for 0, this will give us 1.

We stop when we get to the stage where we need to find the binary equivalent of 0. This leads us to the following function:

```
void decToBin(int n) {
   if (n > 0) {
      decToBin(n / 2);
      printf("%d ", n % 2);
   }
}
```

The call decToBin(13) will print 1101.

Note how much more compact this is than Program P5.5 . However, it is not more efficient. The stacking/unstacking that is done explicitly in Program P5.5 is done by the recursive mechanism provided by the language when a function calls itself. To illustrate, let's trace the call decToBin(13).

1. On the first call, n assumes the value 13.
2. While the call decToBin(13) is executing, the call decToBin(6) is made; 13 is pushed onto the runtime stack, and n assumes the value 6.
3. While the call decToBin(6) is executing, the call decToBin(3) is made; 6 is pushed onto the stack, and n assumes the value 3.
4. While the call decToBin(3) is executing, the call decToBin(1) is made; 3 is pushed onto the stack, and n assumes the value 1.
5. While the call decToBin(1) is executing, the call decToBin(0) is made; 1 is pushed onto the stack, and n assumes the value 0.
6. At this stage, the stack contains 13, 6, 3, 1.
7. Since n is 0, this call of the function returns immediately; so far, nothing has been printed.
8. When the call decToBin(0) returns, the argument on top of the stack, 1, is reinstated as the value of n.

9. Control goes to the `printf` statement, which prints `1 % 2`, that is, `1`.
10. The call `decToBin(1)` can now return, and the argument on top of the stack, `3`, is reinstated as the value of `n`.
11. Control goes to the `printf` statement, which prints `3 % 2`, that is, `1`.
12. The call `decToBin(3)` can now return, and the argument on top of the stack, `6`, is reinstated as the value of `n`.
13. Control goes to the `printf` statement, which prints `6 % 2`, that is, `0`.
14. The call `decToBin(6)` can now return, and the argument on top of the stack, `13`, is reinstated as the value of `n`.
15. Control goes to the `printf` statement, which prints `13 % 2`, that is, `1`.
16. The call `decToBin(13)` can now return, and `1101` has been printed.

We can summarize the previous description as follows:

```
decToBin(13)    →     decToBin(6)
                      print(13 % 2)
                →     decToBin(3)
                      print(6 % 2)
                      print(13 % 2)
                →     decToBin(1)
                      print(3 % 2)
                      print(6 % 2)
                      print(13 % 2)

                →     decToBin(0) = do nothing
                      print(1 % 2) = 1
                      print(3 % 2) = 1
                      print(6 % 2) = 0
                      print(13 % 2) = 1
```

One of the most important properties of recursive functions is that when a function calls itself, the current arguments (and local variables, if any) are pushed onto a stack. Execution of the function takes place with the new arguments and new local variables. When execution is completed, arguments (and local variables, if any) are popped from the stack, and execution resumes (with *these* popped values) with the statement following the recursive call.

Consider the following function fragment and the call `test(4, 9)`:

```
void test(int m, int n) {
   char ch;
      .
   test(m + 1, n - 1);
   printf("%d %d", m, n);
      .
}
```

The function executes with m = 4, n = 9 and the local variable, ch. When the recursive call is made, the following happens:

1. The values of m, n, and ch are pushed onto a stack.
2. test begins execution, again, with m = 5, n = 8, and a new copy of ch.
3. Whenever this call to test finishes (perhaps even after calling itself one or more times), the stack is popped, and the program resumes execution with printf (the statement after the recursive call) and the popped values of m, n, and ch. In this example, 4 9 would be printed.

6.4 Printing a Linked List in Reverse Order

Consider the problem of printing a linked list in reverse order.

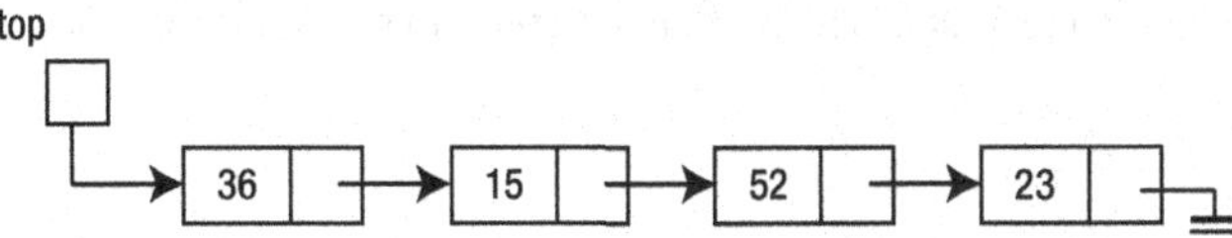

One way of doing this is to traverse the list, pushing items onto an integer stack as we meet them. When we reach the end of the list, the last number would be at the top of the stack, and the first would be at the bottom. We then pop items off the stack and print each one as it is popped.

As we may expect by now, we can use recursion to perform the stacking/unstacking. We use the following idea:

```
to print a list in reverse order
     print the list, except the first item, in reverse order
     print the first item
```

Using the previous list, this says print (15 52 23) in reverse order followed by 36:

- To print (15 52 23) in reverse order, we must print (52 23) in reverse order followed by 15.
- To print (52 23) in reverse order, we must print (23) in reverse order followed by 52.
- To print (23) in reverse order, we must print nothing (the rest of the list when 23 is removed) in reverse order followed by 23.

At the end, we would have printed: 23 52 15 36.

Another way to look at this is as follows:

```
reverse(36 15 52 23)    →    reverse(15 52 23) 36
                        →    reverse(52 23) 15 36
                        →    reverse(23) 52 15 36
                        →    reverse() 23 52 15 36
                        →    23 52 15 36
```

Here is the function, assuming that the pointer to the head of the list is of type `NodePtr` and the node fields are `num` and `next`:

```
void reverse(NodePtr top) {
   if (top != NULL) {
      reverse(top -> next);
      printf("%d ", top -> num);
   }
}
```

The key to working out a recursive solution to a problem is to be able to express the solution in terms of itself but on a "smaller" problem. If the problem keeps getting smaller and smaller, eventually it will be small enough that we can solve it directly.

We see this principle in both the "decimal to binary" and "print a linked list in reverse order" problems. In the first problem, the conversion of `n` is expressed in terms of `n/2`; this will, in turn, be expressed in terms of `n/4`, and so on, until there is nothing to convert. In the second problem, printing the list reversed is expressed in terms of printing a shorter list (the original list minus the first element) reversed. The list gets shorter and shorter until there is nothing to reverse.

6.5 Towers of Hanoi

The Towers of Hanoi puzzle is a classic problem that can be solved using recursion. Legend has it that when the world was created, some high priests in the Temple of Brahma were given three golden pins. On one of the pins were placed 64 golden disks. The disks were all different sizes with the largest at the bottom, the smallest on the top, and no disk placed on top of a smaller one.

They were required to move the 64 disks from the given pin to another one according to the following rules:

- Move one disk at a time; only a disk at the top of a pin can be moved, and it must be moved to the top of another pin.
- No disk must be placed on top of a smaller one.

When all 64 disks have been transferred, the world will come to an end.

This is an example of a problem that can be solved easily by recursion but for which a nonrecursive solution is quite difficult. Let's denote the pins by *A*, *B*, and *C* with the disks originally placed on *A* and the destination pin being *B*. Pin *C* is used for the temporary placement of disks.

Suppose there is one disk. It can be moved directly from *A* to *B*. Next, suppose there are five disks on *A*, as shown in Figure 6-1.

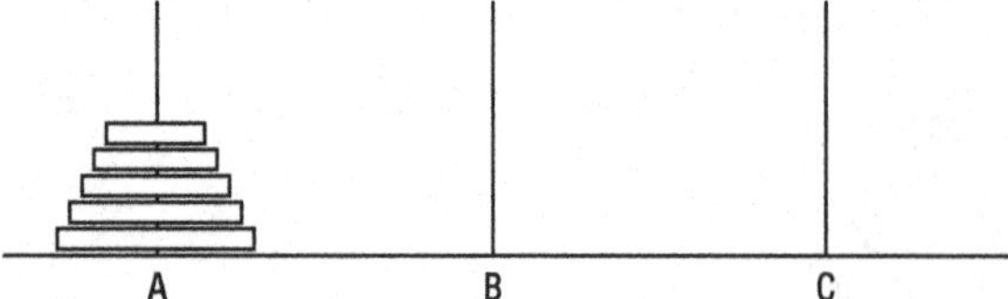

Figure 6-1. *Towers of Hanoi with five disks*

Assume we know how to transfer the top four from *A* to *C* using *B*. When this is done, we have Figure 6-2.

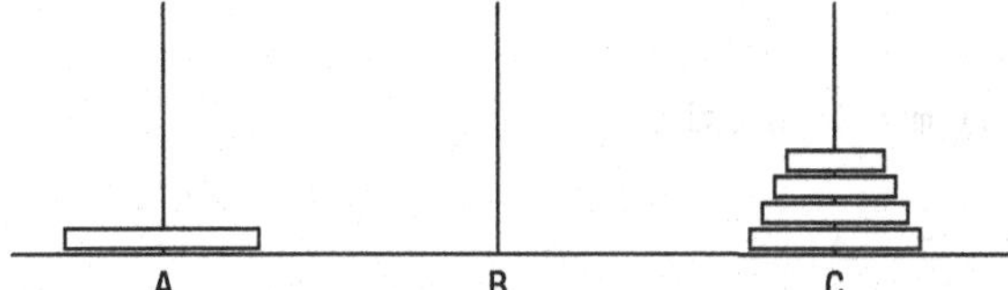

Figure 6-2. *After four disks have been moved from A to C*

We can now move the fifth disk from *A* to *B*, as shown in Figure 6-3.

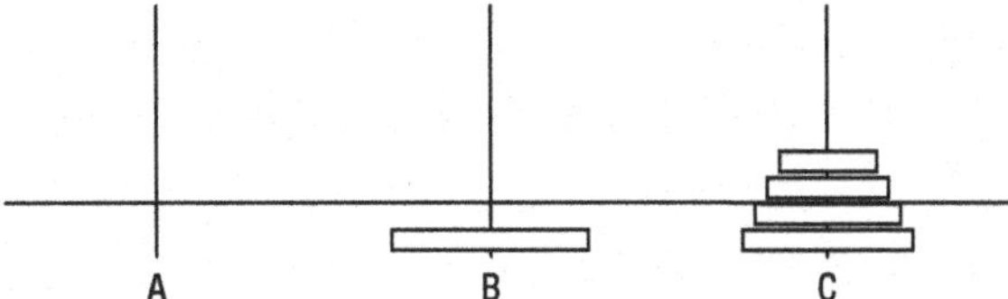

Figure 6-3. *The fifth disk is placed on B*

It remains only to transfer the four disks from *C* to *B* using *A*, which we assume we know how to do. The job is completed as shown in Figure 6-4.

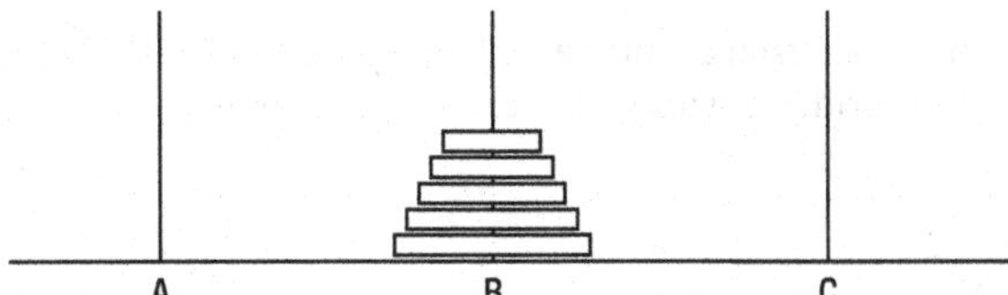

Figure 6-4. *After the four disks have been moved from C to B*

We have thus reduced the problem of transferring five disks to a problem of transferring four disks from one pin to another. This, in turn, can be reduced to a problem of moving three disks from one pin to another, and this can be reduced to two and then to one, which we know how to do. The recursive solution for *n* disks is as follows:

- Transfer *n* - 1 disks from *A* to *C* using *B*.
- Move *n*th disk from *A* to *B*.
- Transfer *n* - 1 disks from *C* to *B* using *A*.

Of course, we can use this same solution for transferring *n* - 1 disks.

The following function transfers `n` disks from `startPin` to `endPin` using `workPin`:

```
void hanoi(int n, char startPin, char endPin, char workPin) {
   if (n > 0) {
      hanoi(n - 1, startPin, workPin, endPin);
      printf("Move disk from %c to %c\n", startPin, endPin);
      hanoi(n - 1, workPin, endPin, startPin);
   }
}
```

When called with the statement:

```
hanoi(3, 'A', 'B', 'C');  //transfer 3 disks from A to B using C
```

the function prints this:

```
Move disk from A to B
Move disk from A to C
Move disk from B to C
Move disk from A to B
Move disk from C to A
Move disk from C to B
Move disk from A to B
```

How many moves are required to transfer *n* disks?

- If *n* is 1, one move is required: ($1 = 2^1 - 1$).
- If *n* is 2, three moves are required: ($3 = 2^2 - 1$).
- If *n* is 3, seven moves (see as shown earlier) are required: ($7 = 2^3 - 1$).

It appears that, for *n* disks, the number of moves is $2^n - 1$. It can be proved that this is indeed the case. When *n* is 64, the number of moves is:

$$2^{64} - 1 = 18,446,744,073,709,551,615$$

Assuming the priests can move one disc per second, never make a mistake, and never take a rest, it will take them almost 600 billion years to complete the task. Rest assured that the world is not about to end any time soon!

6.6 Writing Power Functions

Given a number, *x*, and an integer, $n \geq 0$, how do we calculate *x* raised to the power *n*, that is, x^n? We can use the definition that x^n is *x* multiplied by itself `n - 1` times. Thus, 3^4 is $3 \times 3 \times 3 \times 3$. Here is a function that uses this method:

```
double power(double x, int n) {
   double pow = 1.0;
   for (int h = 1; h <= n; h++) pow = pow * x;
   return pow;
}
```

Note that if *n* is `0`, `power` returns `1`, the correct answer.

As written, this function performs *n* multiplications. However, we can write a faster function if we adopt a different approach. Suppose we want to calculate x^{16}. We can do it as follows:

- If we know `x8` = x^8, we can multiply `x8` by `x8` to get x^{16}, using just one more multiplication.
- If we know `x4` = x^4, we can multiply `x4` by `x4` to get `x8`, using just one more multiplication.
- If we know `x2` = x^2, we can multiply `x2` by `x2` to get `x4`, using just one more multiplication.

We know `x`; therefore, we can find `x2` using one multiplication. Knowing `x2`, we can find `x4` using one more multiplication. Knowing `x4`, we can find `x8` using one more multiplication. Knowing `x8`, we can find x^{16} using one more multiplication. In all, we can find x^{16} using just four multiplications.

What if n were 15? First, we would work out $x^{15/2}$, that is, x^7 (call this x7). We would then multiply x7 by x7 to give x^{14}. Recognizing that n is odd, we would then multiply this value by x to give the required answer. To summarize:

$$x^n = x^{n/2}.x^{n/2}, \text{ if } n \text{ is even and}$$
$$x.x^{n/2}.x^{n/2}, \text{ if } n \text{ is odd}$$

We use this as the basis for a recursive power function that calculates x^n more efficiently than the previous function.

```
double power(double x, int n) {
   double y;
   if (n == 0) return 1.0;
   y = power(x, n/2);
   y = y * y;
   if (n % 2 == 0) return y;
   return x * y;
}
```

As an exercise, trace the execution of the function with n = 5 and n = 6.

6.7 Merge Sort

Consider, again, the problem of sorting a list of *n* items in ascending order. We will illustrate our ideas with a list of integers. In Section 1.8, we saw how to merge two sorted lists by traversing each list once. We now show how to use recursion and merging to sort a list. Consider this:

```
sort a list
   sort first half of list
   sort second half of list
    merge sorted halves into one sorted list
end sort
```

Clearly, if we can sort the two halves and then merge them, we will have a sorted list. But how do we sort the halves? We use the same method! Here's an example:

```
sort first half of list
   sort first half of first half of list (one quarter of the original list)
   sort second half of first half of list (one quarter of the original list)
    merge sorted halves into one sorted list
end sort
```

For each piece we have to sort, we break it into halves, sort the halves, and merge them. When do we stop using this process on a piece? When the piece consists of one element only, there is nothing to do to sort one element. We can modify our algorithm as follows:

```
sort a list
   if the list contains more than one element then
      sort first half of list
      sort second half of list
       merge sorted halves into one sorted list
   end if
end sort
```

We assume the list is stored in an array, A, from A[lo] to A[hi]. We can code the algorithm as a C function as follows:

```
void mergeSort(int A[], int lo, int hi) {
   void merge(int[], int, int, int);
   if (lo < hi) { //list contains at least 2 elements
      int mid = (lo + hi) / 2; //get the mid-point subscript
      mergeSort(A, lo, mid); //sort first half
      mergeSort(A, mid + 1, hi); //sort second half
      merge(A, lo, mid, hi); //merge sorted halves
   }
}
```

This assumes that merge is available and the following statement will merge the sorted pieces in A[lo..mid] and A[mid+1..hi] so that A[lo..hi] is sorted:

```
merge(A, lo, mid, hi);
```

We will show how to write merge shortly.

But first, we show how this function sorts the following list stored in an array, num:

num

57	48	79	65	33	52	15
0	1	2	3	4	5	6

The function will be called with:

```
mergeSort(num, 0, 6);
```

In the function, num will be known as A, lo will be 0, and hi will be 6. From these, mid will be calculated as 3, giving rise to two calls.

```
mergeSort(A, 0, 3);
mergeSort(A, 4, 6);
```

Assuming that the first will sort A[0..3] and the second will sort A[4..6], we will have the following result:

A

48	57	65	79	15	33	52
0	1	2	3	4	5	6

merge will merge the pieces to produce:

A

15	33	48	52	57	65	79
0	1	2	3	4	5	6

Each of these calls will give rise to two further calls. The first will produce:

```
mergeSort(A, 0, 1);
mergeSort(A, 2, 3);
```

The second will produce:

```
mergeSort(A, 4, 5);
mergeSort(A, 6, 6);
```

As long as lo is less than hi, two further calls will be produced. If lo is equal to hi, the list consists of one element only, and the function simply returns. The following shows all the calls generated by the initial call to mergeSort, in the order in which they are generated:

```
mergeSort(A, 0, 6)
   mergeSort(A, 0, 3)
      mergeSort(A, 0, 1);
         mergeSort(A, 0, 0);
         mergeSort(A, 1, 1);
      mergeSort(A, 2, 3);
         mergeSort(A, 2, 2);
         mergeSort(A, 3, 3);
   mergeSort(A, 4, 6);
      mergeSort(A, 4, 5);
         mergeSort(A, 4, 4);
         mergeSort(A, 5, 5);
      mergeSort(A, 6, 6);
```

To complete the job, we need to write merge. We can describe merge as follows:

```
void merge(int A[], int lo, int mid, int hi) {
//A[lo..mid] and A[mid+1..hi] are sorted;
//merge the pieces so that A[lo..hi] are sorted
```

Note what must be done: we must merge two adjacent portions of A back into the *same* locations. The problem with this is that we *cannot* merge into the same locations *while the merge is being performed* since we may overwrite numbers before they are used. We will have to merge into another (temporary) array and then copy the merged elements back into the original locations in A.

We will use a temporary array called T; we just need to make sure it is big enough to hold the merged elements. This implies it must be at least as big as the array to be sorted. In merge, we will denote its size by the symbolic constant MaxSize. Here is merge:

```
void merge(int A[], int lo, int mid, int hi) {
//A[lo..mid] and A[mid+1..hi] are sorted;
//merge the pieces so that A[lo..hi] are sorted
   int T[MaxSize];
   int i = lo;
   int j = mid + 1;
   int k = lo;
   while (i <= mid || j <= hi) {
      if (i > mid) T[k++] = A[j++];
      else if (j > hi) T[k++] = A[i++];
```

```
         else if (A[i] < A[j]) T[k++] = A[i++];
         else T[k++] = A[j++];
      }
      for (j = lo; j <= hi; j++) A[j] = T[j];
   }
```

We use i to subscript the first part of A, j to subscript the second part, and k to subscript T. The function merges A[lo..mid] and A[mid+1..hi] into T[lo..hi].

The while loop expresses the following logic: as long as we haven't processed *all* the elements in *both* parts, we enter the loop. If we are finished with the first part (i > mid), copy an element from the second part to T. (Since (i > mid) would continue to remain true each time through the loop, we will end up copying the remaining elements from the second part to T.) If we are finished with the second part (j > hi), copy an element from the first part to T. (Since (j > hi) would continue to remain true each time through the loop, we will end up copying the remaining elements from the first part to T.) Otherwise, we copy the smaller of A[i] and A[j] to T.

At the end, we copy the elements from T to the corresponding locations in A.

We can test mergeSort with the following:

```
#include <stdio.h>

#define MaxSize 20
int main() {
   void mergeSort(int[], int, int);
   int num[] = {4,8,6,16,1,9,14,2,3,5,18,13,17,7,12,11,15,10};
   int n = 18;
   mergeSort(num, 0, n-1);
   for (int h = 0; h < n; h++) printf("%d ", num[h]);
   printf("\n\n");
}
```

When combined with mergeSort and merge, it produces the following output:

```
1 2 3 4 5 6 7 8 9 10 11 12 13 14 15 16 17 18
```

In passing, we note that merge sort is a much faster sorting method than either selection sort or insertion sort.

Programming note: Each time we enter merge, storage is allocated for T, and this storage is released when the function returns. This is because, as declared, T is a local variable. If we want, we can declare T as a static variable, like this:

```
static int T[MaxSize];
```

We simply put the word static before the normal declaration. We could also write:

```
int static T[MaxSize];
```

Now, storage is allocated for T when we enter the function the first time only. It is not released when the function returns but remains in existence until the program ends. The values in T are also retained between calls to the function. We take a more detailed look at static variables next.

6.8 static Variables

In general, a variable is declared to be `static` by prefixing its normal declaration with the word `static`, as follows:

```
static int lineCount;
```

We could also use the following since the properties of a variable may be stated in any order:

```
int static lineCount;
```

Initialization may be specified, as follows:

```
static int lineCount = 0;
```

In the absence of explicit initialization, C guarantees that `static` variables will be initialized to `0`, but it is better programming practice to initialize your variables explicitly.

A `static` variable can be either *internal or external.*

6.8.1 Internal Static

If the declaration appears inside a function, as follows, then the variable is known only inside the function; in other words, it is *local* to the function:

```
void fun() {
   static int lineCount = 0;
          .
}
```

Variables of the same name in other parts of the program will cause no conflict. Storage is allocated to an *internal static* variable once. If specified, initialization is done at this time. This storage (and the value it contains) is retained between calls to the function.

Thus, if the value of `lineCount` is `5` when the function returns the first time, the second call of the function can assume that the value of `lineCount` is 5. In this example, `lineCount` can be used to count the total number of lines printed by all the calls to this function.

6.8.2 External Static

If the declaration appears outside of all functions, as follows, then the variable is known from the point of declaration to the end of the file containing the declaration:

```
int fun1() {
      .
      .
}

static int lineCount = 0;

void fun2() {
      .
      .
}
```

In this example, `lineCount` is known to `fun2` and any functions that come after it in the file; it is *not* known to `fun1`.

If necessary, `lineCount` can be incremented by any function following the declaration, provided it is in the same file. Thus, it can be used to count the total number of lines printed by all the functions that use it.

Normally, a function name is *external*; that is, it is known throughout the program, which may span several files. If we want to restrict the scope of a function to a particular file, we can precede its normal declaration with the word `static`, as follows:

```
static int fun(...)
```

Here, `fun` will be unknown outside the file in which this declaration appears.

The term `static` denotes permanence. Whether internal or external, a `static` variable is allocated storage only once, which is retained for the duration of the program. A `static` variable also affords a degree of privacy. If it is internal, it is known only in the function in which it is declared. If it is external, it is known only in the file in which it is declared.

6.9 Counting Organisms

Consider the following arrangement:

```
0 1 0 1 1 1 0
0 0 1 1 0 0 0
1 1 0 1 0 0 1
1 0 1 0 0 1 1
1 1 0 0 0 1 0
```

Assume that each `1` represents a cell of an organism; `0` means there is no cell. Two cells are *contiguous* if they are next to each other in the same row or same column. An organism is defined as follows:

- An organism contains at least one 1.
- Two contiguous 1s belong to the same organism.

There are five organisms in the arrangement shown. Count them!

Given an arrangement of cells in a grid, we want to write a program to count the number of organisms present.

A glance at the grid will reveal that, given a cell (`1`), the organism can extend in either of four directions. For *each* of these, it can extend in either of four directions, giving 16 possibilities. Each of these gives rise to four more possibilities, and so on. How do we keep track of all these possibilities, knowing which have been explored and which are still waiting to be explored?

The easiest way to do this is to let the recursive mechanism keep track for us.

To count the number of organisms, we need a way to determine which cells belong to an organism. To begin, we must find a `1`. Next, we must find all `1`s that are contiguous to this `1`, then `1`s that are contiguous to those, and so on.

To find contiguous `1`s, we must look in four directions, North, East, South, and West (in any order). When we look, there are four possibilities:

1. We are outside the grid, and there is nothing to do.
2. We see a 0, and there is nothing to do.
3. We see a 1 that has been seen previously; there is nothing to do.
4. We see a 1 for the first time; we move into that position and look in four directions from there.

Step 3 implies that when we meet a 1 for the first time, we would need to mark it in some way so that if we come across this position later, we will know it has been met before and we will not attempt to process it again.

The simplest thing we can do is to change the value from 1 to 0; this ensures that nothing is done if this position is met again. This is fine if all we want to do is *count* the organisms. But if we also want to identify which cells make up an organism, we will have to mark it differently.

Presumably, we will need a variable that keeps count of the number of organisms. Let's call it `orgCount`. When a 1 is encountered for the first time, we will change it to `orgCount + 1`. Thus, the cells of organism 1 will be labeled 2, the cells of organism 2 will be labeled 3, and so on.

This is necessary since, if we start labeling from 1, we would not be able to distinguish between a 1 representing a not-yet-met cell and a 1 indicating a cell belonging to organism 1.

This "adding 1 to the label" is necessary only *while we are processing the grid.* When we print it, we will subtract 1 from the label so that, on output, organism 1 will be labeled 1, organism 2 will be labeled 2, and so on.

In writing the program, we assume that the grid data is stored in an array `G` and consists of `m` rows and `n` columns. We will use `MaxRow` and `MaxCol` to denote maximum values for `m` and `n`, respectively. Data for the program consists of values for `m` and `n`, followed by the cell data in row order. For example, data for the previous grid will be supplied as follows:

```
5 7
0 1 0 1 1 1 0
0 0 1 1 0 0 0
1 1 0 1 0 0 1
1 0 1 0 0 1 1
1 1 0 0 0 1 0
```

We assume that the data will be read from a file, `cell.in`, and output will be sent to the file `cell.out`.

The gist of the program logic is as follows:

```
scan the grid from left to right, top to bottom
when we meet a 1, we have a new organism
add 1 to orgCount
call a function findOrg to mark all the cells of the organism
```

The function `findOrg` will implement the four possibilities outlined previously. When it sees a 1 in grid position `(i, j)`, say, it will call itself recursively for each of the grid positions to the North, East, South, and West of `(i, j)`. All the details are shown in Program P6.1.

Program P6.1

```
#include <stdio.h>
#define MaxRow 20
#define MaxCol 20

int G[MaxRow][MaxCol];
int orgCount = 0;

int main() {
   void findOrg(int, int, int, int);
   void printOrg(FILE *, int m, int n);
   int i, j, m, n;
   FILE * in = fopen("cell.in", "r");
   FILE * out = fopen("cell.out", "w");
```

```
   fscanf(in, "%d %d", &m, &n);
   for (i = 0; i < m; i++)
      for (j = 0; j < n; j++)
         fscanf(in, "%d", &G[i][j]);

   for (i = 0; i < m; i++)
      for (j = 0; j < n; j++)
         if (G[i][j] == 1) {
            orgCount++;
            findOrg(i, j, m, n);
         }

   printOrg(out, m, n);
} //end main

void findOrg(int i, int j, int m, int n) {
   if (i < 0 || i >= m || j < 0 || j >= n) return; //outside of grid
   if (G[i][j] == 0 || G[i][j] > 1) return; //no cell or cell already seen
   // else G[i][j] = 1;
   G[i][j]= orgCount + 1; //so that this 1 is not considered again
   findOrg(i - 1, j, m, n);
   findOrg(i, j + 1, m, n);
   findOrg(i + 1, j, m, n);
   findOrg(i, j - 1, m, n);
} //end findOrg

void printOrg(FILE * out, int m, int n) {
   fprintf(out, "\nNumber of organisms = %d\n", orgCount);
   fprintf(out, "\nPosition of organisms are shown here\n\n");
   for (int i = 0; i < m; i++) {
      for (int j = 0; j < n; j++)
         if (G[i][j] > 1) fprintf(out, "%2d ", G[i][j] - 1);
            //organism labels are one more than they should be
         else fprintf(out, "%2d ", G[i][j]);
      fprintf(out, "\n");
   }
} //end printOrg
```

When run with the earlier grid, this program produced the following output:

```
Number of organisms = 5

Position of organisms are shown here:

0  1  0  2  2  2  0
0  0  2  2  0  0  0
3  3  0  2  0  0  4
3  0  5  0  0  4  4
3  3  0  0  0  4  0
```

Consider how findOrg identifies organism 1. In main, when i = 0 and j = 1, G[0][1] is 1, so the call findOrg(0, 1, ...) will be made with G as follows:

```
0 1 0 1 1 1 0
0 0 1 1 0 0 0
1 1 0 1 0 0 1
1 0 1 0 0 1 1
1 1 0 0 0 1 0
```

In findOrg, since G[0][1] is 1, it will be set to 2, and four calls to findOrg will be made as follows:

```
findOrg(-1, 1, ...); //immediate return since i < 0
findOrg(0, 2, ...);  //immediate return since G[0][2] is 0
findOrg(1, 1, ...);  //immediate return since G[1][1] is 0
findOrg(0, -1, ...); //immediate return since j < 0
```

All of these calls return immediately, so only G[0][1] is marked with a 2.

Next, consider how findOrg identifies organism 3. In main, when i = 2 and j = 0, G[2][0] is 1, so the call findOrg(2, 0, ...) will be made with G as follows:

```
0 2 0 3 3 3 0
0 0 3 3 0 0 0
1 1 0 3 0 0 1
1 0 1 0 0 1 1
1 1 0 0 0 1 0
```

(Recall that, at this stage, the label of an organism is 1 more than the number of the organism.) For this example, we will use the notation N, E, S, and W (rather than subscripts) to indicate a grid position to the North, East, South, and West, respectively. At this stage, orgCount is 3 so that the cells will be labeled with 4.

The following are the calls generated to findOrg from the initial findOrg(2, 0, ...):

```
findOrg(2, 0, ...) //G[2][0] is labelled with 4
   findOrg(N...) //returns immediately since G[N] is 0
   findOrg(E...) //G[E] is 1, relabelled with 4, gives rise to 4 calls
      findOrg(N...) //returns immediately since G[N] is 0
      findOrg(E...) //returns immediately since G[E] is 0
      findOrg(S...) //returns immediately since G[S] is 0
      findOrg(W...) //returns immediately since G[W] is 4
   findOrg(S...) //G[S] is 1, relabelled with 4, gives rise to 4 calls
      findOrg(N...) //returns immediately since G[N] is 4
      findOrg(E...) //returns immediately since G[E] is 0
      findOrg(S...) //G[S] is 1, relabelled with 4, gives rise to 4 calls
         findOrg(N...) //returns immediately since G[N] is 4
         findOrg(E...) //G[E] is 1, relabelled with 4, gives rise to 4 calls
            findOrg(N...) //returns immediately since G[N] is 0
            findOrg(E...) //returns immediately since G[E] is 0
            findOrg(S...) //returns immediately since G[S] is outside grid
            findOrg(W...) //returns immediately since G[W] is 4
         findOrg(S...) //returns immediately since G[S] is outside grid
         findOrg(W...) //returns immediately since G[W] is outside grid
      findOrg(W...) //returns immediately since G[W] is outside grid
   findOrg(W...) //returns immediately since G[W] is outside grid
```

When the call `findOrg(2, 0, ...)` finally returns, `G` would be changed to this:

```
0 2 0 3 3 3 0
0 0 3 3 0 0 0
4 4 0 3 0 0 1
4 0 1 0 0 1 1
4 4 0 0 0 1 0
```

The third organism (labeled `4`) has been identified. Note that each cell in the organism gave rise to four calls to `findOrg`.

6.10 Finding a Path Through a Maze

Consider the following diagram that represents a maze:

```
##########
# #   #  #
# # # ## #
#   #    #
# ###### #
# # #S##
#     ## #
##########
```

Problem: Starting at S and moving along the open spaces, try to find a way out of the maze. The following shows how to do it with x's marking the path:

```
##########
# #xxx#  #
# #x#x## #
#xxx#xxxx#
#x######x#
#x# #x##xx
#xxxxx## #
##########
```

We want to write a program that, given a maze, determines whether a path exists. If one exists, mark the path with x's.

Given any position in the maze, there are four possible directions in which one can move: North (N), East (E), South (S), and West (W). You will not be able to move in a particular direction if you meet a wall. However, if there is an open space, you can move into it.

In writing the program, we will try the directions in the order N, E, S, and W. We will use the following strategy:

```
try N
if there is a wall, try E
else if there is a space, move to it and mark it with x
```

Whenever we go to an open space, we repeat this strategy. So, for instance, when we go East, if there is a space, we mark it and try the four directions *from this new position.*

Eventually, we will get out of the maze, or we will reach a dead-end position. For example, suppose we get to the position marked C:

```
##########
#C#   #  #
#B# # ## #
#A  #    #
#x###### #
#x# #x##
#xxxxx## #
##########
```

There are walls in all directions except South, from which we came. In this situation, we go back to the previous position and try the next possibility from there. This is called *backtracking*. In this example, we go back to the position south of C (call this B).

When we were at B, we would have gotten to C by trying the North direction. Since this failed, when we go back to B, we will try the "next" possibility, that is, East. This fails since there is a wall. So, we try South; this fails since we have already been there. Finally, we try West, which fails since there is a wall.

So, from B, we go back (we say *backtrack*) to the position from which we moved to B (call this A).

When we backtrack to A, the "next" possibility is East. There is a space, so we move into it, mark it with x, and try the first direction (North) from there.

When we backtrack from a failed position, we must "unmark" that position; that is, we must erase the x. This is necessary since a failed position will not be part of the solution path.

How do we backtrack? The recursive mechanism will take care of that for us, in a similar manner to the "counting organisms" problem. The following shows how:

```
int findPath(P) { //find a path from position P
   if P is outside the maze, return 0
   if P is at a wall, return 0
   if P was considered already, return 0
   //if we get here, P is a space we can move into
   mark P with x
   if P is on the border of the maze, we are out of the maze; return 1
   //try to extend the path to the North; if successful, return 1
   if (findPath(N)) return 1;
   //if North fails, try East, then South, then West
   //however, if North succeeds, there is no need to try other directions
   if (findPath(E)) return 1;
   if (findPath(S)) return 1;
   if (findPath(W)) return 1;
   //if all directions fail, we must unmark P and backtrack
   mark P with space
   return 0; //we have failed to find a path from P
} //end findPath
```

6.10.1 Writing the Program

First we must determine how the maze data will be supplied. In the previous example, the maze consists of eight rows and ten columns. If we represent each wall by 1 and each space by 0, the maze is represented by the following:

```
1 1 1 1 1 1 1 1 1 1
1 0 1 0 0 0 1 0 0 1
1 0 1 0 1 0 1 1 0 1
1 0 0 0 1 0 0 0 0 1
1 0 1 1 1 1 1 1 0 1
1 0 1 0 1 0 1 1 0 0
1 0 0 0 0 0 1 1 0 1
1 1 1 1 1 1 1 1 1 1
```

The start position, S, is at row 6, column 6. The first line of data will specify the number of rows and columns of the maze and the coordinates of S. Thus, the first line of data will be as follows:

```
8 10 6 6
```

This will be followed by the maze data, shown earlier.

When we need to mark a position with an x, we will use the value 2.

Our program will read data from the file `maze.in` and send output to `maze.out`. The complete program is shown as Program P6.2. When this program is run with the previous data, it produces the following output:

```
##########
# #xxx#  #
# #x#x## #
#xxx#xxxx#
#x######x#
#x# #S##xx
#xxxxx## #
##########
```

Program P6.2

```
#include <stdio.h>
#define MaxRow 20
#define MaxCol 20

int m, n, sr, sc;
int G[MaxRow+1][MaxCol+1];

int main() {
   void getData(FILE *);
   int findPath(int, int);
   void printMaze(FILE *);

   FILE * in = fopen("maze.in", "r");
   FILE * out = fopen("maze.out", "w");
```

```
   getData(in);
   if (findPath(sr, sc)) printMaze(out);
   else fprintf(out, "\nNo solution\n");

   fclose(in);
   fclose(out);
} //end main

void getData(FILE * in) {
   fscanf(in, "%d %d %d %d", &m, &n, &sr, &sc);
   for (int r = 1; r <= m; r++)
      for (int c = 1; c <= n; c++)
         fscanf(in, "%d", &G[r][c]);
} //end getData

int findPath(int r, int c) {
   if (r < 1 || r > m || c < 1 || c > n) return 0;
   if (G[r][c] == 1) return 0; //into a wall
   if (G[r][c] == 2) return 0; //already considered

   // else G[r][c] = 0;
   G[r][c] = 2; //mark the path
   if (r == 1 || r == m || c == 1 || c == n) return 1;
   //path found - space located on the border of the maze

   if (findPath(r-1, c)) return 1;
   if (findPath(r, c+1)) return 1;
   if (findPath(r+1, c)) return 1;
   if (findPath(r, c-1)) return 1;
   G[r][c] = 0; //no path found; unmark
   return 0;
} //end findPath

void printMaze(FILE * out) {
   for (int r = 1; r <= m; r++) {
      for (int c = 1; c <= n; c++)
         if (r == sr && c == sc) fprintf(out,"S");
         else if (G[r][c] == 0) fprintf(out," ");
         else if (G[r][c] == 1) fprintf(out,"#");
         else fprintf(out,"x");
      fprintf(out, "\n");
   }
} //end printMaze
```

EXERCISES 6

1. Write an iterative function to return the *n*th Fibonacci number.
2. Print an integer with commas separating the thousands. For example, given 12058, print 12,058.
3. `A` is an array containing *n* integers. Write a recursive function to find the number of times a given integer `x` appears in `A`.
4. Write a recursive function to implement *selection sort.*
5. Write a recursive function to return the largest element in an integer array.
6. Write a recursive function to search for a given number in an `int` array.
7. Write a recursive function to search for a given number in a *sorted* `int` array.
8. What output is produced by the call `W(0)` of the following function?

```
void W(int n) {
   printf("%3d", n);
   if (n < 10) W(n + 3);
   printf("%3d", n);
}
```

9. What output is produced by the call `S('C')` of the following function?

```
void S(char ch) {
   if (ch < 'H') {
      S(++ch);
      printf("%c ", ch);
   }
}
```

10. In 9, what output will be produced if the statements within the `if` statement are interchanged?
11. In 9, what will happen if `++ch` is changed to `ch++`?
12. Write a recursive function, `length`, that, given a pointer to a linked list, returns the number of nodes in the list.
13. Write a recursive function, `sum`, that, given a pointer to a linked list of integers, returns the sum of the values at the nodes of the list.
14. Write a recursive function that, given a pointer to the head of a linked list of integers, returns `1` if the list is in ascending order and `0` if it is not.

15. What is printed by the call `fun(18, 3)` of the following recursive function?

```
void fun(int m, int n) {
   if (n > 0) {
      fun(m-1, n-1);
      printf("%d ", m);
      fun(m+1, n-1);
   }
}
```

16. What is returned by the call `test(7, 2)` of the following recursive function?

```
int test(int n, int r) {
   if (r == 0) return 1;
   if (r == 1) return n;
   if (r == n) return 1;
   return test(n-1, r-1) + test(n-1, r);
}
```

17. Write a recursive function that takes an integer argument and prints the integer with one space after each digit. For example, given `7583`, it prints `7 5 8 3 `.

18. Consider points (*m*, *n*) in the usual Cartesian coordinate system where *m* and *n* are positive *integers*. In a *north-east* path from point A to point B, one can move only *up* and only *right* (no *down* or *left* movements are allowed). Write a function that, given the coordinates of any two points A and B, returns the *number* of north-east paths from A to B.

19. The eight-queens problem can be stated as follows: place 8 queens on a chess board so that no two queens attack each other. Two queens attack each other if they are in the same row, same column, or same diagonal. Clearly, any solution must have the queens in different rows and different columns.

    One approach to solving the problem is as follows. Place the first queen in the first column of the first row. Next, place the second queen so that it does not attack the first. If this is not possible, go back and place the first queen in the next column and try again.

    After the first two queens have been placed, place the third queen so that it does not attack the first two. If this is not possible, go back and place the second queen in the next column and try again.

    At each step, try to place the next queen so that it does not conflict with those already placed. If you succeed, try to place the next queen. If you fail, you must *backtrack* to the previously placed queen and try the next possible column. If all columns have been tried, you must backtrack to the queen before *this* queen and try the next column for *that* queen.

    The idea is similar to finding a path through a maze. Write a program to solve the eight-queens problem. Use recursion to implement the backtracking.

CHAPTER 7

Random Numbers, Games, and Simulation

In this chapter, we will explain the following:

- Random numbers
- The difference between random and pseudorandom numbers
- How to generate random numbers on a computer
- How to write a program to play a guessing game
- How to write a program to drill a user in arithmetic
- How to write a program to play Nim
- How to simulate the collection of bottle caps to spell a word
- How to simulate queues in real-life situations
- How to estimate numerical values using random numbers

7.1 Random Numbers

If you were to throw a six-sided die 100 times, each time writing down the number that shows, you would have written down 100 *random* integers *uniformly distributed* in the range 1 to 6.

If you tossed a coin 144 times and, for each toss, wrote down `0` (for heads) or `1` (for tails), you would have written 144 random integers uniformly distributed in the range 0 to 1.

If you were standing by the roadside and, as vehicles passed, you noted the last two digits of the registration number (for those vehicles that have at least two digits), you would have noted random integers uniformly distributed in the range 0 to 99.

Spin a roulette wheel (with 36 numbers) 500 times. The 500 numbers that appear are random integers uniformly distributed in the range 1 to 36.

The word *random* implies that any outcome is completely independent of any other outcome. For instance, if a 5 showed on one throw of the die, then this has no bearing on what would show on the next throw. Similarly, a 29 on the roulette wheel has no effect whatsoever on what number comes up next.

The term *uniformly distributed* means that all values are equally likely to appear. In the case of the die, you have the same chance of throwing a 1 or a 6 or any other number. And, in a large number of throws, each number will occur with roughly the same frequency.

In the case of a coin, if we toss it 144 times, we would expect heads to appear 72 times and tails to appear 72 times. In practice, these exact values are not normally obtained, but if the coin is a fair one, then the values would be close enough to the expected values to pass certain statistical tests. For example, a result of 75 heads and 69 tails is close enough to the expected value of 72 to pass the required tests.

Random numbers are widely used in simulating games of chance (such as games involving dice, coins, or cards), in playing educational games (such as creating problems in arithmetic), and in modeling real-life situations on a computer.

For example, if we want to play a game of *Snakes and Ladders*, throwing the die is simulated by the computer generating a random number from 1 to 6. Suppose we want to create problems in addition for a child, using only the numbers from 1 to 9. For each problem, the computer can generate two numbers (for example, 7 and 4) in the range 1 to 9 and give these to the child to add.

But suppose we want to simulate the traffic pattern at a road intersection governed by traffic lights. We want to time the lights in such a way that the waiting time in both directions is as short as possible. To do the simulation on a computer, we will need some data as to how fast vehicles arrive at and leave the intersection. This must be done by observation in order for the simulation to be as useful as possible.

Suppose it is determined that a random number of vehicles (between 5 and 15) going in direction 1 arrive at the intersection every 30 seconds. Also, between 8 and 20 vehicles arrive every 30 seconds going in direction 2. The computer can simulate this situation as follows:

1. Generate a random number, `r1`, in the range 5 to 15.
2. Generate a random number, `r2`, in the range 8 to 20.

`r1` and `r2` are taken as the numbers of vehicles that arrive at the intersection from each direction in the first 30 seconds. The process is repeated for successive 30-second periods.

7.2 Random and Pseudorandom Numbers

The value that appears when a die is thrown has no effect on what comes up on the next throw. We say that the throws have independent outcomes and the values thrown are random integers in the range 1 to 6. But when a computer is used to generate a sequence of random numbers in a given interval, it uses an algorithm.

Normally, the next number in the sequence is generated from the previous number in a prescribed and predetermined manner. This means the numbers in the sequence are not independent of each other, like they are when we throw a die, for instance. However, the numbers generated will pass the usual set of statistical tests for *randomness*, so, to all intents and purposes, they are random numbers. But, because they are generated in a very predictable manner, they are usually called *pseudorandom* numbers.

In modeling many types of situations, it does not usually matter whether we use random or pseudorandom numbers. In fact, in most applications, pseudorandom numbers work quite satisfactorily. However, consider an organization running a weekly lottery where the winning number is a six-digit number. Should a pseudorandom number generator be used to provide the winning number from one week to the next?

Since the generator produces these numbers in a completely predetermined way, it would be possible to predict the winning numbers for weeks to come. Clearly, this is not desirable (unless *you* are in charge of the random number generator!). In this situation, a truly random method of producing the winning numbers is needed.

7.3 Generating Random Numbers by Computer

In what follows, we make no distinction between random and pseudorandom numbers since, for most practical purposes, no distinction is necessary. Almost all programming languages provide some sort of random number generator, but there are slight differences in the way they operate.

In C, we can work with random numbers using the predefined constant RAND_MAX and the functions rand and srand. To use them, your program must be preceded by:

```
#include <stdlib.h>
```

The value of RAND_MAX is the maximum possible value that can be returned by rand. On some systems, it is 2147483647, which is the largest signed integer representable in 32 bits. On others, it is 32767, which is the largest signed integer representable in 16 bits.

The prototype for rand is:

```
int rand(void)
```

It returns the next random number in the series. The value is in the range 0 to RAND_MAX.

The prototype for srand is:

```
void srand(unsigned int seed)
```

It uses seed to establish a starting point for a new series of random numbers. We say we must *seed* the random number generator. Normally, you must call srand to seed the generator *before* using rand. If you call rand before srand, it uses the value 1 as a default seed.

In practice, we would hardly ever use rand in the form provided. This is because, most times, we would need random numbers in a specific range (like 1 to 36, say) rather than 0 to 32767. However, we can easily write a function that uses rand and srand to provide random numbers from m to n where m < n. Here it is:

```
int random(int m, int n) {
//returns a random integer from m to n, inclusive
   int offset = rand() / (RAND_MAX + 1.0) * (n - m + 1);
   return m + offset;
} //end random
```

Programming note: Some C libraries may contain a function called random. To avoid conflict, you can use another name for the previous function.

Before using random, we must seed the generator. We can do this in main with this:

```
srand(101); //an arbitrary integer
```

In random, it is important to use 1.0 instead of 1. Since rand returns an integer and RAND_MAX + 1 is also an integer, if 1 is used, an integer division would be performed. This would always give 0 since the maximum value of rand is RAND_MAX. The value returned by random would always be m.

However, using (the double constant) 1.0 causes RAND_MAX + 1.0 to be evaluated as double, in turn causing the value returned by rand to be converted to double and a floating-point division to be performed. The value of (n - m + 1) is also converted to double and the multiplication performed. The result obtained is truncated before being assigned to the integer variable offset. In effect, the following construct returns a random *fraction*, *f*, between 0 (inclusive) and 1 (exclusive):

```
rand() / (RAND_MAX + 1.0)
```

To illustrate how random works, suppose m = 5 and n = 20. There are 20 - 5 + 1 = 16 numbers in the range 5 to 20. We calculate offset as follows, noting that the smallest value of *f* is 0.0 and the largest is 0.9999 (to four decimal places):

1. *f* is multiplied by 16 to give a value from 0.0 to 15.99 (to two decimal places).
2. When assigned to offset (an int), the fraction is discarded so offset assumes a value between 0 and 15.

5 is added to offset, giving a value between 5 and 20. This is the value returned by random.

Another reason for using 1.0 is that, on many systems, the value of RAND_MAX is the largest integer on the system (typically, 32767 for a 16-bit int). If we tried to add the *integer* 1 to it, *overflow* would occur since we would be trying to exceed the largest value that can be stored.

One final note: when we use a given seed (101, say), this determines the sequence of numbers that will be generated. If we rerun the program with the same seed, the same sequence will be generated. We can change the seed, but this will entail changing the program. We can ask the user to enter a seed, but this puts a burden on the user and may confuse her since she may not know the purpose of the number she is being asked to enter.

A common approach is to use the time function provided by C in time.h. In its simplest form, we can use:

```
srand(time(0));
```

This uses the actual time at which the program is being run to seed the generator. Since this will be different each time the program is run, the sequence generated will be different.

Consider the following code that generates and prints 20 random numbers from 1 to 6:

```
#include <stdio.h>
#include <stdlib.h>
int main() {
   int random(int, int);
   srand(101);
   for (int h = 1; h <= 20; h++) printf("%2d", random(1, 6));
   printf("\n\n");
}
```

When run, it prints the following sequence of random numbers:

```
1 3 3 6 4 3 4 1 1 6 5 3 4 4 2 5 4 6 5 4
```

Each call to random produces the next number in the sequence. Note that the sequence may be different on another computer or on the same computer using a different compiler.

If the code is run a second time, the same sequence will be produced since the seed, 101, is the same.

However, if we change srand(101) to srand(time(0)), two runs of the program will produce different sequences, as shown here:

```
2 6 5 6 4 2 1 6 6 3 2 4 6 3 6 3 3 2 2 1
5 5 2 3 4 3 6 4 4 2 1 5 1 3 4 3 6 1 1 5
```

Each time the program is run, a different sequence will be generated.

Programming note: Strictly speaking, in order to use the function time, you should have #include <time.h> at the head of your program. However, some compilers have a declaration for time in stdlib.h, so all you need is #include <stdlib.h>.

7.4 A Guessing Game

To illustrate a simple use of random numbers, let's write a program to play a guessing game. The program will "think" of a number from 1 to 100. You are required to guess the number using as few guesses as possible. The following is a sample run of the program. Underlined items are typed by the user:

```
I have thought of a number from 1 to 100.
Try to guess what it is.

Your guess? 50
Too low
Your guess? 75
Too high
Your guess? 62
Too high
Your guess? 56
Too low
Your guess? 59
Too high
Your guess? 57
Congratulations, you've got it!
```

As you can see, each time you guess, the program will tell you whether your guess is too high or too low and allow you to guess again.

The program will "think" of a number from 1 to 100 by calling `random(1, 100)`. You will guess until you have guessed correctly or until you give up. You give up by entering `0` as your guess. Program P7.1 contains all the details.

Programming note: It is a good idea to remind the user that he has the option of giving up and how to do so. To this end, the prompt can be:

```
Your guess (0 to give up)?
```

Program P7.1

```
#include <stdio.h>
#include <stdlib.h>
#include <time.h>

int main() {
   int answer, guess, random(int, int);

   printf("\nI have thought of a number from 1 to 100.\n");
   printf("Try to guess what it is.\n\n");

   srand(time (0));
   answer = random(1, 100);

   printf("Your guess? ");
   scanf("%d", &guess);
```

```
   while (guess != answer && guess != 0) {
      if (guess < answer) printf("Too low\n");
      else printf("Too high\n");
      printf("Your guess? ");
      scanf("%d", &guess);
   }
   if (guess == 0) printf("Sorry, answer is %d\n", answer);
   else printf("Congratulations, you've got it!\n");
} //end main

int random(int m, int n) {
//returns a random integer from m to n, inclusive
   int offset = rand() / (RAND_MAX + 1.0) * (n - m + 1);
   return m + offset;
} //end random
```

7.5 Drills in Addition

We want to write a program to drill a user in simple arithmetic problems (Program P7.2). More specifically, we want to write a program to create addition problems for a user to solve. The problems will involve the addition of two numbers. But where do the numbers come from? We will let the computer "think" of the two numbers. By now, you should know that, in order to do this, the computer will generate two random numbers.

We also need to decide what size of numbers to use in the problems. This will determine, to some extent, how difficult the problems are going to be. We will use two-digit numbers, that is, numbers from 10 to 99. The program can be easily modified to handle numbers in a different range.

The program will begin by asking the user how many problems he wants to be given. The user will type the number required. He will then be asked how many attempts he wants to be given for each problem. He will enter this number. The program then proceeds to give him the requested number of problems.

The following is a sample run of the program. Underlined items are typed by the user; everything else is typed by the computer.

```
Welcome to Problems in Addition

How many problems would you like? 3
Maximum tries per problem? 2

Problem 1, Try 1 of 2
   80 + 75 = 155
Correct, well done!

Problem 2, Try 1 of 2
   17 + 29 = 36
Incorrect, try again

Problem 2, Try 2 of 2
   17 + 29 = 46
Correct, well done!

Problem 3, Try 1 of 2
   83 + 87 = 160
Incorrect, try again
```

```
Problem 3, Try 2 of 2
   83 + 87 = 180
Sorry, answer is 170

Thank you for playing. Bye...
```

All the details are shown in Program P7.2.

Program P7.2

```
#include <stdio.h>
#include <stdlib.h>
#include <time.h>

int main() {
   int maxTries, numProblems, answer, response;
   int num1, num2, random(int, int);

   printf("\nWelcome to Problems in Addition\n\n");
   printf("How many problems would you like? ");
   scanf("%d", &numProblems);
   printf("Maximum tries per problem? ");
   scanf("%d", &maxTries);

   srand(time(0));

   for (int h = 1; h <= numProblems; h++) {
      num1 = random(10, 99);
      num2 = random(10, 99);
      answer = num1 + num2;
      for (int try = 1; try <= maxTries; try++) {
         printf("\nProblem %d, Try %d of %d\n", h, try, maxTries);
         printf("%5d + %2d = ", num1, num2);
         scanf("%d", &response);
         if (response == answer) {
            printf("Correct, well done!\n");
            break;
         }
         if (try < maxTries) printf("Incorrect, try again\n");
         else printf("Sorry, answer is %d\n", answer);
      } //end for try
   } //end for h
   printf("\nThank you for playing. Bye...\n");
} //end main

int random(int m, int n) {
//returns a random integer from m to n, inclusive
   int offset = rand() / (RAND_MAX + 1.0) * (n - m + 1);
   return m + offset;
} //end random
```

7.6 Nim

One version of the game called Nim is played between two people, A and B, say. Initially, there is a known number of matches (`startAmount`, say) on the table. Each player, in turn, is allowed to pick up any number of matches from 1 to some agreed maximum (`maxPick`, say). The player who picks up the last match loses the game. For example, if `startAmount` is `20` and `maxPick` is `3`, the game may proceed as follows:

A picks up 2, leaving 18 on the table.

B picks up 1, leaving 17 on the table.

A picks up 3, leaving 14 on the table.

B picks up 1, leaving 13 on the table.

A picks up 2, leaving 11 on the table.

B picks up 2, leaving 9 on the table.

A picks up 1, leaving 8 on the table.

B picks up 3, leaving 5 on the table.

A picks up 1, leaving 4 on the table.

B picks up 3, leaving 1 on the table.

A is forced to pick up the last match and, therefore, loses the game.

What is the best way to play the game? Obviously, the goal should be to leave your opponent with one match remaining on the table. Let's call this a *losing position*. The next question to answer is, how many matches must you leave so that, no matter how many he picks up (within the rules of the game), you can leave him with one?

In this example, the answer is 5. Whether he picks up 1, 2, or 3, you can *always* leave him with 1. If he picks up 1, you pick up 3; if he picks up 2, you pick up 2; if he picks up 3, you pick up 1. So, therefore, 5 is the next losing position.

The next question is, how many matches must you leave so that, no matter how many he picks up (within the rules of the game), you can leave him with 5? The answer is 9. Try it!

And so on. Reasoning this way, we discover that 1, 5, 9, 13, 17, and so on, are all losing positions. In other words, if you can leave your opponent with any of these number of matches, you can force a win.

In this example, the moment B left A with 17 matches, B was in a position from which he could not lose, unless he became careless.

In general, losing positions are obtained by adding 1 to multiples of `maxPick + 1`. If `maxPick` is `3`, multiples of 4 are 4, 8, 12, 16, and so on. Adding 1 gives the losing positions 5, 9, 13, 17, and so on.

We will write a program in which the computer plays the best possible game of Nim. If it can force the user into a losing position, it will. If the user has forced *it* into a losing position, it will pick up a random number of matches and hope that the user makes a mistake.

If `remain` is the number of matches remaining on the table, how can the computer determine what is the best move to make?

If `remain` is less than or equal to `maxPick`, the computer picks up `remain - 1` matches, leaving the user with 1. Otherwise, we perform this calculation:

```
r = remain % (maxPick + 1)
```

If `r` is `0`, `remain` is a multiple of `maxPick + 1`; the computer picks up `maxPick` matches, leaving the user in a losing position. In this example, if `remain` is 16 (a multiple of 4), the computer picks up 3, leaving the user with 13—a losing position.

If `r` is `1`, the computer is in a losing position and picks up a random number of matches.

Otherwise, the computer picks up `r - 1` matches, leaving the user in a losing position. In this example, if `remain` is 18, `r` would be 2. The computer picks up 1, leaving the user with 17—a losing position.

This strategy is implemented in the function `bestPick`, part of Program P7.3 that pits the computer against a user in our version of Nim.

Program P7.3

```
#include <stdio.h>
#include <stdlib.h>
#include <time.h>

int main() {
   int remain, maxPick, userPick, compPick;
   int bestPick(int, int), min(int, int);
   printf("\nNumber of matches on the table? ");
   scanf("%d", &remain);
   printf("Maximum pickup per turn? ");
   scanf("%d", &maxPick);
   printf("\nMatches remaining: %d\n", remain);

   srand(time(0));
   while (1) { //do forever...well, until the game ends
      do {
         printf("Your turn: ");
         scanf("%d", &userPick);
         if (userPick > remain)
            printf("Cannot pick up more than %d\n", min(remain, maxPick));
         else if (userPick < 1 || userPick > maxPick)
            printf("Invalid: must be between 1 and %d\n", maxPick);
      } while (userPick > remain || userPick < 1 || userPick > maxPick);
      remain = remain - userPick;
      printf("Matches remaining: %d\n", remain);
      if (remain == 0) {
         printf("You lose!!\n");
         exit(0);
      }
      if (remain == 1) {
         printf("You win!!\n");
         exit(0);
      }
      compPick = bestPick(remain, maxPick);
      printf("I pick up %d\n", compPick);
      remain = remain - compPick;
      printf("Matches remaining: %d\n", remain);
      if (remain == 0) {
         printf("You win!!\n");  exit(0);
      }
      if (remain == 1) {
         printf("I win!!\n");  exit(0);
      }
   } //end while(1)
} //end main
```

```
int bestPick(int remain, int maxPick) {
   int random(int, int);
   if (remain <= maxPick) return remain - 1; //put user in losing position
   int r = remain % (maxPick + 1);
   if (r == 0) return maxPick; //put user in losing position
   if (r == 1) return random(1, maxPick); //computer in losing position
   return r - 1; //put user in losing position
} //end bestPick

int min(int a, int b) {
   if (a < b) return a;
   return b;
} //end min

int random(int m, int n) {
//returns a random integer from m to n, inclusive
   int offset = rand() / (RAND_MAX + 1.0) * (n - m + 1);
   return m + offset;
} //end random
```

Note the use of the do...while statement for getting and validating the user's play. The general form is as follows:

```
do <statement> while (<expression>);
```

As usual, `<statement>` can be simple (one-line) or compound (enclosed in braces). The words do and while and the brackets and semicolon are required. The programmer supplies `<statement>` and `<expression>`. A do...while is executed as follows:

1. `<statement>` is executed.
2. `<expression>` is then evaluated; if it is true (nonzero), repeat from step 1. If it is false (zero), execution continues with the statement, if any, after the semicolon.

As long as `<expression>` is true, `<statement>` is executed. It is important to note that because of the nature of the construct, `<statement>` is *always executed at least once*. This is particularly useful in a situation where we *want* `<statement>` to be executed at least once. In this example, we need to prompt the user at least once for his play, hence the reason for do...while.

A sample run of P7.3 is shown here:

```
Number of matches on the table? 30
Maximum pickup per turn? 5

Matches remaining: 30
Your turn: 2
Matches remaining: 28
I pick up 3
Matches remaining: 25
Your turn: 3
Matches remaining: 22
I pick up 3
Matches remaining: 19
Your turn: 6
Invalid: must be between 1 and 5
```

```
Your turn: 1
Matches remaining: 18
I pick up 5
Matches remaining: 13
Your turn: 4
Matches remaining: 9
I pick up 2
Matches remaining: 7
Your turn: 9
Cannot pick up more than 5
Your turn: 2
Matches remaining: 5
I pick up 4
Matches remaining: 1
I win!!
```

We note, in passing, that it would be useful to provide instructions for the game when it is run.

7.7 Non-uniform Distributions

So far, the random numbers we have generated have been uniformly distributed in a given range. For instance, when we generated numbers from 10 to 99, each number in that range had the same chance of being generated. Similarly, the call `random(1, 6)` will generate each of the numbers 1 to 6 with equal probability.

Now suppose we want the computer to "throw" a six-sided die. Since the computer can't physically throw the die, it has to simulate the process of throwing. What is the purpose of throwing the die? It is simply to come up with a random number from 1 to 6. As we have seen, the computer knows how to do this.

If the die is fair, then each of the faces has the same chance of showing. To simulate the throwing of such a die, all we have to do is generate random numbers uniformly distributed in the range 1 to 6. We can do this with `random(1, 6)`.

Similarly, when we toss a fair coin, heads and tails both have the same chance of showing. To simulate the tossing of such a coin on a computer, all we have to do is generate random numbers uniformly distributed in the range `1` to `2`. We can let `1` represent heads and `2` represent tails.

In general, if all possible occurrences of an event (such as throwing a fair die) are equally likely, we can use uniformly distributed random numbers to simulate the event. However, if all occurrences are not equally likely, how can we simulate such an event?

To give an example, consider a *biased* coin, which comes up heads twice as often as tails. We say that the probability of heads is 2/3 and the probability of tails is 1/3. To simulate such a coin, we generate random numbers uniformly distributed in the range `1` to `3`. If `1` or `2` occurs, we say that heads was thrown; if `3` occurs, we say that tails was thrown.

Thus, to simulate an event that has a nonuniform distribution, we convert it to one in which we can use uniformly distributed random numbers.

For another example, suppose that, for any day of a given month (June, say), we know the following, and only these conditions are possible:

```
probability of sun = 4/9
probability of rain = 3/9
probability of overcast = 2/9
```

We can simulate the weather for June as follows:

```
for each day in June
   r = random(1, 9)
   if (r <= 4) "the day is sunny"
   else if (r <= 7) "the day is rainy"
   else "the day is overcast"
endfor
```

We note, in passing, that we can assign *any* four numbers to sunny, any other three to rainy, and the remaining two to overcast.

7.7.1 Collecting Bottle Caps

The maker of a popular beverage is running a contest in which you must collect bottle caps to spell the word *mango*. It is known that in every 100 bottle caps, there are 40 *A*s, 25 *O*s, 15 *N*s, 15 *M*s, and 5 *G*s. We want to write a program to perform 20 simulations of the collection of bottle caps until we have enough caps to spell *mango*. For each simulation, we want to know how many caps were collected. We also want to know the average number of bottle caps collected per simulation.

The collection of a bottle cap is an event with nonuniform distribution. It is easier to collect an *A* than a *G*. To simulate the event, we can generate random numbers uniformly distributed in the range 1 to 100. To determine which letter was collected, we can use this:

```
c = random(1, 100)
if (c <= 40) we have an A
else if (c <= 65) we have an O
else if (c <= 80) we have an N
else if (c <=95) we have an M
else we have a G
```

In this example, if we want, we can scale everything by a factor of 5 and use the following:

```
c = random(1, 20)
if (c <= 8) we have an A
else if (c <= 13) we have an O
else if (c <= 16) we have an N
else if (c <=19) we have an M
else we have a G
```

Either version will work fine for this problem.
The gist of the algorithm for solving this problem is as follows:

```
totalCaps = 0
for sim = 1 to 20
   capsThisSim = perform one simulation
   print capsThisSim
   add capsThisSim to totalCaps
endfor
print totalCaps / 20
```

The logic for performing one simulation is as follows:

```
numCaps = 0
while (word not spelt) {
   collect a cap and determine the letter
   mark the letter collected
   add 1 to numCaps
}
return numCaps
```

We will use an array `cap[5]` to hold the status of each letter: `cap[0]` for *A*, `cap[1]` for *O*, `cap[2]` for *N*, `cap[3]` for *M*, and `cap[4]` for *G*. A value of `0` indicates that the corresponding letter has not been collected. When we collect an *N*, say, we set `cap[2]` to `1`; we do so similarly for the other letters. We have collected each letter at least once when all the elements of `cap` are `1`.

All these details are incorporated in Program P7.4.

Program P7.4

```
#include <stdio.h>
#include <stdlib.h>
#include <time.h>

#define MaxSim 20
#define MaxLetters 5

int main() {
   int capsThisSim, totalCaps = 0, doOneSim();

   srand(time(0));
   printf("\nSimulation  Caps collected\n\n");
   for (int sim = 1; sim <= MaxSim; sim++) {
      capsThisSim = doOneSim();
      printf("%6d %13d\n", sim, capsThisSim);
      totalCaps += capsThisSim;
   }
   printf("\nAverage caps per simulation: %d\n", totalCaps/MaxSim);
} //end main

int doOneSim() {
   int cap[MaxLetters], numCaps = 0, mango(int []), random(int, int);
   for (int h = 0; h < MaxLetters; h++) cap[h] = 0;
   while (!mango(cap)) {
      int c = random(1, 20);
      if (c <= 8) cap[0] = 1;
      else if (c <= 13) cap[1] = 1;
      else if (c <= 16) cap[2] = 1;
      else if (c <= 19) cap[3] = 1;
      else cap[4] = 1;
      numCaps++;
   }
   return numCaps;
} //end doOneSim
```

```
int mango(int cap[]) {
  for (int h = 0; h < MaxLetters; h++)
      if (cap[h] == 0) return 0;
   return 1;
} //end mango

int random(int m, int n) {
//returns a random integer from m to n, inclusive
   int offset = rand() / (RAND_MAX + 1.0) * (n - m + 1);
   return m + offset;
} //end random
```

When run, this program produced the following output:

```
Simulation  Caps collected
     1           10
     2           10
     3           22
     4           12
     5           36
     6            9
     7           15
     8            7
     9           11
    10           70
    11           17
    12           12
    13           27
    14           10
    15            6
    16           25
    17            8
    18            7
    19           39
    20           71
Average caps per simulation: 21
```

The results range from as few as 6 caps to as many as 71. Sometimes you get lucky, sometimes you don't. Each time the program is run, it will produce different results.

7.8 Simulation of Real-Life Problems

The computer can be used to answer certain questions about many real-life situations by using *simulation*. The process of simulation allows us to consider different solutions to a problem. This enables us to choose, with confidence, the best alternative for a given situation.

However, before the computer simulation is done, we need to collect data to enable the simulation to be as realistic as possible. For example, if we want to simulate serving customers at a bank, we would need to know (or at least estimate) the following:

- The time, *t1*, between arrivals of customers in the queue
- The time, *t2*, to serve a customer

Of course, *t1* could vary greatly. It would depend, for instance, on the time of the day; at certain times, customers arrive more frequently than at other times. Also, different customers have different needs, so *t2* would vary from one customer to the next. However, by observing the system in operation for a while, we can usually make assumptions like the following:

- *t1* varies randomly between one and five minutes.
- *t2* varies randomly between three and ten minutes.

Using these assumptions, we can do the simulation to find out how the queue length varies when there are 2, 3, 4, ..., and so on, service counters. We assume that there is one queue; the person at the head of the queue goes to whichever counter first becomes available. In practice, a bank usually assigns more counters at peak periods than at slow periods. In this case, we can do the simulation in two parts, using the assumptions that apply for each period.

These are other situations in which a similar method of simulation applies:

- *Checkout counters at supermarkets or stores*: We are normally interested in a compromise between the number of checkout counters and the average queue length. The fewer counters we have, the longer the queue will be. However, having more counters means more machines and more employees. We want to find the best compromise between the cost of operation and service to customers.
- *Gasoline stations*: How many pumps will best serve the needs of the customers?
- T*raffic lights*: What is the best timing of the lights so that the average length of the queues in all directions is kept to a minimum? In this case, we would need to gather data such as follows:
    - How often do cars arrive from direction 1 and from direction 2? The answer to this might be something like this:

      Between 5 and 15 cars arrive every minute from direction 1.

      Between 10 and 30 cars arrive every minute from direction 2.

    - How fast can cars leave in direction 1 and in direction 2? The answer might be as follows:

      20 cars can cross the intersection in direction 1 in 30 seconds.

      30 cars can cross the intersection in direction 2 in 30 seconds.

      We assume, in this simple situation, that turning is not allowed.

7.9 Simulating a Queue

Consider the situation at a bank or supermarket checkout, where customers arrive and must queue for service. Suppose there is one queue but several counters. If a counter is free, the person at the head of the queue goes to it. If all counters are busy, the customers must wait; the person at the head of the queue goes to the first available counter.

To illustrate, suppose there are two counters; we denote them by C1 and C2. To perform the simulation, we need to know the frequency with which customers arrive and the time it takes to serve a customer. Based on observation and experience, we may be able to say the following:

- The time between customer arrivals varies randomly from one to five minutes.
- The time to serve a customer varies randomly from three to ten minutes.

For the simulation to be meaningful, this data must be close to what occurs in practice. As a general rule, a simulation is only as good as the data on which it is based.

Suppose we begin at 9 a.m. We can simulate the arrival of the first ten customers by generating ten random numbers from 1 to 5, like this:

```
3 1 2 4 2 5 1 3 2 4
```

This means the first customer arrives at 9:03, the second at 9:04, the third at 9:06, the fourth at 9:10, and so on.

We can simulate the service time for these customers by generating ten random numbers from 3 to 10, like this:

```
5 8 7 6 9 4 7 4 9 6
```

This means the first customer spends five minutes at the teller, the second spends eight minutes, the third spends seven minutes, and so on.

Table 7-1 shows what happens to these ten customers.

Table 7-1. *Tracking Ten Customers*

Customer	Arrives	Start Service	Counter	Service Time	Departs	Wait Time
1	9:03	9:03	C1	5	9:08	0
2	9:04	9:04	C2	8	9:12	0
3	9:06	9:08	C1	7	9:15	2
4	9:10	9:12	C2	6	9:18	2
5	9:12	9:15	C1	9	9:24	3
6	9:17	9:18	C2	4	9:22	1
7	9:18	9:22	C2	7	9:29	4
8	9:21	9:24	C1	4	9:28	3
9	9:23	9:28	C1	9	9:37	5
10	9:27	9:29	C2	6	9:35	2

- The first customer arrives at 9:03 and goes straight to C1. His service time is five minutes, so he will leave C1 at 9:08.
- The second customer arrives at 9:04 and goes straight to C2. His service time is 8 minutes, so he will leave C2 at 9:12.

- The third customer arrives at 9:06. At this time, both C1 and C2 are busy so he must wait. C1 will be the first to become free at 9:08. This customer will begin service at 9:08. His service time is seven minutes, so he will leave C1 at 9:15. This customer had to wait in the queue for ten minutes.
- The fourth customer arrives at 9:10. At this time, both C1 and C2 are busy, so he must wait. C2 will be the first to become free at 9:12. This customer will begin service at 9:12. His service time is six minutes, so he will leave C2 at 9:18. This customer had to wait in the queue for two minutes.

And so on. Work through the rest of the table to make sure you understand how those values are obtained.

Also observe that once the tellers started serving, they had no idle time. As soon as one customer left, another was waiting to be served.

7.9.1 Programming the Simulation

We now show how to write a program to produce Table 7-1. First we observe that it is no more difficult to write the program for several counters than it is for two. Hence, we will assume that there are `n` (`n < 10`) counters.

We will use an array `depart[10]` such that `depart[c]` will hold the time at which counter `c` will next become free. We will not use `depart[0]`. If we need to handle more than nine counters, we just need to increase the size of `depart`.

Suppose the customer at the head of the queue arrives at `arriveTime`. He will go to the first free counter. Counter `c` is free if `arriveTime` is greater than or equal to `depart[c]`. If no counter is free, he must wait. He will go to the counter with the lowest value in the array `depart`; suppose this is `depart[m]`. He will begin service at a time that is the later of `arriveTime` and `depart[m]`.

The program begins by asking for the number of counters and the number of customers to be simulated. The simulation starts from time `0`, and all times are relative to this. The details are shown in Program P7.5.

Program P7.5

```
#include <stdio.h>
#include <stdlib.h>
#include <time.h>

#define MaxCounters 9

int main() {
   int  random(int, int), smallest(int[], int, int), max(int, int);
   int depart[MaxCounters + 1];
   int m, n, numCust, arriveTime, startServe, serveTime, waitTime;

   printf("\nHow many counters? ");
   scanf("%d", &n);
   printf("\nHow many customers? ");
   scanf("%d", &numCust);

   for (int c = 1; c <= n; c++) depart[c] = 0;
   srand(time(0));
   printf("\n                       Start        Service        Wait\n");
   printf("Customer Arrives Service Counter  Time   Departs Time\n\n");
   arriveTime = 0;
   for (int c = 1; c <= numCust; c++) {
      arriveTime += random(1, 5);
```

```
      m = smallest(depart, 1, n);
      startServe = max(arriveTime, depart[m]);
      serveTime = random(3, 10);
      depart[m] = startServe + serveTime;
      waitTime = startServe - arriveTime;
      printf("%5d %8d %7d %6d %7d %8d %5d\n",
         c, arriveTime, startServe, m, serveTime, depart[m], waitTime);
   } //end for
} //end main

int smallest(int list[], int lo, int hi) {
//returns the subscript of the smallest value in list
   int k = lo;
   for (int h = lo + 1; h <= hi; h++)
      if (list[h] < list[k]) k = h;
   return k;
} //end smallest

int max(int a, int b) {
   if (a > b) return a;
   return b;
} //end max

int random(int m, int n) {
//returns a random integer from m to n, inclusive
   int offset = rand() / (RAND_MAX + 1.0) * (n - m + 1);
   return m + offset;
} //end random
```

A sample run of Program P7.5 is shown here:

```
How many counters? 2

How many customers? 10

                  Start            Service          Wait
Customer Arrives Service Counter  Time    Departs  Time

    1        3       3      1        8       11     0
    2        7       7      2        9       16     0
    3       10      11      1        9       20     1
    4       11      16      2        4       20     5
    5       14      20      1        5       25     6
    6       19      20      2        9       29     1
    7       23      25      1        7       32     2
    8       26      29      2        8       37     3
    9       29      32      1        7       39     3
   10       33      37      2        6       43     4
```

As you can see, the waiting time is reasonably short. However, if you run the simulation with 25 customers, you will see that the waiting time increases appreciably. What if we added another counter? With simulation, it's easy to test the effect of this without actually having to buy another machine or hire another employee.

In this case, all we have to do is enter 3 and 25 for the number of counters and customers, respectively. When we do, we will find that there is very little waiting time. We urge you to experiment with different data—counters, customers, arrival times, and service times—to see what happens.

7.10 Estimating Numerical Values Using Random Numbers

We have seen how random numbers can be used to play games and simulate real-life situations. A less obvious use is to estimate numerical values that may be difficult or cumbersome to calculate. We will show how to use random numbers to estimate the square root of a number and π (pi).

7.10.1 Estimating $\sqrt{5}$

We use random numbers to estimate the square root of 5 based on the following:

- It is between 2 and 3.
- x is less than $\sqrt{5}$ if x^2 is less than 5.
- Random numbers, with fractions, between 2 and 3 are generated. A count is kept of those numbers that are less than $\sqrt{5}$.
- Let `maxCount` be the total number of random numbers generated between 2 and 3. The user will supply `maxCount`.
- Let `amountLess` be the count of those numbers less than $\sqrt{5}$.
- An approximation to $\sqrt{5}$ is given by $2+\frac{\text{amountLess}}{\text{maxCount}}$.

To understand the idea behind the method, consider the line segment between 2 and 3 and let the point `r` represent the square root of 5.

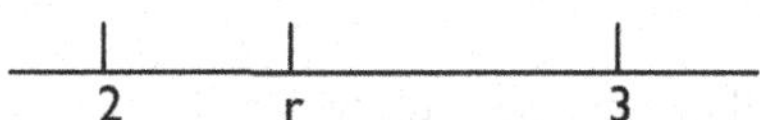

If we imagine the line between 2 and 3 completely covered with dots, we would expect that the number of dots between 2 and `r` would be proportional to the length of that segment. In general, the number of dots falling on any line segment would be proportional to the length of that segment—the longer the segment, the more dots will fall on it.

Now, each random number between 2 and 3 represents a dot on that line. We would expect that the more numbers we use, the more accurate would be our statement that the length of the line between 2 and `r` is proportional to the number of numbers falling on it and, hence, the more accurate our estimate.

Program P7.6 calculates an estimate for $\sqrt{5}$ based on the above explanation.

When run with 1,000 numbers, this program gave 2.234 as the square root of 5. The value of $\sqrt{5}$ is 2.236 to three decimal places.

Program P7.6

```
#include <stdio.h>
#include <stdlib.h>
#include <time.h>
```

```
int main() {
   int maxCount, amountLess;
   double r;

   printf("\nHow many numbers to use? ");
   scanf("%d", &maxCount);

   srand(time(0));
   amountLess = 0;
   for (int h = 1; h <= maxCount; h++) {
      r = 2 + rand() / (RAND_MAX + 1.0);
      if (r * r < 5) ++amountLess;
   }
   printf("\nAn approximation to the square root of 5 is %5.3f\n",
            2 + (double) amountLess / maxCount);
} //end main
```

7.10.2 Estimating π

Consider Figure 7-1, which shows a circle within a square.

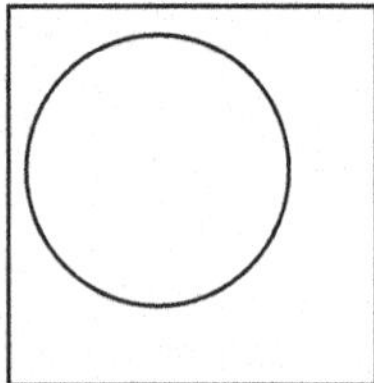

Figure 7-1. *Circle within a square*

If you close your eyes and keep stabbing at the diagram repeatedly with a pencil, you may end up with something like Figure 7-2 (considering only the dots that fall within the diagram).

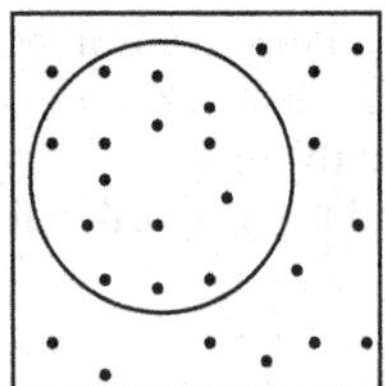

Figure 7-2. *Circle within a square after stabbing with pencil*

Note that some dots fall inside the circle and some fall outside the circle. If the dots were made "at random," it seems reasonable to expect that the number of dots inside the circle is proportional to the area of the circle—the larger the circle, the more dots will fall inside it.

Based on this, we have the following approximation:

$$\frac{\textit{area of circle}}{\textit{area of square}} = \frac{\textit{number of dots inside circle}}{\textit{number of dots inside square}}$$

Note that the number of dots inside the square also includes those inside the circle. If we imagine the entire square filled with dots, then the previous approximation will be quite accurate. We now show how to use this idea to estimate π.

Consider Figure 7-3.

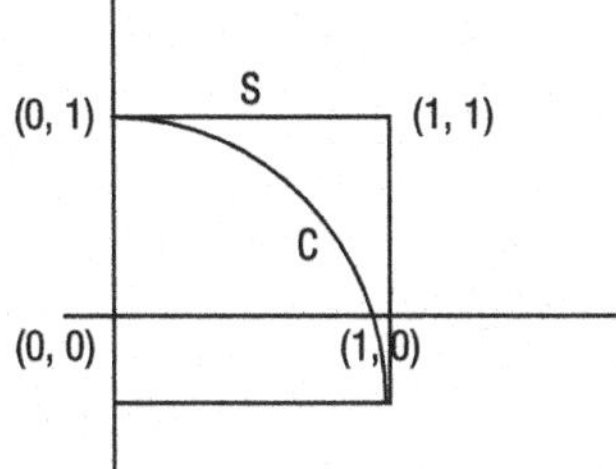

Figure 7-3. *Quarter circle and a square*

C is a quarter circle of radius 1; S is a square of side 1.

Area of C= $\frac{\pi}{4}$ Area of S = 1.

A point (x, y) within C satisfies $x^2 + y^2 \le 1, x \ge 0, y \ge 0$.

A point (x, y) within S satisfies $0 \le x \le 1, 0 \le y \le 1$.

Suppose we generate two random fractions, that is, two values between 0 and 1; call these values *x* and *y*.

Since $0 \le x \le 1$ and $0 \le y \le 1$, it follows that the point (*x*, *y*) lies within S. This point will also lie within C if $x^2 + y^2 \le 1$.

If we generate *n* pairs of random fractions, we have, in fact, generated *n* points within S. For each of these points, we can determine whether the point lies with C. Suppose *m* of these *n* points fall within C. From our discussion earlier, we can assume that the following approximation holds:

$$\frac{\textit{area of C}}{\textit{area of S}} = \frac{m}{n}$$

The area of C is $\frac{\pi}{4}$ and the area of S is 1. So, we have this:

$$\frac{\pi}{4} = \frac{m}{n}$$

Hence: $\pi = \frac{4m}{n}$.

Based on this, we write Program P7.7 to estimate π.

Program P7.7

```
#include <stdio.h>
#include <stdlib.h>

int main() {
   int inS, inC = 0;
   double x, y;

   printf("\nHow many numbers to use? ");
   scanf("%d", &inS);

   srand(time(0));
   for (int h = 1; h <= inS; h++) {
      x = rand() / (RAND_MAX + 1.0);
      y = rand() / (RAND_MAX + 1.0);
      if (x * x + y * y <= 1) inC++;
   }
   printf("\nAn approximation to pi is %5.3f\n", 4.0 * inC / inS);
}
```

The value of π to three decimal places is 3.142. When run with 1,000 numbers, this program gave 3.132 as an approximation to π. When run with 2,000 numbers, it gave 3.140 as the approximation.

EXERCISES 7

1. Write a program to request two numbers, *m* and *n*, and print 25 random numbers from *m* to *n*.
2. Explain what you need to do so that the program in exercise 1 will produce different numbers each time it is run for the same values of *m* and *n*.
3. Modify Program P7.1 to play several games in one run. After each game, ask the user if he wants to play another.
4. Modify Program P7.2 to incorporate a scoring system. For example, for two attempts at a problem, you can give 2 points for a correct answer on the first attempt and 1 point for a correct answer on the second attempt.
5. Modify Program P7.2 to give a user problems in subtraction.
6. Modify Program P7.2 to give a user problems in multiplication.
7. Rewrite Program P7.2 so that it presents the user with a menu that allows her to choose what kinds of problems she gets (addition, subtraction, or multiplication).
8. Write a program to simulate 1,000 throws of a die and determine the number of 1s, 2s, 3s, 4s, 5s, and 6s that show. Write the program (a) without using an array and (b) using an array.
9. Write a program to simulate the weather for 60 days using the probabilities in Section 7.7.
10. In the manufacture of electric bulbs, the probability that a bulb is defective is 0.01. Simulate the manufacture of 5,000 bulbs, indicating how many are defective.

11. A die is weighted such that 1s and 5s come up twice as often as any other number. Simulate 1,000 throws of this die, indicating the frequency with which each number occurs.

12. Modify Program P7.5 to calculate the average waiting time for customers and the total idle time for each counter.

13. One-zero is a game that can be played among several players using a six-sided die. On his turn, a player can throw the die as many times as he wants. His score for that turn is the sum of the numbers he throws *provided he does not throw* a 1. If he throws a 1, his score is 0. Suppose a player decides to adopt the strategy of ending his turn after seven throws. (Of course, if he throws a 1 before the seventh throw, he must end his turn.) Write a program to play ten turns using this strategy. For each turn, print the score obtained. Also, print the average score for the ten turns.

    Generalize the program to request values for `numTurns` and `maxThrowsPerTurn` and print the results as shown earlier.

14. Write a program to simulate the game of *Snakes and Ladders*. The board consists of 100 squares. Snakes and ladders are input as ordered pairs of numbers, *m* and *n*. For example, the pair `17 64` means that there is a ladder from 17 to 64, and the pair `99 28` means that there is a snake from 99 to 28.

    Simulate the playing of 20 games, each game lasting a maximum of 100 moves. Print the number of games that were completed in the 100 moves and the average number of moves per game for completed games.

15. Write a program to play a modified game of Nim (in Section 7.6) in which there are two heaps of matches and a player, on his turn, may choose from either one. However, in this case, a player *wins* if he picks up the last match.

16. Using the traffic lights data Section 7.9, write a program to simulate the situation at the lights for a 30-minute period. Print the number of cars in each queue each time the light changes.

17. Write a program to estimate the square root of 59.

18. Write a program to read a positive integer *n* and estimate the square root of *n*.

19. Write a program to read a positive integer *n* and estimate the cube root of *n*.

20. Write a program to simulate the collection of bottle caps to spell *apple*. In every 100 caps, *A* and *E* occur 40 times each, and *P* and *L* occur 10 times each. Do 50 simulations and print the average number of caps per simulation.

21. The Lotto requires people to pick seven numbers from the numbers 1 to 40. Write a program to randomly generate and print five sets of seven numbers each (one set per line). No number is to be repeated in any of the sets; that is, exactly 35 of the 40 numbers must be used. If a number (*p*, say) is generated that has been used already, the first unused number after *p* is used. (Assume that 1 follows 40.) For example, if 15 is generated but has been used already, 16 is tried, but if this has been used, 17 is tried, and so on, until an unused number is found.

22. A function $f(x)$ is defined for $0 \leq x \leq 1$, and such that $0 \leq f(x) < 1$ for all $0 \leq x < 1$. Write a program to estimate the integral of $f(x)$ from 0 to 1. Hint: estimate the area under the curve by generating points (x, y), $0 \leq x < 1$, $0 \leq y < 1$.

23. A gambler pays $5 to play the following game. He throws two six-sided dice. If the sum of the two numbers thrown is even, he loses his bet. If the sum is odd, he draws a card from a standard pack of 52 playing cards. If he draws an ace, 3, 5, 7 or 9, he is paid the value of the card plus $5 (an ace counts as 1). If he draws any other card, he loses. Write a program to simulate the playing of 20 games and print the average amount won by the gambler per game.

CHAPTER 8

Working with Files

In this chapter, we will explain the following:

- How to read data from a file
- How to send output to a file
- The difference between text files and binary files
- The difference between internal and external file names
- `fopen` and `fclose`
- `getc` and `putc`
- `feof` and `ferror`
- `fgets` and `fputs`
- How to write a program to compare two text files
- How to perform input/output with binary files
- How to work with a binary file of records
- What are random access files
- How to create and retrieve records from random access files
- What are indexed files
- How to update a random access file using an index

8.1 Reading Data from a File

Almost anything we need to store on a computer must be stored in a file. We use text files for storing the kinds of documents we create with a text editor or word processor. We use binary files for storing photographic image files, sound files, video files, and files of "records." In this chapter, we show how to create and manipulate text and binary files. We also explain how to work with that most versatile kind of file—a random access file.

So far, most of our programs have read data from the standard input stream (the keyboard) and written output to the standard output stream (the screen). A few have read from a file and sent output to a file. We now explain file input/output in more detail.

Suppose we want to be able to read data from the file `input.txt`. The first thing we need to do is declare an identifier called a *file pointer*. This can be done with this statement:

```
FILE * in;    // read as "file pointer in"
```

The word `FILE` must be spelled as shown, with all uppercase letters. The spaces before and after * may be omitted. So, you could write `FILE* in`, `FILE *in`, or even `FILE*in`. We have used the identifier `in`; any other will do, such as `inf`, `infile`, `inputFile`, or `payData`.

The second thing we must do is associate the file pointer `in` with the file `input.txt` and tell C we will be reading data from the file. This is done using the function `fopen`, as follows:

```
in = fopen("input.txt", "r");
```

This says to "open the file `input.txt` for reading" (`"r"` indicates reading). We will use `"w"` if we want a file to be opened for writing, that is, to receive output. It is usual to combine the previous two statements into one, like this:

```
FILE * in = fopen("input.txt", "r");
```

Once this is done, a data pointer will be positioned at the beginning of the file. This pointer indicates the position in the file from which C will start looking for the next data item. As items are read, the pointer moves through the file. You can imagine it always being positioned just after the last item read.

We can now write statements that will read data from the file. We will see how shortly.

It is up to us to ensure that the file exists and contains the appropriate data. If not, we will get an error message such as "File not found." If we need to, we can specify the *path* to the file.

Suppose the file is located at `C:\testdata\input.txt`.

We specify that we will be reading data from the file with the following:

```
FILE * in = fopen("C:\\testdata\\input.txt", "r");
```

Recall that the escape sequence \\ is used to represent \ within a string.

8.1.1 fscanf

Once the file has been opened for reading, we use the statement (more precisely, the function) `fscanf` to read data from the file. It is used in the same way as `scanf` except that the first argument is the file pointer `in`. For example, if `num` is `int`, the following statement will read an integer from the file `input.txt` (the one associated with `in`) and store it in `num`:

```
fscanf(in, "%d", &num);
```

Note that the argument is the file pointer and not the name of the file. When we have finished reading data from the file, we should close it. This is done with `fclose`, as follows:

```
fclose(in);
```

There is one argument, the file pointer (not the name of the file). This statement breaks the association of the file pointer `in` with the file `input.txt`. If we need to, we could now link the identifier `in` with another file (`payData.txt`, say) using this:

```
in = fopen("payData.txt", "r");
```

Note that we do not repeat the `FILE *` part of the declaration, since `in` has already been declared as `FILE *`. Subsequent `fscanf(in, ...)` statements will read data from the file `payData.txt`.

8.1.2 Finding the Average of Some Numbers in a File

To illustrate the use of fscanf, let's write Program P8.1 to read several numbers from a file and find their average. Suppose the file is called input.txt and contains several positive integers with 0 indicating the end; here's an example:

```
24 13 55 32 19 0
```

Program P8.1 shows how to define the file as the place from which the data will be read and how to find the average.

Program P8.1

```
//read numbers from a file and find their average; 0 ends the data
#include <stdio.h>
int main() {
   FILE * in = fopen("input.txt", "r");
   int num, sum = 0, n = 0;
   fscanf(in, "%d", &num);
   while (num != 0) {
      n = n + 1;
      sum = sum + num;
      fscanf(in, "%d", &num);
   }
   if (n == 0) printf("\nNo numbers entered\n");
   else {
      printf("\n%d numbers were entered\n", n);
      printf("The sum is %d\n", sum);
      printf("The average is %3.2f\n", (double) sum/n);
   }
   fclose(in);
} //end main
```

If the data file contains this:

```
24 13 55 32 19 0
```

the output will be:

```
5 numbers were supplied
The sum is 143
The average is 28.60
```

The numbers in the file could be supplied in "free format"—any amount could be put on a line. For example, the sample data could have been typed on one line as shown earlier or as follows:

```
24   13
55 32
          19 0
```

or

```
24   13
55
  32 19
0
```

or

```
24
13
55
32
19
0
```

When you try to run this program, it may not run properly because it cannot find the file `input.txt`. This may be because the compiler is looking for the file in the wrong place. Some compilers expect to find the file in the same folder/directory as the program file. Others expect to find it in the same folder/directory as the compiler.

Try placing `input.txt` in each of these folders, in turn, and run the program. If this does not work, then you will need to specify the complete path to the file in the `fopen` statement. For example, if the file is in the folder `data`, which is in the folder `CS10E`, which is on the `C:` drive, you will need to use this statement:

```
FILE * in = fopen("C:\\CS10E\\data\\input.txt", "r");
```

8.2 Sending Output to a File

We have just seen how to read data from a file. We now show you how you can send output to a file.

This is important because when we send output to the screen, it is lost when we exit the program or when we switch off the computer. If we need to save our output, we must write it to a file. Then the output is available as long as we want to keep the file.

The process is similar to reading from a file. We must declare a file pointer (we will use `out`) and associate it with the actual file (`output.txt`, say) using `fopen`. This can be done with the following:

```
FILE * out = fopen("output.txt", "w");
```

This says to "open the file `output.txt` for writing" (`"w"` indicates writing). When this statement is executed, the file `output.txt` is created if it does not already exist. If it exists, its contents are destroyed. In other words, whatever you write to the file will *replace* its original contents. Be careful that you do not open for writing a file whose contents you want to keep. In addition to "r" and **"w"**, there are other *modes* in which a file may be opened. These modes are discussed in Section 8.5.

8.2.1 fprintf

Once the file has been opened for writing, we use the statement (more precisely, the function) `fprintf` to send output to the file. It is used in the same way as `printf` except that the first argument is the file pointer `out`. For example, if `sum` is `int` with value `143`, the statement:

```
fprintf(out, "The sum is %d\n", sum);
```

will write this to the file output.txt:

```
The sum is 143
```

Note that the first argument to fprintf is the file pointer and not the name of the file.

When we have finished writing output to the file, we must close it. This is especially important for output files; because of the way some operating systems are configured,[1] this is the only way to ensure that all output is sent to the file. We close the file with fclose, as follows:

```
fclose(out);
```

There is one argument, the file pointer (not the name of the file). This statement breaks the association of the file pointer out with the file output.txt. If we need to, we could now link the identifier out with another file (payroll.txt, say) using the following:

```
out = fopen("payroll.txt", "w");
```

Note that we do not repeat the FILE * part of the declaration, since out has already been declared as FILE *. Subsequent fprintf(out, ...) statements will send output to the file payroll.txt.

For example, in Program P8.1, we can send the output to the file output.txt by replacing the printf statements with fprintf, like this:

```
if (n == 0) fprintf(out, "No numbers entered\n");
else {
   fprintf(out, "%d numbers were entered\n", n);
   fprintf(out, "The sum is %d\n", sum);
   fprintf(out, "The average is %3.2f\n", (double) sum/n);
}
```

As explained earlier, you can, if you want, specify the complete path to your file in the fopen statement. For instance, if you want to send the output to a file output.txt in the folder results on the C: drive, you can use this:

```
FILE * out = fopen("c:\\results\\output.txt", "w");
```

8.3 Text and Binary Files

A *text* file is a sequence of characters organized into lines. Conceptually, we think of each line as being terminated by a newline character. However, depending on the host environment, certain character translations may occur. For example, if we wrote the newline character \n to a file, it could be translated into two characters—a carriage return and a line-feed character.

Thus, there is not necessarily a one-to-one correspondence between characters written and those stored on an external device. Similarly, there may not be a one-to-one correspondence between the number of characters stored in a file and the number read.

A *binary* file is simply a sequence of bytes, with *no* character translations occurring on input or output. Thus, there *is* a one-to-one correspondence between what is read or written and what is stored in the file.

Apart from possible character translations, there are other differences between text and binary files. To illustrate, if an integer is stored in 2 bytes (16 bits), the number 3371 is stored as 00001101 00101011.

[1]For instance, they send output to a temporary buffer in memory, and only when the buffer is full is it sent to the file. If you do not close the file, some output may be left in the buffer and never sent to the file.

If we were to write this number to a text file, it would be written as the character '3', followed by the character '3', followed by '7', followed by '1', occupying 4 bytes in all. However, we could simply write the 2 bytes as is to a binary file.

Even though we could still think of them as a sequence of two character, the values they contain may not represent any valid characters. In this case, the decimal values of the 2 bytes are 13 and 43, which, interpreted as two ASCII characters, are the carriage return character (CR) and '+'.

Another way to look at it is that, in general, each byte in a text file contains a human-readable character, whereas, in general, each byte in a binary file contains an arbitrary bit pattern. Binary files are important for writing data directly from its internal representation to an external device, usually a disk file.

The standard input and output are considered text files. A disk file may be created as a text file or as a binary file. We will see how to do so shortly.

8.4 Internal vs. External File Name

The usual way of using a computer is via its operating system. We normally create and edit files using a word processor or a text file editor. When we create a file, we give it a name that we use whenever we need to do anything with the file. This is the name by which the file is known to the operating system.

We will refer to such a name as an *external* file name. (The term *external* is used here to mean "external to a C program.") When we are writing a program, we may want to specify, say, the reading of data from a file. The program will need to use a file name, but for several reasons this name should not be an external file name. The major reasons are as follows:

- The file to be read may not have been created as yet.
- If the external name is tied to the program, the program will be able to read a file with that name only. If the data is in a file with a different name, either the program will have to be changed or the file renamed.
- The program will be less portable since different operating systems have different file-naming conventions. A valid external file name on one system may be invalid on another one.

For these reasons, a C program uses an *internal* file name—this is the file pointer referred to earlier. For instance, when we write the following, we associate the internal name, `in`, with the external file, `input.txt`:

```
FILE * in = fopen("input.txt", "r");
```

This is the only statement that mentions the external file name. The rest of the program is written in terms of `in`. Of course, we can be even more flexible and write this:

```
FILE * in = fopen(fileName, "r");
```

When the program is run, we supply the name of the file in `fileName`, like this:

```
printf("Enter file name: ");
gets(fileName);
```

In the next few sections, we discuss some of the common functions needed for working with files.

8.5 fopen and fclose

So far, we've seen how to use fopen and fclose in simple situations. In this section, we take a closer look at these functions.

The standard function fopen returns a pointer to a FILE, and its prototype is declared in stdio.h as follows:

```
FILE *fopen(char name[], char mode[]);
```

or

```
FILE *fopen(char *name, char *mode);
```

or

```
FILE *fopen(char *, char *);
```

Both parameters are strings (or, more accurately, character pointers). The first specifies an external file name, and the second specifies the manner in which the file is to be used, for example, whether text or binary or whether for reading or writing. The valid modes are as follows:

- "r":open text file for reading. The file must exist.
- "w": create text file for writing. If the file exists, its contents are destroyed; otherwise, it is created, if possible.
- "a": open text file for appending (writing at the end). If the file does not exist, it is created, if possible; some systems may report error.
- "r+": open text file for both reading and writing. The file must exist.
- "w+": create text file for both reading and writing. If the file exists, its contents are destroyed; otherwise, it is created, if possible.
- "a+": open text file for reading and appending. If the file exists, its contents are retained. If the file does not exist, it is created, if possible; some systems may report an error.

A file opened for reading ("r" or "r+") must exist. If it doesn't, then fopen returns NULL. As indicated earlier, certain modes (for example, "w" or "a") require that a file be created. If it cannot be created (for example, the user may have exceeded the allotted disk space or the disk may be write-protected), then fopen returns NULL. If the external file exists, then opening it for writing causes the old contents to be destroyed.

If a file is opened with "a" or "a+", all write operations occur at the end of the file. This holds even if the file pointer is repositioned with fseek or rewind (Section 8.10.1). When a write operation is about to occur, the file pointer is positioned at the end of the file. This ensures that existing data cannot be overwritten.

When "b" is added to the previous modes, the files are treated as binary, rather than text. Thus, the following are also valid modes:

- "rb": open binary file for reading. The file must exist.
- "wb": create binary file for writing. If the file exists, its contents are destroyed; otherwise, it is created, if possible.
- "ab": open binary file for appending (writing at the end). If the file does not exist, it is created, if possible; some systems may report an error.
- "rb+": open binary file for both reading and writing. The file must exist.

- "wb+": create binary file for both reading and writing. If the file exists, its contents are destroyed; otherwise, it is created, if possible.
- "ab+": open binary file for reading and appending. If the file exists, its contents are retained. If the file does not exist, it is created, if possible; some systems may report an error.

Observe that the basic modes are reading ("r"), writing ("w"), and appending ("a"). Adding "+" allows both reading and writing, and adding "b" specifies that the file is to be treated as a binary file. The modes "rb+", "wb+", and "ab+" could also be written as "r+b", "w+b", and "a+b", respectively.

Consider this statement:

```
FILE *inPay = fopen("payrollNov.txt", "r");
```

This says to open the external file payrollNov.txt for reading. If such a file does not exist, an error results, and fopen returns NULL. If the file exists, then fopen returns the address of the place in memory where information about the file would be kept.

In the example, this address is assigned to inPay, thus establishing a connection between the external file name payrollNov.txt and the internal name inPay. Subsequent accesses to the external file are done via the internal name only. Once the file has been opened, we can read data from it using fscanf, say. For example, the following statement says to read values for name, hours, and rate from the file associated with inPay:

```
fscanf(inPay, "%s %f %f", name, &hours, &rate);
```

We use fscanf in the same way as scanf, except that the first argument is now a file pointer.

When we are finished using the file, we must close it. This is done via the standard function fclose. The previous file may be closed with the following:

```
fclose(inPay);
```

In the example, this statement severs the association between the internal name inPay and the external file payrollNov.txt. If required, the name inPay can now be used with another external file.

It is important to close all files before your program terminates. Failure to do so could result in output being lost or a file becoming corrupted.

As used earlier, the name of the external file payrollNov.txt is tied to the program, since it is used in the fopen statement. If the data to be processed is in another file, such as payrollDec.txt, then the statement to open the file must be changed to the following:

```
FILE *inPay = fopen("payrollDec.txt", "r");
```

Or, the name of the file must be changed to payrollNov.txt, which may not be desirable.

A more flexible approach is to let the user supply the name of the external file at run time. For instance, if payFile is an array of characters large enough to hold the name of the file, then we can use this:

```
printf("Enter payroll data file name: ");
gets(payFile);
inPay = fopen(payFile, "r");
```

Just in case the user types the file name incorrectly or forgot to create the file, we can use the fact that fopen will return NULL to check for this, as follows:

```
do {
   printf("Enter payroll data file name: ");
   gets(payFile);
   inPay = fopen(payFile, "r");
   if (inPay == NULL) printf("File does not exist or is not available\n");
} while (inPay == NULL);
```

Now, exit from the `do...while` takes place only when an existing file name is entered. As usual, the assignment and test of `inPay` (against `NULL`) can be done in one statement.

```
if ((inPay = fopen(payFile, "r")) == NULL) printf("File does not exist\n");
```

To pursue the example, suppose we want to write the payroll report onto an external file called `payReportNov.txt`. Suppose `outPay` is declared as follows:

```
FILE *outPay;
```

Then the following statement will associate the internal name `outPay` with the file `payReportNov.txt`:

```
outPay = fopen("payReportNov.txt", "w");
```

Output can then be sent to the file using `fprintf`, say, as follows:

```
fprintf(outPay, "Name: %s,  Net pay: $%7.2f\n", name, salary);
```

`fprintf` is identical to `printf`, except that the first argument is now a file pointer, indicating where the output is to be sent.

As shown earlier, it is best to let the user supply the name of the file at run time and to use a character array variable as the first argument to `fopen`.

8.6 getc and putc

Reading and writing characters one at a time is basic to many C programs. We have used `getchar()` to read a character from the standard input and have used `putchar()` to send a character to the standard output.

To read a character from a named file, we use `getc`, as follows, where `filePtr` is the pointer to the file from which characters are being read:

```
int ch = getc(filePtr);
```

The integer value of the next character is returned. On end-of-file, `EOF` (defined in `stdio.h`) is returned. Since `EOF` must be distinguishable from any possible character that *can* be returned, it cannot be the value of any character. The value of `EOF` is an integer (usually 0), which must not be the value of any character. For this reason, `getc` returns an `int` rather than `char`.

To write a character to a file, we can use `putc`, as follows:

```
putc(ch, filePtr);
```

Note that the file pointer is the *second* argument to `putc`.

In C, the file pointers `stdin` and `stdout` are predefined to point to the standard input and output, respectively. Thus, `getchar()` is equivalent to `getc(stdin)` and `putchar(ch)` is equivalent to `putc(ch, stdout)`.

8.7 feof and ferror

To keep our programs simple, we have not worried too much about errors that can arise on input/output. However, while we hope that such errors will not occur, the possibility is very real, and we now discuss the topic in a bit more detail.

When data is being read from a file, several possible conditions can arise.

- The data could be read successfully.
- An attempt may be made to read beyond the end of the file.
- A read error could occur; for example, the disk may be damaged.

The functions that read data return EOF if an attempt has been made to read beyond the end of the file. However, many of these functions also return EOF if an error is encountered (for example, trying to write to a file opened for reading only). How can a program determine which condition obtained?

The function feof can be used to check the end-of-file condition on a file. Its prototype is:

```
int feof(FILE *fp);
```

The argument to feof is a file pointer (fp, say). It returns nonzero (true) if the end of the file linked to fp has been reached; otherwise, it returns zero (false). For example, to copy a file (associated with fp) to the standard output, we could use this:

```
while (!feof(fp)) putchar(getc(fp));
```

However, there is a subtle danger here. If, for whatever reason, the file becomes unavailable, feof will not return true, and the program will be stuck in the loop. As a result, it is better to write the following (ch is an int):

```
while ((ch = getc(fp)) != EOF) putchar(ch);
```

Now, if a file error is encountered, getc will return EOF, and the loop will terminate.

Testing for end-of-file with EOF is fine for *text* files. This is because C guarantees that the (integer) value of EOF is different from that of any other character. Thus, EOF could be returned only when the end of the file is actually reached.

Unfortunately, the same does not hold for binary files. This is because a binary file consists of arbitrary bit patterns (as opposed to bit patterns representing characters). Thus, it is entirely possible that the value of an arbitrary byte could be the same as the value of EOF. Testing such a byte against EOF would lead to the erroneous conclusion that the end of the file had been reached. For binary files, therefore, the safest way to test for end-of-file is to use the function feof.

The function ferror accepts a file pointer (fp, say) and returns nonzero (true) if an error occurred during the last file operation attempted; otherwise, it returns zero (false). Its prototype is as follows:

```
int ferror(FILE *fp);
```

and can be used as in the following example (chFile is a FILE *):

```
fscanf(chFile, "%d %f", &age, &allowance); // int age; float allowance;
if (ferror(chFile)) fprintf(stderr, "Error reading age, allowance\n");
```

Since the error indication (for a given file) could be set by any file operation, it is important to test for it immediately after a given operation. If this is not done, an error may be lost. For example, suppose two scanfs are done and then ferror is called. If it returns true, we would not know whether the error was due to the first or the second call to scanf.

8.8 fgets and fputs

These are two standard functions that can be used with arbitrary files: fgets is used to read an entire string (up to, and including, the next newline), and fputs is used to output a string that may or may not contain a newline.

The prototype of fgets is as follows:

```
char *fgets(char line[], int max, FILE *infile);
```

The character array line must have at least max elements. Characters are read from infile and stored in line until newline is encountered or max-1 characters have been stored, whichever comes first. If newline is encountered and max-1 characters have not yet been stored, \n is added to line. In either case, line is terminated with \0.

If at least one character (other than \0) is stored in line, fgets returns line (which is, in effect, a pointer to the characters stored). If end-of-file is encountered and no characters have been stored in line, fgets returns NULL. If an error occurs, fgets also returns NULL. Since NULL is returned for both end-of-file and error conditions, the functions feof and/or ferror must be used to determine which one occurred. Note that the file pointer is the *last* argument, not the first as in fscanf or fprintf.

fgets is useful for reading strings that may contain blanks or tabs. Recall that the %s option of fscanf cannot be used to read a string containing blanks or tabs.

The prototype for fputs is as follows:

```
int fputs(char strng[], FILE *outFile);
```

strng contains the string (properly terminated by \0) to be written to outFile. It may contain *any* characters, including newlines. The terminating \0 is not written. If successful, fputs returns a non-negative value; if unsuccessful, it returns EOF.

8.8.1 Example: Comparing Two Files

This example uses fgets to compare two files, printing the first lines, if any, where they differ.

Program P8.2 reads lines from both files (using fgets) until a mismatch is found or one of the files comes to an end. It also illustrates one way of verifying the file name that a user enters, using the function getFileName.

Program P8.2

```
#include <stdio.h>
#include <string.h>
#define MaxName 20
#define MaxLine 101
int main() {
   char name1[MaxName], name2[MaxName];
   char line1[MaxLine], line2[MaxLine];
   FILE *file1, *file2, *getFileName(char *, char *);
   char *eof1, *eof2;

   int lineNum = 0;
   file1 = getFileName("First file?", name1);
   file2 = getFileName("Second file?", name2);
```

```
    while (((eof1 = fgets(line1, MaxLine, file1)) != NULL) &&
             ((eof2 = fgets(line2, MaxLine, file2)) != NULL) &&
             (strcmp(line1, line2) == 0))
       lineNum++;
    // at this stage, linenum is the number of matching lines found
    if (eof1 == NULL) //first file ended
       if (fgets(line2, MaxLine, file2) == NULL) //second also ended
          printf("\nFiles are identical\n\n");
       else    //first file ended, second file not ended
          printf("\n%s, with %d line(s), is a subset of %s\n", name1, lineNum, name2);
    else if (eof2 == NULL)  //first file not ended, second file ended
       printf("\n%s, with %d line(s), is a subset of %s\n", name2, lineNum, name1);
    else {  // mismatch found
       printf("\nThe files differ at line %d\n", ++lineNum);
       printf("The lines are \n%s and \n%s\n", line1, line2);
    }
    fclose(file1);
    fclose(file2);
 } //end main

 FILE * getFileName(char *prompt, char *name) {
 //store the filename in 'name' and return the pointer to the file
    FILE *filePtr;
    do {
       printf("%s ", prompt); gets(name);
       if ((filePtr = fopen(name, "r")) == NULL)
          printf("File does not exist or access denied\n");
    } while (filePtr == NULL);
    return filePtr;
 } //end getFileName
```

If the first file contains this:

```
one and one are two
two and two are four
three and three are six
four and four are eight
five and five are ten
six and six are twelve
```

and the second file contains this:

```
one and one are two
two and two are four
three and three are six
four and four are eight
this is the fifth line
six and six are twelve
```

the program will print this:

```
The files differ at line 5
The lines are
five and five are ten
 and
this is the fifth line
```

The following points are for noting:

- The maximum length of the file name catered for is `MaxName-1`.
- The maximum line length (including `\n`) catered for is `MaxLine-1`.
- The file name is read using `gets`, so it may contain blanks. With `gets`, `\n` is never part of the string returned.
- In the interest of brevity and simplicity, we assume that no errors in reading the files occur—the files are read until one or the other comes to an end. To cater for errors, we could use `ferror` to determine whether a reading error caused `fgets` to return `NULL`. Alternatively, we could use `feof` to determine whether the end of file was actually reached.

8.9 Input/Output for Binary File

As mentioned earlier, a binary file contains data in a form that corresponds exactly with the internal representation of the data. For example, if a `float` variable occupies 4 bytes of memory, writing it to a binary file simply involves making an exact copy of the 4 bytes. On the other hand, writing it to a text file causes it to be converted to character form, and the characters obtained are stored in the file.

Normally, a binary file can be created only from within a program, and its contents can be read only by a program. Listing a binary file, for example, produces only "garbage" and, sometimes, generates an error. Compare a text file that can be created by typing into it and whose contents can be listed and read by a human. However, a binary file has the following advantages:

- Data can be transferred to and from a binary file much faster than for a text file since no data conversions are necessary; the data is read and written as is.
- The values of data types such as arrays and structures can be written to a binary file. For a text file, individual elements must be written.
- Data stored in a binary file usually occupies less space than the same data stored in a text file. For example, the integer -25367 (six characters) occupies 6 bytes in a text file but only 2 bytes in a binary file.

C provides the functions `fread` and `fwrite` for use on binary files.

8.9.1 fread and fwrite

Consider the problem of reading integers from the standard input and writing them, in their internal form, to a (binary) file. Assume that the numbers are to be stored in the external file `num.bin`. This can be done with Program P8.3.

Program P8.3

```
#include <stdio.h>
int main() {
   FILE *intFile;
   int num;

   if ((intFile = fopen("num.bin", "wb")) == NULL) {
      printf("Cannot open file\n");
      return -1;
   }
   while (scanf("%d", &num) == 1)
      fwrite(&num, sizeof(int), 1, intFile);
   fclose (intFile);
} //end main
```

The program reads data from the standard input until an invalid integer is read or end of file is met (for instance, if a user types `Ctrl-z`).

In Program P8.3, `num.bin` is opened with `"wb"`, which means "open a binary file for writing." If the file cannot be opened, a message is printed, and the program is stopped. (A `return` statement in `main` returns control to the operating system.)

In the statement:

```
fwrite(&num, sizeof(int), 1, intFile);
```

- `&num` specifies the starting address of the items to be written.
- `sizeof(int)` specifies the size of each item to be written.
- `1` specifies that one item is to be written.
- `intFile` specifies the file to which the items are to be written.

In general, `fwrite` writes a specified number of items to a binary file. Its prototype is (think of `size_t` as `int`):

```
size_t fwrite(void *buffer, size_t unitSize, size_t numItems, FILE *fp);
```

where

- `buffer` is the starting address of the item(s) to be written.
- `unitSize` is the size of each item.
- `numItems` is the number of items to be written.
- `fp` is the file pointer.

`fwrite` returns the number of full items written; this could be less than `numItems` if an error occurs. We usually specify `unitSize` using the `sizeof` operator. This is particularly useful for structures as well as to ensure portability. As another example, if `poly` is a `double` array of size 20, then the following writes the entire array to the file specified by `fp`:

```
fwrite(poly, sizeof(double), 20, fp);
```

Recall that an array name is a synonym for the address of its first element.

Given the declaration:

```
struct child {
   char name[20];
   int age;
   char gender;
   double allowance;
} sassy;
```

we could write the entire structure sassy to a file with:

```
fwrite(&sassy, sizeof(struct child), 1, fp);
```

If class is an array of structures defined as:

```
struct child class[100];
```

then the 100 structure elements could be written to a file with:

```
fwrite(class, sizeof(struct child), 100, fp);
```

The function fread has the same format as fwrite and is used for reading a specified number of items from a binary file. Its prototype is:

```
size_t fread(void *buffer, size_t unitSize, size_t numItems, FILE *fp);
```

where

- buffer is the address where the items read are to be stored.
- unitSize is the size of each item.
- numItems is the number of items to be written.
- fp is the file pointer.

fread returns the number of full items actually read; this could be less than numItems if an error occurs or if the end of file is reached before numItems are read. The functions feof or ferror may be used to distinguish between a read error and an end-of-file condition.

Program P8.4 reads the file of integers created earlier and prints them on the standard output. The file is opened with "rb", which means open a binary file for reading. Each time a number is read, the return value of fread should be 1; if it isn't, then either the end of file was reached or an error occurred.

Program P8.4

```
#include <stdio.h>
int main() {
   FILE *intFile;
   int num;

   if ((intFile = fopen("num.bin", "rb")) == NULL) {
      printf("Cannot open file\n");
      return -1;
   }
```

```
   while (fread(&num, sizeof(int), 1, intFile) == 1)
      printf("%d\n", num);

   if (feof(intFile)) printf("\nEnd of list\n");
   else printf("\nError reading file\n");

   fclose(intFile);
} //end main
```

8.10 Random Access Files

In the normal mode of operation, data is read from a file in the order in which it is stored. When a file is opened, you can think of an imaginary pointer positioned at the beginning of the file. (This is not to be confused with the data type FILE * discussed previously.) As items are read from the file, this pointer moves along by the number of bytes read. Put another way, this pointer indicates where the next read (or write) operation would occur.

Normally, this pointer is moved implicitly by a read or write operation. However, C provides facilities for moving the pointer explicitly to any position in the file. We discuss the functions rewind and fseek. While rewind can be used on either text or binary files, fseek is recommended for use with binary files only. For a text file, character translations would cause fseek to give unexpected results.

8.10.1 rewind and fseek

The function rewind positions the pointer at the beginning of the file. Its prototype is:

```
void rewind(FILE *fp);
```

rewind does not return a value. If the end of file or error condition was set for a file, a call to rewind clears the condition.

The function fseek allows more flexible movement within a file. Its prototype is:

```
int fseek(FILE *fp, long offset, int origin);
```

It moves the file pointer to a position that is offset bytes from origin. If successful, fseek returns zero; otherwise, it returns nonzero.

origin must be one of the following predefined constants (defined in stdio.h):

- SEEK_SET: Beginning of the file
- SEEK_CUR: Current position of file pointer
- SEEK_END: End of the file

offset is a long integer; if the actual argument is not long, then the function prototype causes automatic coercion to long. For example, the following moves the file pointer to a position that is 32 bytes from the beginning of the file, that is, to the beginning of the 33rd byte:

```
fseek(intFile, 32, SEEK_SET);
```

Since 32 is an int, it is automatically converted to long int before being passed to fseek. We could also have used 32L.

One of the most common uses of fseek is to retrieve the records of a file in random order. This is illustrated by the next example.

Consider this declaration:

```
struct partRecord {
   char partNum[7];    // part number
   char name[25];      // name of part
   int amtInStock;     // quantity in stock
   double unitPrice;  // unit selling price
};
```

Suppose we want to create a file containing the records for several parts. The data for each part will be read from a text file, `parts.txt`; stored in a temporary structure; and then written, as one unit, to a binary file.

Suppose that a part number is a six-character string (e.g., PKL070) and a part name is a maximum of 24 characters long. (The extra character declared is used for storing `\0`.) For simplicity, we assume that a part name does not contain any spaces. Some sample data is shown here:

```
PKL070 Park-Lens 8 6.50
BLJ375 Ball-Joint 12 11.95
FLT015 Oil-Filter 23 7.95
DKP080 Disc-Pads 16 9.99
GSF555 Gas-Filter 9 4.50
```

Program P8.5 reads the data and stores it in a binary file, `parts.bin`. The data is stored in the same order as in the text file.

The program confirms that a given part record has been written successfully to the parts file by checking the return value of `fwrite`. If successful, `fwrite` should return `1`, in this example. Note the specification `%lf` ("percent ell f") for reading a value into a `double` variable.

Program P8.5

```
#include <stdio.h>

typedef struct partRecord {
   char partNum[7];
   char name[25];
   int amtInStock;
   double unitPrice;
} PartRecord;

int main() {
   FILE *ftxt, *fbin;
   PartRecord part;

   if ((ftxt = fopen("parts.txt", "r")) == NULL) {
      printf("Cannot open parts file\n");
      return -1;
   }

   if ((fbin = fopen("parts.bin", "wb")) == NULL) {
      printf("Cannot create file\n");
      return -1;
   }
```

```
    while (fscanf(ftxt, "%s %s %d %lf", part.partNum, part.name,
                      &part.amtInStock, &part.unitPrice) == 4)
       if (fwrite(&part, sizeof(PartRecord), 1, fbin) != 1) {
          printf("Error in writing file\n");
          return -1;
       }

    fclose(ftxt);
    fclose(fbin);
 } //end main
```

To understand how fseek may be used on the binary parts file, think of the records as being numbered consecutively from 1 and suppose that each record is 40 bytes long. The records are stored in the file starting at byte 0.

```
Record 1 occupies bytes 0 - 39;
Record 2 occupies bytes 40 - 79;
Record 3 occupies bytes 80 - 119;
```

In general, Record n starts at byte number $(n - 1)$*40 and occupies the next 40 bytes.

Now, suppose we want to read record n; we must do the following:

1. Position the file pointer at the beginning of the nth record.
2. Read a number of bytes equal to the size of a record.

This can be done with:

```
fseek(fbin, (n - 1)*sizeof(PartRecord), SEEK_SET);
fread(&part, sizeof(PartRecord), 1, fbin);
```

As usual, we could check the return values to ensure successful completion of the operations. Program P8.6 requests a record number, reads the record from the file, and prints the record information on the screen. *It assumes that the record number supplied is a valid one,* but keep in mind that a robust program must verify this.

Program P8.6

```
#include <stdio.h>

typedef struct partRecord {
   char partNum[7];
   char name[25];
   int amtInStock;
   double unitPrice;
} PartRecord;

int main() {
   FILE *fbin;
   PartRecord part;
   int n;
```

```
    if ((fbin = fopen("parts.bin", "rb")) == NULL) {
       printf("Cannot open file\n");
       return -1;
    }
    printf("Enter record number: ");
    scanf("%d", &n);
    while (n != 0) {
       fseek(fbin, (n - 1) * sizeof(PartRecord), SEEK_SET);
       fread(&part, sizeof(PartRecord), 1, fbin);

       printf("\nPart number: %s\n", part.partNum);
       printf("Part name: %s\n", part.name);
       printf("Amount in stock: %d\n", part.amtInStock);
       printf("Price: $%3.2f\n\n", part.unitPrice);

       printf("Enter record number: ");
       scanf("%d", &n);
    }
    fclose(fbin);
} //end main
```

Suppose `parts.bin` was created using the sample data shown here:

```
PKL070 Park-Lens 8 6.50
BLJ375 Ball-Joint 12 11.95
FLT015 Oil-Filter 23 7.95
DKP080 Disc-Pads 16 9.99
GSF555 Gas-Filter 9 4.50
```

The following is a sample run of P8.6.

```
Enter a record number: 3
Part number: FLT015
Part name: Oil-Filter
Amount in stock: 23
Price: $7.95

Enter a record number: 1
Part number: PKL070
Part name: Park-Lens
Amount in stock: 8
Price: $6.50

Enter a record number: 4
Part number: DKP080
Part name: Disc-Pads
Amount in stock: 16
Price: $9.99

Enter a record number: 0
```

8.11 Indexed Files

The previous section showed how to retrieve a part record given the record number. But this is not the most natural way to retrieve records. More likely than not, we would want to retrieve records based on some *key*, in this case, the part number. It is more natural to ask, "How many of BLJ375 do we have?" rather than "How many of record 2 do we have?" The problem then is how to retrieve a record given the part number.

One approach is to use an *index*. Just as a book index lets us quickly locate information in a book, a file index enables us to quickly find records in a file. The index is created as the file is loaded. Later, it must be updated as records are added to, or deleted from, the file. In our example, an index entry will consist of a part number and a record number.

We will use the following declaration for an index entry:

```
struct indexEntry {
   char partNum[7];
   int recNum;
};
```

An array of such structures will be used to hold the entire index. For example, if we want to cater for up to 100 items, we could use:

```
struct indexEntry index[100];
```

The index will be kept in order by part number. Let's illustrate how to create an index for the following records:

```
PKL070 Park-Lens    8  6.50
BLJ375 Ball-Joint  12 11.95
FLT015 Oil-Filter  23  7.95
DKP080 Disc-Pads   16  9.99
GSF555 Gas-Filter   9  4.50
```

We assume that the records are stored in the file in the order shown. When the first record is read and stored, the index will contain this, meaning that the record for PKL070 is record number 1 in the parts file:

```
PKL070 1
```

After the second record is read and stored, the index will be as follows, since the index is in order by part number:

```
BLJ375 2
PKL070 1
```

After the third record is read and stored, the index will be:

```
BLJ375 2
FLT015 3
PKL070 1
```

After the fourth record is read and stored, the index will be:

```
BLJ375 2
DKP080 4
FLT015 3
PKL070 1
```

After the fifth record is read and stored, the index will be:

```
BLJ375 2
DKP080 4
FLT015 3
GSF555 5
PKL070 1
```

Program P8.7 illustrates how an index can be created as described above.

Program P8.7

```
#include <stdio.h>
#include <stdlib.h>
#include <string.h>

#define  PartNumSize  6
#define  MaxName  24
#define  MaxRecords  100

typedef struct partRecord {
   char partNum[PartNumSize + 1];
   char name[MaxName + 1];
   int amtInStock;
   double unitPrice;
} PartRecord;
typedef struct indexEntry {
   char partNum[PartNumSize + 1];
   int recNum;
} IndexEntry;

int main() {
   IndexEntry index[MaxRecords + 1];
   void createMaster(char *, IndexEntry[], int);
   void saveIndex(char *, IndexEntry[], int);
   createMaster("parts.bin", index, MaxRecords);
   saveIndex("index.bin", index, MaxRecords + 1);
} //end main

void createMaster(char *fileName, IndexEntry index[], int maxRecords) {
// stores records in 'fileName';  caters for maxRecords index entries;
// sets index[0].recNum to the number of index entries actually used
   FILE *ftxt, *fbin;
   PartRecord part;
   int searchResult, search(char[], IndexEntry[], int);
   int numRecords = 0;

   if ((ftxt = fopen("parts.txt", "r")) == NULL) {
      printf("Cannot open parts file\n"); return;
   }
```

```
   if ((fbin = fopen("parts.bin", "wb")) == NULL) {
      printf("Cannot create file\n");
      return;
   }

   while (fscanf(ftxt, "%s %s %d %lf", part.partNum, part.name,
                     &part.amtInStock, &part.unitPrice) == 4) {
      searchResult = search(part.partNum, index, numRecords);
      if (searchResult > 0)
         printf("Duplicate part: %s ignored\n", part.partNum);
      else { //this is a new part number
         if (numRecords == maxRecords) {
            printf("Too many records: only %d allowed\n", maxRecords);
            exit(1);
         }
         //the index has room; shift entries to accommodate new part

         for (int j = numRecords; j >= -searchResult; j--)
               index[j + 1] = index[j];
         strcpy(index[-searchResult].partNum, part.partNum);
         index[-searchResult].recNum = ++numRecords;
         if (fwrite(&part, sizeof(PartRecord), 1, fbin) != 1) {
            printf("Error in writing file\n"); exit(1);
         }
         printf("%s %-11s %2d %5.2f\n", part.partNum, part.name,
                           part.amtInStock, part.unitPrice);
      }
   }
   index[0].recNum = numRecords;
   fclose(fbin);
} //end createMaster

int search(char key[], IndexEntry list[], int n) {
//searches list[1..n] for key. If found, it returns the location; otherwise
//it returns the negative of the location in which key should be inserted.
   int lo = 1;  int hi = n;
   while (lo <= hi) {               // as long as more elements remain to consider
      int mid = (lo + hi) / 2;
      int cmp = strcmp(key, list[mid].partNum);
      if (cmp == 0) return mid;     // search succeeds
      if (cmp < 0) hi = mid - 1;    // key is 'less than' list[mid].partNum
      else lo = mid + 1;            // key is 'greater than' list[mid].partNum
   }
   return -lo;                      // key not found; insert in location lo
} //end search

void saveIndex(char *fileName, IndexEntry index[], int max) {
//save the index in fileName; max is the size of index.
   FILE *indexFile;
```

```
    if ((indexFile = fopen(fileName, "wb")) == NULL) {
       printf("Cannot create file %s. Index not saved\n", fileName);
       exit(1);
    }
    fwrite(&max, sizeof(int), 1, indexFile);          //save the index size first
    fwrite(index, sizeof(IndexEntry), max, indexFile); //save the index
    fclose(indexFile);
} //end saveIndex
```

When a part number is read, we look for it in the index. Since the index is kept in order by part number, we search it using a binary search. If the part number is present, it means the part has been stored already so this record is ignored. If it is not present, this is a new part, so its record is stored in the parts file, `parts.bin`, provided we have not already stored `MaxRecords` records.

A count is kept (in `numRecords`) of the number of records read. The part number and the record number are then inserted in the proper place in the `index` array.

When all the records have been stored, the index is saved in another file, `index.bin`. The value of `MaxRecords` is the first value sent to the file. This is followed by `index[0]` to `index[MaxRecords]`. Remember that `index[0].recNum` contains the value of `numRecords`.

Given that `parts.txt` contains this:

```
PKL070 Park-Lens 8 6.50
BLJ375 Ball-Joint 12 11.95
PKL070 Park-Lens 8 6.50
FLT015 Oil-Filter 23 7.95
DKP080 Disc-Pads 16 9.99
GSF555 Gas-Filter 9 4.50
FLT015 Oil-Filter 23 7.95
```

Program P8.7 prints the following:

```
PKL070 Park-Lens    8  6.50
BLJ375 Ball-Joint  12 11.95
Duplicate part: PKL070 ignored
FLT015 Oil-Filter  23  7.95
DKP080 Disc-Pads   16  9.99
GSF555 Gas-Filter   9  4.50
Duplicate part: FLT015 ignored
```

Next, we write a program that tests our index by first retrieving it from the file. The user is then asked to enter part numbers, one at a time. For each, it searches the index for the part number. If it finds it, the index entry will indicate the record number in the parts file. Using the record number, the part record is retrieved. If the part number is not found in the index, then there is no record for that part. The program is shown as Program P8.8.

Program P8.8

```
#include <stdio.h>
#include <string.h>
#include <stdlib.h>
#define PartNumSize  6
#define MaxName  24
#define MaxRecords 100
```

```
typedef struct partRecord {
   char partNum[PartNumSize + 1];
   char name[MaxName + 1];
   int amtInStock; double unitPrice;
} PartRecord;
typedef struct indexEntry {
   char partNum[PartNumSize + 1];
   int recNum;
} IndexEntry;

int main() {
   FILE *partFile;
   IndexEntry index[MaxRecords + 1];
   void retrieveIndex(char *, IndexEntry[]);
   void retrieveRecords(IndexEntry[], FILE *);

   if ((partFile = fopen("parts.bin", "rb")) == NULL) {
      printf("Cannot open file\n");  return -1;
   }
   retrieveIndex("index.bin", index);
   retrieveRecords(index, partFile);
   fclose(partFile);
} //end main

void retrieveRecords(IndexEntry index[], FILE *pf) {
   char pnum[PartNumSize * 2]; //to cater for extra characters typed
   PartRecord part;
   int search(char[], IndexEntry[], int);

   int numRecords = index[0].recNum;
   printf("\nEnter a part number (E to end): ");
   scanf("%s", pnum);
   while (strcmp(pnum, "E") != 0) {
      int n = search(pnum, index, numRecords);
      if (n < 0) printf("Part not found\n");
      else {
         fseek(pf, (index[n].recNum - 1)*sizeof(PartRecord), SEEK_SET);
         fread(&part, sizeof(PartRecord), 1, pf);
         printf("\nPart number: %s\n", part.partNum);
         printf("Part name: %s\n", part.name);
         printf("Amount in stock: %d\n", part.amtInStock);
         printf("Price: $%3.2f\n", part.unitPrice);
      }
      printf("\nEnter a part number (E to end): ");
      scanf("%s", pnum);
   } //end while
} //end retrieveRecords
```

```
void retrieveIndex(char *fileName, IndexEntry index[]) {
   FILE *indexFile;
   int maxRecords;

   if ((indexFile = fopen(fileName, "rb")) == NULL){
      printf("cannot open index file.\n");
      exit(1);
   }
   fread(&maxRecords, sizeof(int), 1,indexFile);
   fread(index, sizeof(IndexEntry), maxRecords, indexFile);
   fclose(indexFile);
} //end retrieveIndex

int search(char key[], IndexEntry list[], int n) {
//searches list[1..n] for key. If found, it returns the location; otherwise
//it returns the negative of the location in which key should be inserted.
   int lo = 1;  int hi = n;
   while (lo <= hi) {               // as long as more elements remain to consider
      int mid = (lo + hi) / 2;
      int cmp = strcmp(key, list[mid].partNum);
      if (cmp == 0) return mid;     // search succeeds
      if (cmp < 0) hi = mid - 1;    // key is 'less than' list[mid].partNum
      else lo = mid + 1;            // key is 'greater than' list[mid].partNum
   }
   return -lo;                      // key not found; insert in location lo
} //end search
```

The following is a sample run of Program P8.8:

```
Enter a part number (E to end): DKP080
Part number: DKP080
Part name: Disc-Pads
Amount in stock: 16
Price: $9.99

Enter a part number (E to end): GSF555
Part number: GSF555
Part name: Gas-Filter
Amount in stock: 9
Price: $4.50

Enter a part number (E to end): PKL060
Part not found

Enter a part number (E to end): PKL070
Part number: PKL070
Part name: Park-Lens
Amount in stock: 8
Price: $6.50

Enter a part number (E to end): E
```

If required, we could use the index to print the records in order by part number. We simply print the records in the order in which they appear in the index. For example, using our sample data, we have the following index:

```
BLJ375 2
DKP080 4
FLT015 3
GSF555 5
PKL070 1
```

If we print record 2, followed by record 4, followed by record 3, followed by record 5, followed by record 1, we would have printed them in ascending order by part number. This can be done with the following code:

```
for (int n = 1; n <= numRecords; n++) {
   fseek(partFile, (index[n].recNum - 1)*sizeof(PartRecord), SEEK_SET);
   fread(&part, sizeof(PartRecord), 1, partFile);
   printf("%s %-11s %2d %5.2f\n", part.partNum, part.name, part.amtInStock, part.unitPrice);
}
```

8.12 Updating a Random Access File

The information in a file is not usually static. It must be updated from time to time. For our parts file, we may want to update it to reflect the new quantity in stock as items are sold or to reflect a change in price. We may decide to stock new parts, so we must add records to the file, and we may discontinue selling certain items, so their records must be deleted from the file.

Adding new records is done in a similar manner to loading the file in the first place. We can delete a record logically by marking it as deleted in the index or by simply removing it from the index. Later, when the file is reorganized, the record could be deleted physically (that is, not present in the new file). But how can we *change* the information in an existing record? To do this, we must do the following:

1. Locate the record in the file.
2. Read it into memory.
3. Change the desired fields.
4. Write the updated record to the *same position* in the file from which it came.

This requires that our file be opened for both reading and writing. Assuming that the file already exists, it must be opened with mode `"rb+"`. We explain how to update a record whose part number is stored in `key`.

First we search the index for `key`. If it is not found, no record exists for this part. Suppose it is found in location `k`. Then `index[k].recNum` gives its record number (`n`, say) in the parts file. We then proceed as follows (omitting error checking in the interest of clarity):

```
fseek(partFile, (n - 1) * sizeof(PartRecord), SEEK_SET);
fread(&part, sizeof(PartRecord), 1, partFile);
```

The record is now in memory in the structure variable `part`. Suppose we need to subtract `amtSold` from the amount in stock. This could be done with this:

```
if (amtSold > part.amtInStock)
   printf("Cannot sell more than you have: ignored\n");
else part.amtInStock -= amtSold;
```

Other fields (except the part number, since this is used to identify the record) could be updated similarly. When all changes have been made, the updated record is in memory in `part`. It must now be written back to the file in the same position from which it came. This could be done with the following:

```
fseek(partFile, (n - 1) * sizeof(PartRecord), SEEK_SET);
fwrite(&part, sizeof(PartRecord), 1, partFile);
```

Note that we must call `fseek` again since, after the previous `fread`, the file is positioned at the beginning of the *next* record. We must reposition it at the beginning of the record just read. The net effect is that the updated record overwrites the old one.

Program P8.9 updates the `amtInStock` field of records in the parts file. The user is asked to enter a part number and the amount sold. The program searches the index for the part number using a binary search. If found, the record is retrieved from the file, updated in memory, and written back to the file. This is repeated until the user enters a dummy part number, `"E"`.

Program P8.9

```
#include <stdio.h>
#include <string.h>
#include <stdlib.h>

#define PartNumSize  6
#define MaxName  24
#define MaxRecords 100

typedef struct partRecord {
   char partNum[PartNumSize + 1];
   char name[MaxName + 1];
   int amtInStock;
   double unitPrice;
} PartRecord;

typedef struct indexEntry {
   char partNum[PartNumSize + 1];
   int recNum;
} IndexEntry;

int main() {
   FILE *partFile;
   IndexEntry index[MaxRecords + 1];
   void retrieveIndex(char *, IndexEntry[]);
   void updateRecord(int, FILE *);
   int search(char[], IndexEntry[], int);
   char pnum[PartNumSize + 1];
```

```
    if ((partFile = fopen("parts.bin", "rb+")) == NULL) {
       printf("Cannot open file\n");
       return -1;
    }
    retrieveIndex("index.bin", index);
    int numRecords = index[0].recNum;

    printf("\nEnter a part number (E to end): ");
    scanf("%s", pnum);
    while (strcmp(pnum, "E") != 0) {
       int n = search(pnum, index, numRecords);
       if (n < 0) printf("Part not found\n");
       else updateRecord(index[n].recNum, partFile);
       printf("\nEnter a part number (E to end): ");
       scanf("%s", pnum);
    } // end while
    fclose(partFile);
 } //end main

 void updateRecord(int n, FILE *pf) {
 //update record n in file pf
    PartRecord part;
    int amtSold;

    fseek(pf, (n - 1) * sizeof(PartRecord), SEEK_SET);
    fread(&part, sizeof(PartRecord), 1, pf);
    printf("Enter amount sold: ");
    scanf("%d", &amtSold);
    if (amtSold > part.amtInStock)
       printf("You have %d: cannot sell more, ignored\n", part.amtInStock);
    else {
       part.amtInStock -= amtSold;
       printf("Amount remaining: %d\n", part.amtInStock);
       fseek(pf, (n - 1) * sizeof(PartRecord), SEEK_SET);
       fwrite(&part, sizeof(PartRecord), 1, pf);
       printf("%s %-11s %2d %5.2f\n", part.partNum, part.name, part.amtInStock, part.unitPrice);
    } //end if
 } //end updateRecord

 void retrieveIndex(char *fileName, IndexEntry index[]) {
    FILE *indexFile;
    int maxRecords;

    if ((indexFile = fopen(fileName, "rb")) == NULL){
       printf("cannot open index file.\n");
       exit(1);
    }
    fread(&maxRecords, sizeof(int), 1,indexFile);
    fread(index, sizeof(IndexEntry), maxRecords, indexFile);
    fclose(indexFile);
 } //end retrieveIndex
```

```
int search(char key[], IndexEntry list[], int n) {
//searches list[1..n] for key. If found, it returns the location; otherwise
//it returns the negative of the location in which key should be inserted.
   int lo = 1;  int hi = n;
   while (lo <= hi) {               // as long as more elements remain to consider
      int mid = (lo + hi) / 2;
      int cmp = strcmp(key, list[mid].partNum);
      if (cmp == 0) return mid;     // search succeeds
      if (cmp < 0) hi = mid - 1;    // key is 'less than' list[mid].partNum
      else lo = mid + 1;            // key is 'greater than' list[mid].partNum
   }
   return -lo;                      // key not found; insert in location lo
} //end search
```

The following is a sample run of Program P8.9:

```
Enter part number (E to end): BLJ375
Enter amount sold: 2
Amount remaining: 10
BLJ375 Ball-Joint  10 11.95

Enter part number (E to end): BLJ375
Enter amount sold: 11
You have 10: cannot sell more, ignored

Enter part number (E to end): DKP080
Enter amount sold: 4
Amount remaining: 12
DKP080 Disc-Pads   12  9.99

Enter part number (E to end): GSF55
Part not found

Enter part number (E to end): GSF555
Enter amount sold: 1
Amount remaining: 8
GSF555 Gas-Filter   8  4.50

Enter part number (E to end): E
```

EXERCISES 8

1. What is the difference between a file opened with "r+" and one opened with "w+"?
2. Write a program to determine whether two binary files are identical. If they are different, print the first byte number at which they differ.
3. Write a program to read a (binary) file of integers, sort the integers, and write them back to the same file. Assume that all the numbers can be stored in an array.
4. Repeat exercise 3, but assume that only 20 numbers can be stored in memory (in an array) at any one time. Hint: you will need to use at least two additional files for temporary output.
5. Write a program to read two sorted files of integers and merge the values to a third sorted file.
6. Write a program to read a text file and produce another text file in which all lines are less than some given length. Make sure and break lines in sensible places; for example, avoid breaking words or putting isolated punctuation marks at the beginning of a line.
7. What is the purpose of creating an index for a file?

   The following are some records from an employee file. The fields are employee number (the key), name, job title, telephone number, monthly salary, and tax to be deducted.

   ```
   STF425, Julie Johnson, Secretary, 623-3321, 2500, 600
   COM319, Ian McLean, Programmer, 676-1319, 3200, 800
   SYS777, Jean Kendall, Systems Analyst, 671-2025, 4200, 1100
   JNR591, Lincoln Kadoo, Operator, 657-0266, 2800, 700
   MSN815, Camille Kelly, Clerical Assistant, 652-5345, 2100, 500
   STF273, Anella Bayne, Data Entry Manager, 632-5324, 3500, 850
   SYS925, Riaz Ali, Senior Programmer, 636-8679, 4800, 1300
   ```

   a. How can a record be retrieved given the record number?
   b. How can a record be retrieved given the key of the record?
   c. As the file is loaded, create an index in which the keys are in the order given. How is such an index searched for a given key?
   d. As the file is loaded, create an index in which the keys are sorted. Given a key, how is the corresponding record retrieved?

   Discuss what changes must be made to the index when records are added to and deleted from the file.
8. For the "parts file" application discussed in this chapter, write functions for (i) adding new records and (ii) deleting records.

CHAPTER 9

Introduction to Binary Trees

In this chapter, we will explain the following:

- The difference between a tree and a binary tree
- How to perform pre-order, in-order, and post-order traversals of a binary tree
- How to represent a binary tree in a computer program
- How to build a binary tree from given data
- What a binary search tree is and how to build one
- How to write a program to do a word-frequency count of words in a passage
- How to use an array as a binary tree representation
- How to write some recursive functions to obtain information about a binary tree
- How to delete a node from a binary search tree

9.1 Trees

A *tree* is a finite set of nodes such that

(a) There is one specially designated node called the root of the tree.

(b) The remaining nodes are partitioned into $m \geq 0$ disjoint sets $T_1, T_2, \ldots, T_m$, and each of these sets is a tree.

The trees $T_1, T_2, \ldots, T_m$, are called the *subtrees* of the root. We use a recursive definition since recursion is an innate characteristic of tree structures. Figure 9-1 illustrates a tree. By convention, the root is drawn at the top, and the tree grows downward.

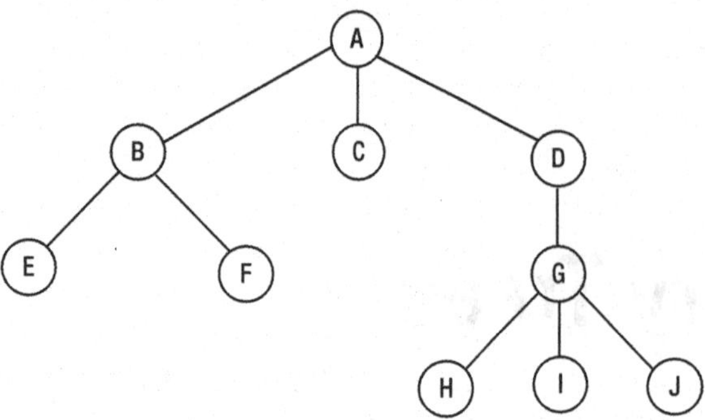

Figure 9-1. *A tree*

The root is A. There are three subtrees rooted at B, C, and D, respectively. The tree rooted at B has two subtrees, the one rooted at C has no subtrees, and the one rooted at D has one subtree. Each node of a tree is the root of a subtree.

The *degree* of a node is the number of subtrees of the node. Think of it as the number of lines leaving the node. For example, degree(A) = 3, degree(C) = 0, degree(D) = 1, and degree(G) = 3.

We use the terms *parent, child,* and *sibling* to refer to the nodes of a tree. For example, the parent A has three children, which are B, C, and D; the parent B has two children, which are E and F; and the parent D has one child, G, which has three children: H, I, and J. Note that a node may be the child of one node but the parent of another.

Sibling nodes are child nodes of the same parent. For example, B, C, and D are siblings; E and F are siblings; and H, I, and J are siblings.

In a tree, a node may have several children but, except for the root, only one parent. The root has no parent. Put another way, a nonroot node has exactly one line leading *into* it.

A *terminal* node (also called a *leaf*) is a node of degree 0. A *branch* node is a nonterminal node. In Figure 9-1, C, E, F, H, I, and J are leaves, while A, B, D, and G are branch nodes.

The *moment* of a tree is the number of nodes in the tree. The tree in Figure 9-1 has moment 10.

The *weight* of a tree is the number of leaves in the tree. The tree in Figure 9-1 has weight 6.

The *level* (or *depth*) of a node is the number of branches that must be traversed on the path to the node from the root. The root has level 0.

In the tree in Figure 9-1, B, C, and D are at level 1; E, F, and G are at level 2; and H, I, and J are at level 3. The level of a node is a measure of the depth of the node in the tree.

The *height* of a tree is the number of levels in the tree. The tree in Figure 9-1 has height 4. Note that the height of a tree is one more than its highest level.

If the relative order of the subtrees $T_1, T_2, \ldots, T_m$ is important, the tree is an *ordered* tree. If order is unimportant, the tree is *oriented.*

A *forest* is a set of zero or more disjoint trees, as shown in Figure 9-2.

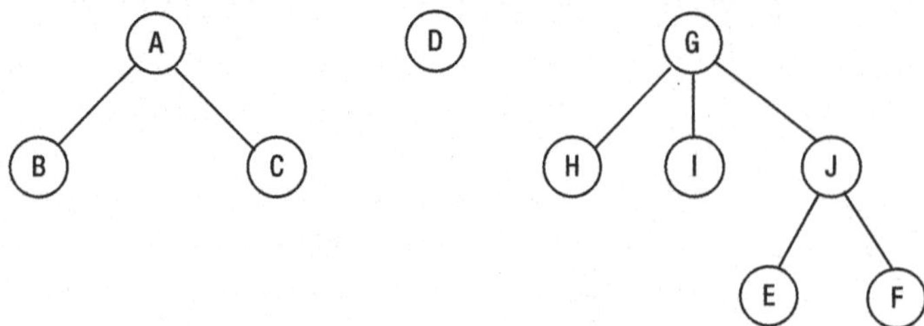

Figure 9-2. *A forest of three disjoint trees*

While general trees are of some interest, by far the most important kind of tree is a binary tree.

9.2 Binary Trees

A *binary tree* is a classic example of a nonlinear data structure—compare this to a linear list where we identify a first item, a next item, and a last item. A binary tree is a special case of the more general *tree* data structure, but it is the most useful and most widely used kind of tree. A binary tree is best defined using the following recursive definition:

A binary tree

(a) is empty

or

(b) consists of a root and two subtrees—a left and a right—with each subtree being a binary tree

A consequence of this definition is that a node always has two subtrees, any of which may be empty. Another consequence is that if a node has *one* nonempty subtree, it is important to distinguish whether it is on the left or right. Here's an example:

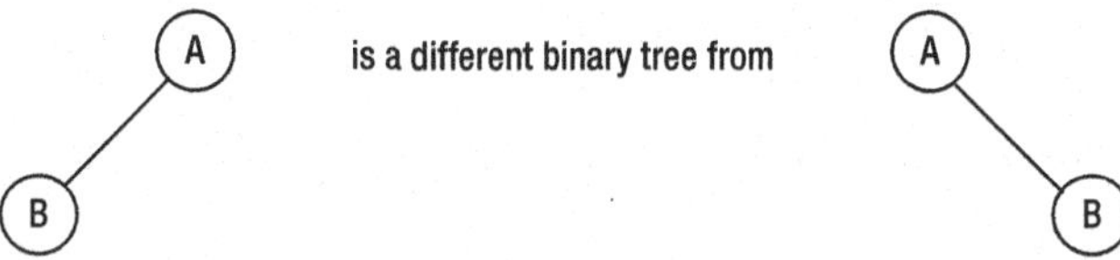

The first has an empty right subtree, while the second has an empty left subtree. However, as *trees*, they are the same.

The following are examples of binary trees.

Here's a binary tree with one node, the root:

Here are binary trees with two nodes:

Here are binary trees with three nodes:

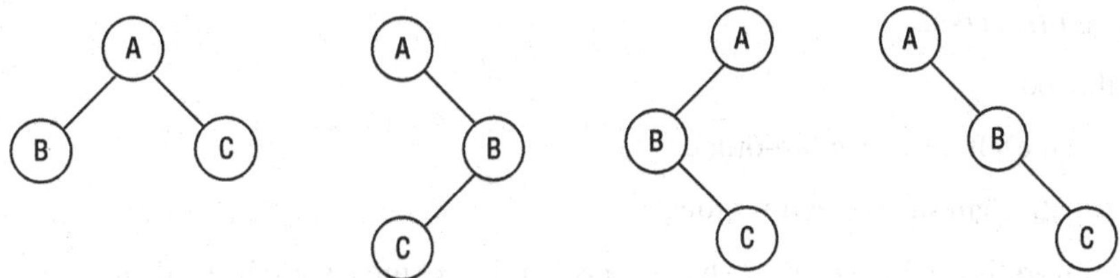

Here are binary trees with all left subtrees empty and all right subtrees empty:

Here is a binary tree where each node, except the leaves, has exactly two subtrees; this is called a *complete* binary tree:

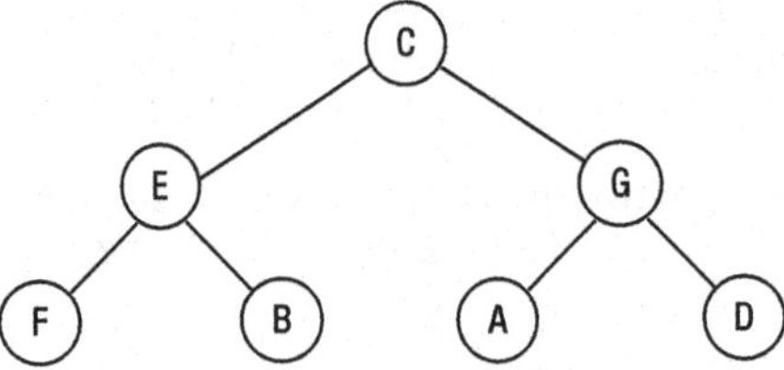

Here is a general binary tree:

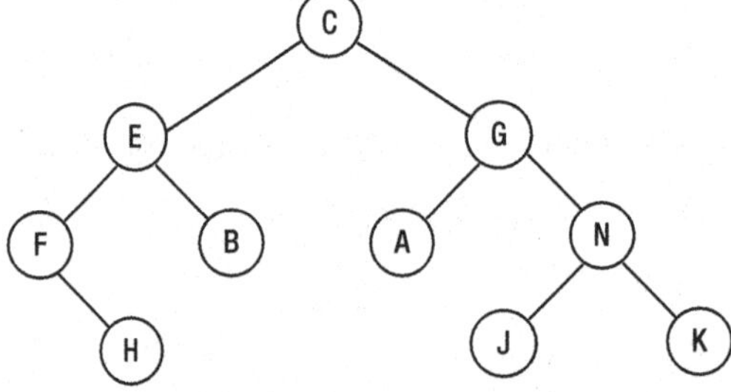

9.3 Traversing a Binary Tree

In many applications, we want to visit the nodes of a binary tree in some systematic way. For now, we'll think of "visit" as simply printing the information at the node. For a tree of *n* nodes, there are *n*! ways to visit them, assuming that each node is visited once.

For example, for a tree with three nodes A, B, and C, we can visit them in any of the following orders: ABC, ACB, BCA, BAC, CAB, and CBA. Not all of these orders are useful. We will define three that are: pre-order, in-order, and post-order.

This is ***pre-order traversal***:

1. Visit the root.
2. Traverse the left subtree in pre-order.
3. Traverse the right subtree in pre-order.

Note that the traversal is defined recursively. In steps 2 and 3, we must reapply the definition of pre-order traversal, which says "visit the root, and so on."

The *pre-order* traversal of

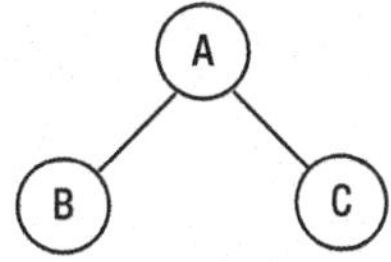

is A B C.

The *pre-order* traversal of

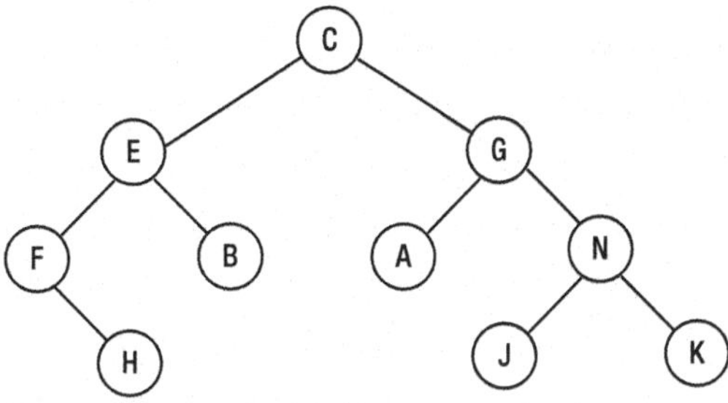

is C E F H B G A N J K.

This is ***in-order traversal***:

1. Traverse the left subtree in in-order.
2. Visit the root.
3. Traverse the right subtree in in-order.

Here we traverse the left subtree first, then the root, and then the right subtree.

The *in-order* traversal of

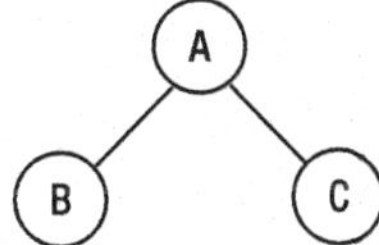

is B A C.

The *in-order* traversal of

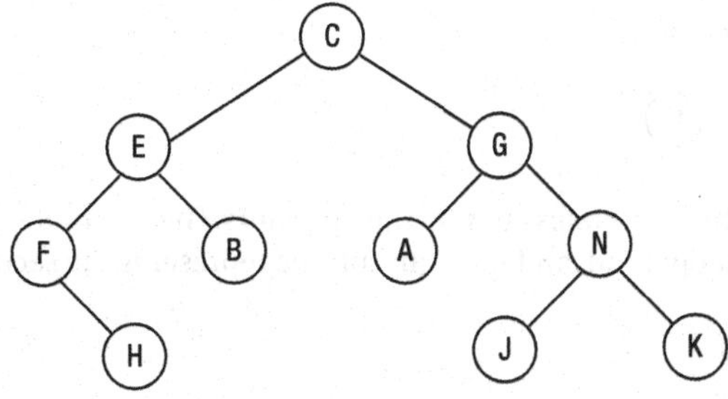

is F H E B C A G J N K.

This is ***post-order traversal***:

1. Traverse the left subtree in post-order.
2. Traverse the right subtree in post-order.
3. Visit the root.

Here we traverse the left and right subtrees *before* visiting the root.

The *post-order* traversal of

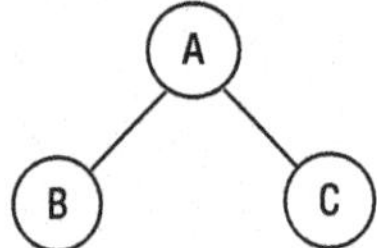

is B C A.

The *post-order* traversal of

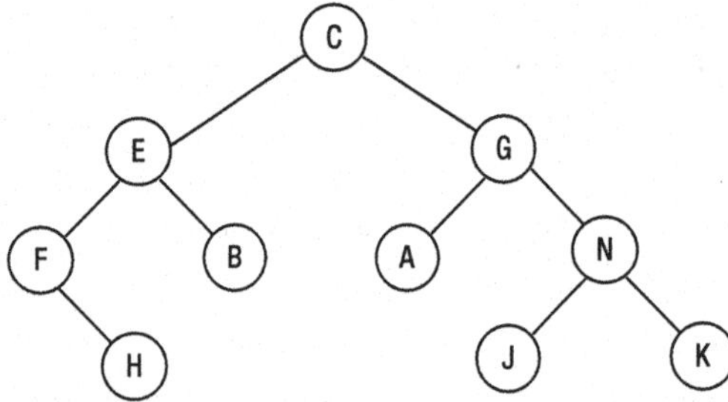

is H F B E A J K N G C.

Note that the traversals derive their names from the place where we visit the root relative to the traversal of the left and right subtrees. As another example, consider a binary tree that can represent the following arithmetic expression:

```
(54 + 37) / (72 - 5 * 13)
```

Here is the tree:

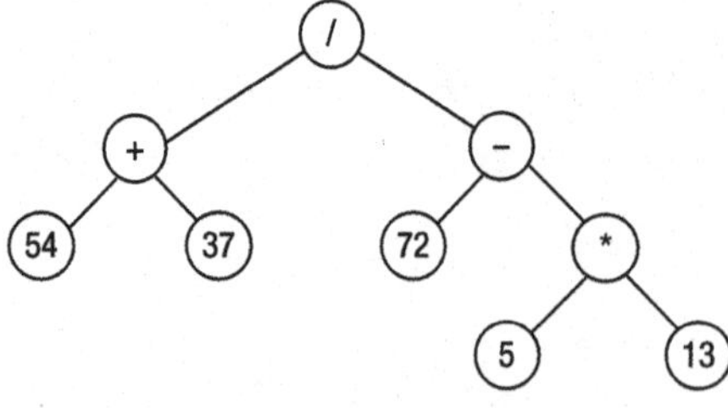

The leaves of the tree contain the operands, and the branch nodes contain the operators. Given a node containing an operator, the left subtree represents the first operand, and the right subtree represents the second operand.

The pre-order traversal is: `/ + 54 37 - 72 * 5 13`
The in-order traversal is: `54 + 37 / 72 - 5 * 13`
The post-order traversal is: `54 37 + 72 5 13 * - /`

The post-order traversal can be used in conjunction with a stack to evaluate the expression. The algorithm is as follows:

```
initialize a stack, S, to empty
while we have not reached the end of the traversal
   get the next item, x
   if x is an operand, push it onto S
   if x is an operator, pop its operands from S, apply the operator and
                           push the result onto S

endwhile
pop S; // this is the value of the expression
```

Consider the post-order traversal: `54 37 + 72 5 13 * - /`. It is evaluated as follows:

1. The next item is 54; push 54 onto S; S contains `54`.
2. The next item is 37; push 37 onto S; S contains `54 37` (the top is on the right).
3. The next item is +; pop 37 and 54 from S; apply + to 54 and 37, giving 91; push 91 onto S; S contains `91`.
4. The next item is 72; push 72 onto S; S contains `91 72`.
5. The next items are 5 and 13; these are pushed onto S; S contains `91 72 5 13`.
6. The next item is *; pop 13 and 5 from S; apply * to 5 and 13, giving 65; push 65 onto S; S contains `91 72 65`.
7. The next item is –; pop 65 and 72 from S; apply - to 72 and 65, giving 7; push 7 onto S; S contains `91 7`.
8. The next item is /; pop 7 and 91 from S; apply / to 91and 7, giving 13; push 13 onto S; S contains `13`.
9. We have reached the end of the traversal; we pop S, getting 13—the result of the expression.

Note that when operands are popped from the stack, the first one popped is the second operand, and the second one popped is the first operand. This does not matter for addition and multiplication but is important for subtraction and division.

9.4 Representing a Binary Tree

At a minimum, each node of a binary tree consists of three fields: a field containing the data at the node, a pointer to the left subtree, and a pointer to the right subtree. For example, suppose the data to be stored at each node is a word. We begin by defining a structure with three fields, like this:

```
typedef struct treenode {
   NodeData data;
   struct treenode *left, *right;
} TreeNode, *TreeNodePtr;
```

To keep our options open, we have defined TreeNode in terms of a general data type that we call NodeData. Any program that wants to use TreeNode must provide its own definition of NodeData.

For example, if the data at a node is an integer, NodeData could be defined like this:

```
typedef  struct {
   int num;
} NodeData;
```

A similar definition can be used if the data is a character. But we are not restricted to single-field data. Any number of fields can be used. Later, we will write a program to do a frequency count of words in a passage. Each node will contain a word and its frequency count. For that program, we define NodeData as follows:

```
typedef  struct {
   char word[MaxWordSize+1];
   int freq;
} NodeData;
```

In addition to the nodes of the tree, we will need to know the root of the tree. Keep in mind that once we know the root, we have access to all the nodes in the tree via the left and right pointers. Thus, a binary tree is defined solely by its root. We define a BinaryTree structure containing a single field, root, like this:

```
typedef struct {
   TreeNodePtr root;
} BinaryTree;
```

9.5 Building a Binary Tree

Let's write a function to build a binary tree. Suppose we want to build a tree consisting of a single node:

The data will be supplied as `A @ @`.

Each @ denotes the position of a null pointer. To build the following, we will supply the data as `A B @ @ C @ @`:

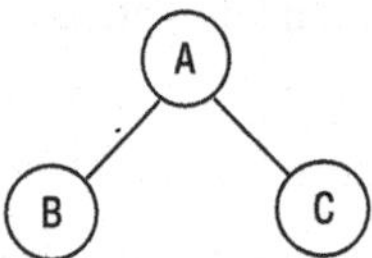

Each node is immediately followed by its left subtree and then its right subtree.

By comparison, to build the following, we will supply the data as `A B @ C @ @ @`.

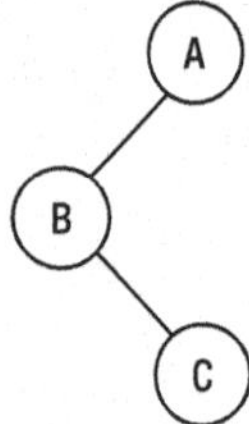

The two @s after C denote its left and right subtrees (null), and the last @ denotes the right subtree of A (null). And to build the following, we supply the data as `C E F @ H @ @ B @ @ G A @ @ N J @ @ K @ @`.

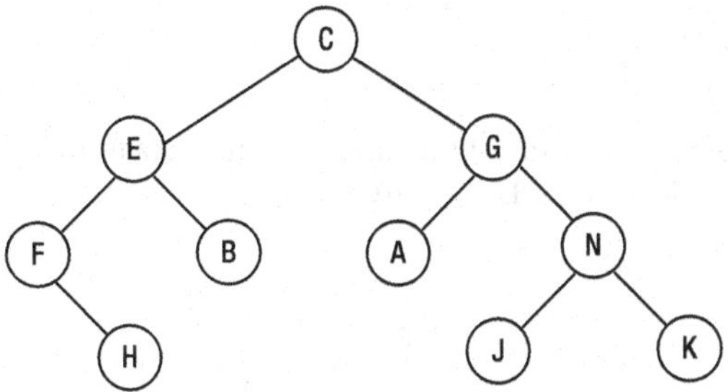

Given data in this format, the following function will build the tree and return a pointer to its root. It reads data from the file specified by `in`. `MaxWordSize` is a `#defined` constant.

```
TreeNodePtr buildTree(FILE * in) {
   char str[MaxWordSize+1];
   fscanf(in, "%s", str);
   if (strcmp(str, "@") == 0) return NULL;
   TreeNodePtr p = (TreeNodePtr) malloc(sizeof(TreeNode));
   strcpy(p -> data.word, str);
   p -> left = buildTree(in);
   p -> right = buildTree(in);
   return p;
} //end buildTree
```

The function uses the following definition of `NodeData`:

```
typedef struct {
   char word[MaxWordSize+1];
} NodeData;
```

Suppose the tree data is stored in the file `btree.in`. We can create a binary tree, `bt`, with the following code:

```
FILE * in = fopen("btree.in", "r");
BinaryTree bt;
bt.root = buildTree(in);
```

Having built the tree, we should want to check that it has been built properly. One way to do that is to perform traversals. Suppose we want to print the nodes of `bt` in pre-order. We could write a function as follows:

```
void preOrder(TreeNodePtr node) {
   void visit(TreeNodePtr);
   if (node != NULL) {
      visit(node);
      preOrder(node -> left);
      preOrder(node -> right);
   }
} //end preOrder
```

where visit could be written as:

```
void visit(TreeNodePtr node) {
   printf("%s ", node -> data.word);
} //end visit
```

We could write similar functions for in-order and post-order. Program P9.1 reads data from a file, builds a binary tree, and prints the pre-order, in-order, and post-order traversals of the tree.

Program P9.1

```
#include <stdio.h>
#include <string.h>
#include <stdlib.h>

#define MaxWordSize 20

typedef struct {
   char word[MaxWordSize+1];
} NodeData;

typedef struct treeNode {
   NodeData data;
   struct treeNode *left, *right;
} TreeNode, *TreeNodePtr;

typedef struct {
   TreeNodePtr root;
} BinaryTree;

int main() {
   TreeNodePtr buildTree(FILE *);
   void preOrder(TreeNodePtr);
   void inOrder(TreeNodePtr);
   void postOrder(TreeNodePtr);

   FILE * in = fopen("btree.in", "r");
   BinaryTree bt;
   bt.root = buildTree(in);
   printf("\nThe pre-order traversal is: ");
   preOrder(bt.root);
   printf("\n\nThe in-order traversal is: ");
   inOrder(bt.root);
   printf("\n\nThe post-order traversal is: ");
   postOrder(bt.root);
   printf("\n\n");
   fclose(in);
} // end main

TreeNodePtr buildTree(FILE * in) {
   char str[MaxWordSize+1];
   fscanf(in, "%s", str);
```

```
   if (strcmp(str, "@") == 0) return NULL;
   TreeNodePtr p = (TreeNodePtr) malloc(sizeof(TreeNode));
   strcpy(p -> data.word, str);
   p -> left = buildTree(in);
   p -> right = buildTree(in);
   return p;
} //end buildTree

void visit(TreeNodePtr node) {
   printf("%s ", node -> data.word);
} //end visit

void preOrder(TreeNodePtr node) {
   void visit(TreeNodePtr);
   if (node != NULL) {
      visit(node);
      preOrder(node -> left);
      preOrder(node -> right);
   }
} //end preOrder

void inOrder(TreeNodePtr node) {
   void visit(TreeNodePtr);
   if (node != NULL) {
      inOrder(node -> left);
      visit(node);
      inOrder(node -> right);
   }
} //end inOrder

void postOrder(TreeNodePtr node) {
   void visit(TreeNodePtr);
   if (node != NULL) {
      postOrder(node -> left);
      postOrder(node -> right);
      visit(node);
   }
} //end postOrder
```

If `btree.in` contains `C E F @ H @ @ B @ @ G A @ @ N J @ @ K @ @`, then the program builds the following tree:

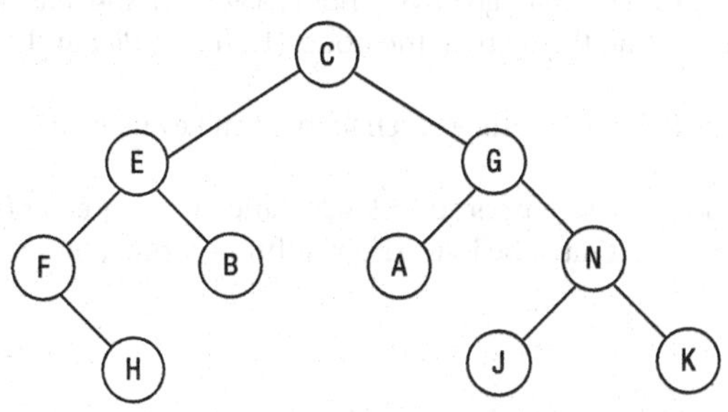

and prints

```
The pre-order traversal is: C E F H B G A N J K
The in-order traversal is: F H E B C A G J N K
The post-order traversal is: H F B E A J K N G C
```

The buildTree method is not restricted to single-character data; any string (not containing whitespace since we use %s to read the data) can be used.

For example, if btree.in contains

```
hat din bun @ @ fan @ @ rum kit @ @ win @ @
```

then Program P9.1 prints

```
The pre-order traversal is: hat din bun fan rum kit win
The in-order traversal is: bun din fan hat kit rum win
The post-order traversal is: bun fan din kit win rum hat
```

As an exercise, draw the tree and verify that these results are correct.

In passing, note that the in-order and pre-order traversals of a binary tree uniquely define that tree. The same holds for in-order and post-order. However, pre-order and post-order do not uniquely define the tree. In other words, it is possible to have two *different* trees A and B where the pre-order and post-order traversals of A are the same as the pre-order and post-order traversals of B, respectively. As an exercise, give an example of such a tree.

9.6 Binary Search Trees

Consider one possible binary tree built with the three-letter words shown in Figure 9-3.

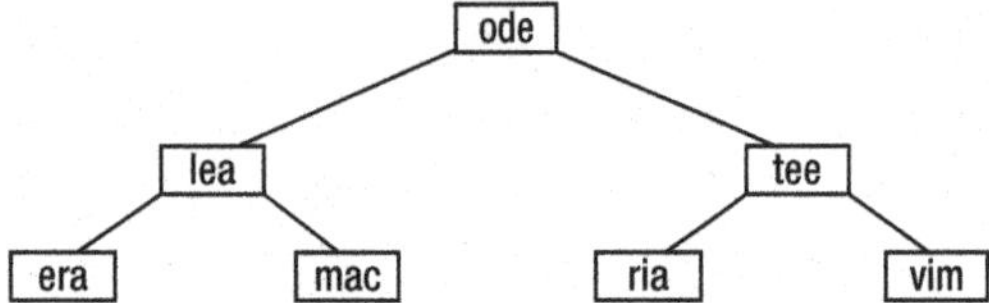

Figure 9-3. *Binary search tree with some three-letter words*

This is a special kind of binary tree. It has the property that, given *any* node, a word in the left subtree is "smaller," and a word in the right subtree is "greater" than the word at the node. (Here, *smaller* and *greater* refer to alphabetical order.)

Such a tree is called a *binary search tree* (BST). It facilitates the search for a given key using a method of searching similar to a binary search of an array.

Consider the search for ria. Starting at the root, ria is compared with ode. Since ria is greater (in alphabetical order) than ode, we can conclude that if it is in the tree, it must be in the right subtree. It must be so since all the nodes in the left subtree are smaller than ode.

Following the right subtree of ode, we next compare ria with tee. Since ria is smaller than tee, we follow the left subtree of tee. We then compare ria with ria, and the search ends successfully.

But what if we were searching for fun?

1. fun is smaller than ode, so we go left.

2. fun is smaller than lea, so we go left again.

3. fun is greater than era, so we must go right.

But since the right subtree of era is empty, we can conclude that fun is not in the tree. If it is necessary to add fun to the tree, note that we have also found the place where it must be added. It must be added as the right subtree of era, as shown in Figure 9-4.

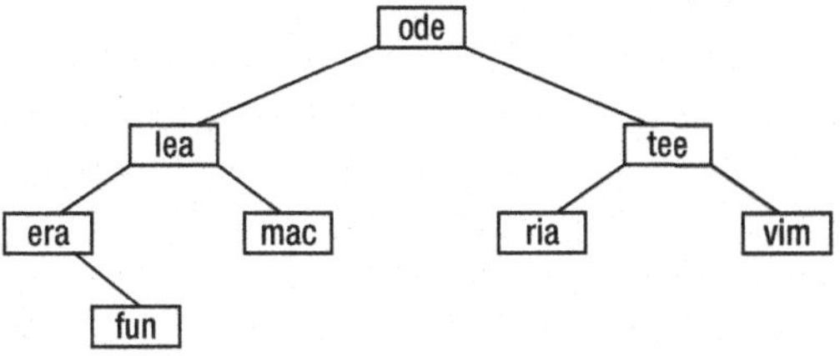

Figure 9-4. *BST after adding fun*

Thus, not only does the binary search tree facilitate searching, but if an item is not found, it can be easily inserted. It combines the speed advantage of a binary search with the easy insertion of a linked list.

The tree drawn in Figure 9-3 is the optimal binary search tree for the seven given words. This means that it is the best possible tree for these words in the sense that no shallower binary tree can be built from these words. It gives the same number of comparisons to find a key as a binary search on a linear array containing these words.

But this is not the only possible search tree for these words. Suppose the words came in one at a time, and as each word came in, it was added to the tree in such a way that the tree remained a binary search tree. The final tree built will depend on the order in which the words came in. For example, suppose the words came in this order:

```
mac  tee  ode  era  ria  lea  vim
```

Initially the tree is empty. When mac comes in, it becomes the root of the tree.

- tee comes next and is compared with mac. Since tee is greater, it is inserted as the right subtree of mac.

- ode comes next and is greater than mac, so we go right; ode is smaller than tee, so it inserted as the left subtree of tee.

- era is next and is smaller than mac, so it is inserted as the left subtree of mac.

The tree built so far is shown in Figure 9-5.

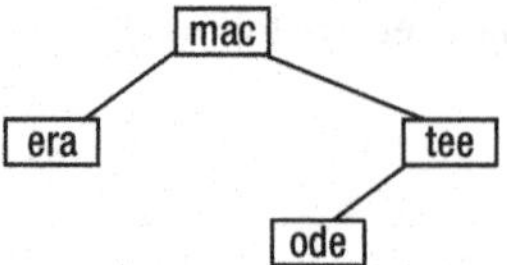

Figure 9-5. *BST after adding mac, tee, ode, era*

- `ria` is next and is greater than `mac`, so we go right; it is smaller than `tee`, so we go left; it is greater than `ode`, so it is inserted as the right subtree of `ode`.

Following this procedure, `lea` is inserted as the right subtree of `era`, and `vim` is inserted as the right subtree of `tee`, giving the final tree shown in Figure 9-6.

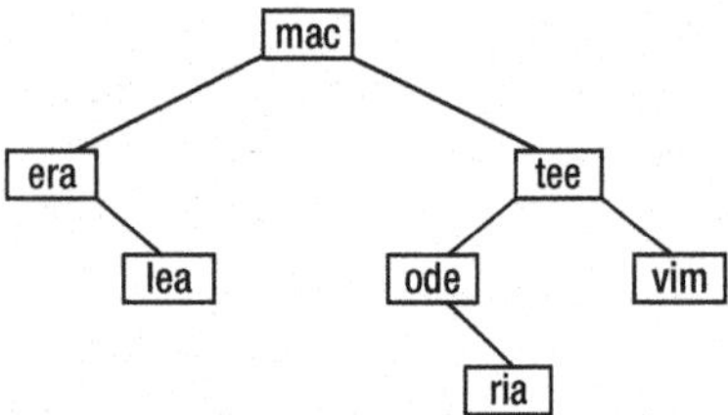

Figure 9-6. *BST after adding all seven words*

Note that the tree obtained is quite different from the optimal search tree. The number of comparisons required to find a given word has also changed. For instance, `ria` now requires four comparisons; it required three previously, and `lea` now requires three as opposed to two previously. But it's not all bad news; `era` now requires two as compared to three previously.

It can be proved that if the words come in random order, then the average search time for a given word is approximately 1.4 times the average for the optimal search tree, that is, $1.4\log_2 n$, for a tree of n nodes.

But what about the worst case? If the words come in alphabetical order, then the tree built will be that shown in Figure 9-7.

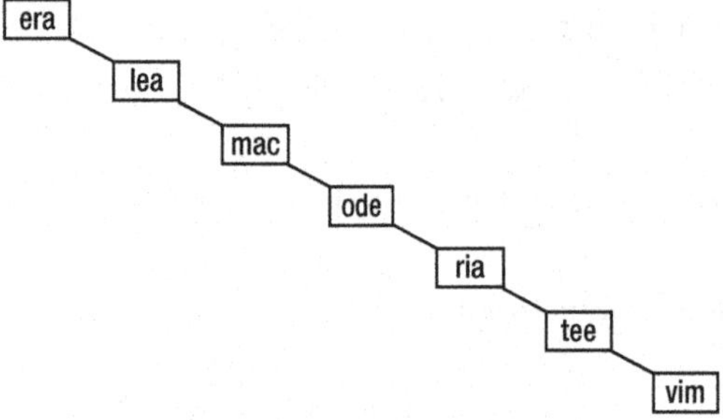

Figure 9-7. *A degenerate tree*

Searching such a tree is reduced to a sequential search of a linked list. This kind of tree is called a *degenerate* tree. Certain orders of the words will give some very unbalanced trees. As an exercise, draw the trees obtained for the following orders of the words:

- vim tee ria ode mac lea era
- era vim lea tee mac ria ode
- vim era lea tee ria mac ode
- lea mac vim tee era ria ode

9.7 Building a Binary Search Tree

We now write a function to find or insert an item in a binary search tree. Assuming the previous definitions of TreeNode and BinaryTree, we write the function findOrInsert. The function searches the tree for a NodeData item, d. If it is found, it returns a pointer to the node. If it is not found, the item is inserted in the tree in its appropriate place, and the function returns a pointer to the new node.

```
TreeNodePtr findOrInsert(BinaryTree bt, NodeData d) {
//searches for d; if found, return pointer to node containing d
//else insert a node containing d and return pointer to new node
   TreeNodePtr newTreeNode(NodeData);

   if (bt.root == NULL) return newTreeNode(d);
   TreeNodePtr curr = bt.root;
   int cmp;
   while ((cmp = strcmp(d.word, curr -> data.word)) != 0) {
      if (cmp < 0) { //try left
         if (curr -> left == NULL) return curr -> left = newTreeNode(d);
         curr = curr -> left;
      }
      else { //try right
         if (curr -> right == NULL) return curr -> right = newTreeNode(d);
         curr = curr -> right;
      }
   }
   //d is in the tree; return pointer to the node
   return curr;
} //end findOrInsert
```

The creation of a new node is delegated to newTreeNode.

```
TreeNodePtr newTreeNode(NodeData d) {
   TreeNodePtr p = (TreeNodePtr) malloc(sizeof(TreeNode));
   p -> data = d;
   p -> left = p -> right = NULL;
   return p;
} //end newTreeNode
```

This allocates storage for the node, stores d in the data field, and sets the left and right pointers to NULL. It returns a pointer to the node created.

9.7.1 Example: Word Frequency Count

We will illustrate the ideas developed so far by writing a program to do a frequency count of the words in a passage. We will store the words in a binary search tree. The tree is searched for each incoming word. If the word is not found, it is added to the tree, and its frequency count is set to 1. If the word is found, then its frequency count is incremented by 1. At the end of the input, an in-order traversal of the tree gives the words in alphabetical order.

First, we must define the `NodeData` structure. This will consist of two fields: a word and its frequency. Here is the definition:

```
typedef struct {
   char word[MaxWordSize+1];
   int freq;
} NodeData;
```

For our program, we will define a word to be any consecutive sequence of uppercase or lowercase letters. All words are converted to lowercase before processing. We will write a function called `getWord` to read a word.

The gist of the algorithm for building the search tree is as follows:

```
create empty tree; set root to NULL
while (there is another word) {
   get the word
   search for word in tree; insert if necessary and set frequency to 0
   add 1 to frequency //for an old word or a newly inserted one
}
print words and frequencies
```

We now write Program P9.2 to do the frequency count of words in the file `wordFreq.in`. It simply reflects the algorithm above.

Program P9.2

```
#include <stdio.h>
#include <string.h>
#include <stdlib.h>
#include <ctype.h>
#define MaxWordSize 20

typedef struct {
   char word[MaxWordSize+1];
   int freq;
} NodeData;

typedef struct treeNode {
   NodeData data;
   struct treeNode *left, *right;
} TreeNode, *TreeNodePtr;

typedef struct {
   TreeNodePtr root;
} BinaryTree;
```

```
int main() {
   int getWord(FILE *, char[]);
   TreeNodePtr newTreeNode(NodeData);
   NodeData newNodeData(char [], int);
   TreeNodePtr findOrInsert(BinaryTree, NodeData);
   void inOrder(FILE *, TreeNodePtr);

   char word[MaxWordSize+1];

   FILE * in = fopen("wordFreq.in", "r");
   FILE * out = fopen("wordFreq.out", "w");

   BinaryTree bst;
   bst.root = NULL;

   while (getWord(in, word) != 0) {
      if (bst.root == NULL)
         bst.root = newTreeNode(newNodeData(word, 1));
      else {
         TreeNodePtr node = findOrInsert(bst, newNodeData(word, 0));
         node -> data.freq++;
      }
   }

   fprintf(out, "\nWords        Frequency\n\n");
   inOrder(out, bst.root); fprintf(out, "\n\n");
   fclose(in);
   fclose(out);
} // end main

int getWord(FILE * in, char str[]) {
// stores the next word, if any, in str; word is converted to lowercase
// returns 1 if a word is found; 0, otherwise
   char ch;
   int n = 0;
   // read over non-letters
   while (!isalpha(ch = getc(in)) && ch != EOF) ; //empty while body
   if (ch == EOF) return 0;
   str[n++] = tolower(ch);
   while (isalpha(ch = getc(in)) && ch != EOF)
      if (n < MaxWordSize) str[n++] = tolower(ch);
   str[n] = '\0';
   return 1;
} // end getWord

TreeNodePtr findOrInsert(BinaryTree bt, NodeData d) {
//searches for d; if found, return pointer to node containing d
//else insert a node containing d and return pointer to new node
   TreeNodePtr newTreeNode(NodeData);
```

```
   if (bt.root == NULL) return newTreeNode(d);
   TreeNodePtr curr = bt.root;
   int cmp;
   while ((cmp = strcmp(d.word, curr -> data.word)) != 0) {
      if (cmp < 0) { //try left
         if (curr -> left == NULL) return curr -> left = newTreeNode(d);
         curr = curr -> left;
      }
      else { //try right
         if (curr -> right == NULL) return curr -> right = newTreeNode(d);
         curr = curr -> right;
      }
   }
   //d is in the tree; return pointer to the node
   return curr;
} //end findOrInsert

TreeNodePtr newTreeNode(NodeData d) {
   TreeNodePtr p = (TreeNodePtr) malloc(sizeof(TreeNode));
   p -> data = d;
   p -> left = p -> right = NULL;
   return p;
} //end newTreeNode

void inOrder(FILE * out, TreeNodePtr node) {
   if (node!= NULL) {
      inOrder(out, node -> left);
      fprintf(out, "%-15s %2d\n", node -> data.word, node -> data.freq);
      inOrder(out, node -> right);
   }
} //end inOrder

NodeData newNodeData(char str[], int n) {
   NodeData temp;
   strcpy(temp.word, str);
   temp.freq = n;
   return temp;
} //end newNodeData
```

Since `newTreeNode` and `findOrInsert` require `NodeData` structures as arguments, we must create a `NodeData` structure from a given `word` to pass as the argument. The function `newNodeData` stores a given word and frequency in a `NodeData` structure and returns the structure. It is used as shown in the `while` loop in `main`.

An in-order traversal of the search tree yields the words in alphabetical order.

When Program P9.2 was run with the following data in `wordFreq.in`:

> The quick brown fox jumps over the lazy dog. Congratulations!
> If the quick brown fox jumped over the lazy dog then
> Why did the quick brown fox jump over the lazy dog?
> Why, why, why? To recuperate! Recuperate?

it produced the following output:

```
Words          Frequency
brown              3
congratulations    1
did                1
dog                3
fox                3
if                 1
jump               1
jumped             1
jumps              1
lazy               3
over               3
quick              3
recuperate         2
the                6
then               1
to                 1
why                4
```

9.8 An Array as a Binary Tree Representation

A *complete* binary tree is one in which every nonleaf node has two nonempty subtrees and all leaves are at the same level. Figure 9-8 shows some complete binary trees.

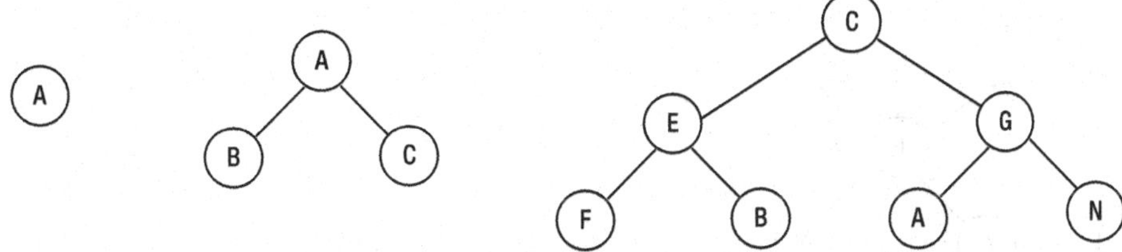

Figure 9-8. *Complete binary trees*

The first is a complete binary tree of height 1, the second is a complete binary tree of height 2, and the third is a complete binary tree of height 3. For a complete binary tree of height n, the number of nodes in the tree is $2^n - 1$.

Consider the third tree. Let's number the nodes as shown in Figure 9-9.

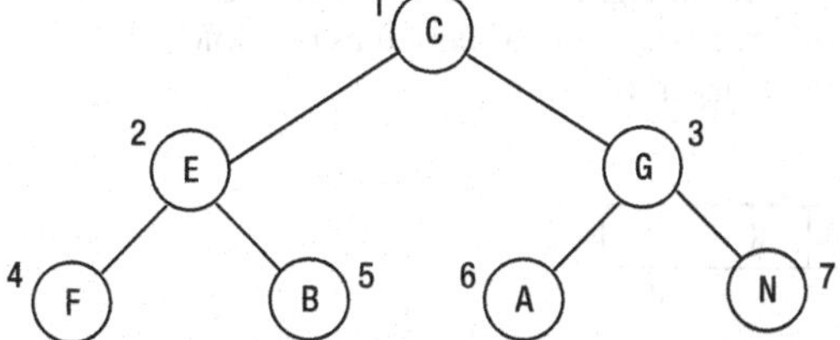

Figure 9-9. *Numbering the nodes, level by level*

Starting from 1 at the root, we number the nodes in order from top to bottom and from left to right at each level. Observe that if a node has label n, its left subtree has label $2n$, and its right subtree has label $2n + 1$.

If the nodes are stored in an array `T[1..7]`, like this:

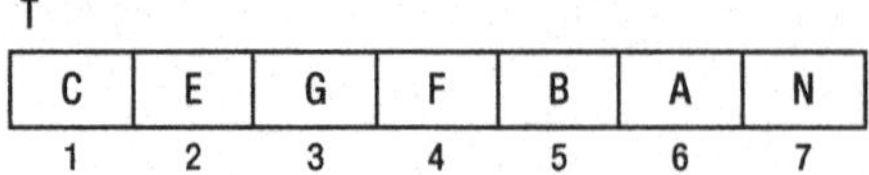

then

- `T[1]` is the root.
- The left subtree of `T[i]` is `T[2i]` if 2i <= 7 and `null` otherwise.
- The right subtree of `T[i]` is `T[2i+1]` if 2i+1 <= 7 and `null` otherwise.
- The parent of `T[i]` is `T[i/2]` (integer division).

Based on this, the array is a representation of a complete binary tree. In other words, given the array, we can easily construct the binary tree it represents.

An array represents a complete binary tree if the number of elements in the array is $2^n - 1$, for some n. If the number of elements is some other value, the array represents an *almost complete* binary tree.

An *almost complete binary tree* is one in which

(a) all levels, except possibly the lowest, are completely filled.

(b) the nodes (all leaves) at the lowest level are as far left as possible.

If the nodes are numbered as shown earlier, then all leaves will be labeled with consecutive numbers from `n/2+1` to `n`. The last nonleaf node will have label `n/2`. For example, consider the tree with ten nodes drawn and labeled as in Figure 9-10.

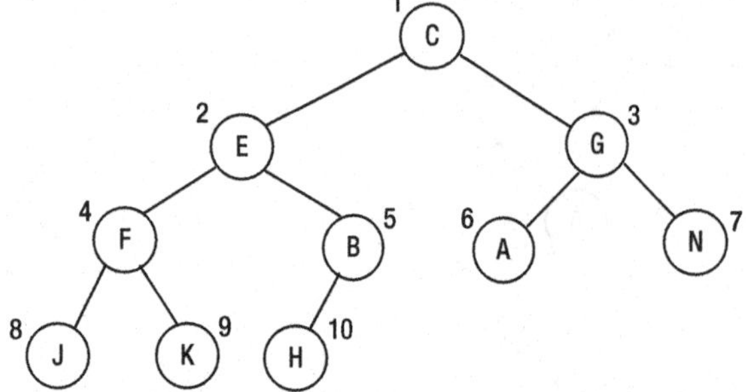

Figure 9-10. *A tree of ten nodes labeled level by level*

Note that the leaves are numbered from 6 to 10. If, for instance, `H` were the right subtree of `B` instead of the left, the tree would not be "almost complete" since the leaves on the lowest level would not be "as far left as possible."

The following array of size 10 can represent this almost complete binary tree:

T

C	E	G	F	B	A	N	J	K	H
1	2	3	4	5	6	7	8	9	10

In general, if the tree is represented by an array `T[1..n]`, the following are true:

- `T[1]` is the root.
- The left subtree of `T[i]` is `T[2i]` if `2i <= n` and `null` otherwise.
- The right subtree of `T[i]` is `T[2i+1]` if `2i+1 <= n` and `null` otherwise.
- The parent of `T[i]` is `T[i/2]` (integer division).

Looked at another way, there is exactly one almost complete binary tree with *n* nodes, and an array of size *n* represents this tree.

An almost complete binary tree has no "holes" in it; there is no room to add a node in between existing nodes. The only place to add a node is after the last one.

For instance, Figure 9-11 is not "almost complete" since there is a "hole" at the right subtree of `B`.

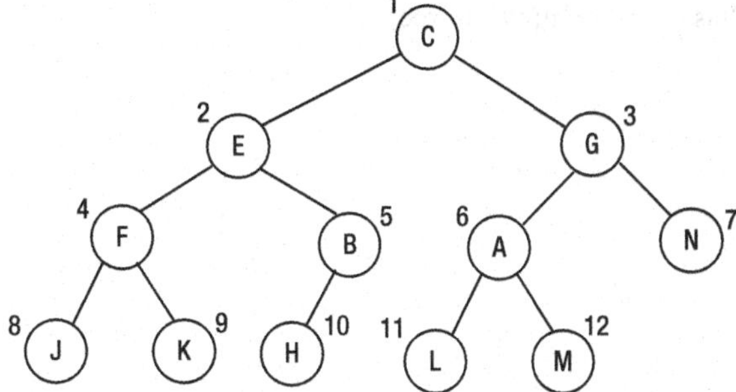

***Figure 9-11.** Empty right subtree of B makes this not "almost complete"*

With the hole, the left subtree of `A` (in position 6) is *not* now in position 6*2 = 12, and the right subtree is not in position 6*2+1 =13. This relationship holds only when the tree is almost complete.

Given an array `T[1..n]` representing an almost complete binary tree with *n* nodes, we can perform an in-order traversal of the tree with the call `inOrder(1, n)` of the following function:

```
void inOrder(int h, int n) {
   if (h <= n) {
      inOrder(h * 2, n);
      visit(h); //or visit(T[h]), if you wish
      inOrder(h * 2 + 1, n);
   }
} //end inOrder
```

We can write similar functions for pre-order and post-order traversals.

By comparison to a complete binary tree, a *full binary tree* is one in which every node, except a leaf, has exactly two nonempty subtrees. Figure 9-12 is an example of a full binary tree.

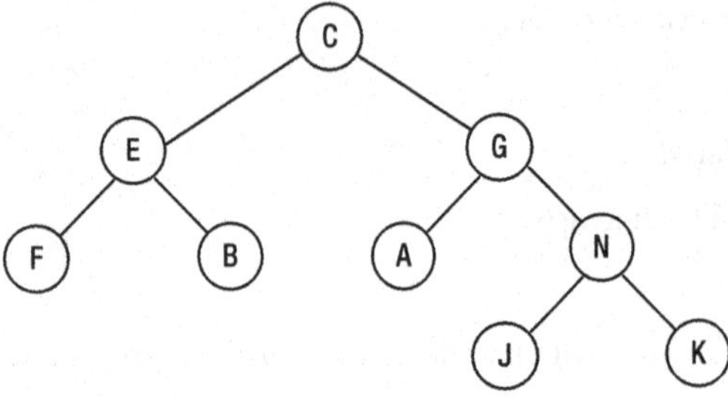

Figure 9-12. *A full binary tree*

Note that a complete binary tree is always full, but as shown in Figure 9-12, a full binary tree is not necessarily complete. An almost complete binary tree may or may not be full.

The tree in Figure 9-13 is almost complete but not full (G has *one* nonempty subtree).

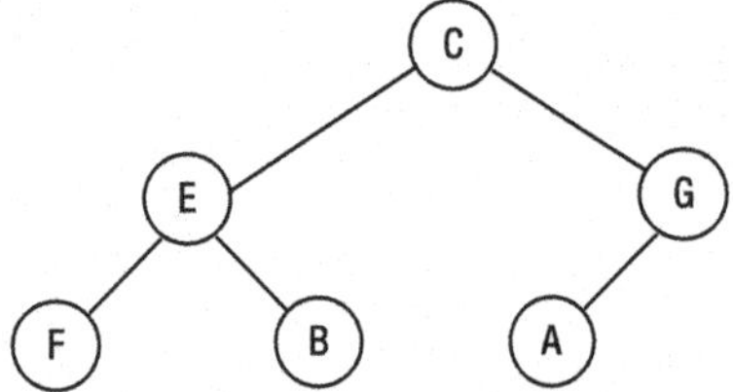

Figure 9-13. *An almost complete but not full binary tree*

However, if node A is removed, the tree will be almost complete *and* full.

In the next chapter, we will explain how to sort an array by interpreting it as an almost complete binary tree.

9.9 Some Useful Binary Tree Functions

We will now show you how to write some functions that return information about a binary tree. The functions are all recursive, reflecting the recursive nature of a binary tree.

The first counts the number of nodes in a tree.

```
int numNodes(TreeNodePtr root) {
   if (root == NULL) return 0;
   return 1 + numNodes(root -> left) + numNodes(root -> right);
}
```

If bt is a BinaryTree, numNodes(bt.root) returns the number of nodes in the tree.

The next function returns the number of leaves in the tree:

```
int numLeaves(TreeNodePtr root) {
   if (root == NULL) return 0;
   if (root-> left == NULL && root-> right == NULL) return 1;
   return numLeaves(root-> left) + numLeaves(root-> right);
}
```

And the next returns the height of the tree:

```
int height(TreeNodePtr root) {
   if (root == NULL) return 0;
   return 1 + max(height (root-> left), height (root-> right));
}
```

where max can be defined as follows:

```
#define max(a, b) ((a) > (b) ? (a) : (b))
```

You are advised to test these functions on some sample trees to verify that they return the correct values.

9.10 Binary Search Tree Deletion

Consider the problem of deleting a node from a binary search tree so that it remains a BST. There are three cases to consider.

1. The node is a leaf.
2. (a) The node has no left subtree

   (b) The node has no right subtree
3. The node has nonempty left and right subtrees.

We illustrate these cases using the BST shown in Figure 9-14.

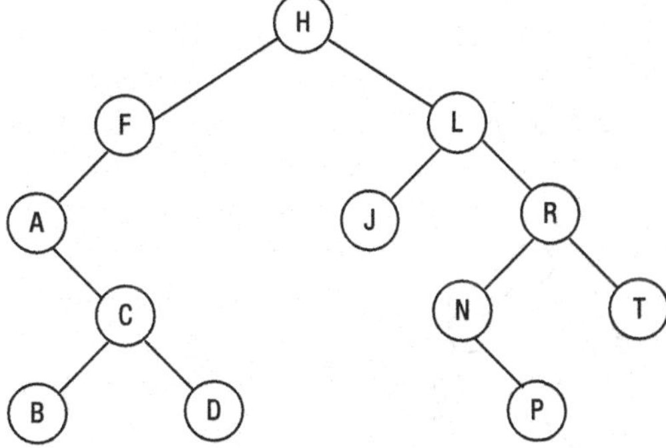

Figure 9-14. *A binary search tree*

Case 1 is easy. For example, to delete P, we simply set the right subtree of N to null. Case 2 is also easy. To delete A (no left subtree), we replace it by C, its right subtree. And to delete F (no right subtree), we replace it by A, its left subtree.

Case 3 is a bit more difficult since we have to worry about what to do with two subtrees. For example, how do we delete L? One approach is to replace L by its in-order successor, N, which *must* have an empty left subtree. Why? Because, by definition, the in-order successor of a node is the first node (in order) in its right subtree. And this first node (in any tree) is found by going as far left as possible.

Since N has no left subtree, we will set its left link to the left subtree of L. We will set the left link of the parent of N (R in this case) to point to P, the right subtree of N. Finally, we will set the right link of N to point to the right subtree of L, giving the tree shown in Figure 9-15.

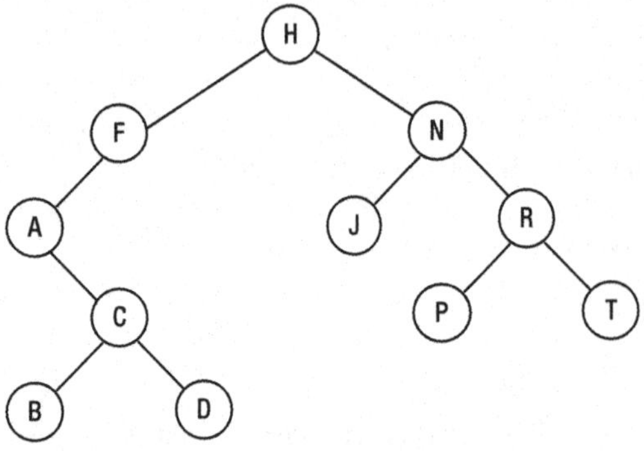

***Figure 9-15.** BST after deletion of L in BST 9.14*

Another way to look at it is to imagine the contents of node N being copied into node L. And the left link of the parent of N is set to point to the right subtree of N.

We will treat the node to be deleted as the root of a subtree. We will delete the root and return a pointer to the root of the reconstructed tree. The following is a function, written in pseudocode, to perform this task:

```
deleteNode(TreeNode T) {
   if (T == null) return null
   if (right(T) == null) return left(T)  //cases 1 and 2b
   R = right(T)
   if (left(T) == null) return R //case 2a
   if (left(R) == null) {
      left(R) == left(T)
      return R
   }

   while (left(R) != null) { //will be executed at least once
      P = R
      R = left(R)
   }
   //R is pointing to the in-order successor of T;
   //P is its parent
   left(R) = left(T)
   left(P) = right(R)
   right(R) = right(T)
   return R
} //end deleteNode
```

Suppose we call deleteNode with a pointer to the node L in Figure 9-14 as argument. The function will delete L and return a pointer to the following tree:

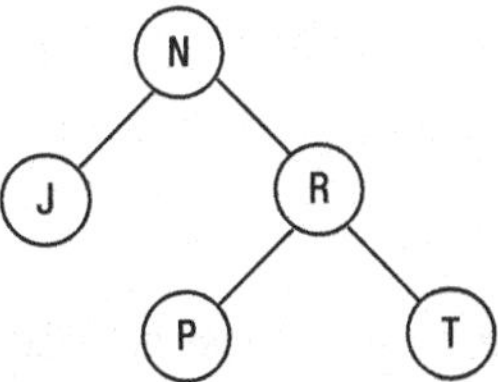

Since L was the right subtree of H, we can now set the right subtree of H to point to this tree.

EXERCISES 9

1. A binary tree consists of an integer key field and pointers to the left subtree, right subtree, and parent. Write the declarations required for building a tree and code to create an empty tree.
2. Each node of a binary tree has fields left, right, key, and parent.

   Write a function to return the in-order successor of any given node x. Hint: if the right subtree of node x is empty and x has a successor y, then y is the lowest ancestor of x, which contains x in its *left* subtree.

   Write a function to return the pre-order successor of any given node x.

   Write a function to return the post-order successor of any given node x.

   Using these functions, write functions to perform the in-order, pre-order, and post-order traversals of a given binary tree.
3. Write a function that, given the root of a binary search tree, deletes the smallest node and returns a pointer to the root of the reconstructed tree.
4. Write a function that, given the root of a binary search tree, deletes the largest node and returns a pointer to the root of the reconstructed tree.
5. Write a function that, given the root of a binary search tree, deletes the root and returns a pointer to the root of the reconstructed tree. Write the function replacing the root by (i) its in-order successor and (ii) its in-order predecessor.
6. Draw a nondegenerate binary tree of five nodes such that the pre-order and level-order traversals produce identical results.
7. Write a function that, given the root of binary tree, returns the *width* of the tree, that is, the maximum number of nodes at any level.
8. Draw two different binary trees such that the pre-order and post-order traversals of the one tree are identical to the pre-order and post-order traversals of the other tree.

9. A binary search tree contains integers. For each of the following sequences, state whether it could be the sequence of values examined in searching for the number `36`. If it cannot, state why.

```
7 25 42 40 33 34 39 36
92 22 91 24 89 20 35 36
95 20 90 24 92 27 30 36
7 46 41 21 26 39 37 24 36
```

10. Draw the binary search tree (BST) obtained for the following keys assuming they are inserted in the order given: `56 30 61 39 47 35 75 13 21 64 26 73 18`.

    There is one almost complete BST for the previous keys. Draw it.

    List the keys in an order that will produce the almost complete BST.

    Assuming that the almost complete tree is stored in a one-dimensional array `num[1..13]`, write a recursive function for printing the integers in post-order.

11. An imaginary "external" node is attached to each null pointer of a binary tree of *n* nodes. How many external nodes are there?

    If `I` is the sum of the levels of the original tree nodes and `E` is the sum of the levels of the external nodes, prove that `E - I` = 2*n*. (`I` is called the *internal path length*.)

    Write a recursive function that, given the root of a binary tree, returns `I`.

    Write a nonrecursive function that, given the root of a binary tree, returns `I`.

12. Draw the binary tree whose in-order and post-order traversals of the nodes are as follows:

```
In-order:    G D P K E N F A T L
Post-order:    G P D K F N T A L E
```

13. Draw the binary tree whose in-order and pre-order traversals of the nodes are as follows:

```
In-order:    G D P K E N F A T L
Pre-order:    N D G K P E T F A L
```

14. Write a recursive function that, given the root of a binary tree and a key, searches for the key using (i) a pre-order, (ii) an in-order, and (iii) a post-order traversal. If found, return the node containing the key; otherwise, return `null`.

15. Each node of a *binary search tree* contains three fields—`left`, `right`, and `data`—with their usual meanings; `data` is a positive integer field. Write an *efficient* function that, given the root of the tree and `key`, returns the *smallest* number in the tree that is *greater* than `key`. If there is no such number, return `-1`.

16. Store the following integers in an array `bst[1..15]` such that `bst` represents a complete binary search tree: 34 23 45 46 37 78 90 2 40 20 87 53 12 15 91.

17. Write a program that takes a C program as input and outputs the program, numbering the lines, followed by an alphabetical cross-reference listing of all user identifiers; that is, a user identifier is followed by the numbers of all lines in which the identifier appears. If an identifier appears more than once in a given line, the line number must be repeated the number of times it appears.

    The cross-reference listing must *not* contain C reserved words, words within character strings, or words within comments.

CHAPTER 10

Advanced Sorting

In this chapter, we will explain the following:

- What a heap is and how to perform heapsort using `siftDown`
- How to build a heap using `siftUp`
- How to analyze the performance of heapsort
- How a heap can be used to implement a priority queue
- How to sort a list of items using quicksort
- How to find the kth smallest item in a list
- How to sort a list of items using Shell (diminishing increment) sort

In Chapter 1, we discussed two simple methods (selection and insertion sort) for sorting a list of items. In this chapter, we take a detailed look at some faster methods—heapsort, quicksort, and Shell (diminishing increment) sort.

10.1 Heapsort

Heapsort is a method of sorting that *interprets* the elements in an array as an almost complete binary tree. Consider the following array, which is to be sorted in ascending order:

num

37	25	43	65	48	84	73	18	79	56	69	32
1	2	3	4	5	6	7	8	9	10	11	12

We can think of this array as an almost complete binary tree with 12 nodes, as shown in Figure 10-1.

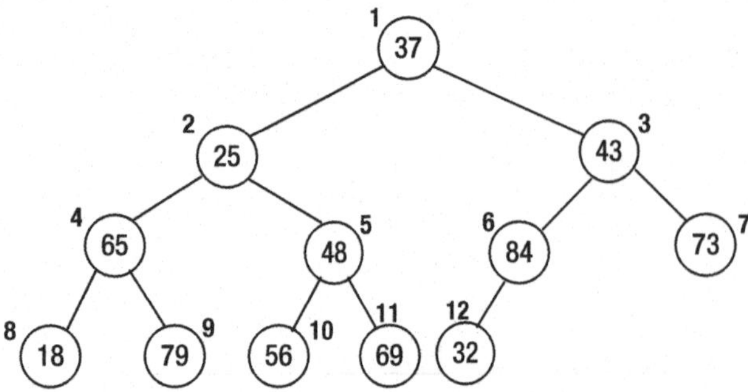

***Figure 10-1.** A binary tree view of the array*

Suppose we now require that the value at each node be greater than or equal to the values in its left and right subtrees, if present. As it is, only node 6 and the leaves have this property. Shortly, we will see how to rearrange the nodes so that *all* nodes satisfy this condition. But, first, we give this condition a name:

> *A **heap** is an almost complete binary tree such that the value at the root is greater than or equal to the values at the left and right children, and the left and right subtrees are also heaps.*

An immediate consequence of this definition is that the largest value is at the root. Such a heap is referred to as a *max-heap*. We define a *min-heap* with the word *greater* replaced by *smaller*. In a min-heap, the *smallest* value is at the root.

Let's now convert the binary tree in Figure 10-1 into a max-heap.

10.1.1 Converting a Binary Tree into a Max-Heap

First, we observe that all the leaves are heaps since they have no children.

Starting at the last nonleaf node (6, in the example), we convert the tree rooted there into a max-heap. If the value at the node is greater than its children, there is nothing to do. This is the case with node 6, since 84 is bigger than 32.

Next, we move on to node 5. The value here, 48, is smaller than at least one child (both, in this case, 56 and 69). We first find the larger child (69) and interchange it with node 5. Thus, 69 ends up in node 5, and 48 ends up in node 11.

Next, we go to node 4. The larger child, 79, is moved to node 4, and 65 is moved to node 9. At this stage, the tree looks like that in Figure 10-2.

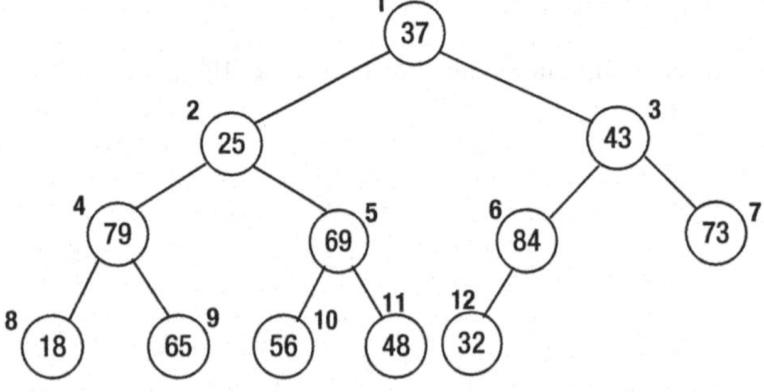

***Figure 10-2.** The tree after nodes 6, 5, and 4 have been processed*

Continuing at node 3, 43 must be moved. The larger child is 84, so we interchange the values at nodes 3 and 6. The value now at node 6 (43) is bigger than its child (32), so there is nothing more to do. Note, however, that if the value at node 6 were 28, say, it would have had to be exchanged with 32.

Moving to node 2, 25 is exchanged with its larger child, 79. But 25 now in node 4 is smaller than 65, its right child in node 9. Thus, these two values must be exchanged.

Finally, at node 1, 37 is exchanged with its larger child, 84. It is further exchanged with its (new) larger child, 73, giving the tree, which is now a heap, shown in Figure 10-3.

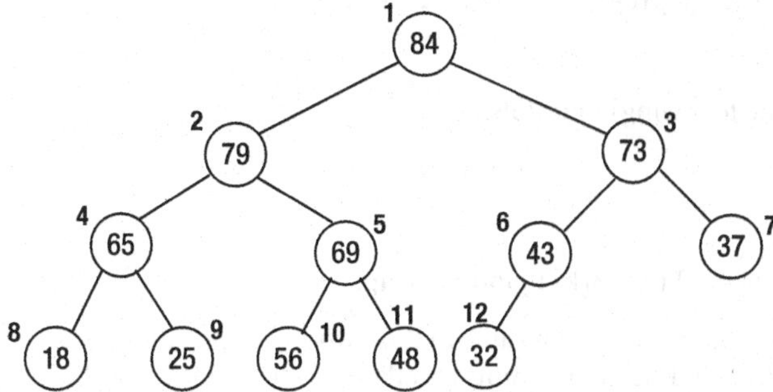

Figure 10-3. *The final tree, which is now a heap*

10.1.2 The Sorting Process

After conversion to a heap, note that the largest value, 84, is at the root of the tree. Now that the values in the array form a heap, we can sort them in ascending order as follows:

> Store the last item, 32, in a temporary location. Next, move 84 to the last position (node 12), freeing node 1. Then, imagine 32 is in node 1 and move it so that items 1 to 11 become a heap. This will be done as follows:
>
> 32 is exchanged with its bigger child, 79, which now moves into node 1. 32 is further exchanged with its (new) bigger child, 69, which moves into node 2.
>
> Finally, 32 is exchanged with 56, giving us Figure 10-4.

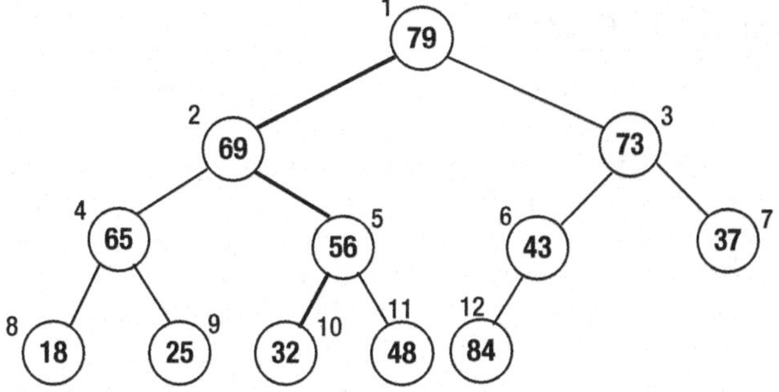

Figure 10-4. *After 84 has been placed and the heap is reorganized*

At this stage, the second largest number, 79, is in node 1. This is placed in node 11, and 48 is "sifted down" from node 1 until items 1 to 10 form a heap. Now, the third largest number, 73, will be at the root. This is placed in node 10, and so on. The process is repeated until the array is sorted.

After the initial heap is built, the sorting process can be described with the following:

```
for k = n downto 2 do
   item = num[k]   //extract current last item
   num[k] = num[1]   //move top of heap to current last node
   siftDown(item, num, 1, k-1)  //restore heap properties from 1 to k-1
end for
```

where `siftDown(item, num, 1, k-1)` is based on the following conditions:

- `num[1]` is empty.
- `num[2]` to `num[k-1]` form a heap.
- Starting at position 1, `item` is inserted so that `num[1]` to `num[k-1]` form a heap.

In the sorting process described above, each time through the loop, the value in the current last position (`k`) is stored in `item`. The value at node 1 is moved to position `k`; node 1 becomes empty (available), and nodes 2 to `k-1` all satisfy the heap property.

The call `siftDown(item, num, 1, k-1)` will add `item` so that `num[1]` to `num[k-1]` contain a heap. This ensures that the next highest number is at node 1.

The nice thing about `siftDown` (when we write it) is that it can be used to create the initial heap from the given array. Recall the process of creating a heap described in Section 10.1.1. At each node (`h`, say), we "sifted the value down" so that we formed a heap rooted at `h`. To use `siftDown` in this situation, we generalize it as follows:

```
void siftDown(int key, int num[], int root, int last)
```

This assumes the following:

- `num[root]` is empty.
- `num[root+1]` to `num[last]` form a heap.
- Starting at `root`, `key` is inserted so that `num[root]` to `num[last]` form a heap.

Given an array of values `num[1]` to `num[n]`, we could build the heap with this:

```
for h = n/2 downto 1 do // n/2 is the last non-leaf node
      siftDown(num[h], num, h, n)
```

We now show how to write `siftDown`.

Consider Figure 10-5.

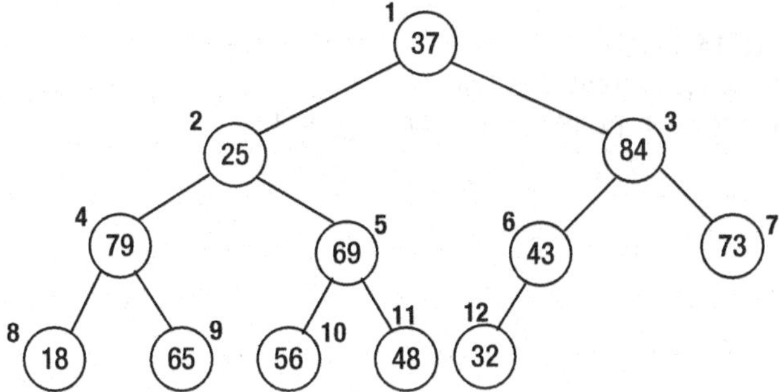

Figure 10-5. *A heap, except for nodes 1 and 2*

Except for nodes 1 and 2, all the other nodes satisfy the heap property that they are bigger than or equal to their children. Suppose we want to make node 2 the root of a heap. As it is, the value 25 is smaller than its children (79 and 69). We want to write `siftDown` so that the call `siftDown(25, num, 2, 12)` will do the job. Here, `25` is the key, `num` is the array, 2 is the root, and 12 is the position of the last node.

After this, each of nodes 2 to 12 will be the root of a heap, and the call `siftDown(37, num, 1, 12)` will ensure that the entire array contains a heap.

The gist of `siftDown` is as follows:

```
find the larger child of num[root]; //suppose it is in node m
if (key >= num[m]) we are done; put key in num[root]
//key is smaller than the bigger child
store num[m] in num[root]  //promote bigger child
set root to m
```

The process is repeated until the value at `root` is bigger than its children or there are no children. Here is `siftDown`:

```
void siftDown(int key, int num[], int root, int last) {
   int bigger = 2 * root;
   while (bigger <= last) { //while there is at least one child
      if (bigger < last) //there is a right child as well; find the bigger
         if (num[bigger+1] > num[bigger]) bigger++;
      //'bigger' holds the index of the bigger child
      if (key >= num[bigger]) break;
      //key is smaller; promote num[bigger]
      num[root] = num[bigger];
      root = bigger;
      bigger = 2 * root;
   }
   num[root] = key;
} //end siftDown
```

We can now write heap`Sort` as follows:

```
void heapSort(int num[], int n) {
//sort num[1] to num[n]
   void siftDown(int, int[], int, int);
   //convert the array to a heap
   for (int h = n / 2; h >= 1; h--) siftDown(num[h], num, h, n);
```

```
      for (int k = n; k > 1; k--) {
         int item = num[k]; //extract current last item
         num[k] = num[1];    //move top of heap to current last node
         siftDown(item, num, 1, k-1); //restore heap properties from 1 to k-1
      }
   } //end heapSort
```

We can test it with the following:

```
   #include <stdio.h>
   int main() {
      void heapSort(int[], int);
      int num[] = {0, 37, 25, 43, 65, 48, 84, 73, 18, 79, 56, 69, 32};
      int n = 12;
      heapSort(num, n);
      for (int h = 1; h <= n; h++) printf("%d ", num[h]);
      printf("\n");
   } //end main
```

This produces the following output (`num[1]` to `num[12]` sorted):

```
   18 25 32 37 43 48 56 65 69 73 79 84
```

Programming note: As written, `heapSort` sorts an array assuming that *n* elements are stored from subscripts `1` to `n`. If they are stored from `0` to `n-1`, appropriate adjustments would have to be made. They would be based mainly on the following observations:

- The root is stored in `num[0]`.
- The left child of node `h` is node `2h + 1` if `2h + 1` < `n`.
- The right child of node `h` is node `2h + 2` if `2h + 2` < `n`.
- The parent of node `h` is node `(h - 1) / 2` (integer division).
- The last nonleaf node is `(n - 1) / 2` (integer division).

You can verify these observations using the tree (n = 12) shown in Figure 10-6.

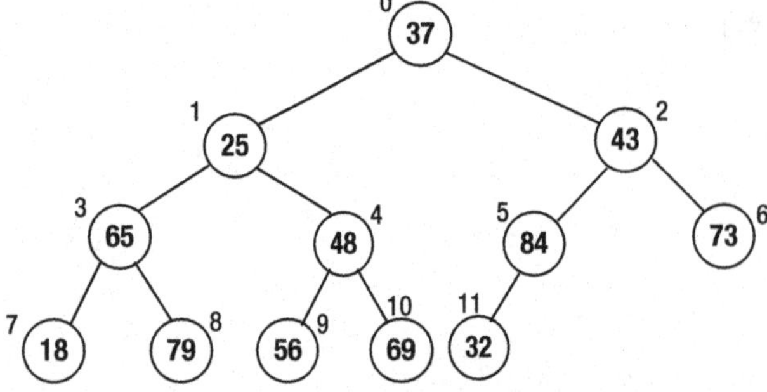

Figure 10-6. *A binary tree stored in an array starting at 0*

You are urged to rewrite heapSort so that it sorts the array num[0..n-1]. As a hint, note that the only change required in siftDown is in the calculation of bigger. Instead of 2 * root, we now use 2 * root + 1.

10.2 Building a Heap Using siftUp

Consider the problem of adding a new node to an existing heap. Specifically, suppose num[1] to num[n] contain a heap. We want to add a new number, newKey, so that num[1] to num[n+1] contain a heap that includes newKey. We assume the array has room for the new key.

For example, suppose we have the heap shown in Figure 10-7 and we want to add 40 to the heap. When the new number is added, the heap will contain 13 elements. We imagine 40 is placed in num[13] (but do not store it there, as yet) and compare it with its parent 43 in num[6]. Since 40 is smaller, the heap property is satisfied; we place 40 in num[13], and the process ends.

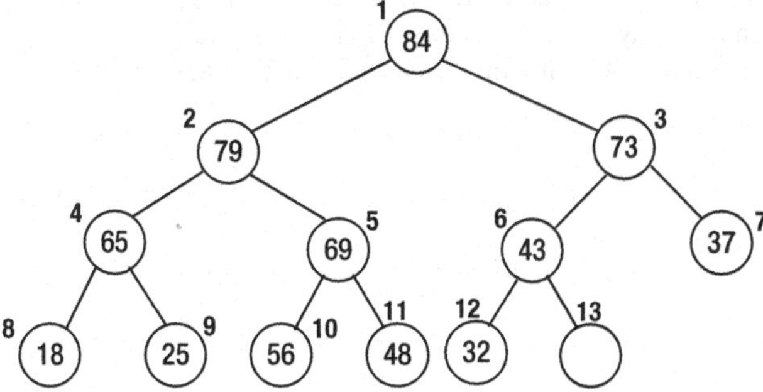

Figure 10-7. *A heap to which we will add a new item*

But suppose we want to add 80 to the heap. We imagine 80 is placed in num[13] (but do not actually store it there, as yet) and compare it with its parent 43 in num[6]. Since 80 is bigger, we move 43 to num[13] and imagine 80 being placed in num[6].

Next, we compare 80 with its parent 73 in num[3]. It is bigger, so we move 73 to num[6] and imagine 80 being placed in num[3].

We then compare 80 with its parent 84 in num[1]. It is smaller, so we place 80 in num[3], and the process ends.

Note that if we were adding 90 to the heap, 84 would be moved to num[3], and 90 would be inserted in num[1]. It is now the largest number in the heap.

Figure 10-8 shows the heap after 80 is added.

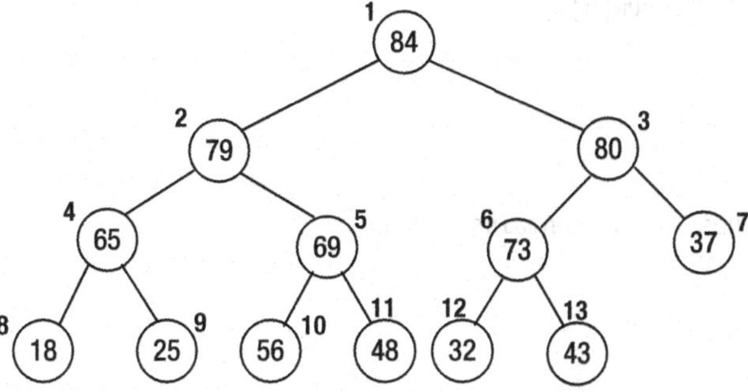

Figure 10-8. *The heap after 80 is added*

The following algorithm adds newKey to a heap stored in num[1] to num[n]:

```
child = n + 1;
parent = child / 2;
while (parent > 0) {
   if (newKey <= num[parent]) break;
   num[child] = num[parent]; //move down parent
   child = parent;
   parent = child / 2;
}
num[child] = newKey;
n = n + 1;
```

The process described is usually referred to as *sifting up*. We can rewrite this algorithm as a function siftUp. We assume that siftUp is given an array heap[1..n] such that heap[1..n-1] contains a heap and heap[n] is to be sifted up so that heap[1..n] contains a heap. In other words, heap[n] plays the role of newKey in the algorithm above.

We show siftUp as part of Program P10.1, which creates a heap out of numbers stored in a file, heap.in.

Program P10.1

```
#include <stdio.h>
#include <stdlib.h>
#define MaxHeapSize 100
int main() {
   void siftUp(int[], int);
   int num[MaxHeapSize + 1];
   int n = 0, number;
   FILE * in = fopen("heap.in", "r");

   while (fscanf(in, "%d", &number) == 1) {
      if (n < MaxHeapSize) { //check if array has room
         num[++n] = number;
         siftUp(num, n);
      }
      else {
         printf("\nArray too small\n");
         exit(1);
      }
   }
   for (int h = 1; h <= n; h++) printf("%d ", num[h]);
   printf("\n");
   fclose(in);
} //end main

void siftUp(int heap[], int n) {
//sifts up the value in heap[n] so that heap[1..n] contains a heap
   int siftItem = heap[n];
   int child = n;
   int parent = child / 2;
   while (parent > 0) {
      if (siftItem <= heap[parent]) break;
      heap[child] = heap[parent]; //move down parent
```

```
            child = parent;
            parent = child / 2;
         }
         heap[child] = siftItem;
      } //end siftUp
```

If heap.in contains the following:

```
37 25 43 65 48 84 73 18 79 56 69 32
```

Program P10.1 will build the heap (described next) and print the following:

```
84 79 73 48 69 37 65 18 25 43 56 32
```

After 37, 25, and 43 are read, we will have Figure 10-9.

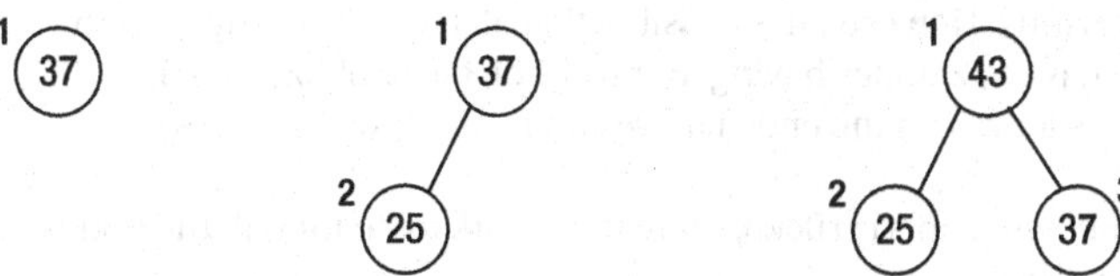

Figure 10-9. *Heap after processing 37, 25, 43*

After 65, 48, 84, and 73 are read, we will have Figure 10-10.

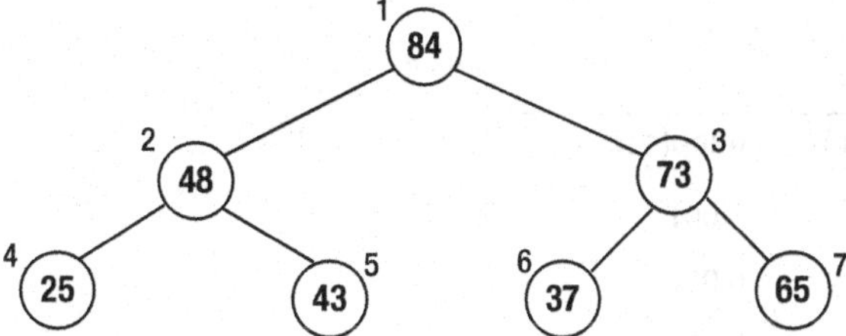

Figure 10-10. *Heap after processing 65, 48, 84, 73*

And after 18, 79, 56, 69, and 32 are read, we will have the final heap shown in Figure 10-11.

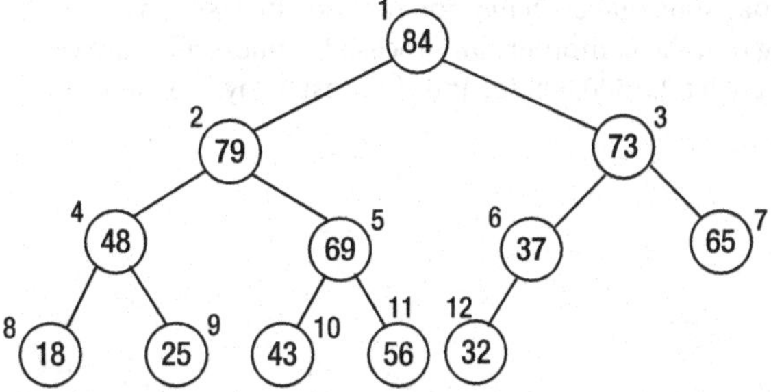

Figure 10-11. *Final heap after processing 18, 79, 56, 69, 32*

Note that the heap in Figure 10-11 is different from that of Figure 10-3 even though they are formed from the same numbers. What hasn't changed is that the largest value, 84, is at the root.

If the values are already stored in an array `num[1..n]`, we can create a heap with the following:

```
for (k = 2; k <= n; k++) siftUp(num, k);
```

10.3 Analysis of Heapsort

Is `siftUp` or `siftDown` better for creating a heap? Keep in mind that the most times any node will ever have to move is $\log_2 n$.

In `siftDown`, we process $n/2$ nodes, and at each step, we make two comparisons: one to find the bigger child and one to compare the node value with the bigger child. In a simplistic analysis, in the worst case, we will need to make $2*n/2*\log_2 n = n\log_2 n$ comparisons. However, a more careful analysis will show that we need to make, at most, only $4n$ comparisons.

In `siftUp`, we process n-1 nodes. At each step, we make one comparison: the node with its parent. In a simplistic analysis, in the worst case, we make $(n\text{-}1)\log_2 n$ comparisons. However, it is possible that all the leaves may have to travel all the way to the top of the tree. In this case, we have $n/2$ nodes having to travel a distance of $\log_2 n$, giving a total of $(n/2)\log_2 n$ comparisons. And that's only for the leaves. In the end, a more careful analysis still gives us approximately $n\log_2 n$ comparisons for `siftUp`.

The difference in performance is hinged on the following: in `siftDown`, there is no work to do for half the nodes (the leaves); `siftUp` has the most work to do for these nodes.

Whichever method we use for creating the initial heap, heapsort will sort an array of size n making at most $2n\log_2 n$ comparisons and $n\log_2 n$ assignments. This is very fast. In addition, heapsort is *stable* in the sense that its performance is always at worst $2n\log_2 n$, regardless of the order of the items in the given array.

To give an idea of how fast heapsort (and all sorting methods that are of order $O(n\log_2 n)$, such as quicksort and mergesort) is, let's compare it with selection sort, which makes roughly ½ n^2 comparisons to sort n items (Table 10-1).

Table 10-1. *Comparison of Heapsort with Selection Sort*

n	selection(comp)	heap(comp)	select(sec)	heap(sec)
100	5,000	1,329	0.005	0.001
1,000	500,000	19,932	0.5	0.020
10,000	50,000,000	265,754	50	0.266
100,000	5,000,000,000	3,321,928	5000	3.322
1,000,000	500,000,000,000	39,863,137	500000	39.863

The second and third columns show the number of comparisons that each method makes. The last two columns show the running time of each method (in seconds) assuming that the computer can process 1 million comparisons per second. For example, to sort 1 million items, selection sort will take 500,000 seconds (almost 6 days!), whereas heapsort will do it in less than 40 seconds.

10.4 Heaps and Priority Queues

A *priority queue* is one in which each item is assigned some "priority" and its position in the queue is based on this priority. The item with top priority is placed at the head of the queue. The following are some typical operations that may be performed on a priority queue:

- Remove (serve) the item with the highest priority
- Add an item with a given priority
- Remove (delete without serving) an item from the queue
- Change the priority of an item, adjusting its position based on its new priority

We can think of priority as an integer—the bigger the integer, the higher the priority.

Immediately, we can surmise that if we implement the queue as a max-heap, the item with the highest priority will be at the root, so it can be easily removed. Reorganizing the heap will simply involve "sifting down" the last item from the root.

Adding an item will involve placing the item in the position after the current last one and sifting it up until it finds its correct position.

To delete an arbitrary item from the queue, we will need to know its position. Deleting it will involve replacing it with the current last item and sifting it up or down to find its correct position. The heap will shrink by one item.

If we change the priority of an item, we may need to sift it either up or down to find its correct position. Of course, it may also remain in its original position, depending on the change.

In many situations (for example, a job queue on a multitasking computer), the priority of a job may increase over time so that it eventually gets served. In these situations, a job moves closer to the top of the heap with each change; thus, only sifting up is required.

In a typical situation, information about the items in a priority queue is held in another structure that can be quickly searched, for example a binary search tree. One field in the node will contain the index of the item in the array used to implement the priority queue.

Using the job queue example, suppose we want to add an item to the queue. We can search the tree by job number, say, and add the item to the tree. Its priority number is used to determine its position in the queue. This position is stored in the tree node.

If, later, the priority changes, the item's position in the queue is adjusted, and this new position is stored in the tree node. Note that adjusting this item may also involve changing the position of other items (as they move up or down the heap), and the tree will have to be updated for these items as well.

10.5 Sorting a List of Items with Quicksort

At the heart of quicksort is the notion of *partitioning* the list with respect to one of the values called a *pivot*. For example, given the following list to be sorted:

num

53	12	98	63	18	32	80	46	72	21
1	2	3	4	5	6	7	8	9	10

we can *partition* it with respect to the first value, 53. This means placing 53 in such a position that all values to the left of it are smaller and all values to the right are greater than or equal to it. Shortly, we will describe an algorithm that will partition the above array as follows:

num

21	12	18	32	46	53	80	98	72	63
1	2	3	4	5	6	7	8	9	10

The value 53 is used as the *pivot*. It is placed in position 6. All values to the left of 53 are smaller than 53, and all values to the right are greater. The location in which the pivot is placed is called the *division point* (dp, say). By definition, 53 is in its final sorted position.

If we can sort num[1..dp-1] and num[dp+1..n], we would have sorted the entire list. But we can use the same process to sort these pieces, indicating that a recursive procedure is appropriate.

Assuming a function partition is available that partitions a given section of an array and returns the division point, we can write quicksort as follows:

```
void quicksort(int A[], int lo, int hi) {
//sorts A[lo] to A[hi] in ascending order
   int partition(int[], int, int);
   if (lo < hi) {
      int dp = partition(A, lo, hi);
      quicksort(A, lo, dp-1);
      quicksort(A, dp+1, hi);
   }
} //end quicksort
```

The call quicksort(num, 1, n) will sort num[1..n] in ascending order.

We now look at how partition may be written. Consider the array:

num

53	12	98	63	18	32	80	46	72	21
1	2	3	4	5	6	7	8	9	10

We will partition it with respect to num[1], 53 (the pivot) by making one pass through the array. We will look at each number in turn. If it is bigger than the pivot, we do nothing. If it is smaller, we move it to the left side of the array. Initially, we set the variable lastSmall to 1; as the method proceeds, lastSmall will be the index of the last item that is known to be smaller than the pivot. We partition num as follows:

1. Compare 12 with 53; it is smaller, so add 1 to lastSmall (making it 2) and swap num[2] with itself.
2. Compare 98 with 53; it is bigger, so move on.
3. Compare 63 with 53; it is bigger, so move on.
4. Compare 18 with 53; it is smaller, so add 1 to lastSmall (making it 3) and swap num[3], 98, with 18.

At this stage, we have this:

num

53	12	18	63	98	32	80	46	72	21
1	2	3	4	5	6	7	8	9	10

5. Compare 32 with 53; it is smaller, so add 1 to lastSmall (making it 4) and swap num[4], 63, with 32.
6. Compare 80 with 53; it is bigger, so move on.
7. Compare 46 with 53; it is smaller, so add 1 to lastSmall (making it 5) and swap num[5], 98, with 46.

At this stage, we have the following:

num

53	12	18	32	46	63	80	98	72	21
1	2	3	4	5	6	7	8	9	10

8. Compare `72` with `53`; it is bigger, so move on.
9. Compare `21` with `53`; it is smaller, so add `1` to `lastSmall` (making it 6) and swap `num[6]`, `63`, with `21`.
10. We have come to the end of the array; swap `num[1]` and `num[lastSmall]`; this moves the pivot into its final position.

We end up with this:

num

21	12	18	32	46	53	80	98	72	63
1	2	3	4	5	6	7	8	9	10

The division point is denoted by `lastSmall` (6).
We can express the previous procedure as a function `partition1`.

```
int partition1(int A[], int lo, int hi) {
//partition A[lo] to A[hi] using A[lo] as the pivot
   void swap(int[], int, int);
   int pivot = A[lo];
   int lastSmall = lo;
   for (int h = lo + 1; h <= hi; h++)
      if (A[h] < pivot) {
         ++lastSmall;
         swap(A, lastSmall, h);
      }
   //end for
   swap(A, lo, lastSmall);
   return lastSmall;  //return the division point
} //end partition1

void swap(int list[], int i, int j) {
//swap list[i] and list[j]
   int hold = list[i];
   list[i] = list[j];
   list[j] = hold;
} //end swap
```

We can test quicksort and partition1 with this:

```
#include <stdio.h>
int main() {
   void quicksort(int[], int, int);
   int num[] = {0, 53, 12, 98, 63, 18, 32, 80, 46, 72, 21};
   int n = 10;
   quicksort(num, 1, n);
   for (int h = 1; h <= n; h++) printf("%d ", num[h]);
   printf("\n");
} //end main
```

When run, this produces the following output (num[1] to num[10] sorted):

```
12 18 21 32 46 53 63 72 80 98
```

Quicksort is one of those methods whose performance can range from very fast to very slow. Typically, it is of order $O(n\log_2 n)$, and for random data, the number of comparisons varies between $n\log_2 n$ and $3n\log_2 n$. However, things can get worse.

The idea behind partitioning is to break up the given portion into two fairly equal pieces. Whether this happens depends, to a large extent, on the value that is chosen as the pivot.

In the function, we choose the first element as the pivot. This will work well in most cases, especially for random data. However, if the first element happens to be the smallest, the partitioning operation becomes almost useless since the division point will simply be the first position. The "left" piece will be empty, and the "right" piece will be only one element smaller than the given sublist. Similar remarks apply if the pivot is the largest element.

While the algorithm will still work, it will be slowed considerably. For example, if the given array is sorted, quicksort will become as slow as selection sort.

One way to avoid this problem is to choose a random element as the pivot, not merely the first one. While it is still possible that this method will choose the smallest (or the largest), that choice will be merely by chance.

Yet another method is to choose the median of the first (A[lo]), last (A[hi]), and middle (A[(lo+hi)/2]) items as the pivot.

You are advised to experiment with various ways of choosing the pivot.

Our experiments showed that choosing a random element as the pivot was simple and effective, even for sorted data. In fact, in many cases, the method ran faster with sorted data than with random data, an unusual result for quicksort.

One possible disadvantage of quicksort is that, depending on the actual data being sorted, the overhead of the recursive calls may be high. We will see how to minimize this in Section 10.5.3. On the plus side, quicksort uses very little extra storage. On the other hand, mergesort (which is also recursive) needs extra storage (the same size as the array being sorted) to facilitate the merging of sorted pieces. Heapsort has neither of these disadvantages. It is *not* recursive and uses very little extra storage. And, as noted in Section 10.3, heapsort is *stable* in that its performance is always at worst $2n\log_2 n$, regardless of the order of the items in the given array.

10.5.1 Another Way to Partition

There are many ways to achieve the goal of partitioning—splitting the list into two parts such that the elements in the left part are smaller than the elements in the right part. Our first method, shown earlier, placed the pivot in its final position. For variety, we will look at another way to partition. While this method still partitions with respect to a pivot, it does *not* place the pivot in its final sorted position. As we will see, this is not a problem.

Consider, again, the array num[1..n] where n = 10.

num

53	12	98	63	18	32	80	46	72	21
1	2	3	4	5	6	7	8	9	10

We choose 53 as the pivot. The general idea is to scan from the right looking for a key that is smaller than, or equal to, the pivot. We then scan from the left for a key that is greater than, or equal to, the pivot. We swap these two values; this process effectively puts smaller values to the left and bigger values to the right.

We use two variables, `lo` and `hi`, to mark our positions on the left and right. Initially, we set `lo` to `0` and `hi` to `11` (`n+1`). We then loop as follows:

1. Subtract `1` from `hi` (making it `10`).
2. Compare `num[hi]`, `21`, with `53`; it is smaller, so stop scanning from the right with `hi` = `10`.
3. Add `1` to `lo` (making it `1`).
4. Compare `num[lo]`, `53`, with `53`; it is not smaller, so stop scanning from the left with `lo` = `1`.
5. `lo` (`1`) is less than `hi` (`10`), so swap `num[lo]` and `num[hi]`.
6. Subtract `1` from `hi` (making it `9`).
7. Compare `num[hi]`, `72`, with `53`; it is bigger, so decrease `hi` (making it `8`). Compare `num[hi]`, `46`, with `53`; it is smaller, so stop scanning from the right with `hi` = `8`.
8. Add `1` to `lo` (making it `2`).
9. Compare `num[lo]`, `12`, with `53`; it is smaller, so add `1` to `lo` (making it `3`). Compare `num[lo]`, `98`, with `53`; it is bigger, so stop scanning from the left with `lo` = `3`.
10. `lo` (`3`) is less than `hi` (`8`), so swap `num[lo]` and `num[hi]`.

At this stage, we have `lo` = `3`, `hi` = `8` and `num` as follows:

num

21	12	46	63	18	32	80	98	72	53
1	2	3	4	5	6	7	8	9	10

11. Subtract `1` from `hi` (making it `7`).
12. Compare `num[hi]`, `80`, with `53`; it is bigger, so decrease `hi` (making it `6`). Compare `num[hi]`, `32`, with `53`; it is smaller, so stop scanning from the right with `hi` = `6`.
13. Add `1` to `lo` (making it `4`).
14. Compare `num[lo]`, `63`, with `53`; it is bigger, so stop scanning from the left with `lo` = `4`.
15. `lo` (`4`) is less than `hi` (`6`), so swap `num[lo]` and `num[hi]`, giving this:

num

21	12	46	32	18	63	80	98	72	53
1	2	3	4	5	6	7	8	9	10

16. Subtract `1` from `hi` (making it `5`).
17. Compare `num[hi]`, `18`, with `53`; it is smaller, so stop scanning from the right with `hi` = `5`.
18. Add `1` to `lo` (making it `5`).
19. Compare `num[lo]`, `18`, with `53`; it is smaller, so add `1` to `lo` (making it `6`). Compare `num[lo]`, `63`, with `53`; it is bigger, so stop scanning from the left with `lo` = `6`.
20. `lo` (`6`) is *not* less than `hi` (`5`), so the algorithm ends.

The value of hi is such that the values in num[1..hi] are smaller than those in num[hi+1..n]. Here, the values in num[1..5] are smaller than those in num[6..10]. Note that 53 is not in its final sorted position. However, this is not a problem since, to sort the array, all we need to do is sort num[1..hi] and num[hi+1..n].

We can implement the procedure described above as partition2:

```
int partition2(int A[], int lo, int hi) {
//return dp such that A[lo..dp] <= A[dp+1..hi]
   void swap(int[], int, int);
   int pivot = A[lo];
   --lo; ++hi;
   while (lo < hi) {
      do --hi; while (A[hi] > pivot);
      do ++lo; while (A[lo] < pivot);
      if (lo < hi) swap(A, lo, hi);
   }
   return hi;
} //end partition2
```

With this version of partition, we can write quicksort2 as follows:

```
void quicksort2(int A[], int lo, int hi) {
//sorts A[lo] to A[hi] in ascending order
   int partition2(int[], int, int);
   if (lo < hi) {
      int dp = partition2(A, lo, hi);
      quicksort2(A, lo, dp);
      quicksort2(A, dp+1, hi);
   }
} //end quicksort2
```

In partition2, we choose the first element as the pivot. However, as discussed, choosing a random element will give better results. We can do this with the following:

```
swap(A, lo, random(lo, hi));
int pivot = A[lo];
```

where random can be written like this:

```
int random(int m, int n) {
//returns a random integer from m to n, inclusive
   int offset = rand()/(RAND_MAX + 1.0) * (n - m + 1);
   return m + offset;
} //end random
```

You are reminded to declare the prototype of random in partition2 and to add the following statement to your program since random uses rand and RAND_MAX:

```
#include <stdlib.h>
```

10.5.2 Nonrecursive Quicksort

In the versions of quicksort shown earlier, after a sublist is partitioned, we call quicksort with the left part followed by the right part. For most cases, this will work fine. However, it is possible that, for a large n, the number of pending recursive calls can get so large so as to generate a "recursive stack overflow" error.

In our experiments, this occurred with n = 7000 if the given data was already sorted and the first element was chosen as the pivot. However, there was no problem even for n = 100000 if a random element was chosen as the pivot.

Another approach is to write quicksort nonrecursively. This would require us to stack the pieces of the list that remain to be sorted. It can be shown that when a sublist is subdivided, if we process the *smaller* sublist first, the number of stack elements will be restricted to at most $\log_2 n$.

For example, suppose we are sorting A[1..99] and the first division point is 40. Assume we are using partition2, which does not put the pivot in its final sorted position. Thus, we must sort A[1..40] and A[41..99] to complete the sort. We will stack (41, 99) and deal with A[1..40] (the shorter sublist) first.

Suppose the division point for A[1..40] is 25. We will stack (1, 25) and process A[26..40] first. At this stage we have two sublists—(41, 99) and (1, 25)—on the stack that remain to be sorted. Attempting to sort A[26..40] will cause another sublist to be added to the stack, and so on. In our implementation, we will also add the shorter sublist to the stack, but this will be taken off immediately and processed.

The result mentioned above assures us that there will never be more than $\log_2 99 = 7$ (rounded up) elements on the stack at any given time. Even for n = 1,000,000, we are guaranteed that the number of stack items will not exceed 20.

Of course, we will have to manipulate the stack ourselves. Each stack element will consist of two integers (left and right, say), meaning that the portion of the list from left to right remains to be sorted. We will assume the stack implementation described in Chapter 5 is stored in an include file, stack.h.

We define StackData and newStackData as follows:

```
typedef struct {
   int left, right;
} StackData;

StackData newStackData(int a, int b) {
   StackData temp;
   temp.left = a;
   temp.right = b;
   return temp;
} //end newStackData
```

We now write quicksort3 based on the above discussion.

```
void quicksort3(int A[], int lo, int hi) {
   int partition2(int[], int, int);
   StackData newStackData(int, int);
   Stack S = initStack();
   push(S, newStackData(lo, hi));
   int stackItems = 1, maxStackItems = 1;
   while (!empty(S)) {
      --stackItems;
      StackData d = pop(S);
      if (d.left < d.right) { //if the sublist is > 1 element
         int dp = partition2(A, d.left, d.right);
         if (dp - d.left + 1 < d.right - dp) {  //compare lengths of sublists
            push(S, newStackData(dp+1, d.right));
            push(S, newStackData(d.left, dp));
         }
```

```
         else {
            push(S, newStackData(d.left, dp));
            push(S, newStackData(dp+1, d.right));
         }
         stackItems += 2;    //two items added to stack
      } //end if
      if (stackItems > maxStackItems) maxStackItems = stackItems;
   } //end while
   printf("Max stack items: %d\n\n", maxStackItems);
} //end quicksort3
```

When partition2 returns, the lengths of the two sublists are compared, and the longer one is placed on the stack first followed by the shorter one. This ensures that the shorter one will be taken off first and processed before the longer one.

We also added statements to quicksort3 to keep track of the maximum number of items on the stack at any given time. When used to sort 100,000 integers, the maximum number of stack items was 13; this is less than the maximum possible, $\log_2 100000 = 17$, rounded up.

As written, even if a sublist consists of two items only, the method will go through the whole process of calling partition, checking the lengths of the sublists, and stacking the two sublists. This seems an awful lot of work to sort two items.

We can make quicksort more efficient by using a simple method (insertion sort, say) to sort sublists that are shorter than some predefined length (8, say). You are urged to write quicksort with this change and experiment with different values of the predefined length.

10.5.3 Finding the kth Smallest Number

Consider the problem of finding the kth smallest number in a list of n numbers. One way to do this is to sort the n numbers and pick out the kth one. If the numbers are stored in an array A[1..n], we simply retrieve A[k] after sorting.

Another, more efficient way is to use partitioning. We will use the version of partition that places the pivot in its final sorted position. Consider an array A[1..99], and suppose a call to partition returns a division point of 40. This means the pivot has been placed in A[40] with smaller numbers to the left and bigger numbers to the right. In other words, the 40th smallest number has been placed in A[40]. So, if k is 40, we have our answer immediately.

What if k were 59? We know that the 40 smallest numbers occupy A[1..40]. So, the 59th must be in A[41..99], and we can confine our search to this part of the array. In other words, with one call to partition, we can eliminate 40 numbers from consideration. The idea is similar to binary search.

Suppose the next call to partition returns 65. We now know the 65th smallest number and the 59th will be in A[41..64]; we have eliminated A[66..99] from consideration. We repeat this process, each time reducing the size of the part that contains the 59th smallest number. Eventually, partition will return 59, and we will have our answer.

The following is one way to write kthSmall; it uses partition1:

```
int kthSmall(int A[], int k, int lo, int hi) {
//returns the kth smallest from A[lo] to A[hi]
   int partition1(int[], int, int);
   int kShift = lo + k - 1; //shift k to the given portion, A[lo..hi]
   if (kShift < lo || kShift > hi) return -9999;
   int dp = partition1(A, lo, hi);
   while (dp != kShift) {
      if (kShift < dp) hi = dp - 1;    //kth smallest is in the left part
      else lo = dp + 1;       //kth smallest is in the right part
      dp = partition1(A, lo, hi);
   }
   return A[dp];
} //end kthSmall
```

For instance, the call `kthSmall(num, 59, 1, 99)` will return the 59th smallest number from `num[1..99]`. Note, however, that the call `kthSmall(num, 10, 30, 75)` will return the 10th smallest number from `num[30..75]`.

As an exercise, write the recursive version of `kthSmall`.

10.6 Shell (Diminishing Increment) Sort

Shell sort (named after Donald Shell) uses a series of *increments* to govern the sorting process. It makes several passes over the data, with the last pass being the same as insertion sort. For the other passes, elements that are a fixed distance apart (for instance, five apart) are sorted using the same technique as insertion sort.

For example, to sort the following array, we use three increments—8, 3, and 1:

num

67	90	28	84	29	58	25	32	16	64	13	71	82	10	51	57
1	2	3	4	5	6	7	8	9	10	11	12	13	14	15	16

The increments decrease in size (hence the term *diminishing increment sort*), with the last one being 1.

Using increment 8, we eight-sort the array. This means we sort the elements that are eight apart. We sort elements 1 and 9, 2 and 10, 3 and 11, 4 and 12, 5 and 13, 6 and 14, 7 and 15, and 8 and 16. This will transform `num` into this:

16	64	13	71	29	10	25	32	67	90	28	84	82	58	51	57
1	2	3	4	5	6	7	8	9	10	11	12	13	14	15	16

Next, we three-sort the array; that is, we sort elements that are three apart. We sort elements (1, 4, 7, 10, 13, 16), (2, 5, 8, 11, 14), and (3, 6, 9, 12, 15). This gives us the following:

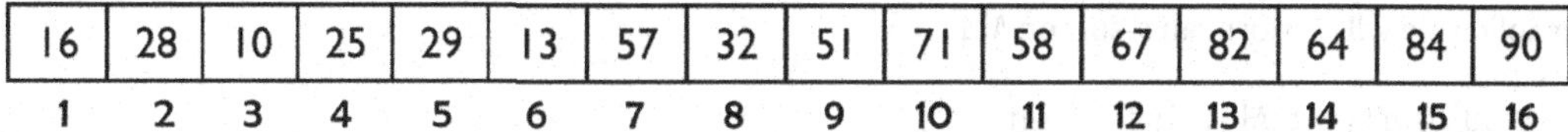

16	28	10	25	29	13	57	32	51	71	58	67	82	64	84	90
1	2	3	4	5	6	7	8	9	10	11	12	13	14	15	16

Note that, at each step, the array is a little closer to being sorted. Finally, we perform a one-sort, sorting the entire list, giving this:

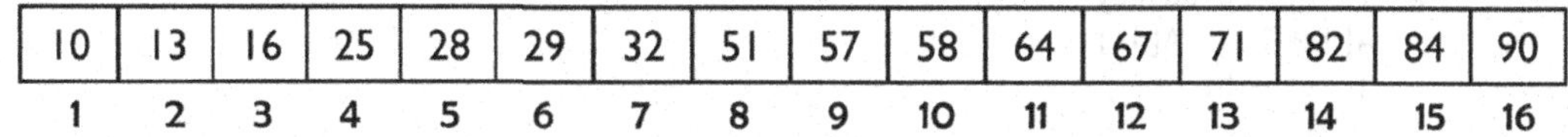

10	13	16	25	28	29	32	51	57	58	64	67	71	82	84	90
1	2	3	4	5	6	7	8	9	10	11	12	13	14	15	16

You may ask, why didn't we just do a one-sort from the beginning and sort the entire list? The idea here is that when we reach the stage of doing a one-sort, the array is more or less in order, and if we use a method that works better with partially ordered data (such as insertion sort), then the sort can proceed quickly.

When the increment is large, the pieces to sort are small. In the example, when the increment is eight, each piece consists of two elements only. Presumably, we can sort a small list quickly. When the increment is small, the pieces to sort are bigger. However, by the time we get to the small increments, the data is partially sorted, and we can sort the pieces quickly if we use a method that takes advantage of order in the data.

We will use a slightly modified version of insertion sort to sort elements that are *h* apart rather than one apart.

Recall that, in insertion sort, when we come to process num[k], we assume that num[1..k-1] are sorted and insert num[k] among the previous items so that num[1..k] are sorted.

Suppose the increment is h and consider how we might process num[k] where k is any valid subscript. Remember, our goal is to sort items that are h apart. So, we must sort num[k] with respect to num[k-h], num[k-2h], num[k-3h], and so on, provided these elements fall within the array. When we come to process num[k], if the previous items that are h apart are sorted among themselves, we must simply insert num[k] among those items so that the sublist ending at num[k] is sorted.

To illustrate, suppose h = 3 and k = 4. There is only one element before num[4] that is three away; that is num[1]. So, when we come to process num[4], we can assume that num[1], by itself, is sorted. We insert num[4] relative to num[1] so that num[1] and num[4] are sorted.

Similarly, there is only one element before num[5] that is three away; that is num[2]. So, when we come to process num[5], we can assume that num[2], by itself, is sorted. We insert num[5] relative to num[2] so that num[2] and num[5] are sorted. Similar remarks apply to num[3] and num[6].

When we get to num[7], the two items before num[7] (num[1] and num[4]) are sorted. We insert num[7] such that num[1], num[4], and num[7] are sorted.

When we get to num[8], the two items before num[8] (num[2] and num[5]) are sorted. We insert num[8] such that num[2], num[5], and num[8] are sorted.

When we get to num[9], the two items before num[9] (num[3] and num[6]) are sorted. We insert num[9] such that num[3], num[6], and num[9] are sorted.

When we get to num[10], the three items before num[10] (num[1], num[4], and num[7]) are sorted. We insert num[10] such that num[1], num[4], num[7], and num[10] are sorted.

And so on. Starting at h+1, we step through the array processing each item with respect to previous items that are multiples of h away.

In the example, when h = 3, we said we must sort elements (1, 4, 7, 10, 13, 16), (2, 5, 8, 11, 14), and (3, 6, 9, 12, 15). This is true, but our algorithm will not sort items (1, 4, 7, 10, 13, 16), followed by items (2, 5, 8, 11, 14) followed by items (3, 6, 9, 12, 15).

Rather, it will sort them in parallel by sorting the pieces in the following order: (1, 4), (2, 5), (3, 6), (1, 4, 7), (2, 5, 8), (3, 6, 9), (1, 4, 7, 10), (2, 5, 8, 11), (3, 6, 9, 12), (1, 4, 7, 10, 13), (2, 5, 8, 11, 14), (3, 6, 9, 12, 15), and finally (1, 4, 7, 10, 13, 16). This may sound more difficult, but it is actually easier to code.

The following will perform an h-sort on A[1..n]:

```
void hsort(int A[], int n, int h) {
   for (int k = h + 1; k <= n; k++) {
      int j = k - h; //j will index elements k - h, k - 2h, k - 3h, etc
      int key = A[k];
      while (j > 0 && key < A[j]) {
         A[j + h] = A[j];
         j = j - h;
      }
      A[j + h] = key;
   }
} //end hsort
```

Alert readers will realize that if we set h to 1, this becomes insertion sort.

Programming note: If we want to sort A[0..n-1], we must use j >= 0 in the while statement and change the for statement to:

```
for (int k = h; k < n; k++)
```

Given a series of increments $h_t, h_{t-1}, ..., h_1 = 1$, we simply call hsort with each increment, from largest to smallest, to effect the sort. For example, if the file shell.in contains the following numbers:

```
67 90 28 84 29 58 25 32 16 64 13 71 82 10 51 57
```

we could read and sort them as described earlier (using increments 8, 3, and 1) with the following main routine:

```
#include <stdio.h>
#include <stdlib.h>
#define MaxSize 100
int main() {
   void hsort(int[], int, int);
   int num[MaxSize + 1];
   int n = 0, number;
   FILE * in = fopen("shell.in", "r");

   while (fscanf(in, "%d", &number) == 1) {
      if (n < MaxSize) num[++n] = number;
      else {
         printf("\nArray too small\n");
         exit(1);
      }
   }
   //perform Shell sort with increments 8, 3 and 1
   hsort(num, n, 8);
   hsort(num, n, 3);
   hsort(num, n, 1);

   for (int h = 1; h <= n; h++) printf("%d ", num[h]);
   printf("\n");
   fclose(in);
} //end main
```

We note, in passing, that our code would be more flexible if the increments are stored in an array (incr, say) and hsort is called with each element of the array in turn. For example, suppose incr[0] contains the number of increments (m, say), and incr[1] to incr[m] contain the increments in decreasing order with incr[m] = 1. We could call hsort with each increment as follows:

```
for (int i = 1; i <= incr[0]; i++) hsort(num, n, incr[i]);
```

One question that arises is how do we decide which increments to use for a given n? Many methods have been proposed; the following gives reasonable results:

```
let h₁ = 1
generate hₛ₊₁ = 3hₛ + 1, for s = 1, 2, 3,...
and stop with hₜ when hₜ₊₂ ≥ n
```

For example, if n = 100, we generate $h_1 = 1, h_2 = 4, h_3 = 13, h_4 = 40, h_5 = 121$. Since $h_5 > 100$, we use h_1, h_2, and h_3 as the increments to sort 100 items.

The performance of Shell sort lies somewhere between the simple $O(n^2)$ methods (insertion, selection) and the $O(n\log_2 n)$ methods (heapsort, quicksort, mergesort). Its order is approximately $O(n^{1.3})$ for n in a practical range tending to $O(n(\log_2 n)^2)$ as n tends to infinity.

As an exercise, write programming code to sort a list using Shell sort, counting the number of comparisons and assignments made in sorting the list.

EXERCISES 10

1. Write a program to compare the performance of all the sorting methods discussed with respect to "number of comparisons" and "number of assignments." For quicksort, compare the performance of choosing the first element as the pivot with choosing a random element.

   Run the program to sort 10, 100, 1,000, 10,000, and 10,0000 elements supplied in random order.

   Run the program to sort 10, 100, 1,000, 10,000, and 100,000 elements that are already sorted.

2. A function `makeHeap` is passed an integer array `A`. If `A[0]` contains `n`, then `A[1]` to `A[n]` contain numbers in arbitrary order. Write `makeHeap` such that `A[1]` to `A[n]` contain a max-heap (*largest* value at the root). Your function must create the heap by processing the elements in the order `A[2]`, `A[3]`, ..., `A[n]`.

3. A heap is stored in a one-dimensional integer array `num[1..n]` with the *largest* value in position 1. Give an efficient algorithm that deletes the root and rearranges the other elements so that the heap now occupies `num[1]` to `num[n-1]`.

4. A heap is stored in a one-dimensional integer array `A[0..max]` with the *largest* value in position 1. `A[0]` specifies the number of elements in the heap at any time. Write a function to add a new value `v` to the heap. Your function should work if the heap is initially empty and should print a message if there is no room to store `v`.

5. Write code to read a set of positive integers (terminated by 0) and create a heap in an array `H` with the *smallest* value at the top of the heap. As each integer is read, it is inserted among the existing items such that the heap properties are maintained. At any time, if *n* numbers have been read, then `H[1..n]` must contain a heap. Assume that `H` is large enough to hold all the integers.

   Given the data `51 26 32 45 38 89 29 58 34 23 0`, show the contents of `H` after each number has been read and processed.

6. A function is given an integer array, `A`, and two subscripts, `m` and `n`. The function must rearrange the elements `A[m]` to `A[n]` and return the subscript `d` such that all elements to the left of `d` are less than or equal to `A[d]` and all elements to the right of `d` are greater than `A[d]`.

7. Write a function that, given an integer array `num` and an integer `n`, sorts the elements `num[1]` to `num[n]` using Shell sort. The function must return the number of key comparisons made in performing the sort. You may use any reasonable method for determining increments.

8. A single integer array `A[1..n]` contains the following: `A[1..k]` contains a min-heap, and `A[k+1..n]` contains arbitrary values. Write efficient code to merge the two portions so that `A[1..n]` contains one min-heap. Do *not* use any other array.

9. Write a recursive function for finding the kth smallest number in an array of *n* numbers, without sorting the array.

10. Write insertion sort using a binary search to determine the position in which `A[j]` will be inserted among the sorted sublist `A[1..j-1]`.

11. An *integer* max-heap is stored in an array (`A`, say) such that the size of the heap (`n`, say) is stored in `A[0]` and `A[1]` to `A[n]` contain the elements of the heap with the *largest* value in `A[1]`.

    Write a function `deleteMax` that, given an array like `A`, deletes the largest element and reorganizes the array so that it remains a heap.

    Given two arrays, `A` and `B`, containing heaps as described earlier, write programming code to merge the elements of `A` and `B` into another array, `C`, such that `C` is in ascending order. Your method must proceed by comparing an element of `A` with one in `B`. You may assume that `deleteMax` is available.

12. A sorting algorithm is said to be *stable* if equal keys retain their original relative order after sorting. Which of the sorting methods discussed are stable?

13. You are given a list of *n* numbers. Write efficient algorithms to find (i) the smallest (ii), the largest, (iii) the mean, (iv) the median (the middle value), and (v) the mode (the value that appears most often).

    Write an efficient algorithm to find all five values.

14. It is known that every number in a list of *n distinct* numbers is between 100 and 9,999. Devise an efficient method for sorting the numbers.

    Modify the method to sort the list if it may contain duplicate numbers.

15. Modify mergesort and quicksort so that if a sublist to be sorted is smaller than some predefined size, it is sorted using insertion sort.

16. You are given a list of *n* numbers and another number, `x`. You must find the smallest number in the list that is greater than or equal to `x`. You must then delete this number from the list and replace it by a new number, `y`, retaining the list structure. Devise ways of solving this problem using (i) an unsorted array, (ii) a sorted array, (iii) a sorted linked list, (iv) a binary search tree, and (v) a heap.

    Which of these is the most efficient?

17. You are given a (long) list of English words. Write a program to determine which of those words are anagrams of each other. Output consists of each group of anagrams (two or more words) followed by a blank line. Two words are anagrams if they consist of the same letters, such as (teacher, cheater) and (sister, resist).

18. Each value in `A[1..n]` is either 1, 2, or 3. You are required to find the *minimal* number of *exchanges* to sort the array. For example, the following array can be sorted with four exchanges, in this order: (1, 3) (4, 7) (2, 9) (5, 9):

2	2	1	3	3	3	2	3	1
1	2	3	4	5	6	7	8	9

    Another solution is (1, 3) (2, 9) (4, 7) (5, 9). This array cannot be sorted with fewer than four exchanges.

CHAPTER 11

Hashing

In this chapter, we will explain the following:

- The fundamental ideas on which hashing is based
- How to solve the search and insert problem using hashing
- How to delete an item from a hash table
- How to resolve collisions using linear probing
- How to resolve collisions using quadratic probing
- How to resolve collisions using chaining
- How to resolve collisions using linear probing with double hashing
- How to link items in order using arrays

11.1 Hashing Fundamentals

Searching for an item in a (large) table is a common operation in many applications. In this chapter, we discuss *hashing*, a fast method for performing this search. The main idea behind hashing is to use the key of an item (for example, the vehicle registration number of a vehicle record) to determine *where* in the table (the *hash table*) the item is stored. The key is first converted to a number (if it is not already one), and this number is mapped (we say *hashed*) to a table location. The method used to convert a key to a table location is called the *hash function*.

It is entirely possible, of course, for two or more keys to hash to the same location. When this happens, we say we have a *collision*, and we must find a way to resolve the collision. The efficiency (or otherwise) of hashing is determined to a large extent by the method used to resolve collisions. Much of the chapter is devoted to a discussion of these methods.

11.1.1 The Search and Insert Problem

The classical statement of the search and insert problem is as follows:

> *Given a list of items (the list may be empty initially), search for a given item in the list. If the item is not found, insert it in the list.*

Items can be things such as numbers (student, account, employee, vehicle, and so on), names, words, or strings in general. For example, suppose we have a set of integers, not necessarily distinct, and we want to find out how many distinct integers there are.

We start with an empty list. For each integer, we look for it in the list. If it is not found, it is added to the list and counted. If it is found, there is nothing to do.

In solving this problem, a major design decision is how to search the list, which, in turn, will depend on how the list is stored and how a new integer is added. The following are some possibilities:

1. The list is stored in an array, and a new integer is placed in the next available position in the array. This implies that a sequential search must be used to look for an incoming integer. This method has the advantages of simplicity and easy addition, but searching takes longer as more numbers are put in the list.

2. The list is stored in an array, and a new integer is added in such a way that the list is always in order. This may entail moving numbers that have already been stored so that the new number may be slotted in the right place.

   However, since the list is in order, a binary search can be used to search for an incoming integer. For this method, searching is faster, but insertion is slower than in method 1. Since, in general, searching is done more frequently than inserting, this method might be preferable to method 1.

   Another advantage here is that, at the end, the integers will be in order, if this is important. If method 1 is used, the numbers will have to be sorted.

3. The list is stored as an unsorted linked list so must be searched sequentially. Since the entire list must be traversed if an incoming number is not present, the new number can be added at the head or tail; both are equally easy.

4. The list is stored as a sorted linked list. A new number must be inserted "in place" to maintain the order. Once the position is found, insertion is easy. The entire list does not have to be traversed if an incoming number is not present, but we are still restricted to a sequential search.

   The list is stored in a binary search tree. Searching is reasonably fast provided the tree does not become too unbalanced. Adding a number is easy—it's only a matter of setting a couple links. An in-order traversal of the tree will give the numbers in sorted order, if this is required.

Yet another possibility is the method called *hashing*. As we will see, this has the advantages of extremely fast search times and easy insertion.

11.2 Solving the Search and Insert Problem by Hashing

We will illustrate how hashing works by solving the "search and insert" problem for a list of integers. The list will be stored in an array `num[1]` to `num[n]`. In our example, we will assume `n` is `12`.

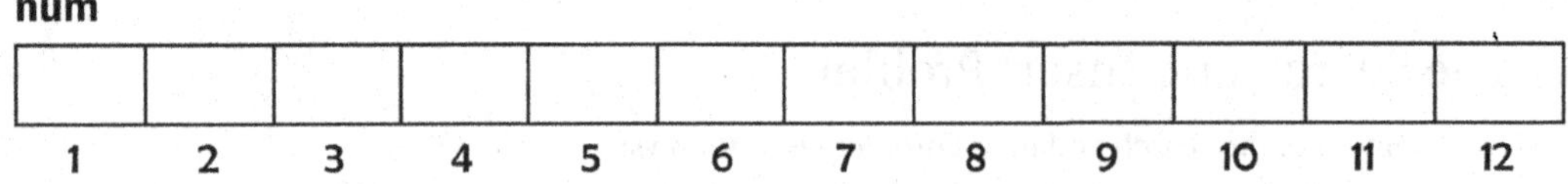

Initially, there are no numbers in the list. Suppose the first incoming number is `52`. The idea behind hashing is to convert `52` (usually called the *key*) into a valid table location (`k`, say). Here, the valid table locations are `1` to `12`.

If there is no number in `num[k]`, then `52` is stored in that location. If `num[k]` is occupied by another key, we say a *collision* has occurred, and we must find another location in which to try to place `52`. This is called *resolving the collision*.

The method used to convert a key to a table location is called the *hash function* (`H`, say). Any calculation that produces a valid table location (array subscript) can be used, but, as we shall see, some functions give better results than others.

For example, we could use `H1(key) = key % 10 + 1`. In other words, we add 1 to the last digit of the key. Thus, `52` would hash to `3`. Note that `H1` produces locations between 1 and 10 only. If the table had 100 locations, say, the function would be valid, but it may not be a good function to use.

Note also that `H(key) = key % 10` would not be a proper hash function here since, for instance, `50` would hash to `0` and there is no table location `0`. Of course, if locations started from subscript `0`, then `key % 10` would be valid, provided there were at least ten locations.

Another function is `H2(key) = key % 12 + 1`. The expression `key % 12` produces a value between `0` and `11`; adding `1` gives values between `1` and `12`. In general, `key % n + 1` produces values between `1` and `n`, inclusive. We will use this function in our example.

`H2(52)` = 52 % 12 + 1 = 5. We say, "52 hashes to location 5." Since `num[5]` is empty, we place 52 in `num[5]`.

Suppose, later, we are searching for 52. We first apply the hash function, and we get 5. We compare `num[5]` with 52; they match, so we find 52 with just one comparison.

Now suppose the following keys come in the order shown:

```
52  33  84  43  16  59  31  23  61
```

- 52 is placed in `num[5]`.
- 33 hashes to 10; `num[10]` is empty, so 33 is placed in `num[10]`.
- 84 hashes to 1; `num[1]` is empty, so 84 is placed in `num[1]`.
- 43 hashes to 8; `num[8]` is empty, so 43 is placed in `num[8]`.

At this stage, we have this:

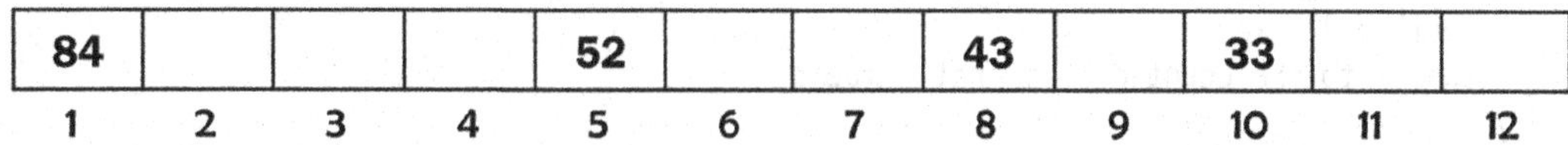

- 16 hashes to 5; `num[5]` is occupied and not by 16—we have a collision. To resolve the collision, we must find another location in which to put 16. One obvious choice is to try the very next location, 6; `num[6]` is empty, so 16 is placed in `num[6]`.
- 59 hashes to 12; `num[12]` is empty, so 59 is placed in `num[12]`.
- 31 hashes to 8; `num[8]` is occupied and not by 31—we have a collision. We try the next location, 9; `num[9]` is empty, so 31 is placed in `num[9]`.

At this stage, we have this:

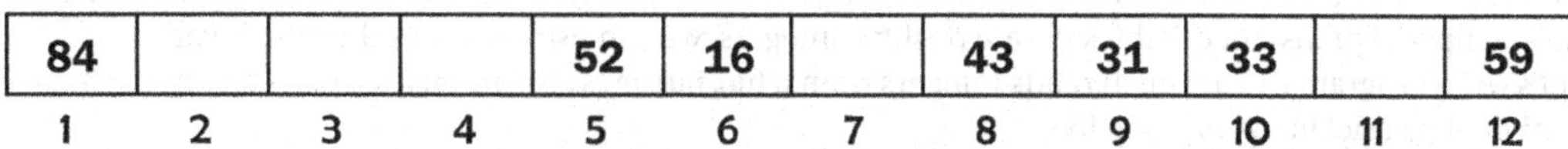

- 23 hashes to 12; `num[12]` is occupied and not by 23—we have a collision. We must try the next location, but what is the next location here? We pretend that the table is "circular" so that location 1 follows location 12. However, `num[1]` is occupied and not by 23. So, we try `num[2]`; `num[2]` is empty, so 23 is placed in `num[2]`.
- Finally, 61 hashes to 2; `num[2]` is occupied and not by 61—we have a collision. We try the next location, 3; `num[3]` is empty, so 61 is placed in `num[3]`.

The following shows the array after all the numbers have been inserted:

num

1	2	3	4	5	6	7	8	9	10	11	12
84	23	61		52	16		43	31	33		59

Note that if a number is already in the array, the previous method would find it. For example, suppose we are searching for 23.

- 23 hashes to 12.
- `num[12]` is occupied and not by 23.
- We try the next location, 1; `num[1]` is occupied and not by 23.
- We next try `num[2]`; `num[2]` is occupied by 23—we find it.

Suppose we are searching for 33; 33 hashes to 10, and `num[10]` contains 33—we find it immediately.

As an exercise, determine the state of `num` after the previous numbers have been added using the hash function `H1(key) = key % 10 + 1`.

We can summarize the process described with the following algorithm:

```
//find or insert 'key' in the hash table, num[1..n]
loc = H(key)
while (num[loc] is not empty && num[loc] != key) loc = loc % n + 1
if (num[loc] is empty) { //key is not in the table
   num[loc] = key
   add 1 to the count of distinct numbers
}
else print key, " found in location ", loc
```

Note the expression `loc % n + 1` for going to the next location. If `loc` is less than `n`, `loc % n` is simply `loc`, and the expression is the same as `loc + 1`. If `loc` *is* `n`, `loc % n` is 0, and the expression evaluates to 1. In either case, `loc` takes on the value of the next location.

Alert readers will realize that we exit the `while` loop when either `num[loc]` is empty or it contains the key. What if neither happens so the `while` loop *never* exits? This situation will arise if the table is completely full (no empty locations) and does not contain the key we are searching for.

However, *in practice*, we never allow the hash table to become completely full. We always ensure that there are a few "extra" locations that are not filled by keys so that the `while` statement *will* exit at some point. In general, the hash technique works better when there are more free locations in the table.

How does the algorithm tell when a location is "empty"? We will need to initialize the array with some value that indicates "empty." For instance, if the keys are positive integers, we can use `0` or `-1` as the empty value.

Let's write Program P11.1, which reads integers from a file, `numbers.in`, and uses a hash technique to determine the number of distinct integers in the file.

Program P11.1

```
#include <stdio.h>
#include <stdlib.h>
#define MaxNumbers 20
#define N 23
#define Empty 0
```

```
int main() {
   FILE * in = fopen("numbers.in", "r");
   int key, num[N + 1];
   for (int h = 1; h <= N; h++) num[h] = Empty;
   int distinct = 0;
   while (fscanf(in, "%d", &key) == 1) {
      int loc = key % N + 1;
      while (num[loc] != Empty && num[loc] != key) loc = loc % N + 1;
      if (num[loc] == Empty) { //key is not in the table
         if (distinct == MaxNumbers) {
            printf("\nTable full: %d not added\n", key);
            exit(1);
         }
         num[loc] = key;
         distinct++;
      }
   }
   printf("\nThere are %d distinct numbers\n", distinct);
   fclose(in);
} //end main
```

If `numbers.in` contains this:

```
25 28 29 23 26 35 22 31 21 26 25 21 31 32 26 20 36 21 27 24
```

Program P11.1 prints the following:

```
There are 14 distinct numbers
```

Notes on Program P11.1:

- `MaxNumbers` (20) is the maximum amount of distinct numbers catered for.
- `N` (23) is the hash table size, a little bigger than `MaxNumbers` so that there is always at least three free locations in the table.
- The hash table occupies `num[1]` to `num[N]`. If you want, `num[0]` may be used; in this case, the hash function could simply be `key % N`.
- If key is not in the table (an empty location is encountered), we first check whether the number of entries has reached `MaxNumbers`. If it has, we declare the table full and do not add key. Otherwise, we put key in the table and count it.
- If key is found, we simply go on to read the next number.

11.2.1 The Hash Function

In the previous section, we saw how an integer key can be "hashed" to a table location. It turns out that the "remainder" operation (%) often gives good results for such keys. But what if the keys were non-numeric, for example, words or names?

The first task is to convert a non-numeric key to a number and then apply the "remainder." Suppose the key is a word. Perhaps the simplest thing to do is add up the *numeric value* of each letter in the word. If the word is stored in a character array, word, properly terminated by \0, we can do this as follows:

```
int h = 0, wordNum = 0;
while (word[h] != '\0') wordNum += word[h++];
loc = wordNum % n + 1; //loc is assigned a value from 1 to n
```

This method will work, but one objection is that words that contain the same letters would hash to the same location. For example, *mate, meat,* and *team* will all hash to the same location. In hashing, we must try to avoid deliberately hashing keys to the same location. One way around this is to assign a weight to each letter depending on its position in the word.

We can assign weights arbitrarily—the main goal is to avoid hashing keys with the same letters to the same location. For instance, we can assign 3 to the first position, 5 to the second position, 7 to the third position, and so on. The following shows how:

```
int h = 0, wordNum = 0;
int w = 3;
while (word[h] != '\0') {
   wordNum += w * word[h++];
   w = w + 2;
}
loc = wordNum % n + 1; //loc is assigned a value from 1 to n
```

The same technique will work if a key contains arbitrary characters.

In hashing, we want the keys to be scattered all over the table. If, for instance, keys are hashed to one area of the table, we can end up with an unnecessarily high number of collisions. To this end, we should try to use *all* of the key. For example, if the keys are alphabetic, it would be unwise to map all keys beginning with the same letter to the same location. Put another way, we should avoid systematically hitting the same location.

And since hashing is meant to be fast, the hash function should be relatively easy to calculate. The speed advantage will be diminished if we spend too much time computing the hash location.

11.2.2 Deleting an Item from a Hash Table

Consider, again, the array after all the sample numbers have been inserted:

num

84	23	61		52	16		43	31	33		59
1	2	3	4	5	6	7	8	9	10	11	12

Recall that 43 and 31 both hashed initially to location 8. Suppose we want to delete 43. The first thought might be to set its location to empty. Assume we did this (set num[8] to empty) and were now looking for 31. This will hash to 8; but since num[8] is empty, we will conclude, wrongly, that 31 is not in the table. So, we cannot delete an item simply by setting its location to empty since other items may become unreachable.

The easiest solution is to set its location to a *deleted* value—some value that cannot be confused with empty or a key. In this example, if the keys are positive integers, we can use 0 for empty and -1 for deleted.

Now, when searching, we still check for the key or an empty location; deleted locations are inspected and skipped. A common error is to stop the search at a deleted location; doing so would lead to incorrect conclusions.

If our search reveals that an incoming key is not in the table, the key can be inserted in an empty location or a deleted one, if one was encountered along the way. For example, suppose we had deleted 43 by setting num[8] to -1. If we now search for 55, we will check locations 8, 9, 10, and 11. Since num[11] is empty, we conclude that 55 is not in the table.

We can, if we want, set num[11] to 55. But we could write our algorithm to remember the deleted location at 8. If we do, we can then insert 55 in num[8]. This is better since we will find 55 faster than if it were in num[11]. We would also be making better use of our available locations by reducing the number of deleted ones.

What if there are several deleted locations along the way? It is best to use the first one encountered since this will reduce the search time for the key. With these ideas, we can rewrite our search/insert algorithm as follows:

```
//find or insert 'key' in the hash table, num[1..n]
loc = H(key)
deletedLoc = 0
while (num[loc] != Empty && num[loc] != key) {
   if (deletedLoc == 0 && num[loc] == Deleted) deletedLoc = loc
   loc = loc % n + 1
}
if (num[loc] == Empty) { //key not found
   if (deletedLoc != 0) loc = deletedLoc
   num[loc] = key
}
else print key, " found in location ", loc
```

Note that we still search until we find an empty location or the key. If we meet a deleted location and deletedLoc is 0, this means it's the first one. Of course, if we *never* meet a deleted location and the key is not in the table, it will be inserted in an empty location.

11.3 Resolving Collisions

In Program P11.1, we resolve a collision by looking at the next location in the table. This is, perhaps, the simplest way to resolve a collision. We say we resolve the collision using *linear probing*, and we will discuss this in more detail in the next section. After this, we will take a look at more sophisticated ways to resolve collisions. Among these are *quadratic probing*, *chaining*, and *double hashing*.

11.3.1 Linear Probing

Linear probing is characterized by the statement loc = loc + 1. Consider, again, the state of num after the nine numbers have been added:

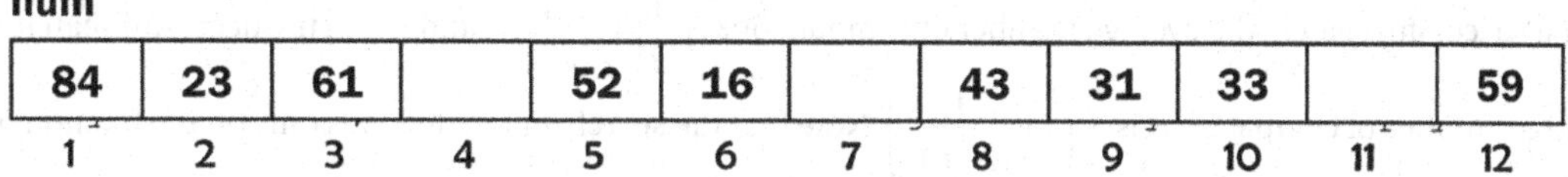

As you can see, the chances of hashing a new key to an empty location decrease as the table fills up.

Suppose a key hashes to location 12. It will be placed in num[4] after trying locations 12, 1, 2, and 3. In fact, any new key that hashes to 12, 1, 2, 3, or 4 will end up in num[4]. When that happens, we will have a long, unbroken chain of keys from location 12 to location 6. Any new key hashing to this chain will end up in num[7], creating an even longer chain.

This phenomenon of *clustering* is one of the main drawbacks of linear probing. Long chains tend to get longer since the probability of hashing to a long chain is usually greater than that of hashing to a short chain. It is also easy for two short chains to be joined, creating a longer chain that, in turn, will tend to get longer. For example, any key that ends up in `num[7]` will create a long chain from locations 5 to 10.

We define two types of clustering.

- *Primary clustering* occurs when keys that hash to different locations trace the same sequence in looking for an empty location. Linear probing exhibits primary clustering since a key that hashes to 5, say, will trace 5, 6, 7, 8, 9, and so on, and a key that hashes to 6 will trace 6, 7, 8, 9, and so on.
- *Secondary clustering* occurs when keys that hash to the *same* location trace the same sequence in looking for an empty location. Linear probing exhibits secondary clustering since keys that hash to 5, say, will trace the same sequence 5, 6, 7, 8, 9, and so on.

Methods of resolving collisions that hope to improve on linear probing will target the elimination of primary and/or secondary clustering.

You may wonder if using `loc = loc + k` where `k` is a constant greater than 1 (for example, 3) will give any better results than `loc = loc + 1`. As it turns out, this will not alter the clustering phenomenon since groups of `k`-apart keys will still be formed.

In addition, it can even be worse than when `k` is 1 since it is possible that not all locations will be generated. Suppose the table size is 12, `k` is 3, and a key hashes to 5. The sequence of locations traced will be 5, 8, 11, 2 (11 + 3 - 12), 5, and the sequence repeats itself. By comparison, when `k` is 1, all locations are generated.

However, this is not really a problem. If the table size is `m` and `k` is "relatively prime" to `m` (their only common factor is 1), then all locations are generated. Two numbers will be relatively prime if one is a prime and the other is not a multiple of it, such as 5 and 12. But being prime is not a necessary condition. The numbers 21 and 50 (neither of which is prime) are relatively prime since they have no common factors other than 1.

If `k` is 5 and `m` is 12, a key hashing to 5 will trace the sequence 5, 10, 3, 8, 1, 6, 11, 4, 9, 2, 7, 12—all locations are generated. A key hashing to any other location will also generate all locations.

In any case, being able to generate all locations is academic since if we had to trace many locations to find an empty one, the search would be too slow, and we would probably need to use another method.

Notwithstanding what we've just said, it turns out that `loc = loc + k`, where `k` *varies* with the key, gives us one of the best ways to implement hashing. We will see how in Section 11.3.4.

So, how fast is the linear method? We are interested in the average *search length*, that is, the number of locations that must be examined to find or insert a given key. In the previous example, the search length of 33 is 1, the search length of 61 is 2, and the search length of 23 is 3.

The search length is a function of the *load factor*, *f*, of the table, where:

$$f = \frac{\textit{number of entries in table}}{\textit{number of table locations}} = \text{fraction of table filled}$$

For a successful search, the average number of comparisons is $\frac{1}{2}\left(1+\frac{1}{1-f}\right)$, and for an unsuccessful search, the average number of comparisons is $\frac{1}{2}\left(1+\frac{1}{(1-f)^2}\right)$. Note that the search length depends only on the fraction of the table filled, *not* on the table size.

Table 11-1 shows how the search length increases as the table fills up.

Table 11-1. Search Length Increases as the Table Fills Up

f	Successful Search Length	Unsuccessful Search Length
0.25	1.2	1.4
0.50	1.5	2.5
0.75	2.5	8.5
0.90	5.5	50.5

At 90% full, the average successful search length is a reasonable 5.5. However, it can take quite long (50.5 probes) to determine that a new key is not in the table. If linear probe is being used, it would be wise to ensure that the table does not become more than about 75% full. This way, we can guarantee good performance with a simple algorithm.

11.3.2 Quadratic Probing

In this method, suppose an incoming key collides with another at location `loc`; we go forward $ai + bi^2$ where a, b are constants and i takes on the value 1 for the first collision, 2 if the key collides again, 3 if it collides yet again, and so on. For example, if we let $a = 1$ and $b = 1$, we go forward $i + i^2$ from location `loc`. Suppose the initial hash location is 7 and there is a collision.

We calculate $i + i^2$ with $i = 1$; this gives 2, so we go forward by 2 and check location 7 + 2 = 9.

If there is still a collision, we calculate $i + i^2$ with $i = 2$; this gives 6, so we go forward by 6 and check location 9 + 6 = 15.

If there is still a collision, we calculate $i + i^2$ with $i = 3$; this gives 12, so we go forward by 12 and check location 15 + 12 = 27.

And so on. Each time we get a collision, we increase i by 1 and recalculate how much we must go forward this time. We continue this way until we find the key or an empty location.

If, at any time, going forward takes us beyond the end of the table, we wrap around to the beginning. For example, if the table size is 25 and we go forward to location 27, we wrap to location 27 - 25, that is, location 2.

For the next incoming key, if there is a collision at the initial hash location, we set i to 1 and continue as explained above. It is worth noting that, for each key, the sequence of "increments" will be 2, 6, 12, 20, 30.... We can, of course, get a different sequence by choosing different values for a and b.

We can summarize the process just described with the following algorithm:

```
//find or insert 'key' in the hash table, num[1..n]
loc = H(key)
i = 0
while (num[loc] != Empty && num[loc] != key) {
   i = i + 1
   loc = loc + a * i + b * i * i
   while (loc > n) loc = loc - n      //while instead of if; see note below
}
if (num[loc] == Empty) num[loc] = key
else print key, " found in location ", loc
```

■ **Note** We use `while` instead of `if` to perform the "wrap around" just in case the new location is more than twice the table size. For instance, suppose n is 25, the increment is 42, and we are going forward from location 20. This will take us to location 62. If we had used `if`, the "wrap around" location would be 62 – 25 = 37, which is still outside the range of the table. With `while`, we will get the valid location 37 – 25 = 12.

Could we have used `loc % n` instead of the `while` loop? In this example, we would get the correct location, but if the new location were a multiple of `n`, `loc % n` will give `0`. This will be an invalid location if the table starts from `1`.

With quadratic probing, keys that hash to different locations trace different sequences; hence, primary clustering is eliminated. However, keys that hash to the same location will trace the same sequence, so secondary clustering remains.

Here are some other points to note:

- If n is a power of 2, that is, $n = 2^m$ for some m, this method explores only a small fraction of the locations in the table and is, therefore, not very effective.
- If n is prime, the method can reach half the locations in the table; this is usually sufficient for most practical purposes.

11.3.3 Chaining

In this method, all items that hash to the same location are held on a linked list. One immediate advantage of this is that items that hash "near" to each other will not interfere with each other since they will not be vying for the same free space in the table, as happens with linear probing. One way to implement chaining is to let the hash table contain "top of list" pointers. For instance, if `hash[1..n]` is the hash table, then `hash[k]` will point to the linked list of all items that hash to location k. An item can be added to a linked list at the head, at the tail, or in a position such that the list is in order.

To illustrate the method, suppose the items are integers. Each linked list item will consist of an integer value and a pointer to the next item. We define the following structure:

```
typedef struct node {
   int num;
   struct node *next;
} Node, *NodePtr
```

and create a new node containing n with:

```
Node newNode(int n) {
   Node temp;
   temp.num = n;
   temp.next = NULL;
   return temp;
}
```

We can now define hash as follows:

```
NodePtr hash[MaxItems+1]; //MaxItems is a symbolic constant
```

and initialize it with:

```
for (int h = 0; h <= MaxItems; h++) hash[h] = NULL;
```

Suppose an incoming key, `inKey`, hashes to location k. We must search the linked list pointed to by `hash[k]` for `inKey`. If it is not found, we must add it to the list. In our program, we will add it such that the list is in ascending order.

We write Program P11.2 to count the number of distinct integers in the input file, `numbers.in`. The program uses *hashing with chaining*. At the end, we print the list of numbers that hash to each location.

Program P11.2

```
#include <stdio.h>
#include <stdlib.h>
#define N 13
#define Empty 0

typedef struct node {
   int num;
   struct node *next;
} Node, *NodePtr;

NodePtr newNode(int n) {
   NodePtr p = (NodePtr) malloc(sizeof(Node));
   p -> num = n;
   p -> next = NULL;
   return p;
}

int main() {
   int key, search(int, NodePtr[], int);
   void printList(NodePtr);
   FILE * in = fopen("numbers.in", "r");
   NodePtr hash[N+1];
   for (int h = 1; h <= N; h++) hash[h] = NULL;
   int distinct = 0;
   while (fscanf(in, "%d", &key) == 1)
      if (!search(key, hash, N)) distinct++;

   printf("\nThere are %d distinct numbers\n\n", distinct);
   for (int h = 1; h <= N; h++)
      if (hash[h] != NULL) {
         printf("hash[%d]:  ", h);
         printList(hash[h]);
      }
   fclose(in);
} //end main

int search(int inKey, NodePtr hash[], int n) {
//return 1 if inKey is found; 0, otherwise
//insert a new key in its appropriate list so list is in order
   NodePtr newNode(int);
   int k = inKey % n + 1;
   NodePtr curr = hash[k];
   NodePtr prev = NULL;
   while (curr != NULL && inKey > curr -> num) {
      prev = curr;
      curr = curr -> next;
   }
   if (curr != NULL && inKey == curr -> num) return 1; //found
   //not found; inKey is a new key; add it so list is in order
   NodePtr np = newNode(inKey);
```

```
      np -> next = curr;
      if (prev == NULL) hash[k] = np;
      else prev -> next = np;
      return 0;
   } //end search

   void printList(NodePtr top) {
      while (top != NULL) {
         printf("%2d ", top -> num);
         top = top -> next;
      }
      printf("\n");
   } //end printList
```

If numbers.in contains the following numbers:

```
24 57 35 37 31 98 85 47 60 32 48 82 16 96 87 46 53 92 71 56
73 85 47 46 22 40 95 32 54 67 31 44 74 40 58 42 88 29 78 87
45 13 73 29 84 48 85 29 66 73 87 17 10 83 95 25 44 93 32 39
```

then Program P11.2 produces the following output:

```
There are 43 distinct numbers

hash[1]: 13 39 78
hash[2]: 40 53 66 92
hash[3]: 54 67 93
hash[4]: 16 29 42
hash[5]: 17 56 82 95
hash[6]: 31 44 57 83 96
hash[7]: 32 45 58 71 84
hash[8]: 46 85 98
hash[9]: 47 60 73
hash[10]: 22 35 48 74 87
hash[11]: 10 88
hash[12]: 24 37
hash[13]: 25
```

If m keys have been stored in the linked lists and there are n hash locations, the average length of a list is $\frac{m}{n}$, and since we must search the lists sequentially, the average successful search length is $\frac{m}{2n}$. The search length can be reduced by increasing the number of hash locations.

Another way to implement hashing with chaining is to use a single array and use array subscripts as links. We can use the declarations:

```
typedef struct node {
   int num;   //key
   int next;   //array subscript of the next item in the list
} Node;

Node hash[MaxItems+1];
```

The first part of the table, hash[1..n], say, is designated as the hash table, and the remaining locations are used as an *overflow* table, as shown in Figure 11-1.

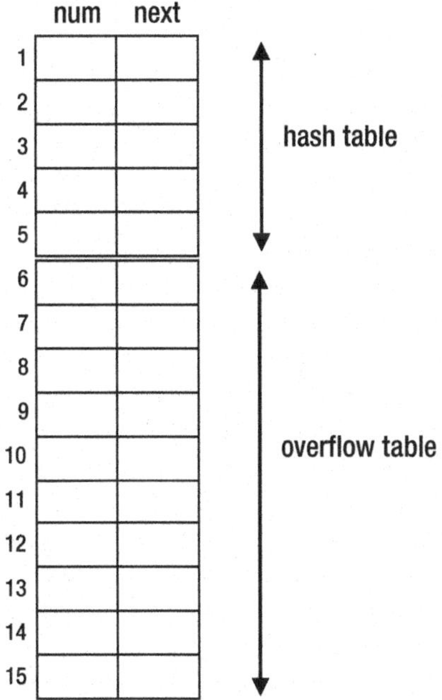

Figure 11-1. *Array implementation of chaining*

Here, hash[1..5] is the hash table, and hash[6..15] is the overflow table.

Suppose key hashes to location k in the hash table:

- If hash[k].num is empty (0, say), we set it to key and set hash[k].next to -1, say, to indicate a null pointer.
- If hash[k].num is not 0, we must search the list starting at k for key. If it is not found, we put it in the next free location (f, say) in the overflow table and link it to the list starting at hash[k]. One way to link it is as follows:

```
hash[f].next = hash[k].next;
hash[k].next = f;
```

- Another way to link the new key is to add it at the end of the list. If L is the location of the last node in the list, this could be done with the following:

```
hash[L].next = f;
hash[f].next = -1;    //this is now the last node
```

If deletions are possible, we will have to decide what to do with deleted locations. One possibility is to keep a list of all available locations in the overflow table. When one is needed to store a key, it is retrieved from the list. When an item is deleted, its location is returned to the list.

Initially, we can link all the items in the overflow table as shown in Figure 11-2 and let the variable `free` point to the first item in the list; here, `free` = 6. Item 6 points to item 7, which points to item 8, and so on, with item 15 at the end of the list.

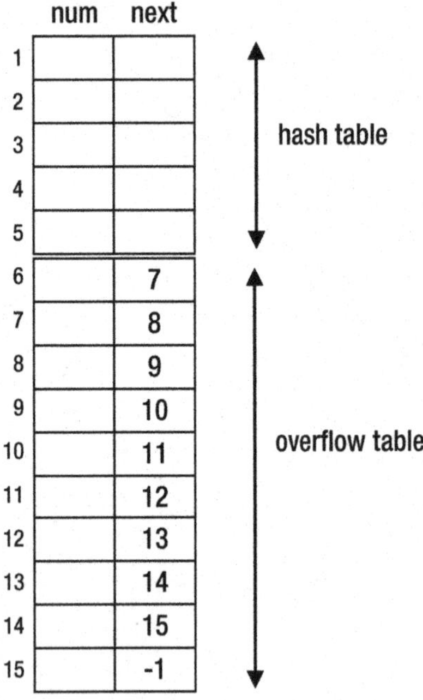

***Figure 11-2.** Link items in overflow table to form "free list"*

Suppose 37 hashes to location 2. This is empty, so 37 is stored in `hash[2].num`. If another number (24, say) hashes to 2, it must be stored in the overflow table. First we must get a location from the "free list." This can be done with:

```
f = free;
free = hash[free].next;
return f;
```

Here, 6 is returned, and `free` is set to 7. The number 24 is stored in location 6, and `hash[2].next` is set to 6. At this stage, we have `free` = 7, with the tables having the values shown in Figure 11-3.

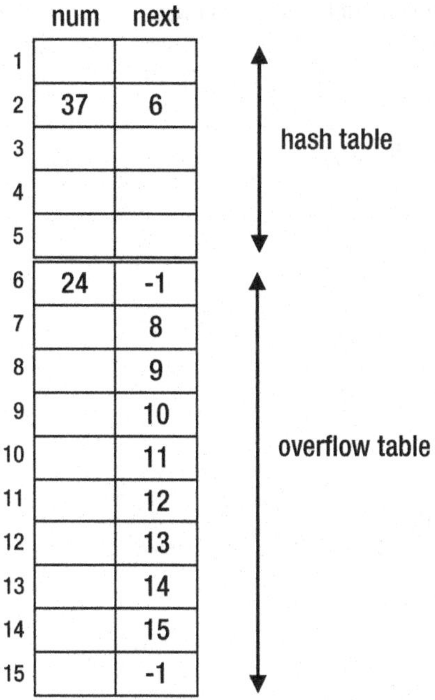

Figure 11-3. *After adding 24 to the overflow table*

Now, consider how an item may be deleted. There are two cases to consider:

1. If the item to be deleted is in the hash table (at k, say), we can delete it with this:

```
if (hash[k].next == -1) set hash[k].num to Empty //only item in the list
else { //copy an item from the overflow table to the hash table
   h = hash[k].next;
   hash[k] = hash[h];   //copy information at location h to location k
   return h to the free list   //see next
}
```

   We can return a location (h, say) to the free list with this:

```
hash[h].next = free;
free = h;
```

2. If the item to be deleted is in the overflow table (at curr, say) and prev is the location of the item that points to the one to be deleted, we can delete it with this:

```
hash[prev].next = hash[curr].next;
return curr to the free list
```

Now consider how an incoming key might be processed. Suppose `free` is 9 and the number 52 hashes to location 2. We search the list starting at 2 for 52. It is not found, so 52 is stored in the next free location, 9. Location 6 contains the last item in the list, so `hash[6].next` is set to 9, and `hash[9].next` is set to -1.

In general, we can perform a search for key and, if not found, insert it at the end of the list with this:

```
k = H(key)    //H is the hash function
if (hash[k].num == Empty) {
   hash[k].num = key
   hash[k].next = -1
}
else {
   curr = k
   prev = -1
   while (curr != -1 && hash[curr].num != key) {
      prev = curr
      curr = hash[curr].next
   }
   if (curr != -1) key is in the list at location curr
   else {  //key is not present
      hash[free].num = key   //assume free list is not empty
      hash[free].next = -1
      hash[prev].next = free
      free = hash[free].next
   } //end else
} //end else
```

11.3.4 Linear Probing with Double Hashing[1]

In Section 11.3.1, we saw that using `loc = loc + k`, where k is a constant greater than 1, does not give us a better performance than when k is 1. However, by letting k vary with the key, we can get excellent results since, unlike linear and quadratic probing, keys that hash to the same location will probe different sequences of locations in searching for an empty one.

The most natural way to let k vary with the key is to use a second hash function. The first hash function will generate the initial table location. If there is a collision, the second hash function will generate the increment, k. If the table locations run from 1 to n, we can use the following:

```
convert key to a numeric value, num (if it is not already numeric)
loc = num % n + 1         //this gives the initial hash location
k = num % (n - 2) + 1   //this gives the increment for this key
```

We mentioned before that it is wise to choose n (the table size) as a prime number. In this method, we get even better results if n - 2 is also prime (in this case, n and n - 2 are called *twin primes*, for example 103/101, 1021/1019).

Apart from the fact that k is not fixed, the method is the same as *linear probing*. We describe it in terms of two hash functions, H1 and H2. H1 produces the initial hash location, a value between 1 and n, inclusive. H2 produces the increment, a value between 1 and n - 1 that is relatively prime to n; this is desirable so that, if required, many locations will be probed. As discussed earlier, if n is prime, any value between 1 and n - 1 will be relatively prime to it. In the previous example, the second hash function produces a value between 1 and n - 2. Here is the algorithm:

[1]The technique is sometimes referred to as *open addressing with double hashing*.

```
//find or insert 'key' using "linear probing with double hashing"
loc = H1(key)
k = H2(key)
while (hash[loc] != Empty && hash[loc] != key) {
   loc = loc + k
   if (loc > n) loc = loc - n
}
if (hash[loc] == Empty) hash[loc] = key
else print key, " found in location ", loc
```

As before, to ensure that the while loop exits at some point, we do not allow the table to become completely full. If we want to cater for MaxItems, say, we declare the table size to be bigger than MaxItems. In general, the more free locations in the table, the better the hash technique works.

However, with double hashing, we do not need as many free locations as with normal linear probe to guarantee good performance. This is because double hashing eliminates both primary and secondary clustering.

Primary clustering is eliminated since keys that hash to different locations will generate different sequences of locations. Secondary clustering is eliminated since different keys that hash to the same location will generate different sequences. This is so since, in general, different keys will generate different increments (k, in the algorithm). It would be a rare coincidence indeed for two keys to be hashed to the same values by both H1 and H2.

In practice, the performance of any hashing application can be improved by keeping information on how often each key is accessed. If we have this information beforehand, we can simply load the hash table with the most popular items first and the least popular last. This will lower the average access time for all keys.

If we do not have this information beforehand, we can keep a counter with each key and increment it each time the key is accessed. After some predefined time (a month, say), we reload the table with the most popular items first and the least popular last. We then reset the counters and garner statistics for the next month. This way we can ensure that the application remains fine-tuned since different items may become popular in the next month.

11.4 Example: Word Frequency Count

Consider, once again, the problem of writing a program to do a frequency count of the words in a passage. Output consists of an alphabetical listing of the words with their frequencies. Now, we will store the words in a hash table using linear probing with double hashing.

Each element in the table consists of three fields: word, freq, and next. We will use the following structure for items to be stored in the table:

```
typedef struct {
   char word[MaxWordSize + 1];
   int freq, next;
} WordInfo;
```

We declare and initialize the table with this:

```
WordInfo wordTable[N+1]; //N - table size
for (int h = 1; h <= N; h++) strcpy(wordTable[h].word, Empty); //Empty - symbolic constant
```

The table is searched for each incoming word. If the word is not found, it is added to the table, and its frequency count is set to 1. If the word is found, then its frequency count is incremented by 1.

In addition, when a word is added to the table, we set links such that we maintain a linked list of the words in alphabetical order. The variable first points to the first word in order. For example, suppose five words have been stored in the hash table. We link them, via next, as shown in Figure 11-4, with first = 6.

	word	freq	next
1	for	2	7
2			
3	the	4	-1
4	man	1	3
5			
6	boy	1	1
7	girl	2	4

Figure 11-4. *Words linked in alphabetical order (first = 6)*

Thus, the first word is boy, which points to for (1), which points to girl (7), which points to man (4), which points to the (3), which does not point to anything (-1). The words are linked in alphabetical order: boy for girl man the. Note that the linking works no matter where the hash algorithm places a word.

The hash algorithm first places the word. Then, regardless of where it is placed, that location is linked to maintain the words in order. For example, suppose the new word kid hashes to location 2. Then the link of kid will be set to 4 (to point to man), and the link of girl will be set to 2 (to point to kid).

We print the alphabetical listing by traversing the linked list. Program P11.3 shows all the details.

Program P11.3

```
#include <stdio.h>
#include <ctype.h>
#include <string.h>
#define MaxWordSize 20
#define MaxWords 10
#define N 13
#define Empty ""
typedef struct {
   char word[MaxWordSize + 1];
   int freq, next;
} WordInfo;

int main() {
   int getWord(FILE *, char[]);
   void printResults(FILE *, WordInfo [], int);
   int search(WordInfo [], char []);
   int addToTable(WordInfo [], char [], int, int);
   char word[MaxWordSize+1];
   WordInfo wordTable[N+1]; //N - table size

   for (int h = 1; h <= N; h++) strcpy(wordTable[h].word, Empty);

   FILE * in = fopen("wordFreq.in", "r");
   FILE * out = fopen("wordFreq.out", "w");

   int first = -1; //points to first word in alphabetical order
   int numWords = 0;
```

```
   while (getWord(in, word) != 0) {
      int loc = search(wordTable, word);
      if (loc > 0) wordTable[loc].freq++;
      else //this is a new word
         if (numWords < MaxWords) { //if table is not full
            first = addToTable(wordTable, word, -loc, first);
            ++numWords;
         }
         else fprintf(out, "'%s' not added to table\n", word);
   }
   printResults(out, wordTable, first);
   fclose(in);
   fclose(out);
} // end main

int getWord(FILE * in, char str[]) {
// stores the next word, if any, in str; word is converted to lowercase
// returns 1 if a word is found; 0, otherwise
   char ch;
   int n = 0;
   // read over non-letters
   while (!isalpha(ch = getc(in)) && ch != EOF) ; //empty while body
   if (ch == EOF) return 0;
   str[n++] = tolower(ch);
   while (isalpha(ch = getc(in)) && ch != EOF)
      if (n < MaxWordSize) str[n++] = tolower(ch);
   str[n] = '\0';
   return 1;
} // end getWord

int search(WordInfo table[], char key[]) {
//search for key in table; if found, return its location; if not,
//return -loc if it must be inserted in location loc
   int convertToNumber(char []);
   int keyNum = convertToNumber(key);
   int loc = keyNum % N + 1;
   int k = keyNum % (N - 2) + 1;

   while ((strcmp(table[loc].word, Empty) != 0) &&
         (strcmp(table[loc].word, key) != 0)) {
      loc = loc + k;
      if (loc > N) loc = loc - N;
   }
   if (strcmp(table[loc].word, Empty) == 0) return -loc;
   return loc;
} // end search
```

```
int convertToNumber(char key[]) {
   int h = 0, keyNum = 0, w = 3;
   while (key[h] != '\0') {
      keyNum += w * key[h++];
      w = w + 2;
   }
   return keyNum;
} //end convertToNumber

int addToTable(WordInfo table[], char key[], int loc, int head) {
//stores key in table[loc] and links it in alphabetical order
   strcpy(table[loc].word, key);
   table[loc].freq = 1;
   int curr = head;
   int prev = -1;
   while (curr != -1 && (strcmp(key, table[curr].word) > 0)) {
      prev = curr;
      curr = table[curr].next;
   }
   table[loc].next = curr;
   if (prev == -1) return loc; //new first item
   table[prev].next = loc;
   return head; //first item did not change
} //end addToTable

void printResults(FILE *out, WordInfo table[], int head) {
   fprintf(out, "\nWords        Frequency\n\n");
   while (head != -1) {
      fprintf(out, "%-15s %2d\n", table[head].word, table[head].freq);
      head = table[head].next;
   }
} //end printResults
```

Using a table size of 13 and MaxWords set to 10, when Program P11.3 was run with the following data in wordFreq.in:

```
The quick brown fox jumps over the lazy dog. Congratulations!
If the quick brown fox jumped over the lazy dog then
Why did the quick brown fox jump over the lazy dog?
```

it produced the following output:

```
'jumped' not added to table
'then' not added to table
'why' not added to table
'did' not added to table
'jump' not added to table

Words          Frequency

brown            3
congratulations  1
dog              3
fox              3
if               1
jumps            1
lazy             3
over             3
quick            3
the              6
```

EXERCISES 11

1. Integers are inserted into a hash table `H[1..11]` using the primary hash function `h1(k) = 1 + k mod 11`. Show the state of the array after inserting the keys `10`, `22`, `31`, `4`, `15`, `28`, `17`, `88`, and `58` using (a) linear probing, (b) quadratic probing with probe function `i + i2`, and (c) double hashing with `h2(k) = 1 + k mod 9`.

2. Integers are inserted in an integer hash table `list[1]` to `list[n]` using linear probe with double hashing. Assume that the function `h1` produces the initial hash location and the function `h2` produces the increment. An available location has the value `Empty`, and a deleted location has the value `Deleted`.

   Write a function to search for a given value `key`. If found, the function returns the location containing `key`. If not found, the function inserts `key` in the *first* deleted location encountered (if any) in searching for `key`, or an `Empty` location, and returns the location in which `key` was inserted. You may assume that `list` contains room for a new integer.

3. In a hashing application, the key consists of a string of letters. Write a hash function that, given a key and an integer `max`, returns a hash location between 1 and `max`, inclusive. Your function must use *all* of the key and should not deliberately return the same value for keys consisting of the same letters.

4. A hash table of size `n` contains two fields—an integer data field and an integer link field—called *data* and *next*, say. The *next* field is used to link data items in the hash table in ascending order. A value of -1 indicates the end of the list. The variable `top` (initially set to -1) indicates the location of the smallest data item. Integers are inserted in the hash table using hash function `h1` and linear probing. The `data` field of an available location has the value `Empty`, and no item is ever deleted from the table. Write programming code to search for a given value `key`. If found, do nothing. If not found, insert `key` in the table and *link it in its ordered position*. You may assume that the table contains room for a new integer.

5. In a certain application, keys that hash to the same location are held on a linked list. The hash table location contains a pointer to the first item on the list, and a new key is placed at the end of the list. Each item in the linked list consists of an integer `key`, an integer `count`, and a pointer to the next element in the list. Storage for a linked list item is allocated as needed. Assume that the hash table is of size *n* and the call `H(key)` returns a location from `1` to *n*, inclusive.

   Write programming code to initialize the hash table.

   Write a function that, given the key `nkey`, searches for it if not found, adds `nkey` in its appropriate position, and sets `count` to `0`. If found, add `1` to `count`; if count reaches `10`, delete the node from its current position, place it at the head of its list, and set `count` to `0`.

6. Write a program to read and store a thesaurus as follows:

   Data for the program consists of lines of input. Each line contains a (variable) number of distinct words, all of which are synonyms. You may assume that words consist of letters only and are separated by one or more blanks. Words may be spelled using any combination of uppercase and lowercase letters. All words are to be stored in a hash table using open addressing with double hashing. A word can appear on more than one line, but each word must be inserted only once in the table. If a word appears on more than one line, then all words on those lines are synonyms. This part of the data is terminated by a line containing the word `EndOfSynonyms`.

   The data structure must be organized such that, given any word, all synonyms for that word can be quickly found.

   The next part of the data consists of several commands, one per line. A valid command is designated by P, A, D, or E.

   P *word* prints, in alphabetical order, all synonyms of *word*.

   A *word1 word2* adds *word1* to the list of synonyms for *word2*.

   D *word* deletes *word* from the thesaurus.

   E, on a line by itself, indicates the end of the data.

7. Write a program to compare quadratic probing, linear probing with double hashing, and chaining. Data consists of an English passage, and you are required to store all the distinct words in the hash tables. For each word and each method, record the number of probes required to insert the word in the hash table.

   Cater for 100 words. For quadratic probing and double hashing, use a table size of 103. For chaining, use two table sizes—23 and 53. For each of the four methods, use the same basic hash function.

   Print an alphabetical listing of the words and the number of probes for each of the four methods. Organize your output so that the performance of the methods can be easily compared.

Index

I, J, K

L

M

N, O

P

Q

R

S

T

U

V

W, X, Y, Z

Get the eBook for only $10!

ow you can take the weightless companion with you anywhere, anytime. Your purchase of this book entitles you to 3 electronic versions for only $10.

Apress title will prove so indispensible that you'll want to carry it with you ywhere, which is why we are offering the eBook in 3 formats for only $10 if have already purchased the print book.

venient and fully searchable, the PDF version enables you to easily find and code—or perform examples by quickly toggling between instructions and ications. The MOBI format is ideal for your Kindle, while the ePUB can be ed on a variety of mobile devices.

o www.apress.com/promo/tendollars to purchase your companion eBook.

ss eBooks are subject to copyright. All rights are reserved by the Publisher, whether the whole or part of the material is concerned, ally the rights of translation, reprinting, reuse of illustrations, recitation, broadcasting, reproduction on microfilms or in any other l way, and transmission or information storage and retrieval, electronic adaptation, computer software, or by similar or dissimilar ology now known or hereafter developed. Exempted from this legal reservation are brief excerpts in connection with reviews or y analysis or material supplied specifically for the purpose of being entered and executed on a computer system, for exclusive use ourchaser of the work. Duplication of this publication or parts thereof is permitted only under the provisions of the Copyright Law of lisher's location, in its current version, and permission for use must always be obtained from Springer. Permissions for use may be d through RightsLink at the Copyright Clearance Center. Violations are liable to prosecution under the respective Copyright Law.